Facing Barriers

Palestinian women have slowly become active in the formal labor market in Israel. In this book, Vered Kraus and Yuval P. Yonay describe and analyse the labor experience of these Palestinian women, and explain why Palestinian and Jewish women have different rates and outcomes in the labor market. Challenging popular views that ascribe these differences to Arab culture and Islam, they instead find that it is state policies and widespread discrimination that hinder Palestinian women's participation and success. By including the various Palestinian sub-groups – Muslims, Bedouins, Druze, Christians, non-citizen residents of Jerusalem – this book shows how the specific life circumstances of the women from these subgroups affect their employment and achievements. The book thus enriches the acute discussion on the labour market experiences of Muslim and Arab women in the Middle East and North Africa and in advanced industrialized societies.

Vered Kraus is Professor Emerita at the University of Haifa. She has published numerous books and articles, including *Promises in the Promised Land: Mobility and Inequality in Israel* (with Robert William Hodge, 1991) and *Secondary Breadwinners: Israeli Women in the Labor Market, 1955–1995* (2002).

Yuval P. Yonay is Associate Professor at the University of Haifa. He is the author of *The Struggle over the Soul of Economics: Institutionalist and Neoclassical Economists in America between the Wars* (1998).

Facing Barriers

Palestinian Women in a Jewish-Dominated Labor Market

Vered Kraus and Yuval P. Yonay

University of Haifa

CAMBRIDGE
UNIVERSITY PRESS

University Printing House, Cambridge CB2 8BS, United Kingdom

One Liberty Plaza, 20th Floor, New York, NY 10006, USA

477 Williamstown Road, Port Melbourne, VIC 3207, Australia

314-321, 3rd Floor, Plot 3, Splendor Forum, Jasola District Centre, New Delhi - 110025, India

79 Anson Road, #06-04/06, Singapore 079906

Cambridge University Press is part of the University of Cambridge.

It furthers the University's mission by disseminating knowledge in the pursuit of
education, learning and research at the highest international levels of excellence.

www.cambridge.org
Information on this title: www.cambridge.org/9781316649978
DOI: 10.1017/9781108227070

First published 2018
First paperback edition 2020

A catalogue record for this publication is available from the British Library

Library of Congress Cataloging in Publication data
Names: Kraus, Vered, author. | Yonay, Yuval P., 1958– author.
Title: Facing barriers : Palestinian women in a Jewish-dominated labor
market / Vered Kraus, Yuval P. Yonay.
Description: Cambridge, United Kingdom : Cambridge University
Press, 2018. | Includes index.
Identifiers: LCCN 2017026025 | ISBN 9781316510476
Subjects: LCSH: Women, Arab – Employment – Israel. | Muslim
women – Employment – Israel.
Classification: LCC HD6182.2 .K69 2018 | DDC 331.4089/927405694–dc23
LC record available at https://lccn.loc.gov/2017026025

ISBN 978-1-316-51047-6 Hardback
ISBN 978-1-316-64997-8 Paperback

Cambridge University Press has no responsibility for the persistence or
accuracy of URLs for external or third-party internet websites referred to in
this publication, and does not guarantee that any content on such websites is,
or will remain, accurate or appropriate.

In honor of all Palestinians and Jews who fight for social justice and especially to Palestinian women who insist on being equal partners at all times.

And in memory of two true friends, Nurit Kadish and Professor Michael Saltman, who loved people and deeply believed in truth and justice.

Contents

List of Figures   *page* viii
List of Tables   x
Acknowledgments   xiii

1 Why Arab and Muslim Women Participate Less in the
   Labor Market Than Other Women   1

2 The Subordinated Citizens: Palestinian Israelis in
   Historical, Social, and Economic Contexts   13

3 Changing Demography: Trends of Educational
   Attainment, Marriage Patterns, and Fertility   39

4 Slowly But Steadily: Muslim Women Enter the Labor
   Market   61

5 Limited Success: Muslim Women's Standing in the Labor
   Market   84

6 Far and Isolated: Bedouin Women in the Naqab   118

7 Residents But Not Citizens: The Annexed Muslim
   Women of Jerusalem   145

8 The "Favorite Minority"? Druze Women in the Labor
   Market   178

9 The Half-Full Glass: Christian Women in the Labor
   Market   201

10 Conclusion: The Politics of Employment in an Ethnocracy   225

References   245
Index   280

Figures

3.1 Mean Years of Schooling of Respondents Aged 18–52 by
Gender, Ethno-Religious Group, and Year   *page* 45
3.2A Percentage of Respondents Aged 18–52 without
Schooling by Gender, Ethno-Religious Group, and Year   46
3.2B Percentage of Respondents Aged 18–52 Attending At Least
Secondary Education   47
3.2C Percentage of Respondents Aged 18–52 Attending Academic
Education by Gender, Ethno-Religious Group, and Year   49
3.3 Median Age at First Marriage for Brides and Grooms by
Ethno-Religious Group and Year   51
3.4 Fertility Rates by Ethno-Religious Group and Year   54
3.5 Fertility Rates for Selected MENA Countries by Year   55
4.1 Labor Force Participation of Muslim and Jewish Women
Aged 18–52   63
4.2 Labor Force Participation of Muslim and Jewish Women
Aged 25–52 by Marital Status and Year   67
4.3 Labor Force Participation of Muslim and Jewish Married
Women Aged 25–52 by Education and Year   69
4.4 Labor Force Participation of Muslim and Jewish Married
Women Aged 25–38 by Number of Children (<15) and Year   72
4.5 Labor Force Participation of Married Muslim Women Aged
25–52 by Place of Residence and Year   75
5.1 Part-Time Employment among Muslim Women and Men
and Jewish Women Aged 18–52 by Year   87
5.2 Involuntary Part-Time Work of Women Aged 25–52 by
Ethno-Religious Group and Year   90
5.3 Commuting to Work of Muslim and Jewish Women Aged
18–52 by Education and Year   93
5.4 Index of Concentration on Economic Branches of Muslims
and Jews Aged 18–52 by Gender and Year   97
6.1 Highest School Attended of Muslims Aged 18 52 in
Bedouin Towns and Other Muslims by Gender and Year   128

6.2 Labor Force Participation of Muslim Women Aged 18–52 in
Bedouin Towns and Other Muslim Women by Age Group
and Year   131
6.3 Labor Force Participation of Muslim Women Aged 25–52 in
Bedouin Towns and Other Muslim Women by Education
and Year   132
6.4 Marital Status of Bedouins in Unrecognized Villages by
Gender and Age Group, 2008   137
6.5 Highest School Attended of Bedouin Men and Women Aged
18–52 in Unrecognized Villages and in Bedouin Towns by
Birth Years, 2008   138
7.1 Mean Age of Current Marriage of Muslims in Jerusalem and
Selected Groups Aged 18–52 by Gender and Year   157
7.2 Fertility Rates of Muslim Women in Jerusalem and Selected
Groups by Year   158
7.3 Highest School Attended of Muslims Women Aged 18–52 in
Jerusalem and Selected Groups by Year   159
7.4 Labor Force Participation of Muslims in Jerusalem and
Selected Groups Aged 18–52 by Gender and Year   160
7.5 Labor force Participation of Muslim Women in Jerusalem
and Selected Groups Aged 25–52 by Education and Year   162
8.1 Labor Force Participation of Druze and Muslims Aged
18–52 by Gender and Year   183
8.2 Labor Force Participation of Druze and Muslim Women
Aged 25–52 by Education and Year   185
8.3 Part-Time Employment of Druze and Muslim Workers Aged
18–52 by Gender and Year   187
8.4 Commuting to Work of Druze and Muslim Workers Aged
18–52 by Gender and Year   190
9.1 Labor Force Participation of Christian and Jewish Women
Aged 18–52 by Year   204
9.2 Labor Force Participation of Christian and Jewish Women
Aged 25–52 by Education and Year   206
9.3 Labor Force Participation of Christian Women Aged 25–52
by Education, Locality, and Year   207
9.4 Involuntary Part-Time Work of Christian and Jewish
Women Aged 18–52 by Year   214

Tables

3.1 Percentage of Never-Married Women Aged 45–54 by Ethno-Religious Group and Year   *page* 52

4.1 Labor Force Participation of Muslims and Jews Women Aged 18–52 by Birth Cohort and Age   65

5.1 Part-Time Employment of Muslim and Jewish Women Aged 18–52 by Birth Cohort and Age Group   88

5.2 Gender and Ethnic Ratios of Median Monthly Earnings of Workers Aged 25–52 by Gender and Year   102

10.1 Selected Characteristics of Israeli Women by Ethno-Religious Group and Year   229

Appendix Tables

3.1 Percentage of Women Aged 18–52 without Schooling by Age Group, Birth Cohort, and Ethno-Religious Group   57

3.2 Percentage of Women Aged 18–52 Attending At Least Secondary Education by Age Group, Birth Cohort, and Ethno-Religious Group   58

3.3 Percentage of Women Aged 18–52 Attending Academic Education by Age Group, Birth Cohort, and Ethno-Religious Group   59

3.4 Percentage of Married Women Aged 15–19, Israel and Selected MENA Countries   60

4.1 Labor Force Participation of Muslim Women Aged 25–52 by Their and Their Husbands' Education and Year   80

4.2 Logistic Coefficients and Standard Errors (in parentheses) Predicting LFP of Married Muslim Women Aged 25–52 by Year   81

4.3 Logistic Coefficients and Standard Errors (in parentheses) Predicting LFP of Single Muslim Women Aged 25–52 by Year   83

5.1 Logistic Coefficients and Standard Errors (in parentheses) Predicting Part-Time vs. Full-Time Employment of Muslim Women Aged 25–52 by Year 107

5.2 Economic Branch Distribution of Muslims and Jews Age 18–52 by Gender and Year 108

5.3 Occupational Distribution of Muslim and Jewish Women Aged 18–52 by Year 111

5.4 Ethnicity and Gender Coefficients and Standard Errors (in Parentheses) Predicting Occupational Enrollment of Highly Educated Workers Aged 25–52 by Year 112

5.5 Distribution and Means of Selected Variables among Muslim and Jewish Employees Aged 25–52 by Gender and Year 114

5.6 Regression Coefficients and Standard Errors (in parentheses) Predicting Monthly Earnings among Muslim and Jewish Employees Aged 25–52 by Gender and Year 116

6.1 Logistic Coefficients and Standard Error (in parentheses) Predicting LFP of Bedouin Women Aged 25–52 by Year 141

6.2 Economic Branch Distribution of Muslims Aged 18–52 in Bedouin Towns and Other Muslims by Gender and Year 142

6.3 Occupational Distribution of Muslims Aged 18–52 in Bedouin Towns and Other Muslims by Gender and Year 143

7.1 Logistic Coefficients and Standard Errors (in parentheses) Predicting LFP of Muslim Women Aged 18–52 in Jerusalem by Year 172

7.2 Economic Branch Distribution of Muslims in Jerusalem and Selected Groups Aged 18–52 by Gender and Year 173

7.3 Occupational Distribution of Muslims in Jerusalem Aged 18–52 by Gender and Year 174

7.4 Mean Gross Monthly Earnings in NIS of Muslim Workers Aged 25–52 in Jerusalem and Selected Groups by Gender, 2008 175

7.5 Mean and Standard Deviation (in parentheses) for Selected Variables of Muslim Workers and Jewish Women Aged 25–52 in Jerusalem by Gender, 2008 175

7.6 Regression Coefficients and Standard Errors (in parentheses) Predicting Gross Monthly Earnings for

Muslim Workers in Jerusalem and Jewish Women Aged
25–52 by Gender, 2008   176
8.1 Logistic Coefficients and Standard Errors (in parentheses)
Predicting LFP of Druze and Muslim Women Aged
25–52 by Year   197
8.2 Economic Branch Distribution of Druze and Muslims
Aged 18–52 by Gender, 2007–2009   198
8.3 Occupational Distribution of Druze and Muslim Women
Aged 18–52 by Year   199
8.4 Regression Coefficients and Standard Errors (in
parentheses) Predicting Gross Monthly Earnings of
Druze and Muslim Workers Aged 25–52 by Gender,
2008   200
9.1 Labor Force Participation of Christian Women Aged
18–52 by Age Group and Birth Cohort   218
9.2 Logistic Coefficients and Standard Errors (in
parentheses) Predicting LFP of Christian Palestinian
Women Aged 25–52 by Year   219
9.3 Economic Branch Distribution of Christians and Jews
Aged 18–52 by Gender and Year   220
9.4 Occupational Distribution of Christians and Jews Aged
18–52 by Gender and Year   222
9.5 Occupational Distribution of Christian and Jewish
Women Aged 25–52 by Education and Locality,
2007–2009   223
9.6 Regression Coefficients and Standard Errors (in
parentheses) Predicting Monthly Earnings of Christian
and Jewish Workers Aged 25–52 by Gender, 2008   224

Acknowledgments

This book is the product of many years' work. We began thinking about the question of Palestinian women's employment when Vered was writing her previous book on Israeli women's work, *Secondary Breadwinners*. One of its chapters focuses on Palestinian women citizens of Israel; however, a single chapter was clearly insufficient to address the complex social, cultural, and political relationships affecting Palestinian women's employment in the Israeli state. We immediately saw the glaring need for another extended research project.

During a sabbatical year (2004–05) at the Max Planck Institute for Education Research in Berlin (Vered) and the Technische Universität-Berlin (Yuval), we took the first step of submitting a research proposal to the Israeli Science Foundation. We wish to thank Professors Karl Ulrich Mayer and Hubert Knoblauch for facilitating our stay in Berlin and for many inspiring conversations then and since. Our efforts resulted in ISF Grant No. 637/06, for which we are indebted to the Israeli Science Foundation. The grant allowed us to gather the data we needed for our analysis from the Central Bureau of Statistics. We would like to especially thank Mark Feldman and Hadas Yaffe for patiently preparing the data and answering nagging queries about sampling techniques and variable definitions.

We wrote a very preliminary draft of this book during another sabbatical year, this time at the Center for the Study of Societal Issues at the University of California-Berkeley (2010–11). We are grateful to the Center for providing us with space for writing and a nurturing scholarly community. We wish to express our deep appreciation to Martin Sanchez-Jankowski, Mike Hout, Roi Livne, and Christine Trost for their warm welcome and encouragement at Berkeley and their ongoing help and support ever since.

When not on sabbatical, our primary appointment is at the University of Haifa. We wish to thank the university, and especially the secretaries in the Department of Sociology and Anthropology, for providing us with an intellectual home and invaluable administrative support. Over the years, we have shared our questions and ideas with our dear friends and colleagues in the department, who have kindly listened and extended helpful comments. Our friend and mentor, Judah Matras, deserves special mention. He has accompanied this project from its inception and has given us unbounded encouragement all along the way. Meir Yaish has also been a constant adviser and friend. We could always rely on him to provide clear insight when facing trying decisions. Amalya Sa'ar's valuable ethnographic work on Palestinian women has provided an ongoing source of thought-provoking inspiration and challenge. Debbie Bernstein has been a patient sounding board for examining our interpretations. Her clarifying questions have helped us sharpen and fine-tune our ideas. We are ever in their debt.

Outside our department, many other scholars have listened and encouraged us. We want to especially mention two firm supporters at the University of Haifa. Ilan Pappé, who moved during the time we worked on this book to the University of Exeter, has been an endless source of knowledge and insight into the intricacies of the Palestinian-Jewish conflict. Ilan Saban has perhaps been the most enthusiastic believer in our project's importance. Other colleagues in Israel who have kindly listened to our thoughts and given theirs in return include Hanna Ayalon, Haya Stier, Nabil Khattab, Nitza Berkovich, Sami Miaari, and Yinon Cohen.

Our great fortune also includes an international group of friends and colleagues with whom we were able to share our project and hear their opinions. While their names are too numerous to display here, we wish to make sure to mention Wout Ultee, with whom we have discussed methodological and substantive issues constantly. Catherine Silver and Seymour Spilerman have steadfastly accompanied us in our work for years. We also wish to thank Rhoda Kanaaneh for her incisive comments on our concluding chapter, along with two anonymous readers who provided encouraging and invaluable comments on our manuscript.

Nira Reiss performed the first round of editing. Her help went far beyond correcting errors and improving linguistic style to giving substantive advice and helping us avoid erroneous arguments. Beverly Katz conducted the second round of devoted and careful editing. Our research assistants, Alexander Zibenberg, Tanya Kolobov, Fany Pesakhov, and Guy Paikowsky, provided dependable and dexterous work. Noga Yeselevich helped us with the drawing of maps. Nadav Azoulay's help in the last stage was priceless. To them all, we are grateful.

During the long period of research and writing, we have talked about our project endlessly with our many friends. We deeply appreciate their tolerance, support, friendship, and intellectual engagement. Ultimately, the love of our families is what gave us the energy and resilience to bring this book to fruition.

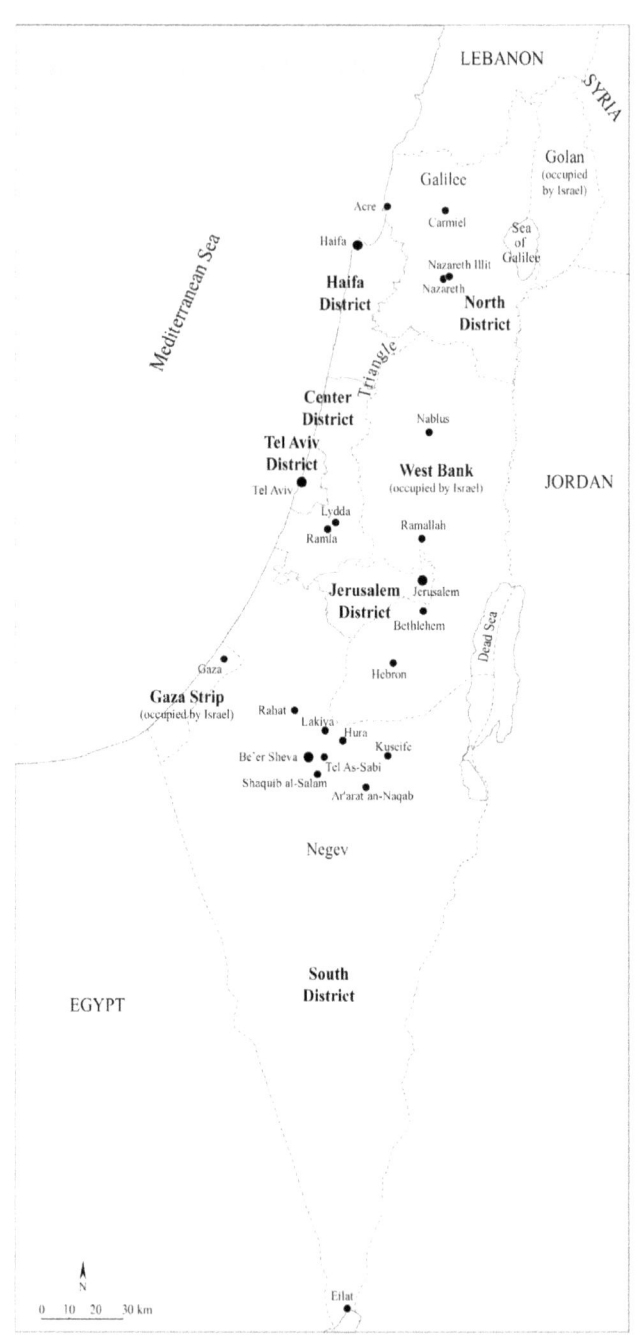

Israel and the Occupied Territories
Source: Created by Noga Yoselevich, Department of Geography and
Environmental Studies, University of Haifa.

1 Why Arab and Muslim Women Participate Less in the Labor Market Than Other Women

1.1 Common Explanations for the Low Labor Force Participation of Muslim Women

At the end of the first decade of the twenty-first century, only one out of four Palestinian women in Israel worked outside her home. Among Jewish women in Israel, the rate was about three times as high: three women out of four were gainfully employed. Middle East scholars would not be surprised by this fact. In most Middle Eastern countries and the Arab countries of North Africa (MENA), women's labor force participation (LFP) rates are not much different from those of Palestinian women in Israel, and they are notoriously lower than women's employment rates in other regions of the world (Hijab 1988 and 2001; Khoury and Moghadam 1995; Cinar 2001; Hosni and Chanmala 2001; Karshenas 2001; Moghadam 2003, 2004; Read 2004; Spierings et al. 2009). This is not a problem of the MENA region only. Muslim women of MENA origins living in Western countries, both first- and second-generation, are also less likely to be employed compared to immigrant women from other regions (Algan et al. 2010; Fleischmann and Hohne 2013; Holland and De Valk 2013; Khoudja and Fleischmann 2015, 2017; Koopmans 2016).

Why are Muslim and Arab women less likely to be part of the modern labor force?[1] A popular answer claims that it is the unique cultural and religious heritage of these women that leads them to choose or to follow

---

[1] We refer somewhat interchangeably to "Arabs" and "Muslims" because of the large overlap of these two big groups. In all Arab countries, with the exception of Lebanon, Muslims constitute the vast majority (90 percent and more), and Islam is a religion that originated in the Arab world, is based on Arabic texts, and was propagated by Arab empires. Thus, the culture of Muslims everywhere carries the insignias of Arab culture. In Europe, similar issues, including women's employment, have arisen in regard to Arab and non-Arab Muslims, and hence it would be too cumbersome to separate the discussion of these two groups, although one should, of course, be aware also of the differences between them, as well as of differences within each group.

options other than participating in the labor force. In many Muslim countries, legislation is explicitly based on the Shari'a (Islamic law), and family laws and practices treat women as inferior to men (Hajjar 2004). Many Muslim countries also deliberately avoid labor laws that ban gender discrimination, do not provide maternity leaves, do not legislate afford-able child care, and formally resist the UN Convention on the Elimination of All Forms of Discrimination against Women (CEDAW) (Sonbol 2010; cf. Afkhami and Friedl 1997; Anwar 2009; Sadiqi and Annaji 2011).

Testing the culturalist perspective requires the comparison of Muslims and non-Muslims under similar political and economic con-ditions. Such comparison is not feasible in Arab countries, where the populations are (with the exception of Lebanon) Muslim and Arab. Researchers therefore resorted to non-Arab countries with large native populations of Muslims and non-Muslims. Amin and Alam (2008), for instance, compared Muslim women in Malaysia with their Hindu and Buddhist compatriots, and found that the former were much less likely to be employed than the latter two groups. This gap, however, was found mostly in rural areas and not in urban ones, indicating that Islam influences women's economic participation only under certain conditions. Spierings (2014) conducted a multilevel comparison of Muslims and Christians within Muslim-dominated and Christian-dominated districts in Indonesia and Nigeria, and found that the impact of Islam on female labor force participation (FLFP) depended on theological interpretation: the difference between people holding different interpretations of Islam were more important than the dif-ference between Muslims and Christians.

To test the importance of religion and culture in the religiously homo-geneous Arab world, Spierings et al. (2010) compared more traditional households and districts to less traditional ones. They identified tradi-tional households in six Arab countries as those where (1) the husbands were much older than wives; (2) members of the extended family lived in the household; (3) a member of the household was involved in a polygynous relationship; and (4) women were young at first birth. Traditional districts were defined as those with higher proportions of traditional households. They found that women from more traditional households and from districts with a relatively higher share of traditional families were less likely to be employed relative to women from less traditional households and from less traditional districts. Yet economic needs and opportunities played a major role as well, leading Spierings and his associates to reject narrow culturalist and modernization theories (ibid., 1405).

Another strategy to study the impact of Islam and Arab culture on women's employment is by comparing FLFP of Muslim and Arab immigrant women in Western countries with that of native women and with non-Muslim and non-Arab immigrant women. The fact that fewer immigrant than native women work outside the home is not very telling, because immigrants suffer from many drawbacks that limit their ability to find suitable jobs: they may not master the local language, may lack understanding of local social norms and expectations, and their educational credentials are frequently not recognized by employers (Koopmans 2016). Second-generation immigrants may overcome some of these obstacles, at least partially, and researchers looking for the effect of culture therefore try to find differences between them and the local natives (Dale et al. 2002; Algan et al. 2010; Hermansen 2013; Holland and de Valk 2014; Connor and Koenig 2015; Koopmans 2016).

The findings of these studies are not consistent, but most conclude that the labor market behavior of second-generation immigrant women is much more similar to that of local native women than is the behavior of their first-generation immigrant mothers (e.g. Algan et al. 2010, F27). Dale et al. (2002), who interviewed first- and second-generation Bangladeshi and Pakistani women in the UK, found that second-generation women were much more determined to combine paid employment with child rearing, and that adherence to Islamic faith was not, in itself, "a deterrent to women's participation in the labour market" (Dale et al. 2002, 23). Holland and de Valk (2014) compared second-generation Turks in four European countries and found large differences in women's employment rates between these immigrants and local native women, but lower educational achievements accounted for a large part of these differences. In France and the Netherlands, second-generation Turkish women were more likely than local native women to withdraw from the labor market when they had two children or more, but in Sweden and Germany no such effect was found, demonstrating that cultural differences do not necessarily hinder Muslim women's entry to the labor force.

Another way to study the impact of Islam on immigrants' integration is to compare them to non-Muslim immigrants rather than to natives. Although immigrants vary in terms of the resources they come with (including education, proficiency in the local language, cultural similarity to the host country, and work skills), at least they share the vulnerabilities associated with arriving at a foreign place. Read's study was among the first to conduct such a comparison, referring merely to women with academic education. She found that, controlling for other potentially relevant variables, academically educated American women of Arab origin (Christian and Muslim) were less likely to be employed outside their homes than women of other origins. She ascribed this result to a cultural tendency that is shared by Christian and Muslim Arab women alike (Read 2004; Read and Oselin 2008). It should be noted, however, that although exhibiting the lowest employment rate among the groups Read examined, two-thirds of the Arab women in her sample were gainfully employed. Thus even if the gaps in women's employment between Arab women and women from other groups are related to the former's cultural preferences, they seem more like lingering effects of past traditions and not like domineering cultural barriers that keep Arab women away from the labor market.

While Read simply compares the behavior of various groups, Fernández (2007) looks for connections between labor behavior in the US and cultures in the countries of origin as approximated by FLFP and attitudes toward women's work in those countries. She found that "women whose parents were born in countries with lower female LFP in 1990 tended to work less themselves in the US in 1970" (315). Köbrich León (2013) replicated this design in a study of immigrant groups in Germany and also found that the culture in the country of origin affected women of that origin. She compared 20 diverse groups of immigrants in Germany and found that culture in country of origin played a much weaker role in determining FLFP of second-generation women compared to first-generation women. Yet among Muslim immigrants, religious identity did have a negative impact on employment among second-generation women as well.

1.2   Doubts about the Role of Culture and Alternative Explanations

Is culture really the main key for changing women's labor force behavior? The idea that cultural uniqueness accounts for the exceptional labor market situation of Arab and Muslim women may seem most immediately appealing. Many observers seem willing to infer – in our opinion too easily and unreflectively – from the above facts, that the main culprit is something inherent to all these communities, i.e. their shared Arab (or more broadly, Muslim) culture. Such views resonate with the deep-rooted orientalist images of Arab and Muslim women that have been current in the European narrative of the Muslim world for centuries, supposedly indicating "quintessential otherness and inferiority of Islam" (Ahmed 1992, 149; cf. Said 1978; Keddie 1991; Abu-Lughod 2002).

It is indeed impossible to deny that deep beliefs and expectations about proper gender roles affect women's decisions about labor market work, but it should be noted that the evidence cited above is not clear-cut and unequivocal. Amin and Alam's (2008) findings were restricted to rural areas, and Spierings (2014) found that FLFP in Muslim regions depended on the version of Islam practiced. In the uniquely elaborate analysis of Spierings et al. (2010), comparing traditional to non-traditional districts in Arab countries, they demonstrated quite convincingly the importance of both values and economic development for women's employment. Yet there is always a possibility of reverse causation: regions with less-developed economies, and therefore fewer employment opportunities for women, lead to the preservation and even strengthening of traditional patterns. For example, women at a younger age marry older husbands and are more likely to enter a polygynous relationship (all are indicators of traditional households according to Spierings et al.) because the prospects of employment are meager. Their analysis also does not take into consideration differences in the state's treatment of women. Studies on second-generation immigrants found that employment gaps between immigrants and native populations were much narrower than in the first generation and had disappeared in some European countries, perhaps due to broader job opportunities.

Moreover, the relevant question is not whether there are some differences between Muslims and non-Muslims with regard to women's work that stem from cultural differences. The crucial question is whether cultural differences are the *main* force keeping Muslim and Arab women's employment rates below those found in other regions. At the end of her article, Fernández sets the goal for future research to

... understand, for example, how culture propagates and evolves. When and why does culture change abruptly whereas at other times it proceeds glacially? ... To what extent is cultural transmission purposeful (optimizing on the part of an individual or group in society) and to what extent is it involuntary? (2007, 329).

These questions fit our approach. Culture is a dynamic force that changes continuously together with, and in response to, changing economic practices and social organization. We should remember that the deeply entrenched division of labor between women and men, which is supported by internalized cultural images and beliefs, characterized most societies, non-Muslim and Muslim, in the not-so-far past. As recently as a century ago, very low FLFP rates characterized all Western societies as well (Fernández 2007; Davis and Greenstein 2009; Walby 2010).

Gender relations in Arab and Muslim societies have also changed tremendously along their histories, and have varied from one Arab (or Muslim) society to another. More recently, gender ideologies have stood in the center of social controversy in modern Arab and Muslim societies for more than a century and have created changes in many of them. Consequently there is wide variance among Arab societies as to the place of women and men, and as to attitudes toward their proper roles (e.g. Mernissi 1985; Sharabi 1988; Kandiyoti 1991b; Ahmed 1992; Hatem 1993; Tucker 1993; Badran 1996; Haddad and Esposito 1998; Sadiqi and Ennaji 2011; Efrati 2012). To understand more comprehensively why Muslim and Arab women are less likely to be part of the modern labor force, one has to study the specific historical processes and the evolving political and economic conditions that have shaped the opportunities and constraints both women and men have faced.

As in Europe and North America (Walby 1986; Goldin 1990; Lewis 1992, 2001; Cooke 2011), the economic structure – level of income, types of industry, ownership patterns, labor supply, and so on – shapes the opportunities available for women in the MENA region (Khoury and Mogadam 1985; Moghadam 1998; Cinar 2001; Hijab 2001). Expansion of state services, education, and health creates a demand for female workers in the Middle East just as it does elsewhere. The impact of economic circumstances is mediated by political forces and state policies (Kandiyoti 1991a, 1991b). Revolutionary regimes, as in Turkey, Algiers, Egypt, Syria, and Iraq, have implemented radical social changes that have opened new opportunities to women, although they are a far cry from those promised by the revolutionary rhetoric (e.g. Hatem 1992; Efrati 2012, 160–162). In countries such as Morocco, Jordan, and Saudi Arabia, the traditional social order has not undergone radical transformation; women have entered the labor force, but the change has occurred within traditional structures and institutions (Samergandi 1992; Moghadam 1993, 2000). The three Maghreb countries of North Africa – all having similar experiences in terms of religion, gender relations, traditional kinship structure, French colonialism, and reformist ideology of national movements – have diverged greatly in terms of family law and women's rights. Charrad (2001, 233) explains that these diverging trajectories were "shaped by the process of state formation in each country, especially the degree of autonomy of the state from – versus reliance upon – kin-based solidarities."

Different modes of production are accompanied by different structures of opportunities for women. According to Ross (2008), for example, mineral-rich states discourage FLFP in the market, due to the enlarged weight of manufacturing industries relative to the services where women have more suitable jobs. In his view, this is the key to understanding the persistence of patriarchy in oil-producing countries in the Middle East and in other regions of the world. Without demand for women's work, the political power of women remains marginal, and without their political participation, "traditional patriarchal institutions will go unchallenged" (ibid., 120). This is true for all kinds of natural resources, but especially relevant for those economies that heavily rely upon oil. "Petroleum per-petuates patriarchy," in Ross's words (120).

The oil industry has hampered women's employment in several ways. First, as a capital intensive industry, it requires a lesser work force and thus discourages the utilization of women's labor (Moghadam 1998). Secondly, revenues from the oil industry enable conservative govern-ments to maintain separated public services for women and men. This may provide employment for women but at the price of strengthening the ideology of sexual segregation (Posusney and Doumato 2003). Thirdly, with high wages in the oil industry, households may not require an additional income beyond the man's (Karshenas and Moghadam 2001; cf. Shami et al. 1990).

Karshenas (2001) develops the last explanation and argues more gen-erally that women's status depends not on economic development per se, but on the specific type of transition from a traditional to a modern market economy. Economies that produce a large income (e.g. the oil econo-mies) enable male workers to provide for their families, decreasing the need for women's paid employment. In contrast, in poorer countries, such as those in South Asia, the need of households for additional income has been strong enough to offset patriarchal norms, and women's employment has become normative.

1.3   Discrimination and Minority Women's Labor Force Opportunities

When we consider minority women's economic activity, their marginality is extremely relevant. When minority members behave differently than the racially and ethnically dominant group, researchers – who often belong to the latter – are often tempted to attribute the dissimilarity to the culture of the minority. This inclination raises the threat that cultural explanations of minority women's lower participation in the labor market are an example of a "blaming the victim" tendency.

Such cultural explanations ignore the fact that those groups suffer from discrimination, prejudice, and negatively skewed allocation of resources and social services, and these obstacles are some of the most harmful factors that block the ability of disadvantaged minorities to find jobs, to advance to higher positions, and to earn higher incomes (e.g. England 1992; Knouse et al. 1992; Feagin and Sikes 1994; Bobo and Suh 1995; Browne 1999). Since women are typically considered to be secondary breadwinners while still having household responsibilities, they must find jobs that pay enough to cover the household expenses of their joining the labor market and that are not too far from home. Discrimination in hiring, promotion, and remuneration lowers the chances that they can find such suitable jobs and may thus keep many minority women away from employment.

In Europe, discrimination against Arabs and Muslims has become more pervasive and severe in recent years due to the increasingly negative images of Islam in many parts of the Western world (Weller at. el. 2001; Allen and Nielson 2002; Sheridan 2006; Bloul 2008; Mastnak 2010; Connor and Koenig 2015). Such attitudes have a long history (Said 1978). The expansion of Arab communities in Europe, coupled with the strengthening of extreme and violent Islamist movements in the Middle East, has exacerbated negative prejudices against Muslims and Arabs and fostered an Islamophobic atmosphere of religious intolerance. "It is basically a phobia against those who are Muslims, look Middle Eastern, speak Arabic, and wear Middle Eastern dress (e.g. head cover of Muslim women) and have names like Muhammad, Saud, Malik, etc." (Cabili 2011: 12). Islam is perceived as a threat to the West, an inherently violent political ideology rather than a faith and spirituality. It is accused of encouraging its followers to launch a global jihad against all non-Muslims – and particularly against the West (Cabili 2011). Muslims' preservation of their customs and traditions is being perceived as hostile to Western culture. Muslims are "commonly devalued as a group which is unfit or unwilling to integrate; which places religious values such as the honor of the Prophet above core principles of Western liberal democracies such as the freedom of expression" (Fleischmann 2011: 1). As we will see in the next chapter, such devaluation of Muslims and Arabs is also common among segments of Jewish society in Israel.

In sum, although cultural beliefs and values are important in shaping women's economic behavior, culture cannot serve as the main explanation for the low LFP rates of Muslim and Arab women in the MENA region and in Western societies. A suitable explanation must refer also to the economic circumstances available for women of various groups and to the state's differential treatment of those groups. Discriminatory practices toward minority groups must be added to any account that seeks to offer a full explanation of women's labor force patterns.

1.4   Goals and Plan of This Book

In this book, we try to follow the guidelines set at the end of the previous section in explaining the work patterns of a unique group of Arab women: the Palestinian citizens and residents of Israel. We assume that studying the exceptional circumstances of their lives will yield important insights that have bearing on other groups of Arab and Muslim women. The uniqueness of this group is related to the fact that, unlike other Arabs in the region, Palestinian women in Israel live in a country with a developed economy. Yet they face the economic opportunities of development from the extremely disadvantaged position of a marginalized minority. Other women in the Arab world might have fewer opportunities for women's work, but whatever opportunities emerge, they are first in line to pick them up. Palestinian women in Israel, in contrast, have to compete with Jewish women, who as part of the dominant group have many more resources and more power.

Their status as a minority makes the Palestinians in Israel similar to Arab (and Muslim) immigrants in Europe and elsewhere: The latter also enjoy improved economic opportunities but have to compete for them from enfeebled positions as members of a discriminated and excluded ethnic minority. *Unlike* these immigrants, however, Palestinians in Israel are a native population whose demographic composition is not the outcome of the selective process of migration. Furthermore, the geographical and religious diversity of the Palestinian minority in Israel and the different treatment of subgroups (Muslims, Druze, Christians, Bedouins)[2] by the state enable us to gain even more insights by comparing the subgroups not only to the Jewish majority but among themselves as well. Thus, while there are only about one million and a half of them – a small fraction of the more than 400 million Arabs worldwide – we believe that the story of the women among them carries important lessons for other Arab and Muslim women, as well as for theories about gender and work in general.

In order to examine patterns in the employment of these women, we apply statistical methods used in studies on the labor market and stratification since the 1970s. These studies elucidate the relationship between women's personal characteristics, social structures and conditions, and the economic activity and achievements of women in the labor market. But because of the lack of reliable and detailed statistics in developing nations, most of these studies have been limited to advanced industrial societies. Israel is among those societies, but the numerous labor force studies conducted in and about it have focused on Jews, or have compared Jews to Palestinians (usually referred to as "Israeli Arabs") without distinguishing among various Palestinian subgroups. Very few quantitative studies have been carried out on Arab women, whether they are residing in Middle Eastern and North African countries or in Europe and other destinations of Arab immigrants. This book offers such a study.

---

[2] This diversity is described in detail in the next chapter.

Our strategy is based on doing an extensive analysis of Arab women's working patterns over a period of 35 years. We use official statistics collected by the Israeli state's Central Bureau of Statistics (CBS), including labor force surveys (LFSs), income surveys, and the last two population censuses, which were conducted in 1995 and 2008. Together, these sources provide detailed information about women, their households, and their work. We examine and analyze relationships between women's personal characteristics (education, marital status, number of children) and their LFP, including number of hours per week, occupation, place of work, and earnings. As will be described in the book plan below, we study these issues separately for each distinct group of Palestinian women, comparing them with each other and with Jewish women, as well as with men of these groups.

Book Plan. In order to understand the meaning of our findings and their significance for theories of FLFP, Chapter 2 places our study in its social, historical, and economic context and is divided into five sections. The first provides a general description of Israeli society, with emphasis on the composition of the Palestinian minority and its geographical distribution. The second section explains the state's policies toward its Palestinian population, emphasizing the lack of economic development, the unequal provision of social services, and the various means used to control this population. The third section describes the ethnic composition of Israel, the relationships between Palestinians and Jews, and the divisions among both Palestinians and Jews. The fourth section presents the geographical aspects related to Palestinian and Jewish relations, emphasizing the segregation between the two groups and the differential policies regarding their communities. Finally, the fifth section is about the economic infrastructure of Palestinian communities.

Women's opportunities in the labor market depend to a large extent on their education, marital status, and the number and age of their children. Chapter 3 provides elaborate information on these topics by describing trends of educational attainment, marriage, and fertility among the various groups of Palestinian women in Israel. The chapter opens with a description of the separate educational systems that serve Israeli citizens according to their national and religious affiliations. The chapter then describes the changes in educational achievements of the various Palestinian groups in Israel along the 35-year span of our study. The last part of the chapter deals with changes in family composition, again distinguishing among the separate subcategories of Palestinians in Israel.

The largest bulk of Arab Palestinians in Israel, 80.5 percent, are Muslims who reside in the northern part of Israel (the Galilee) and in the central part of Israel along the border between Israel and the West Bank ("the Triangle"). The size of this group enables us to make more detailed analyses in Chapters 4 and 5 in which we examine the economic behavior of Muslim women from these regions. Chapter 4 looks at Muslim women from the northern and central districts with respect to their participation in the labor market from the mid-1970s to 2009. Chapter 5 deals with various characteristics of employment of those Muslim women who work. There are four main topics that we examine in this chapter. First we look at part-time employment, analyzing the factors involved in part-time work and the reasons given by women for working part time. The second part of the chapter looks into commuting patterns and asks what we may learn from differences in commuting patterns between highly educated and less-educated women. Next, the chapter moves to an investigation of the positions Palestinian women occupy in the Israeli labor market: we describe in what occupations and segments of the Israeli economy they work, and examine whether being a Muslim as compared to a Jew increases women's probability of working in such occupations and segments. In the fourth and last section we examine Muslim women's earnings compared with that of Muslim men on the one hand, and with that of Jewish women on the other, and based on multivariate analysis, we examine the sources that generate these gender and ethnic gaps.

The above two chapters deal only with the majority of the Muslim population, and do not include two distinct Muslim groups, the Bedouins who live mostly in the south of Israel and the Palestinians of Jerusalem. The next two chapters are dedicated to these two groups. Chapter 6 describes the unique case of Bedouin women. The nomadic past of the Bedouins and their separate social organization have kept them as a socially distinctive group. They live all over the country, but in the north and center of Israel, they cannot be distinguished from other Muslims in official statistics, and therefore this chapter deals only with Muslims in the south of Israel, almost all of them Bedouins. Our analysis compares Bedouins who live in the officially recognized towns with those who live in the so-called 'unrecognized villages.' Chapter 7 deals with Muslim women who reside in Jerusalem. East Jerusalem and its vicinity were annexed by Israel in 1967, but their inhabitants have remained part of the social organization of the Palestinian West Bank. This is especially important with regard to their education, which is conducted according to the Palestinian curriculum (or the Jordanian curriculum prior to the establishment of the Palestinian Authority). Furthermore, almost all Palestinian Jerusalemites refuse to apply for Israeli citizenship (and the few who do often encounter red tape). They are officially considered to be residents who may work freely in Israel, but they do not take part in its political life. Due to these circumstances, we expect Palestinian women in Jerusalem to have different work patterns than the Palestinian citizens of Israel. We study only the Muslim inhabitants because they constitute 97 percent of Palestinians in the city, while the Christian inhabitants are too few in our data to enable statistical analysis. The chapter compares Jerusalemite Muslim women to those Palestinian Muslim citizens of Israel who live, like the Jerusalemites, in mixed cities.

Chapter 8 brings the story of Druze women. The Druze community in Israel has an exceptional position as an Arab minority allied with the Jewish state. Chapter 9 deals with Christian Palestinian women. Although divided into about a dozen denominations, the Christian Palestinians in Israel constitute a single social group, which is socially separate from their Muslim counterparts. The relationship between these two groups is complex: Christians feel uneasy with the strong Islamist movement among Muslims, and there is a class gap between the (more affluent) Christians and the (less prosperous) Muslims. But the two groups share the same Palestinian national sentiments and aspirations.

In Chapter 10 we summarize our study. We use our results to reconsider the question of how women make decisions about their involvement in the labor market under the specific cultural and economic conditions of their communities, as they are shaped by state policies, legal arrangements, and intergroup relations. We conclude the book with a discussion of how culture is profoundly intertwined with economic structures and political action, affecting people's behavior while at the same time being rearranged and transformed. We end with a discussion of the implications of our findings for other Arab and Muslim women in the MENA region, as well as for Arab women who live in other Western countries. We believe that our study will contribute to a comparative understanding of the processes that generate women's activities in the labor market.

2   The Subordinated Citizens
Palestinian Israelis in Historical, Social, and Economic Contexts

In order to understand the situation of Palestinian women in the Israeli labor market, we need to understand the structure of Israeli society. This chapter describes the ethno-religious composition of Israel, focusing on the relationship between the Palestinian minority and the ruling Jewish majority.[1] We begin with a short introduction to the history between these two groups, and then show the standing of Palestinians in Israel today. After discussing the geographical segregation of the two national groups, we present some general features of the Israeli economy and show the place of Palestinian citizens in it.

2.1   Historical Background

Until modern times, most of the residents of the region known as Palestine – including the area covered currently by Israel, the West Bank (of the Jordan River), and the Gaza Strip[2] – were Arabs, most of them Muslims but with a large Christian minority and a smaller group of Druze. For most in the Jewish diaspora worldwide, this region was known as *Eretz Israel*, the Land of Israel, the sacred place where all members of the Jewish people would be reunited in messianic times. Small Jewish communities existed in several towns in Palestine for many centuries as well, but numerically they were a very small fraction of the local population. The rise of nationalism and modern anti-Semitism in Eastern Europe during the nineteenth century, as well as economic scarcity, aggravated the threat to Jews and caused millions of them to seek new places to live. Influenced by the nationalist trends of the time, some Jews came to believe that the only solution for the Jewish people's troubles

---

[1] We use the vague term "ethno-religious group" as the most general term to capture all the socially distinct categories that are based either on national, religious, language, or origin (cf. McGahern 2011).
[2] Some would add the area known today as the Hashemite Kingdom of Jordan. The definition, names, and borders of this land are a major subject of controversy and we try to follow the most common English terminology.

13

would be the establishment of a modern Jewish state in Eretz Israel, Palestine. The Zionist movement was the political instrument aimed at realizing this goal by settling Jews in Palestine and gradually building a new modern state as the homeland of all Jews (Tibawi 1969; Lesch 1979, 2006; Owen 1982; Kimmerling 1983, 2001; Wiemer 1983; Pappé 1988, 1992, 2004; Shafir 1989; McCarthy 1990; Masalha 1992, 2012; Kimmerling and Migdal 1993;Piterberg 2013).

The slow growth of the Jewish population in Palestine – first under the Ottoman regime and later under British rule – and the explicit aspiration to turn the land into a Jewish homeland met the resistance of the local Arab population, which was itself in the process of change and deliberation over its national identity, both as a separate community and as part of the larger Arab nation. The intensifying violence of the Palestinian-Jewish conflict led to Britain's decision to withdraw from Palestine and to the subsequent 1947 UN decision to divide the country into two separate states, a Palestinian and a Jewish one (Pappé 1992; Yakobson and Rubinstein 2009). At that time the Palestinian population, amounting to about 1.3 million, constituted two-thirds of the country's inhabitants, while Jews, most of them immigrants from Eastern Europe and Germany, comprised one-third (Pappé 1992; McCarthy 1990; Kimmerling 2001, 35).[3] Palestinians and the Arab states around Palestine perceived the Jewish state as an institutionalization of the colonial regime in the middle of the Arab world, and rejected the UN decision to divide the country. One day after the decision, the hostilities between Palestinians and Jews all over the country escalated and led to the 1948 war (Pappé 1992).

On May 15, 1948, the British rule ended formally, and the last British troops left the country. A day earlier, the new Jewish state, officially named Israel, was declared and immediately invaded by armies from the four neighboring countries. Starting even before the official end of the Mandatory regime, Jewish forces managed to take control of 78 percent of Palestine by the end of the 1948 war, including large areas that had been designated as part of the Palestinian state. The war, which was labeled by Jews as the War of Independence, became known in Palestinian history as the *Nakba*, the "disaster," since it crushed Palestinian society. More than a half of the population, 750,000 people, became refugees: some in the neighboring countries (especially in Jordan, Syria, and Lebanon), some in the areas of Palestine beyond the borders of Israel, and some within the new Jewish state. Within Israel, entire areas

[3] According to the most accurate study of population in Mandatory Palestine, Jews accounted for 30 percent of the population, but this figure is for 1944, four years before the end of the British rule (McCarthy 1990, Chart 3).

were cleansed of their inhabitants, more than 500 villages were completely destroyed, and almost all of the Palestinian urban population of big cities such as Haifa, Jaffa, Ramla, Lydda, Acre, and West Jerusalem[4] was uprooted and deported (Masalha 1992; Morris 1987; Pappé 1992, 2006). Against the wishes of Palestinians and without international recognition (but with British support and Israeli silent approval), the West Bank was annexed by the Hashemite Kingdom of Jordan, and the Gaza Strip was left under Egyptian control (Pappé 1988, 1992; Shlaim 1988).

Thirteen percent of the original Palestinian population of 1947, about 150,000 people, remained within the internationally recognized borders of the new state of Israel and became its citizens. The expulsion of the urban population left Palestinians in Israel without the institutional basis of a civil society and without cultural and political leadership (Haklai 2011; Pappé 2011; Masalha 2012). Most of those who remained had been subsistence farmers before the war. The burden of the war and of the new state's rule further exhausted their meager resources (Ben-Porath 1966; Haidar 2009; Haklai 2011; Pappé 2011, Bäuml 2007). Between one-sixth (Cohen 2005, 56) and one-quarter (Bronstein 2005, 216; Masalha 2005, 23) of the Palestinians who remained within Israel's borders were "internal refugees" – deported from their homes during the Nakba; having to find a place to live in other Palestinian communities in Israel and having lost all of their economic resources, they had to start over from scratch. This fact may have bearing on the economic standing of the refugees' families even to this day (Boqa'i 2005; Masalha 2005, Kanaaneh and Nusair 2010; Sabbagh-Khoury 2011).

2.2   A "Jewish and Democratic" State?

The Declaration of Independence that heralded the birth of the new state professed that the State of Israel will "foster the development of the country for the benefit of all its inhabitants" and "will ensure complete equality of social and political rights to all its inhabitants irrespective of religion, race or sex" (Official translation, Israel Foreign Ministry; cf. Halabi 1995, 7; Peleg and Waxman 2011, 32). Although this statement has often been quoted, the reality has been far from the promise (Herzog et al. 2008; Peleg and Waxman 2011). The military rule imposed on the Palestinians during the 1948 war was lifted only in December 1966, but the movement limitations continued until after the 1967 war (Bäuml 2007, 242–245). During this period, Palestinians were administered by

---

[4] Prior to the war, many Palestinians lived in the part of Jerusalem that was under Israeli rule after the war ("West Jerusalem").

army officers who intervened in all aspects of their lives. They were prohibited from leaving their villages without permits, no matter for what purpose: work, study, a family event, a bureaucratic chore, or a medical examination. This tight control was used to thwart political organization. Arab citizens were allowed to vote, but they could choose only among Jewish-controlled political parties and Arab parties affiliated with the governing Mapai (the dominant labor party in the government between 1948 and 1977). The limitation on organic political activity (to borrow Gramsci's term) enhanced the power of local leaders who were co-opted by the state. These leaders were socially conservative, and they used their power and connections in the state to curb modernizing forces within the Palestinian communities, including those aiming at gender equality (Zureik 1979; Lustick 1980; Wiemer 1983; Korn 2000; Sa'di 2003a, 2003b; Cohen 2010; Haklai 2011; Pappé 2011).[5]

Along with promising equal rights to all, The Declaration of Independence also made it clear that the state would be a Jewish state. The tension between the principle of equality and the privileged status of Jewishness has accompanied life in Israel since its founding. During the 1990s, new Basic Laws officially stamped the state as "Jewish and Democratic." Since then, political philosophers and legal students have debated the question of whether these two concepts could be harmoniously reconciled. Standing on the one side are those who think that many exemplary democracies have a commitment to a specific ethnic or national group (e.g. Gavison 1999; Gans 2008; Yakobson and Rubinstein 2009). On the other hand, there are many critics who have argued that a true democracy cannot use state resources to advance the goals of some citizens, thus treating the rest as citizens of a lesser status (e.g. Halabi 1995; Zeedani 1995; Ghanem 1998, 2001; Rouhana 2006; Yiftachel 2006).

This legal debate is mirrored in a controversy among social scientists. Comparative political sociologist Sammy Smooha argued that none of the familiar types of democracies discussed in the literature fit the Israeli case. He originated the concept of an "ethnic democracy" to characterize the type of regime in which all individuals had the basic individual rights of modern democracies and were equal before the law, but some ethnic and national groups were identified with the state and consequently had

---

[5] The military administration used its control especially to curb the activities of the Communist Party (Maki). Maki was committed to the egalitarian treatment of all citizens and therefore found many supporters among Palestinian citizens. It was also more supportive of women's rights than the Palestinian parties allied with the government. Many other parties – including those in the governing coalition – argued that Mapai used the military rule to advance narrow political interests and called to terminate it.

certain collective rights that other groups lacked. According to Smooha, Israel is an exemplary case of this type of democracy, but there are many other examples, such as Hungary, Slovakia, and Latvia (Smooha 1997; 2002).

For Jews, collective rights in Israel extend beyond the borders of the state. According to the official ideology of Israel, which is strongly supported by almost all Israeli Jews, non-citizen Jews who live outside Israel are considered as legitimate "stakeholders" of the state (Smooha 1997; Rouhana 1989). This approach is most evident in the Law of Return, which grants immediate citizenship to any Jew who wishes to settle in Israel. The state proactively encourages and subsidizes Jewish immigration while making it extremely difficult for non-Jews to receive citizenship (Gans 2008). For non-citizen Arabs, Palestinian or not, gaining citizenship is next to impossible,[6] and the return of Palestinian refugees is considered anathema for most Jews in Israel, many of whom perceive such a return as "the end of the Jewish state" (Halabi 1995; Smooha 1997, 2004).

On the eve of independence, the number of Jews in Israel was about 600,000. The vitality of the Jewish state project required many more people in order to build a modern economy, to settle the "cleansed" areas, and to establish a military force. Israel therefore initiated a widespread project of moving the old Jewish communities of the Middle East to Israel.[7] Together with the arrival of those European Jews who survived World War II, the Jewish population was doubled in a year and tripled in seven years. The successful integration of these immigrants required providing residence, social services, and employment for the newcomers and establishing schools for their children. The realization of these goals put a huge burden on the small, new, and poor state, and together with security concerns, preoccupied the national policy-makers (Lissak 1999; Kimmerling 2001).

With no representation in the government and no political power, the needs of the wrecked Palestinian population were far down on the list of national priorities. The state's main concern about its Palestinian citizens was to secure their docility, and it had little interest in their well-being and economic advancement (Haklai 2011; Pappé 2011). As will be elaborated below, the state built new neighborhoods, towns, and settlements for Jews, gave Jews preference in the allocation of jobs, and invested much

---

[6] According to the 2003 Amendment to the Citizenship Law, even Arab spouses of Israeli citizens cannot apply for citizenship.
[7] Sporadic immigration of Jews from MENA countries took place in the centuries that preceded the establishment of Israel, but in 1948, the Jews who originated in those countries constituted only a fifth of the Jewish population.

more in Jewish schools. Furthermore, the state confiscated large portions of land belonging to the Palestinians who remained in their villages and the land of those whose villages were demolished (regardless of their presence in Israel or not). The Palestinians who were mostly farmers had to look for livelihoods outside of agriculture, but not until the late 1950s were industrial labor markets opened to them (Wiemer 1983; Ozacky-Lazer 2000). Palestinians benefited from the overall economic development of the country and from the provision of universal services such as basic medical care and education, but their communities were last in line and underfunded compared to the Jewish ones (Kretzmer 1990; Bäuml 2007; Peled 2001; Pappé 2011).[8]

The disregard of the needs of Palestinian communities and their discrimination in public services and budgets have continued to this day and are well documented in numerous studies (e.g. Smooha 1978, 1982, 1997; Wiemer 1983; Falah 1989a, 1990, 1995; Haidar 1991; Carmi and Rosenfeld 1992; Al-Haj 1995; Halabi 1995; Ghanem 1998, 2001; Jabareen 1998; Rouhana 1998; Rosenhek 1999; Jamal 2002; Lewin and Stier 2002; Coursen-Neff 2003; Abu-Saad 2004b; Bäuml 2010; Friedman and Shalev 2010; Khamaisi 2011; Jabareen and Mustafa 2013; Sa'ar 2016; Shalev and Lazarus 2016), but perhaps the best summary of the underprivileged condition of Israeli Palestinians was given by the Or Commission, which was appointed by the Israeli government to investigate the October 2000 riots.[9] Justice Or himself summarized the situation of the Israeli Palestinians as follows:

The Arab citizens of Israel live in a reality in which they experience discrimination as Arabs. This inequality has been documented in a large number of professional surveys and studies, has been confirmed in court judgments and government

---

[8] The changes in Palestinians' place in the Israeli economy are presented in much more detail in Section 2.5 below.

[9] The October 2000 riots of Palestinian citizens in Israel started in a protest against the killing of many Palestinians in Jerusalem following the provocative visit of the then opposition leader Ariel Sharon on the Temple Mount. The riots continued for more than a week and included violent clashes between Palestinian rioters and the police, during which 13 Palestinians and one Jewish civilian were killed. The Palestinian public was infuriated by the use of live ammunition by the police, a practice not used against Jewish protesters. The State Investigation Commission, headed by Supreme Court Judge Theodore Or, was charged with the examination of the events that had led to the riots and with the way the government responded. The Commission also delved into the deprivation of the Palestinian citizens in order to understand the frustration and anger that fed the riots. The Commission was aided by a legion of research assistants who collected an impressive number of academic studies and various reports of government bodies and agencies, including classified reports written by internal security experts worried about the specter of violent explosion due to the continuing neglect of Arab Palestinians by the state (Peleg and Waxman 2011, 93–97).

resolutions, and has also found expression in reports by the state comptroller and in other official documents (Or 2006, 30).

As these words demonstrate, claims as to discrimination in the allocation of resources and in meeting the needs of the Palestinian population are made not only by critical social scientists; they are also acknowledged again and again by state bodies and political leaders. Measures to alleviate their difficulties and to make up for long years of neglect are occasionally announced, but in the absence of political clout, no significant improvements have been undertaken (cf. Shamir 2005; Peleg and Waxman 2011, 97).

2.3   The Ethnic Composition of Israel and Intergroup Relations

Ethnic Composition. The major ethnic division in Israel is between Jews and Palestinians. According to the state's CBS, the Israeli population in 2012 numbered 7,810,500 people, of which 5,949,000 (76.2 percent) were classified as Jewish, and 1,628,500 (20.9 percent) as Palestinians. The rest of the population (233,000 or 2.9 percent) consists mostly of immigrants from the former Soviet Union, who are not Jewish according to Halachic Law but have Jewish ancestry. From the point of view of the Palestinian-Jewish cleavage, they are on the Jewish side, so the socially significant numerical ratio of Palestinian to Jews is 21 to 79 (CBS 2013, Tables 2.19 and 2.20).

The last figure, however, is not fully accurate; 296,300 Palestinians included in the above calculation (3.8 percent) reside in what the Israeli authorities call East Jerusalem (ibid., Table 2.20). An additional 21,200 are Druze Syrians from the Golan Heights, which has been occupied by Israel since 1967. These populations are included in Israeli official statistics, but the vast majority of them are merely permanent residents and not citizens of Israel. East Jerusalem is part of the West Bank that includes the pre-1967 Jordanian side of Jerusalem and more than a dozen villages in its vicinity. This area was annexed by Israel a few weeks after the 1967 war and was added to the municipal jurisdiction of Jerusalem. This annexation violated international law and is not recognized by any international body outside of Israel. Moreover, most of the Palestinian residents of the so-called East Jerusalem do not have Israeli citizenship. They have the status of permanent residents and may work and move freely inside Israel, but they cannot take part in the election to the Knesset and do not have an Israeli passport (Quigley 1996; Rempel 1997; Klein 2001; Lapidoth 2002). In order to know the proportion of Palestinians and Jews inside the internationally recognized borders of Israel, we should exclude the non-Israeli Jerusalemites. Such a calculation changes the ratio of Palestinians to Jews to 17.5 to 82.5. Throughout this book, unless otherwise indicated, we do not include East Jerusalem in our statistical analyses. Since the CBS collects data on this population, we use it to advance our understanding of how women's employment depends on political and economic conditions but it must be emphasized that our analyses do not imply the legitimacy of the annexation. In Chapter 7, we tell the story of its residents.

Understanding the ethnic composition of Israel involves considering ethnic divisions among both Jews and Palestinians. Among Jews, one may distinguish between Ashkenazi Jews (those originating from Europe) and Mizrahi Jews (those originating from Asia and Africa). Additional diversity is related to the immigration of a million Russian-speaking immigrants from the FSU and a much smaller group of Jews from Ethiopia. The Palestinians include three religious affiliations: Muslims (all Sunni) make up 83.0 percent of all Palestinians in Israel; Christians (who belong to a dozen of different denominations) account for 8.7 percent; and the rest, 8.3 percent, are Druze (CBS 2013, Tables 2.19 and 2.20).[10] Among the Muslims, the Bedouins are a socially distinctive group, as will be explained in Chapter 6. They constitute almost all the Palestinians in southern Israel (about 200,000 people in 2012), but they are a minority in other regions where statistical data do not distinguish them from other Muslims.

Jews' Perceptions and Attitudes toward Palestinians. Anti-Palestinian sentiments are very common among Jews. One explanation of this animosity is the prolonged conflict between the two peoples, but racist attitudes were part of the way European Jews looked not only at Arabs and other indigenous peoples, but were also a fundamental component of their view of non-European (Mizrahi) Jews. In this regard, European Jews did not differ from other Europeans of the time in perceiving native peoples as belonging to primitive cultures lower on the scale of cultural evolution. Khazoom depicts a chain of "othering" that characterized the attitudes of French and German Jews toward Eastern European Jews (*Ostjuden*), of all European Jews toward the Mizrahi Jews, and of all Jews toward the Arabs (Khazoom 2003). Yet there was a basic difference in the approach of European Jews toward Mizrahi Jews as compared to Arabs. The former were part of the Jewish nation who could be "saved" and brought into civilization with the help of Ashkenazi Jews; the latter were part of an even more primitive world (Motzafi-Haller 2001). In

---

[10] As said before, Palestinians in the East Jerusalem and Druze from the Golan Heights are not included.

Theodore Herzl's utopia of a Jewish state, the Arabs appear in the role of the grateful natives who thank Jews for modernizing Palestine and accelerating the modernization of local Arabs as well (Herzl 1960[1902]).

In fact, the attitudes of most early Jewish immigrants to Palestine followed the pattern of other settler societies (Memmi 1965; Lustick 1993; Mitchell 2000). Beyond pervasive racist perceptions and images, the settlers needed the land of the indigenous people and depended on the latter as a source of labor. The Zionist project was a Jewish project, aimed at solving a Jewish problem, and it could not imagine the Palestinians as an equal partner.[11] The resistance of the latter to the Zionist project was therefore unavoidable (Shafir 1989; Masalha 1992; Lustick 1993; Abdo and Yuval-Davis 1995; Rouhana and Sabbagh-Khoury 2015). Jews failed to understand the roots of the Palestinian hostility and responded with intensified antagonism toward them (Ben-Eliezer 1998).

The year 1948 was a crossroads. Rather than integrating the few Palestinians who became citizens in Israel into the new society, the logic of national separation dominated the relations between the groups. The continuing conflict with the neighboring Arab states, the omnipresent racist images, and, perhaps most importantly, the idea of a state which is Jewish, have kept the Palestinians as the "Other" in the thinking of policy-makers and of the majority of intellectuals and the Jewish population (Bäuml 2007). When Mizrahi Jews arrived from Arab countries, deliberate measures were taken to "de-Arabize" them. In order to keep them away from the Palestinians with whom they shared the Arabic language as well as many other cultural views and practices, housing policies created separate neighborhoods for the Mizrahi immigrants and the Palestinians (Shohat 1988; Nurieli 2005; Shenhav 2006).

Studies of Jewish Israelis of all ages and groups – from preschool children to adults – show that cultural constructs reflecting racist attitudes are internalized by children and become part of the way they conceive of the Arab Other.[12] For example, Adir Cohen (1985), who studied the ways Arabs appear in 520 Hebrew children's books, found that the Arab figures have often been pictured in a very negative way,

---

[11] Smaller political groups (e.g. Brit Shalom, the Canaanite movement) had different visions of Jewish-Palestinian cooperation and equality, but they were completely marginalized and lacked significant influence.

[12] Jews have a general perception of all Arabs, regardless of their specific nationality. Furthermore, in Israeli discourse, the term "Arabs" is used to designate Israeli Palestinians, keeping the term "Palestinian" for those living in the Occupied Territories and the neighboring countries.

presenting them as aggressive, murderous, and ruthless.[13] In his conversations with children, Cohen found that the latter often echoed these grossly distorted images and integrated them into their cognitive constructs. Based on a series of studies of the way Jewish children perceive Arabs in Israel, Bar-Tal reached similar conclusions, finding that "children acquire the word and the concept 'an Arab' very early" and although "little knowledge is associated with the concept, it has negative connotations" (1996, 341). Stereotypical and one-dimensional presentations of Arabs are not limited to children's books. Aburaya and Abu-Raiya (2012) found that even well-educated and well-informed Jews in Israel held false views about Islam and Muslims in general and saw Muslims as belonging to an inferior culture (for more examples see Bar-Tal 1998; First 1998; Avraham et al. 2000; Podeh 2002; Bar-Tal and Teichman 2005; Nets-Zehngut 2008; Bar-Tal et al., 2010; Peled-Elhanan 2010, 2012).

Surveys of the Israeli Jewish public conducted continuously since the 1980s by Smooha document the pervasive anti-Arab attitudes of Jews in Israel. In his interpretations of successive surveys, Smooha seeks to refute frequent claims that Jews have become more extreme in their negative views about Israeli Palestinians. He shows that while these views have not become increasingly hostile, a strong and constant negative attitude toward Palestinians in Israel persists. In the six surveys conducted between 1985 and 2004, about a third of all Jews believed that Arabs should not have even the right to vote for the Knesset; an even greater number (39.5–43.8) thought that the state should encourage Arabs to leave Israel. About half were not willing to have an Arab neighbor, and two-thirds refrained from entering Arab localities (Smooha 2004). A PEW survey conducted in 2016 found a similarly disturbing finding. According to this study, 48 percent of all Jews concurred that "Arabs should be expelled or transferred from Israel" (2016, 153).[14]

Racist views and negative attitudes toward racial, religious, and ethnic minorities are, of course, common in many countries. But in many of those countries, the state has proactive programs to fight racism and

---

[13] Cohen also lists books that portray Arabs in a positive ways and depict friendly relations between Arabs and Jews; however, such books are not only fewer in number, but they also belong to less popular literary genres.

[14] Smooha's studies also use the term "Arabs," for Palestinians who live in Israel. In fact, one finding of Smooha is that more than 70 percent of Jews believe that "an Arab citizen who defines him/herself as a 'Palestinian Arab in Israel' cannot be loyal to the state and to its laws" (2010, 23). While there are numerous other studies on Jew's attitudes toward Arabs, Smooha's studies are widely considered as the most reliable, and they have the extra value of repeating the same questions every year, thus enabling us to identify stable patterns and follow changes along the years.

reduce its harmful fallouts by means of legislation, education, and a variety of other symbolic and practical measures. In Israel, the central agencies of the state have been extremely tepid in fighting anti-Arab sentiments. Although official statements emphasize the principle of equality, and racism is often denounced, anti-Arab incidents against Palestinians elicit much milder denunciations than insults against subordinate Jewish groups.[15]

Palestinian Attitudes. Palestinians' responses to their exclusion from the mainstream of Israeli society and to the expressions of racism and hostility they face are complex and may seem contradictory. On the one hand, there are many indications of what Smooha calls "Israelization" – Palestinians seek ways to join the mainstream of Israeli society and be part of it; 64 percent of all Palestinians said that they felt proud when Israel had a significant achievement, and only one in eight would avoid having a Jewish friend (Smooha 2004). The aspiration to integrate with Jews is evident also in the positive responses of Palestinians during dialogue workshops and intergroup encounters. They are frustrated when they feel that Jews do not understand their vulnerability and pain as a national minority within Israel, but they do not give up on their wish to reach mutual understanding with Jewish participants and gain their respect (Maoz 2000a, 2000b; Halabi 2004; Hertz-Lazarowitz and Zelniker 2004; Maoz et al. 2004).

Parallel to the "Israelization" of Palestinians, Smooha identifies a process of "Palestinization" – feelings and expressions of belonging to the Palestinian nation, supporting its struggle for independence, and caring for the well-being of Palestinians in the Occupied Territories and elsewhere. Palestinization does not contradict Israelization, explains Smooha. On the contrary, Palestinians feel that as citizens they are entitled to equal rights not only as individuals but also as a separate national group entitled to receive recognition and to express its collective sentiments and aspirations (Smooha 1999). They have learned how to combine their daily practice as citizens in a Jewish-dominated environment with the "middle-ground politics" of developing and maintaining their Palestinian identity (Schölch 1983; Ben-Ze'ev and Aburaiya 2004; cf. Levy 2005; Haklai 2011; Peleg and Waxman 2011). Al-Haj

---

[15] Expressions denigrating Jews cause an immediate uproar and public denunciation of those who dare to break the appearance of Jewish unity. Similar and worse insults against Arabs are considered normal and meet with apathetic responses by state agencies and the media. On the soccer turfs, for example, "Kill the Arabs" is a shout heard constantly against teams representing Palestinian communities or against Palestinian players in teams of mixed ethnicity. Except for lip-service condemnation, little is done to stop it (Shor and Yonay 2011; Yonay and Shor 2014).

similarly talks about two components in the identity of Israeli Palestinians:

> The Palestinians in Israel developed two central identity components. One, the civic element, is manifested in connecting their future to the State of Israel, which they see as their homeland. Having no other homeland except Israel, they struggle for full equality of rights in this state. The national component is reflected in their perception of themselves as part of the Palestinian people and in their support of the right of self-determination for the Palestinians, including the establishment of a Palestinian state alongside Israel" (2005, 202).

The experience of living in a Jewish state has thus shaped a unique Palestinian consciousness that differs from that of Palestinians in other parts of the world. They "have over time developed a 'strategy of adjustment,' which combines profound elements of bilingualism, biculturalism and a strong desire to fit into Israeli society" (ibid., 202). This strategy is expressed in the Vision Documents, four statements drafted in 2006–2007 by Palestinian activists and scholars. These documents best summarize the agenda shared by the mainstream of the Palestinian society in Israel and its "attempt to restore trust in the viability and feasibility of coexistence and reconciliation between Israeli citizenship and Palestinian nationality" (Agbaria and Mustafa 2012, 719; cf. Peleg and Waxman 2011, 68–76; Haklai 2012).

The only alternative approach among Palestinians has been developed by the Islamist movement whose goal has not been "to democratize the state, but to Islamize the Palestinian society in Israel" (Agbaria and Mustafa 2012, 728). Yet the Islamist movement in Israel deviates from the anti-nationalist Pan-Islamism of most Islamist movements in the area, due to its tendency "to emphasize the nationalist and local Palestinian perspective, with religious activities being used as a means of mobilization" (Ali 2004, 90; cf. Jad 2013 on the Islamist movement in the Palestinian Occupied Territories). The movement in Israel builds a Muslim community and provides alternative services to those insufficiently provided by the state. It does not aspire to an integrated Palestinian-Jewish society but rather accepts the political reality of a Jewish state in which it aims to preserve the integrity of a Muslim community (Ali 2004; Rosmer 2012; cf. Aburaiya 2004).[16]

---

[16] The last decade witnesses abundant research on the unique identity of Palestinians in Israel. We discussed a small fraction of that literature. A non-exhaustive list is Ashkenasi 1992; Rouhana 1997; Rekhess 1998, 2007a, 2007b; Abdel-Malek and Jacobson 1999; Suleiman 2002; Amara 2003; Sorek 2003, 2005, 2008; Dwairy 2004; Jamal 2004; Sa'di 2004a, 2004b; Rabinowitz and Abu-Baker 2008; Kanaaneh 2009; Pappé 2011; Peleg and Waxman 2011; Haklai 2012.

Intergroup Relations among Palestinians. The above description treats Palestinians in Israel as one group. Yet social divisions of ethno-religion and class run across Palestinian society in general, including within the Palestinian minority in Israel. Palestinian nationalists under-play the importance of internal differences among Palestinians. In the Israeli context the claim has been made that state policy has been to maintain separation among the Palestinian groups in order to prevent them from establishing a collective identity (Lustick 1980: 135; Jakubowska 1992, 85; Firro 2001, 41; Kanaaneh 2002, 140; Kanaaneh 2009; Kanaaneh and Nusair 2010, 3; Peleg and Waxman 2011, 23–25). This divide-and-rule policy "hindered the crystallization of a united Arab bloc and enabled Arab public figures and politicians to deal with the interests of their subgroups rather than the interests of the Arab minority as a whole" (Soen and Shmuel 1987, 331). Counteracting the divide-and-rule policy, Palestinian political and cultural elites, especially among Muslims and Christians, have advanced a common national identity and have resisted the Jewish establishment's emphasis on their separate reli-gious identities (Peleg and Waxman 2011).

Religious boundaries, however, do not vanish easily. Christians and Muslims in Israel hardly intermarry, and some prejudice and hostility between them persist in spite of leaders' attempts to eradicate them. Class differences between Muslims and Christians – the latter are on the aver-age much more likely to have higher education and middle-class occupa-tions – also keep the two groups apart. The relationship between the two religious communities has hardly been studied, partly because of the political sensitivity involved, but there are many indications that there is substantial tension and hostility (Shdema 2012; McGahern 2011).

The state has been much more successful in separating the Druze from other Palestinian Arabs. Although some Druze activists share the project of Palestinian nationalism, the majority have followed the Druze faction that reached an agreement with the state in the 1950s, which turned the Druze into an ally of the Israeli state in its conflict with other Palestinians.[17] Druze men are the only Palestinian group for whom military service is mandatory, and consequently the Druze have differ-ent ties with the Jewish majority than the other two religious groups. Druze politicians have joined Zionist parties, and Druze schools empha-size the difference of the Druze from Palestinians and the alliance of the Druze with Jews. Many Druze refuse to be called Palestinians, and some

[17] According to Frisch (1993, 52), the main interest of the state in constructing the alliance with the Druze was not necessarily to separate them from other Palestinians but to make a precedent of an agreement between the Jewish state and an Arab group.

avoid even the label "Arab," although Arabic is their native language (Frisch 1993; Hajjar 1996; Yiftachel and Segal 1998; Firro 1999; Kanaaneh 2009). At the same time, the Druze do share a language and a cultural heritage with Muslim and Christian Palestinians, and in several Palestinian communities they live side by side with Muslims and Christians. Because their language is Arabic and their appearance is similar to that of other Palestinians, the Druze suffer from discrimination and prejudice by those Jews for whom all Arab-speakers are the same (Wolkinson 1999, 68). We will elaborate on the Druze in Chapter 8. Another distinct Palestinian group is the Bedouins. Although most Bedouins have undergone a long and gradual process of sedentarization in the last century, the social boundaries between them and other Muslims have not disappeared; however, the nature of their relations with other Palestinian groups in Israel has not been studied. We will elaborate on this issue in Chapter 6.

2.4   Land, Development Policies, and Residential Segregation

Palestinians and Jews in Israel live in different places. About 92 percent of the former live in homogeneous separate communities with no Jewish inhabitants at all. Only about 8 percent reside in mixed Palestinian-Jewish towns and cities, but even in such municipalities, most neighborhoods are homogeneous.[18] Of course, the same situation is mirrored on the Jewish side. Most Jews live in separate Jewish communities or in Jewish neighborhoods in mixed cities. Israeli social scientists have therefore never bothered to calculate segregation indexes between Arab Palestinians and Jews. The reality of almost complete segregation is well known in advance and does not change over time. A very small number of Palestinians and Jews rent apartments and houses in each other's communities, but such cases are too few to really matter (Falah 1996; Falah et al. 2000; Yiftachel and Yacobi 2003; Nurieli 2005; Leibovitz 2007; Rekhess 2007b).

Israeli Palestinians and Jews are differentially distributed across the regions of the country (Yiftachel 1997, 1999). More than half of the

---

[18] The same is true for Jerusalem, which, as explained above, we do not treat its eastern side as part of the State of Israel. The mixed cities are Tel Aviv-Jaffa, Haifa, Acre, Ramla, Lydda, Maalot-Tarshiha, Carmiel, and Nazarat Ilit. In the first five, neighborhoods are quite segregated; the sixth is actually two separate communities, one Palestinian and one Jewish put together under one municipality for administrative reasons. The last two were purely Jewish, but Palestinians moved in gradually due to housing shortages in nearby Arab localities.

Palestinians (58 percent) are concentrated in the northern part (Galilee, Haifa and its vicinity), 21 percent in the so-called "Triangle" area (located along the border between Israel and the West Bank)[19], and around 16 percent reside in the south. In the Triangle area and in the south, the Palestinians are all Muslims; the Christians live in the north and in mixed cities, and the Druze only in the north. The Jewish population is very differently located: one out of two Jews live in the two most economically developed areas, the Central District and Tel Aviv District (CBS 2013, Tables 2.17, Table 2.20). More than half the Muslim Palestinians (52 percent) and almost all of the Druze reside in rural localities, while only 33 percent of the Christian population, and 19 of the Jewish, reside in such communities (CBS 2013, Table 2.20; cf. Cohen 2015).[20]

Land, settlement, and housing policies in Israel have always been formulated to serve Jews, often at the expense of Palestinians (Halabi 1995; Wesley 2006; Yiftachel 2006; Hananel and Alterman 2015; Rouhana and Sabbagh-Khoury 2015). After the expulsion of Palestinians from hundreds of villages during the 1948 war, Israel used the emptied areas to settle the new Jewish immigrants. A major motivation behind this settlement was the fear of Palestinian repatriation according to the UN 194 resolution that called for Israel to allow the refugees to return to their homes (Rouhana and Sabbagh-Khoury 2015). Urban residences that had belonged to Arab Palestinians were transferred to the state and allocated to Jewish residents (Golan 2003; Nurieli 2005); most of the Palestinian villages were demolished, while dozens of economically unviable "development towns" and hundreds of agrarian settlements (*kibbutzim* and *moshavim*) were built for Jews on the sites of the destroyed villages (Kadman 2015). The establishment of the new settlements required not only taking over the land of the villages demolished after the 1948 war but also confiscating the land of remaining Palestinian villages in the Galilee and the Triangle (Or Commission 2003, §33–34; Falah 1989a, 2003; Yiftachel 1992; Firro 1999; Kedar 2001; Golan 2003; Forman and Kedar 2004; H. Cohen 2005; Y. Cohen 2015). Since many villagers lost the land from which they made their living,

---

[19] The term "Triangle" referred originally to the three largest towns in the Samaria Mountains (Nablus, Jenin, and Tulkarem), which became part of the Jordanian West Bank. The so-called Triangle in Israel is actually a long, densely populated strip of land at the western outskirts of the original Triangle that became part of Israel after the 1948 war (Shmueli et al. 1983).

[20] We include localities with 2,000–20,000 residents as rural although they are classified as urban by the CBS because they have maintained their rural character and have not developed many of the features typical of urban spaces (Falah 1993; Cohen 2015).

they had to look for work in Jewish urban areas (Carmi and Rosenfeld 1974; Rosenfeld 1978; Khalidi 1988).[21]

The appropriation of village lands has also aggravated land shortages in other Palestinian localities. Palestinian towns and villages have become overly crowded, with not enough space left for developing commerce and industry (Or Commission 2003, §35–36; Wesley 2006; Jabareen and Mustafa 2013). While hundreds of new Jewish communities have been erected, Palestinians have not been allowed to establish even one new settlement (Rosenhek and Shalev 2000).[22] Another major problem that has hurt the development of Palestinian communities is that, in many places, the state has not issued the required official development plan, thus preventing the installation of modern infrastructure and the establishment of industrial and commercial projects, and placing a constant threat of demolition over many residential houses built out of necessity without permits (which could not be granted without the official plan; Or Commission 2003, §37; Wesley 2006).

Residential patterns and the lack of land have contributed to the persistence of the traditional institution of patrilocality. This means that men tend to build their homes near their fathers' houses, and women who marry move to those houses and thus have to live in proximity to the husbands' parents, brothers, and other relatives (Abou-Tabickh, 2010). The endurance of this pattern in modern Israel is exceptional in the Middle East, where widespread migration to large urban centers has been the rule (Joseph and Slyomovics, 2001: 3). The endurance of patrilocality might be attributed to the small size of Israel, but it is undoubtedly reinforced by the barriers Palestinians meet in moving to large urban areas. As mentioned above, most neighborhoods in Jewish communities have hardly any Palestinians, and Jewish owners are very reluctant to rent or sell to Palestinians. Moreover, local authorities do not provide necessary services to Arab-speaking residents. When, in spite of these problems, thousands of Palestinians have found places to live in nearby Jewish towns – especially in the Galilee in Nazareth Illit (Upper

---

[21] Even today the dominant ideology in Israel sees establishing a new Jewish community as a pioneering act, and all Israeli governments have encouraged and subsidized Jews to move to new settlements in spite of the high cost of developing new infrastructures, the ecological costs, and the frustration of Palestinians whose residence in these new settlements has been blocked.

[22] The only exception are several small towns built for the Bedouins in the Galilee and the Negev, where it was the state's interest to evacuate residents of many small villages and encampments in order to free more land for Jewish communities and for other state goals (Abu-Sa'ad 2005; Falah 1985; see more in Chapter 6). According to Cohen (2015), from 1961 to 2013 the number of officially recognized Palestinian communities in the North increased from 66 to 83, but the reason for this is state recognition of old communities rather than the establishment of new ones.

Nazareth) and Carmiel – they have faced great obstacles. Expressions of hostility have been not only frequent but also publicly stated by mayors and other officials who refuse to fulfill even their legal obligations to provide basic services (Cohen 2015). Arab schools are yet to be built in Nazareth Illit, for example, where there are almost 2,000 children who have to be bussed to schools in nearby Arab communities (ACRI 2013a). The official reply by Mayor Shimon Gapso to the demand to establish Arab schools (20 percent of the residents of this town are Palestinian) is telling and demonstrates the implications of identifying the state as Jewish:

Nazareth-Illit is a town established to Judeize the Galilee ... That was its mission in the past, and this is its mission at present ... Indeed, there are Arab residents with Israeli citizenship who live in the city and benefit equally from city services but still, Nazareth Illit is a Jewish city, exactly as Nazareth is an Arab city ... The establishment of Arab educational institutions in Nazareth-Illit, the same as establishing a Muslim cemetery or a mosque, would mean total relinquishing of the city's character as Jewish and a failure of the mission for which it was established (ACRI 2013b).[23]

The story of Nazareth Illit is not an exception but a typical case that demonstrates the logic of ethnic relations in Israel. The fundamental assumption is separation: There are Jewish communities and Palestinian ones. When Palestinians violate this logic and move to communities considered by Jews to be Jewish it is assumed that the "host" city does not have to provide them with services. Mayor Gapso insists that Palestinian residents "benefit equally from city services" but believes that such equality does not include the establishment of Arab schools, mosques, and even cemeteries.[24] He says so in spite of the fact that Nazareth Illit was founded on lands expropriated from Palestinian residents of Nazareth and its neighboring Palestinian villages. Furthermore, the state expanded Nazareth Illit's jurisdiction so that this city has much more land per capita than the neighboring Arab Palestinian communities.[25] Within this jurisdiction the

---

[23] Following a discussion in the Knesset education Committee, the then Minister of Education promised to ensure the opening of Arab school in the city, but a few years later nothing changed except for the despair of the Palestinian parents who stopped fighting and the mayor's conviction of bribery (http://www.timesofisrael.com/nazareth-illit-mayor-convicted-of-bribery/). In June 2016, the parents petitioned the Supreme Court to order a school construction but withdrew their petition following a promise of the Ministry of Education and Nazareth Illit to reconsider the issue. In July 2017, the parents filed another petition to the Supreme Court due to the refusal of the state to advance the establishment of Arab schools.

[24] Burial places in Israel are separate according to religion and are provided by municipal authorities.

[25] The Or Commission Reports compares the land available per capita in Sakhnin and Karmiel, a Jewish town established on lands confiscated from Sakhnin residents in the

regional industrial area was built, enriching the city with regional business taxes. In the next section we describe the place of Palestinians in the Israeli economy in consequence of the differential development policy of the state.

2.5   The Palestinians in the Israeli Economy

The Israeli economy has undergone two major periods: During the first 25 years of its existence (1948–1973), it was highly regulated and tightly managed under the leadership of a dominant party (Mapai, headed by Ben-Gurion) that controlled both the government and the Histadrut (the labor federation which encompassed most workers in Israel). After the 1973 war, Israel witnessed a long economic crisis related to the war expenses, the worldwide stagflation crisis, the shift of power in Israel politics (Begin's victory in 1977), and the hyperinflation of the first half of the 1980s when prices rose by 445 percent in 1984 alone. The hyper-inflation provided economic policy-makers with the opportunity to trans-form the Israeli economy and move from tight regulation and intensive state interference in the running of the economy to a neoliberal regime.[26] In what follows we describe these economic policies in more detail and highlight their impact on the Palestinians in particular.

During the first 25 years of the state, rapid industrialization took place by attracting private capital to medium-size industries (e.g. tex-tile, food) and by establishing heavy industry with public capital that came from aid from the US and world Jewry and from reparations paid by Germany for the Nazi destruction of Jewish lives and property. These funds were invested in large corporations owned by the state and the Histadrut. Mapai's control of the government, heavy industry and labor unions (through the Histadrut) facilitated corpora-tist arrangements that supported fast growth and the development of an extensive welfare state. Such development was geared toward the Jewish population. Millions of new Jewish immigrants needed employ-ment, housing, and social services, and their needs came first (Ozacky-Lazer 2000). The state also had to maintain the newly established "development towns," which housed new Jewish immigrants and strengthened Israel's claim over Palestinian lands. It subsidized new factories in these towns to provide employment for the new immigrants (Ofer 1967; Patinkin 1967; Ben-Porath 1986; Sharkansky 1987; Aharoni 1991; Grinberg 1991; Shalev 1992; Khamaisi 2011).

1960s and 1970s. In 2000, Karmiel residents had 524 m² per capita, much more than the 191 m² per capita in Sakhnin (2003, §35).

[26] Kristal (2013) divides our first period into two, distinguishing between a stage of "mixed economy" (from 1948 to the late 1960s) and a stage of "coordinated capitalism."

The Standing of Palestinians. The Palestinians who remained in Israel were mostly farmers who depended on their land for subsistence. The expropriation of a large part of this land reduced their livelihood resources. They also could not compete with the growing Jewish agricultural sector, which benefited from state favoritism and support. The Jewish communal agricultural settlements and the new *moshavim* created for the new immigrants benefited from a more advanced technology, professional supervision, and preference in the allocation of water and marketing outlets. Palestinian farmers could produce for local consumption but were limited in their ability to market to the Jewish sector. Farming thus accounted for less and less employment among Palestinians. In 1961, 38 percent of Palestinians – once mostly farmers – worked in agriculture, and this figure further dropped to 16 percent in 1970, 6 percent in 1983, and 3 percent in 2004 (Haidar 2009, 259; cf. Wiemer 1983; Khalidi 1988; Manna 2008, Table B8; Gozansky 2014).

The diminishing opportunities in agriculture pushed Arab Palestinian men to employment in industrial production and construction, but they were placed at the bottom of the queue of workers waiting for jobs. Until 1959, Palestinian workers could not even join the Histadrut, the powerful union federation and one of Israel's biggest employers, which also controlled the supply of workers to private employers. Even after it opened its gates for them, the Histadrut's policies continued to favor and support Jewish workers (Wiemer 1983; Wolkinson 1999, ch. 5; Ozacky-Lazer 2000; Gozansky 2014).[27] The anthropologist Henry Rosenfeld, who studied the transformation of Arab villages during the first decades of the state, described the Palestinians as the "reserve army" of Israeli industry: working in the least desirable jobs and being pushed out of employment in periods of economic slack[28] (Carmi and Rosenfeld 1974, 1992; Rosenfeld 1978; Zureik 1979; Lustick 1980;

---

[27] According to Ozacky-Lazer, the Histadrut preceded the state in providing basic services to Arab villages and defended to some extent Palestinian workers. As early as 1927, the Histadrut also established the Palestinian Labor League as an affiliated but separate organization for Palestinian workers. Controlled by the Histadrut itself, the League represented Palestinian workers who might have brought all workers' wages down had they remained unorganized. The League continued its activities after 1948, but Palestinian workers kept pushing for membership in the Histadrut itself (Bernstein 1998; Ozacky-Lazer 2000; Gozansky 2014). In 1953, Palestinians were admitted for the first time to specific unions within the Histadrut but it took a few years more until they gained full membership (Ozacky-Lazer 2000; Gozansky 2014).

[28] During the Military Administration (in place until 1967), the fact that Palestinians needed permits to go out of their communities enabled the state to control who could gain employment outside his or her locality, and political considerations often dictated such decisions. The prevention of good employment for Palestinians suspected as 'disloyal' further slowed down the economic mobility of Arab Palestinian citizens.

Khalidi 1988; Lewin-Epstein and Semyonov 1992; Goldscheider 1996; Firro 1999). The share of Palestinians working in industry increased continuously from 13 percent in 1961 to 26 percent 1983, and then declined to 15.5 percent in 2004, the latter probably reflecting a relative decline of industry in the Israeli economy in general; the share of those working in construction increased from 12.5 to 19 percent in 1983, and to 20 percent in 2004 (Haider 2009: 259; Manna 2008, Table B8).

Discrimination has been a major hindrance to the occupational advancement of the Palestinians (Gozansky 2014). Although Israel has a progressive law that proscribes discrimination on, *inter alia*, the basis of nationality, enforcement is very weak. It seems that Palestinian workers are afraid to file suits and suspect the willingness of the court to use the law to protect their rights (Margalioth 2004). While there are few studies that directly prove discrimination, it is unlikely that the prejudices against Palestinians and the level of hostility toward them discussed above (Section 2.3) would not gravely affect the behavior of Jewish employers, managers, and coworkers. One finding in the surveys conducted by Smooha is that 43 percent of Jews said they were "not ready to have an Arab as a superior in a job" (Smooha 2004, 23). Given the frequent hostilities between Israel and the Palestinians outside of Israel, the presence of a mixed Palestinian-Jewish workforce is widely considered as a source of tension, and even employers who do not share the hostility toward Palestinians may dodge hiring or promoting them in order to avoid such potential tension among their workers. Indirect evidence of the impact of Israeli-Palestinian violent clashes on labor market discrimination was provided by Miaari et al. (2011) during the Second Intifada. They found that the likelihood of Palestinian workers to be laid off by private employers increased relative to the years before the Intifada. A direct proof of discrimination of Palestinian sellers and potential buyers was found in a field experiment of an online market for used cars (Zussman 2013). The existence of discrimination in this market increases the likelihood of discrimination in the labor market, where relationships are expected to continue for a long time.

Discrimination is also evident by the absence of Arab Palestinians (or their scarce presence) in many workplaces. Wolkinson (1999), who studied a sample of 48 industrial facilities employing more than 100 workers, found that almost half of them (22) did not employ any Palestinian workers; among the rest, in only one facility were there Palestinians in a managerial capacity, and in only six facilities were they present in professional, technical or clerical positions. In a bit of an understatement, Wolkinson concludes that

Given the thousands of Israeli Arabs who are university graduates, it is reasonable to conclude that but for discriminatory practices, more Arabs would be employed in white-collar positions. This conclusion is strongly reaffirmed by the acknowledged practice of many of the personnel managers of the plants employing Arabs to afford preferences to Jews when filling of white-collar positions (1999, 67).

In workplaces linked to the army and to the weapons industry, official restrictions (such as security clearance) limit the employment of Palestinians (Margalioth 2004, 864–868). In a country with a strong military sector, this limitation has been consequential. Since most of the high-tech industry has catered to the army and its surrounding industries and services, this restriction has severely limited opportunities for Palestinians in one of the most lucrative sectors of the economy. The utilities in Israel are also tightly linked to the army and the related services, and they too have also limited the hiring of Palestinians. In the electricity and water industrial branches, only 6.5 percent of all workers in 2008 were Arab Palestinian (4.8 if we exclude the Druze), much fewer than their share in the Israeli population.[29] The "security" rationale is used as a pretext to exclude Arabs even when there is no relation to a military or security function (Wolkinson 1999, 68).

Palestinian workers are keenly aware of the everyday racism and microaggression directed at them in the workplace (Gozansky 2014; Shoshana 2016), and this awareness undoubtedly affects their decisions and labor-market strategies. For example, Palestinians may have to compromise on lower salaries in order to secure employment. Studies examining net earning gaps among different ethnic and gender groups in Israel found that both Muslim men and women earned much less than their Jewish counterparts for comparable work characteristics (Asali 2006; Bental et al. 2017; Haberfeld and Cohen 2007; Khattab 2005). In the case of women, lower salaries due to discrimination might be critical for deciding whether or not to go out to work. Women earn less than men, and if Palestinian women earn even less than Jewish women, it may make their market employment unprofitable if wages are too low to compensate for childcare expenses.

The barriers Palestinians encounter in entering Jewish-owned or Jewish-managed firms, and in being promoted to good jobs, push many of them in two directions: self-employment and the public sector. We turn now to these two options before moving on to describe the changes that took place in the Israeli economy in the last decades.

---

[29] Calculated by the authors from census data for all ages but without Jews born outside Israel. Had we included Jewish immigrants, this low figure would be even smaller.

Self-Employment and the Ethnic Economy. Many minorities who face discrimination and barriers to entering and advancing in big firms and corporations owned and managed by majority members establish their own businesses (e.g. Waldinger et al. 1990; Clark and Drinkwater 1998; Fairlie 2007). This is the case among Palestinians in Israel. About a fifth of Muslim Palestinian male workers were self-employed in 2007–2009, compared with 12 percent among Jews. Among Christian Palestinians, the rate was even higher (24 percent; Yonay and Kraus 2011). As is the case in many ethnic economies worldwide (e.g. Portes and Jensen. 1989; Waldinger et al. 1990; Clark and Drinkwater 2000), the Palestinian economy in Israel has been composed mostly of small businesses, which employ a few workers at most. These "ethnic businesses" are usually in competitive branches with low profits and pay low salaries to employees (Khalidi 1988; Yonay and Kraus 2001; Schnell and Sofer 2002, 2003; Gozansky 2014).

In Israel, the tendency of minority firms to be small is even more pronounced due to the neglect of Palestinian communities by state development policies. While new industrial zones were established in Jewish towns, very few Arab municipalities – which have a much inferior infrastructure – have industrial zones within their jurisdiction (Yiftachel 1992; Schnell and Sofer 2003; Wesley 2006; Khamaisi 2011). Jews have been preferred in the allocation of state aid to new businesses. Arab Palestinians also face more difficulties in getting credit, and they face discrimination by Jewish producers and consumers. In spite of these difficulties, Palestinians have had successes in several fields, including construction, transportation (where small companies have filled the void left so far by the big bus companies), garages, carpentries, welding workshops, and retail (Khalidi 1988; Schnell 1994; Schnell et al. 1995).[30]

The Public Sector. Racism, prejudice, and intergroup tension do not stop at the threshold of the public sector, but public accountability, political pressures by minorities, and a greater emphasis on formal procedures have turned the public sector, especially in democratic countries, more egalitarian in employing and promoting minority workers. The

---

[30] Palestinian professionals cater mostly to the Palestinian population, but they have started to compete for Jewish customers as well recently. Yet, some Palestinian clients prefer Jewish lawyers and accountants whom they believe have better contacts with state and local authorities. In retail, Palestinian shops attract Jewish clients from nearby communities due to their low prices, but their sales fluctuate with the level of Palestinian-Jewish tension. After the 2000 riots, for example, many Jewish clients either wanted to punish the Palestinians or were afraid to enter their communities.

expansion of educational and health services in Israel in the 1990s and 2000s provided job opportunities not only for Jewish women but for Palestinians women as well. The growing educational attainment among Palestinian women enabled them to enter teaching, nursing, and clerical positions (Semyonov and Lewin-Epstein 1994; Yonay and Kraus 2001, 2011; Winckler 2003; Shalev and Lazarus 2013). Consequently, the share of Palestinians working in the social services increased from 9.2 in 1961 to 27 percent in 2012, mainly in educational and health services (CBS 2012, Table 12.12).

Studies show that Palestinian males employed in the public sector in Israel attain higher socioeconomic status and earnings than in the private sector (Lewin-Epstein and Semyonov 1994; Yonay and Kraus 2001; Bental et al. 2017). Earning gaps between Palestinians and Jews have also been found to be smaller in the public sector than in the private sector, probably due to the existence of strict pay scales and to the examination of budgetary expenditures by special authorities (Kraus 1992; Yaish and Kraus 2003; Bental et al. 2017). Shalev and Lazarus (2013) compared the earning advantage of Palestinians at two points of time. In 2002, Israeli Palestinians who worked in social services (mostly in the public sector) experienced two kinds of gains: "a sectorial premium vis-à-vis comparably qualified workers employed in other branches, and equality of earnings with the members of more socially advantaged groups within the social services (ibid., 177–178)." However, by 2010 these achievements were weakened; the premium for working in the social services has become smaller, and a gap in favor of Jewish workers has developed (ibid., 177; cf. Bental et al. 2017).

The protection the public services provide to Palestinians in Israel is very partial and unsatisfactory. Most Palestinian employees in this sector work in public services within their own communities (either in Palestinian municipalities or in providing services to Palestinian publics in the mixed cities). These employees are teachers in Arab schools, social workers, and the staff of the municipal administration. The positions in local public services attract many highly educated women and men, and since men have fewer opportunities than their Jewish counterparts, Palestinian women face harsher competition from their male compatriots, compared with Jewish women (Yonay and Kraus 2011, 2013; Bental et al. 2017).

In branches of the public service outside their own localities, Palestinians face the same obstacles that hinder their hiring and promotion in the private sector and are consequently greatly underrepresented. That is why, in 2008, only 4.2 percent of employees in public administration were Palestinians, much less than their share in the population.[31] The only public service outside Palestinian communities that seems to provide a more egalitarian employment for Palestinians is that of medical services. Indeed, the latter have become one of the biggest niches for Palestinians, both women and men. Relatively to Jewish men, many more Palestinian men are employed as nurses, in other paramedical occupations, and as physicians (Keshet et al. 2015; Popper-Giveon et al. 2015; Popper-Giveon and Keshet 2016). Yet even in the medical services which are often brought as a model for equal treatment of Palestinian and Jewish workers, a recent study showed the high level of abuse of Palestinians by managers, colleagues, and their own patients (Keshet and Popper-Giveon 2017).

The Neoliberal Period. The neoliberal turn started in Israel in 1985 (under the disguise of the stabilization program of 1985 to stop hyperinflation) and accelerated in the 1990s (Shalev 2000; Ben-Bassat 2002; Hanieh 2003; Ben-Porath 2008; Maman and Rosenhek 2009, 2012; Kristal 2013). This period is characterized by deregulation, a decrease in state interference in industrial decisions, a weakening in the power of unions, an increase in the share of outsourced workers, and cuts in welfare services.

During the neoliberal period the growth of the Israeli economy was led by the high-tech sector, while labor-intensive industries such as the textile industry have gradually moved to countries with cheaper labor (Justman 2002). This industrial restructuring has had a major impact on the position of various groups of workers. The high-tech industry absorbed some Palestinian workers, but it is still very difficult for Palestinians to find work there (Habib et al. 2010). The transfer of the textile industry to the Far East and, following the peace process in the Middle East, to neighboring countries such as Egypt and Jordan was especially inimical to Palestinian women with a low level of education, who depended on this industry.[32]

Neoliberal labor policies worsened the work conditions of workers in the public sector, reducing their relative income, and providing less job security. Many permanent positions in the public sector were either canceled or filled with workers from human resource companies – a change that reduced benefits, job security, and worker bargaining power. Government contracts were moved to subcontractors, resulting in reduced compensation and benefits for workers (Artstein 2002, Dahan 2002; Strawczynski and Zeira 2002; Cohen et al. 2003; Haidar 2009;

---

[31] See note 29 for explanation on the data.
[32] While 12,600 Palestinian women worked in the textile industry in 1998, only three years later, in 2001, a mere 6,000 women found employment in this industry (Haidar 2009, 262).

Shalev and Lazarus 2013). Palestinians depended more heavily than Jews on the public sector for good jobs, and were therefore more negatively influenced by the neoliberal turn (Bental et al. 2017; Sa'ar 2016). Another aspect of neoliberal reforms was the employment of a growing number of foreign workers, especially in construction, agriculture, and caregiving. Although originally the foreign workers were brought to replace the Palestinian workers from the territories occupied by Israel in 1967 (the West Bank and the Gaza Strip), the opening of this channel and the infinite number of potential workers abroad had an adverse impact on the salary and work conditions of the local workers, many of whom were Palestinians (Haidar 1995; Schnell et al. 1995; Hovsepian 2004; Habib et al. 2010; Sa'ar 2016). The arrival of about one million immigrants from the former Soviet Union during the 1990s – about a fifth of the Israeli population at the time – also weakened local workers' bargaining power with employers (Al-Haj 2004; Remennick 2007). The newcomers competed with Arab workers in some of the latter's labor niches, for example, in occupations as nurses, saleswomen, and cashiers.

2.6   Summary

This chapter laid the ground for our study by describing the unique case of the Palestinian minority in Israel. We began with a very brief history of the encounter between the Jewish settlers and the indigenous Palestinians from the late nineteenth century to Israel independence in 1948. In the second section of this chapter, we reviewed the legal standing of Palestinians in Israel, focusing on the controversy around the definition of the state as "Jewish and Democratic." Next we described the complex ethnic structure of Israel and the relationships among the various groups that make up the Israeli society. We emphasized the social barriers between the Palestinian and the Jewish communities, the pervasive racist attitudes of the Jewish population, and the perception of Palestinians among Jews as not really belonging to the Israeli society. We also discussed the relationships among Palestinian subgroups. Although Palestinian leaders in Israel aspire to maintain the unity of all Palestinians, social and religious distinctions among them obstruct such unity, and the state has encouraged divisive forces among Palestinians in an attempt to weaken their national solidarity. The state was especially successful in separating the Druze from other groups and turning most of them into an ally of Jews in their struggle with Palestinians. In the fourth section, we examined in more detail the geographical segregation of the two national groups. We saw that the Palestinians lived mostly in separate communities or in separate neighborhoods in mixed cities. Development efforts have been concentrated in Jewish communities, leaving Palestinians with lacking infrastructure for modern industrialization and relatively few opportunities for employment. Israeli control of agricultural resources and marketing and extensive confiscation of Palestinian-owned agricultural lands pushed Palestinians out of agricultural work and turned them into the "reserve army" of the Israeli industry. They worked in the least desired jobs and were widely discriminated against in the main economy. As an alternative to dead-end jobs in the main Jewish sector, many Palestinian men established their own businesses, but due to undeveloped infrastructure, lack of resources, and discrimination in capital and marketing, their success has been limited.

The picture depicted in this chapter attests to the marginal position of Palestinians in Israel. They became a minority group that is considered foreign in its own homeland. Palestinians are excluded from major institutions and are discriminated against in the labor market and in the allocation of public resources. How have these circumstances shaped the standing of Palestinian women in the labor market? The goal of this book is to answer this question by analyzing various sources of data, looking separately at the achievements of each Palestinian group over time and comparing them to each other.

3   Changing Demography
Trends of Educational Attainment, Marriage Patterns, and Fertility

This chapter prepares the ground for our research by examining two important determinants of women's place in the economy: Sections 3.1 and 3.2 focus on the educational achievements of the various ethno-religious groups in Israel since the 1970s, and Section 3.3 describes marriage and fertility trends.

Macro-level studies on labor force enrollment in many countries have emphasized the importance of schooling in facilitating women's entrance into paid employment. Studying Palestinian women's educational achievements is therefore essential for understanding their labor market behavior. In this chapter we present the results of such a study, but in order to put our results in a broader context, we begin with a general description of the educational opportunities available to Palestinians in Israel.

3.1   The Development of the Education System in Israel

The development of a good education system was a major concern of the Israeli state during its first decades. It was considered to be a vital instrument for absorbing and integrating the numerous immigrants and an investment in developing a skilled labor force. Thus, the Compulsory Education Law, requiring that all children finish primary school (grades 1–8), was one of the first laws enacted by the Knesset in 1949. This law has been changed several times since then, expanding the span of compulsory education to the ages of five to eighteen. An amendment from 1984 mandates preschool education from the age of three, but due to budgetary limitations, the implementation of this amendment has been postponed for many years and has been gradually executed only in the last years (Kalekin-Fishman 2004).

The Structure of the Educational System. Since the enactment of the Law of State Education in 1953, the education system in Israel has been highly centralized. The Ministry of Education directly controls all public schools and tightly supervises private schools as well. The Ministry is also responsible for the training and certification of all teachers, and it determines the curricula to be taught. In accordance with the logic of national separation between Jews and Palestinians, a separate system was established for Palestinian students.[1] The language of these schools is Arabic, and they have separate curricula. The separate system for Palestinians does not, however, mean more autonomy. On the contrary, it enables Jewish officials in the Ministry of Education to tightly control the personnel and curricula of Palestinian schools.[2] Consequently, Palestinian students barely study their own literary and historical heritage, and the Ministry of Education does not include in the curricula any materials that may encourage Palestinian nationalism. Rather than pointing out the connection between Israeli Palestinians and Palestinians elsewhere, the curriculum emphasizes the uniqueness of this Israeli population (Al-Haj 1995; Jabareen 1998; Or Commission 2003, §62; Kalekin-Fishman 2004; Levy 2005; Abu-Saad 2006; Mor-Sommerfeld et al. 2007; Nusair 2010).[3] Only in 2000 were the goals of the Arabic school system as defined in the Public Education Law amended to include familiarity with "the language, the culture, the history, the heritage, and the unique tradition of the Arab population," but at present it is still questionable how much has actually changed in the wake of this amendment (Or Commission 2003, §62.).

When the state established special relations with the Druze and Bedouin communities, two special school systems were founded for these two relatively small groups. The Druze and the Bedouins have more control of the systems that serve them and the curricula taught in their schools than the other Palestinians in Israel (Al-Haj 1995, 72–75; Halabi 1997).[4]

---

[1] See Levy and Shavit (2015) for the very few cases in which Palestinian pupils study with Jews.

[2] Due to political compromises, when the public system was established, a separate system was established for religious Jews as well, but unlike the Arab system, religious Jews were appointed to run this system according to their own views.

[3] Rhoda Ann Kanaaneh wrote, for example, that "the Israeli school system never taught me about the Islamic era in Palestine, which lasted about 1,300 years; it tried to keep that out of my mind" (2002, 7).

[4] Since many municipalities have a religiously mixed Palestinian population, the type of the public school depends on the majority. Thus, the big Druze communities in Shefa'Amr and Rameh notwithstanding, the schools in these towns belong to the regular Arab system. Yet certain schools might be identified with the Druze, be managed by a Druze principal, employ mostly Druze teachers, and draw mostly Druze students. Individual school choices are not determined strictly based on group affiliation. Parents may send their children to a close-by school or to a school they consider better even if it is identified with a different religious affiliation (We thank Ahmad Badran for this information; see also Badran 2012).

In addition to the public education system with its separate branches, numerous private schools also exist. The state participates in funding these schools at a level similar to that of the public schools, but parents and NGO's frequently add extra funding to these schools, which are usually smaller and more exclusive than the public schools. In Jewish communities, such schools are usually founded to advance specific pedagogical and philosophical doctrines (e.g. "open and democratic" schools; anthroposophic schools) but are often used to provide higher-quality teaching than in the public schools, and a better educational environment (Swirski 1999, ch. 9). Among the Palestinian population, private schools are mostly run by churches and are used even by non-Christians to avoid their public schools, which are poorly funded and of low quality compared to the Jewish schools (Yonay et al. 2015).

Expansion of the Arabic Education System. In the early years of Israeli statehood, the educational opportunities available to the Palestinian population were very limited. Their previous educational infrastructure had been destroyed, most of the urban intelligentsia had left Palestine or had been expelled, and the remaining population lived mostly in rural areas, under military administration (Mazawi 1994). The Compulsory Education Law of 1949 was not implemented immediately or equally. During the first years of the state, there were not enough teachers to teach all children, and the education of Palestinians was not a priority of the state, so many minority children remained out of school. Yet the state gradually expanded the educational system so that during the 1960s, primary education became universal. Secondary schooling was also expanded, and during the 1960s eleven new high schools were added to the Arabic system (Al-Haj 1995; Mazawi 1994). Further expansion has continued since then, with most Palestinian teenagers currently completing 12 grades.

Despite the major improvements in the educational opportunities of Palestinians, their schools are still underprivileged compared to the Jewish schools. Studies show that funding per student is lower in the Arab systems, and the average class size in Arab schools is larger than in Jewish ones[5] (Shavit 1990; Al-Haj 1995; Jabareen 1998; Mazawi 1994, 1996, 1999; Kraus and Yonay 2000; Khattab 2003; Coursen-Neff 2003; Okun and Friedlander 2005; Abu-Saad 2004a, 2004b). The poor condition of Arab education is well known and acknowledged by the official authorities. In 1997 the Supreme Court officially stated that a petition served against the Israeli Ministry of Education by the High Follow-Up

---

[5] The average number of pupils in a primary-school class is 24 in Jewish schools and 28 in Palestinian ones, and in post-primary schools the respective figures are 26 and 29 (data are for 2009–10, CBS 2013, Tables 8.8 and 8.19).

Committee (the major coordinating body representing the Palestinian citizens of Israel) "exposed a difficult picture of deprivation" of Arabic schools. This statement was based, *inter alia*, on an admission by the state (Or Commission 2003, §31).

Consequently, the educational achievements of Palestinian students are lesser than those of their Jewish peers. Their scores on the Growth and Effectiveness Measures of Schools (GEMS) tests in the eighth grade were much lower compared to those of Jewish students.[6] Israeli Palestinian pupils also have a much higher school dropout rate. In 2012, 9.8 percent of Palestinian pupils graduating from middle school (ninth grade) did not continue to high school, and 6.0 percent dropped out after one year in a high school (tenth grade). Among Jewish pupils the respective figures are 2.9 and 2.7 percent only (CBS 2013, Table 8.35). The fact that about a sixth of Palestinian students did not reach eleventh grade puts a severe limitation on their job prospects as adults, and the picture gets even gloomier if we consider that only 36.0 percent of Palestinian high school graduates passed the matriculation tests and obtained the matriculation certificate that is a prerequisite for higher education. Among Jews, almost half (49.7 percent) were awarded this crucial certificate (CBS 2013, Table 8.26).

Tertiary Education. The tertiary level is the only one where integration between Palestinians and Jews occurs. The teaching language is Hebrew,[7] and for students whose previous schoolwork was in Arabic, this is a very difficult transition. They have to listen to lectures in a language many of them are not used to hearing and have to write term papers and exams in a language they have learned as a foreign language. Not only is the Hebrew language foreign, but the cultural environment is as well. Almost all the lecturers, teaching assistants, and administrative workers are Jews (Ali 2013), and Palestinian students sometimes encounter prejudices, avoidance, discriminatory behavior, and explicit expressions of hostility. Cultural sensitivity training for academic and administrative staff and students does not exist, and almost no effort is made to bring Jewish and Palestinian students together. Moreover, the academic settings are established and managed by Jews. Their academic year is based on the

---

[6] In 2009/10, the average score of an Arab-Palestinian child was 53.3 in English and 39.0 in mathematics; Jewish pupils' mean score was 70.6 in English and 50.1 for mathematics (CBS 2013, Table 8.24).

[7] There are four colleges that cater only to the Palestinian population and the language of teaching is mostly Arabic. The first was a teachers college in Haifa, and the three others were established quite recently: the Sakhnin College in 2005, the Elkasami College in 2003, and the academic institute in Nazareth established in 2009. Altogether these four institutions provide a very limited number of academic programs and serve only a small fraction of Palestinian students.

Jewish calendar, ignoring major Muslim, Christian, and Druze holidays;[8] signs are in Hebrew and sometimes in English; the ceremonies are based on Jewish culture and history and are conducted in Hebrew. These features of Israeli academic institutions hamper the chances of Palestinian students to succeed relative to their Jewish classmates (Hendin 2011; Hertz-Lazarowitz 2003; Hertz-Lazarowitz and Zelniker 2004; Maayan 2013; Dirasat et al. 2014).

Although universities and colleges are officially private bodies, state supervision is tight and academic degrees require state certification. The state financially supports academic institutions and controls wages and tuition. The state has used its power to shape the academic system by regulating the number of institutions and the academic programs they are allowed to run. When Israel gained independence, it had only two institutions of higher learning (The Hebrew University and the Technion), and academic education was limited to talented students and to those who were economically privileged. During the decades that followed four more universities were opened – Bar-Ilan, Tel Aviv, Haifa, and Ben-Gurion (Be'er Sheva) universities – and even so, the number of students was still limited. Countrywide standard exams and high school matriculation grades determined students' prospects in general and their admittance to prestigious departments in particular (Troen 1992; Ayalon and Yogev 2005; U. Cohen 2007, 2014).

In 1995 the state initiated structural changes in the academic system by establishing a less competitive tier of regional colleges and permitting the establishment of private institutions in addition to the seven older and more prestigious universities. These changes have significantly expanded educational opportunities, increasing the number of students by a factor of 2.5 between 1990 and 2005 (to over 200,000 in 62 institutions; Knesset 2009). The change was particularly important for people in the Israeli periphery, Palestinians and Jews alike. Among the former, in 1991 only 11 percent of high school graduates enrolled in tertiary education; this figure rose to 18 percent in 2003. In 1995, only 6.7 percent of all undergraduate students in Israel were Palestinians; by 2007, this figure rose to 11 percent (ibid.). However, the expansion of the academic system brought an increasing stratification within it. Most of the new regional colleges serve the Palestinian population alongside the population of *Mizrahim* from Jewish "development towns." While facilitating the road these previously excluded populations can take toward academic degrees, the relative value of such

---

[8] Students are allowed to miss classes on the holidays they respect and are entitled to an alternative date for an exam if they miss one because of a holiday, but even if such entitlements allow students to join their families for the holiday, it still constitutes a burden that makes their studies more difficult.

degrees has been less than the degrees awarded by the established universities (Ayalon and Yogev 2005).

Given this difference in value, the fact that a much higher percentage of Palestinian applicants with a matriculation certificate are not accepted by Israeli universities as compared with their Jewish counterparts (39.5 and 19.6 percent, respectively; CBS 2013, Table 8.47) is another impediment Palestinians encounter. In addition, the new colleges do not satisfy the demand among Palestinians to study in the lucrative medical and paramedical fields. Due to their difficulties in Israel in pursuing the professions in which they are interested, many Palestinian citizens of Israel now study in Jordan and, to a smaller degree, in the Palestinian Authority or at European universities. Studying in foreign countries is more expensive than in Israel, and prospective employers in Israel prefer Israeli academic degrees, yet for many students, this is the only way to achieve the profession to which they aspire, especially in the medical field (Abu-Rabia-Queder and Arar 2011; Arar and Haj-Yehia 2013).

3.2   Trends in Educational Attainment

In this section we look at educational attainment among the major ethno-religious groups in Israel. Our analysis is based on labor force surveys conducted by the state CBS from 1974 to 2009 (collapsed into three-year intervals). We included only individuals in the age bracket 18–52. Our analysis here does not include Muslim Bedouins from the southern part of Israel since until 1995 they were not interviewed regularly in the labor force surveys (more about this group in Chapter 6). Nor does it include Palestinians residing in Jerusalem (on whom we write in Chapter 7). We included only those born in Israel to avoid the interfering impact of immigration.

Looking at the educational attainment of the various groups over the years, we see that all groups considerably increased their educational levels (Figure 3.1). The changes are most striking for Muslim and Druze women. Both of these groups monotonically increased their level of education from very low in 1974–1976 (a mean of 3.8 and 3.2 years of schooling, respectively) to a mean of about 11.2 years for both groups in 2007–2009. In spite of this impressive upswing, both groups' educational attainments in 2007–2009 were still lower than the level that Jewish women had already achieved in 1974–1976 (11.7). Christian women had a mean of 7.8 years of education in 1974–1976, and they increased their average years of schooling to 13.2 in 2007–2009 – close to the level attained by Jewish women in those years (13.9 years).

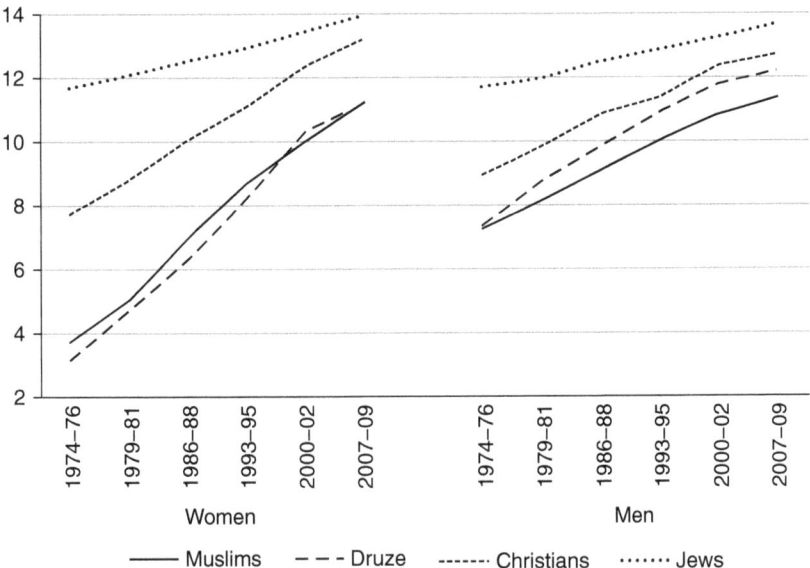

Figure 3.1 Mean Years of Schooling of Respondents Aged 18–52 by
Gender, Ethno-Religious Group, and Year
Source: Labor Force Surveys 1974–2009.
Note: Respondents born in Israel, excluding Palestinians from the Southern
District and from Jerusalem, and Druze from the Golan Heights.

As Palestinian women's educational achievements increased, they closed
the educational gap between them and their male counterparts. Whereas in
1974–1976 Muslim women attended three and half fewer years of schooling
than their male counterparts, in 2007–2009 both men and women had
almost the same number of years of education (11.2 and 11.4, respectively).
Christian women surpassed their male counterparts by half a year in 2007–
2009, while Druze women remained behind Druze men, although the gap
between the men and the women was narrowed to one year only. For Jewish
men and women, the mean educational levels in all years were very similar.

In order to further elaborate on the educational achievements
of the ethno-religious groups, we examined the levels of schooling
attended by the four groups, taking into account age groups and
birth cohorts. Starting with women and men who did not attend school
at all,[9] Figure 3.2A shows that despite the implementation of the Law of

---

[9] We started our analysis in 1979, since only from this year respondents were asked about
the type of last school attended. In previous years they were only asked on number of years
of schooling completed.

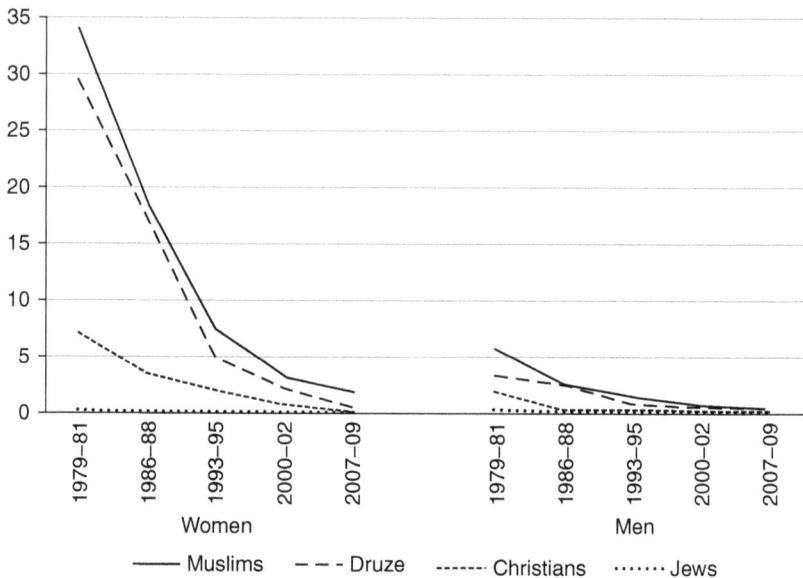

Figure 3.2A Percentage of Respondents Aged 18–52 without Schooling by Gender, Ethno-Religious Group, and Year
Source: Labor Force Surveys 1979–2009.
Note: Respondents born in Israel, excluding Palestinians from the Southern District and from Jerusalem, and Druze from the Golan Heights.

Compulsory Education introduced in 1949, even thirty years later (in 1979–1981) quite a high number of Muslim and Druze women did not attend any school (34.0 and 29.5 percent, respectively). Although the proportion among Christian women was much lower, still, more than 7 percent of them did not attend any school in 1979–1981. Almost all Jewish women (99.7 percent) had some education at that time. This is a norm that all the other groups of women reached only by 2000–2002. On the other hand, almost all men, regardless of ethnicity and religion, already had some education in 1986–1988.

The increase in school attendance stems mainly from successive cohort replacement (Appendix 3.1). That is, if we compare people of the same age across birth cohorts, the later the birth cohort, the higher the rate of school attendance. School attendance approached a universal level among Muslim and Druze women only beginning with the cohort born in 1956–1962, about ten years after the beginning of Israeli statehood. Among Christian women, almost the entire cohort born just before 1948

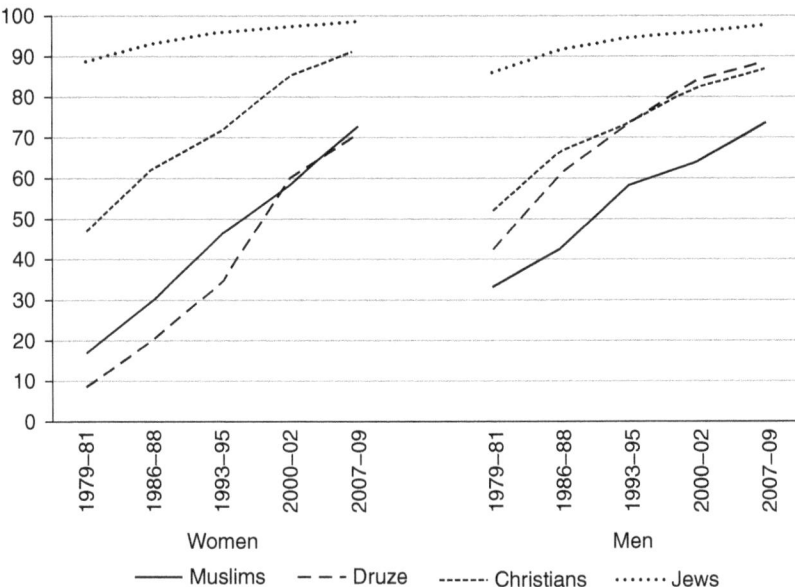

Figure 3.2B Percentage of Respondents Aged 18–52 Attending At
Least Secondary Education by Gender, Ethno-Religious Group, and
Year
Source: Labor Force Surveys 1979–2009.
Note: Respondents born in Israel, excluding Palestinians from the
Southern District and from Jerusalem, and Druze from the Golan Heights.

(born 1942–1948, reaching school age in 1948–1954) already had some
school attendance (94 percent).

As to secondary education, only 8.6 percent of Druze women and 16.7
percent of Muslim women attended at least secondary education in
1979–1981. Among Christian women, the rate was much higher at 47.2
percent, but it was significantly lower than the rate among Jewish women,
almost 90 percent of whom attended secondary education by then. Since
1979–1981 the percentage of women who have attended secondary
schooling has increased among all ethno-religious groups, most notice-
ably among Muslim and Druze women. Nevertheless, only among Jewish
women has attendance of secondary schooling been practically universal
since the mid-1990s, whereas among Muslim and Druze women, the
rates of those who have not attended high school remained high even in
2007–2009 (27 and 29 percent, respectively). Here too Christian women
are between these two poles; 8 percent of these women did not attend
secondary education in 2007–2009 (Figure 3.2B).

As in the case of formal schooling discussed above, the increase in women's share of secondary school attendance also stems mainly from cohort replacement. Both Druze and Muslim women monotonically increased their numbers having high school education, with the last cohort of Druze women (born 1984–1990) reaching universal high school attendance (98.1 percent), a level that Muslim women have yet to reach (their attendance rate is 94 percent). Christian women's cohorts reached a high rate of high school attendance much earlier (e.g. 76 percent of those born 1956–1962), and among those born after the mid-1970s, high school attendance is universal (Appendix 3.2).

Since the share of Muslim and Druze women who have completed secondary education has been relatively low, it is not surprising that the share of tertiary education among those women has been extremely small for most of the period under consideration. In 1979–1981, a negligible percentage of both Druze and Muslim women enrolled in an academic institution (1.3 and 3.5 percent, respectively; Figure 3.2C). During the following years these two groups increased their academic education, but until 2000–2002 the increase was very slow, and only thereafter did the rates reach significant levels. Thus by 2007–2009 about one-fifth of the women in each of these two groups had some academic education. An even more impressive change is observed among Christian women, among whom only 9.9 percent had some academic education in 1979–1981. This rate has risen monotonically so that by 2007–2009 it was 39 percent, still below the rate of 45,4 percent of Jewish women with academic education. The latter have also had a substantial increase in academic education, but since their rate was already 28 percent in 1979–1981, the rise looks less impressive. The increases in the rates of academic education stem not only from cohort replacement but occur also within birth cohorts as women get older, which means that significant numbers of women who did not continue to academic education have returned to school after their children were older and they were freed from many family duties.[10]

One of the features of patriarchal societies is that investment in boys' education is greater than in girls' in order to enable men, when married, to be able to support their wives and children (Karshenas 2001, 175–176). With the modern expansion of the service industry and the growing employment of women, investment in girls' and women's education has grown. This trend has been observed in Israel as well as in other MENA countries, making women's educational achievements in many

[10] For example, among Muslim women born in 1970–1976, 4.1 percent had an academic education when they were 18–24, and seven years later this percentage among the same cohort was 7.3 percent; when they reached the age of 32–38, almost 14 percent have had an academic education (Appendix 3.3).

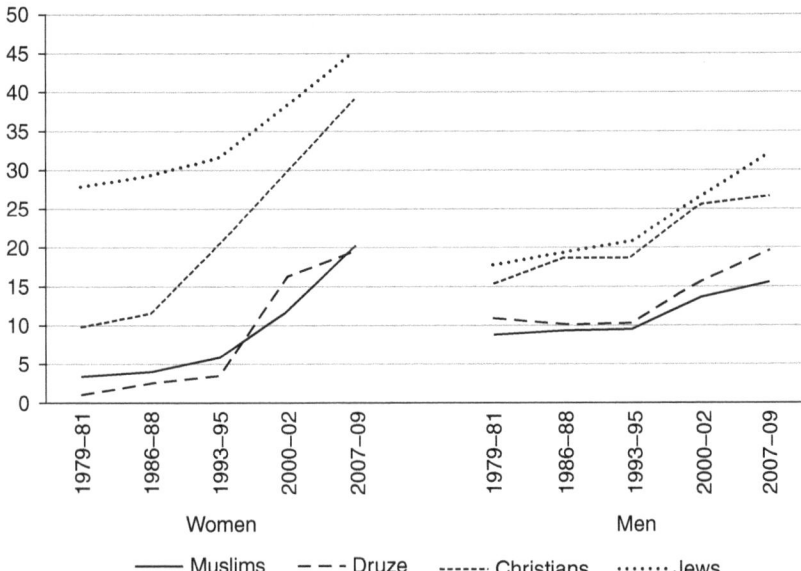

Women   Men

———— Muslims   – – - Druze   ------ Christians   ······· Jews

Figure 3.2C Percentage of Respondents Aged 18–52 Attending
Academic Education by Gender, Ethno-Religious Group, and Year
Source: Labor Force Surveys 1979–2009.
Note: Respondents born in Israel, excluding Palestinians from the
Southern District and from Jerusalem, and Druze from the Golan
Heights.

cases equal to or even exceeding those of men. Such a shift obviously
increases women's chances of gaining economic independence and of
achieving higher social standing in their communities (Smits 2007).

The gender equalization of academic education is thus an indication
of changing gender relations. It occurred in different periods for the
four groups in our study (Figure 3.2C). In all the years studied here,
Jewish women have had higher academic attendance than men, while
for Christian women educational advantage over men began in the mid-
1990s and has continued since then. Muslim women surpassed Muslim
men for the first time only in the last period of our study (2007–2009),
while Druze women have so far only achieved equality with their male
counterparts.

To put the Israeli case in a comparative perspective, we see that the share
of Muslim and Druze women in Israel in the age bracket 25–30 with some
tertiary education (around 21 percent) is much lower than among Libyan
women in the same age group (58 percent), slightly lower than among

Tunisian and Jordanian women (29 and 25 percent, respectively), much the same as among women in Algeria (22 percent), and much higher compared with women in Egypt, Morocco, or Syria (16, 10, and 6 percent, respectively; World Bank 2016).

3.3   Family Structure and Fertility

Marital patterns are important determinants of women's economic behavior. Changes in women's rates of marriage and age of marriage are related to changes in women's educational attainments, affect fertility rates, and influence women's incentives to take part in the paid-labor market (Blossfeld and Huinink 1991; Oppenheimer 1988; Rashad and Osman 2003). In this section we analyze trends of five family features among Palestinian women in Israel: Age at first marriage, rate of early marriage, age difference between spouses, rate of never-married women, and women's fertility rate. We will compare these trends to these features among Jewish women born in Israel, as well as among women in selected MENA countries, including in the Occupied West Bank and the Gaza Strip.

In patriarchal societies men are considered the main breadwinners in the family, and they delay marriage until they establish themselves economically. When these men get married, they choose much younger women, and as a result, women's fertility rates are high (Bergstrom and Bagnoli 1993; Danziger and Neuman 1999; Rashad et al. 2005).[11] Figure 3.3 presents trends of women's age at first marriage. Comparing the three Palestinian groups in Israel shows that throughout the years studied, Christian women married at an older age than women of the other two groups: In 1970 their average age at first marriage was 21.5 years, and this age rose to 25.2 in 2014. In 1970 Druze and Muslim women were the youngest to marry: Druze women at the age of 18.9 and Muslim women at 19.3. Since then the two groups have diverged. After more than four decades, Muslim women's average age at first marriage occurs two years later than in 1970, while Druze women average age at first marriage occurs almost four years later. Thus, in 2014 it is Muslim women who marry at the youngest age (21.3 years), followed by Druze women (22.9) and by Christian women (25.2). For all years (save 1970) Jewish women's first marriage is at a later age than among the three Arab-Palestinian groups, so that in 2014 Jewish brides were on the average older by 4.4 years than Muslim brides, by 2.8 years older than Druze brides, and only by half a year older than Christian Brides.

---

[11] Marriage at a young age extends the period of being fertile while married, and therefore women have more time to get pregnant, intentionally and unintentionally.

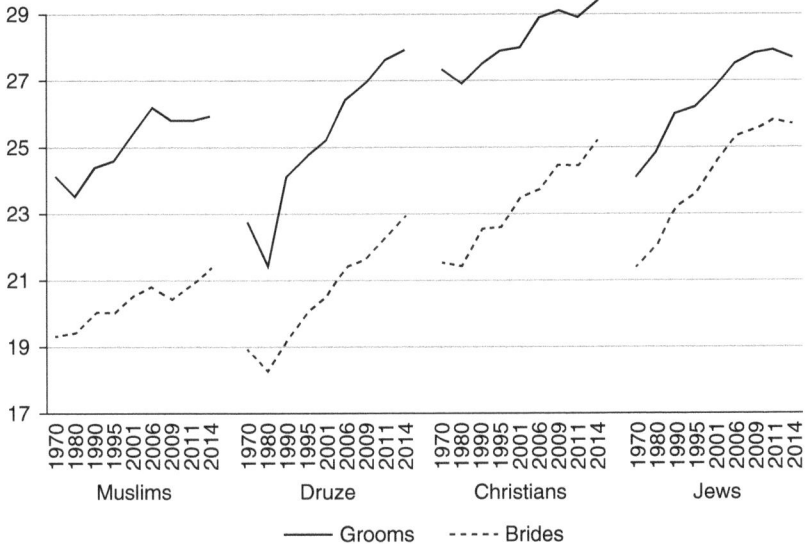

Figure 3.3 Median Age at First Marriage for Brides and Grooms by
Ethno-Religious Group and Year
Source: CBS (2013, 2016), Table 3.6.

Additional evidence of the relatively early marriage of Muslim and
Druze women is the share of women already married at the very young
age bracket of 15–19 (Part A, Appendix 3.4). In 1997 a relatively high
share of Muslim and Druze women in this young age bracket were already
married (15.6 percent among Muslim women and 14.4 among Druze)
while among Christian and Jewish women the rates were significantly
lower: 4.5 percent for Christian women and 2.3 for Jewish women.
Although throughout the years the rate of marriage at age 15–19 declined
both for Muslim and Druze women, in 2014 there were still about 6.6
percent of Muslim women and 3.5 percent of Druze women at that young
age who were already married.[12] Further inspection of Appendix 3.4
shows that very few men, Jewish or Palestinian, were married at this
young age bracket.

The share of married women in the age bracket 15–19 in some selected
MENA countries is presented in Part B of Appendix 3.4. Examining these
figures shows a great variance among these countries. The share of
married women at the age of 15–19 is very low in Libya, Algeria, and

---

[12] In 2014, 1.2 percent of Jewish women and 0.7 percent of Christian women were married
at the age 15–19.

Table 3.1 *Percentage of Never-Married Women Aged 45–54 by Ethno-Religious Group and Year*

	Muslim	Druze	Christian	Jews
1995	5.6	5.5	10.7	4.5
1997	6.8	7.8	12.5	5.1
2000	7.4	8.5	11.1	5.3
2002	8.1	8.1	10.3	5.6
2004	8.5	9.3	10.8	5.6
2006	9.1	10.4	10.1	5.8
2008	10.0	9.6	11.4	6.3
2010	11.7	10.0	11.6	6.9
2012	12.1	10.8	12.0	7.7
2014	12.2	10.2	12.2	8.0

Sources: CBS (1998, 2000, 2003–04, 2006, 2008–09), Table 2.19; CBS (2010–2012), Table 2.20; CBS (2014, 2016), Table 2.4.

Tunisia but relatively high among Egyptian and Moroccan women, as well as among Arab-Palestinians living in the West Bank and Gaza.[13]

As we saw earlier, grooms from the four ethno-religious groups marry on average at an older age than brides, but the age gaps differ among these groups (see Figure 3.3). They are lower for Jews than Palestinians. The biggest age difference in 1970 was among Christians, where grooms were on average older by 5.8 years than their brides. For Muslims this gap was 4.8 years, and for Druze 3.8 years. During the span of our study the age gap between grooms and brides increased to five years for Druze, remained the same for Muslims, and declined to 4.2 among Christians (all data is for 2014). Among Jews this gap declined from about 2.6–2.8 until the mid-1990s to two in 2014. One consequence of the relatively large age difference between Palestinian grooms and brides is the emergence of a marriage squeeze, that is, the number of potential grooms is smaller than that of potential brides, and consequently, a relatively high share of Palestinian women never marry. This is our next topic.

Trends in the share of never-married women are presented in Table 3.1. In contrast to the prevalent image of Palestinian women as married wives and mothers, we find that men in these groups are more likely to

---

[13] Early marriage in MENA countries sharply declined during the years, as reported by Rashad et al. 2005. Focusing on Kuwait and Libya, they report that while in 1970 around 40 percent of women aged 15–19 were married in Kuwait and Libya, these figures dropped by the mid-1990s to 5 percent and around 1 percent, respectively.

get married than women. In Table 3.1 we see that the share of never-married women in the age group 45–54 is high in all years for all three Palestinian groups as compared to Jewish women. In the mid-1990s Christian women's odds of being single (at age 45–54) were 10.7 percent, significantly higher than these odds for Muslim and Druze women (5.6 and 5.5 percent, respectively). Since then a monotonic increase in the share of single women (in the age bracket 45–54) among both Muslim and Druze women occurred, so that in 2014, 12.2 percent of both Muslim and Christian women and 10.2 of Druze women had never married.[14] Hlihel (2008) relates this rise to the expansion of the marriage squeeze. Other factors which may account for the increase in never-married women are the increase in educational achievements of Palestinian women and the decline in the frequency of arranged marriage as a social institution (Rosenfeld 1968; Matras 1973; Kanaaneh 2002; Sa'ar 2004; Zlotogora et. al. 2002; Lewin 2012).[15]

Israeli Palestinians have experienced a striking decline in fertility rates, similar to that among women in other MENA countries (Nahmias and Stecklov 2007; Schellekens and Eisennbach 2007). Before 1970, Muslim and Druze women had the highest rates of fertility among the four ethno-religious groups (an average of more than nine births per Muslim woman, and more than seven births on average per Druze woman; Figure 3.4). Fifteen years later, in 1985–1989, the birth rates among both Muslim and Druze women declined by about a half, to an average of 4.7 and 4.2 births per woman, respectively. Druze women's fertility rate has continued to decline: In 2000–2004 it was an average of 2.9 births per woman, and by 2014 it was a low average of 2.2 births per woman (a decline of almost 70 percent during the years of this study). Meanwhile, Muslim women's fertility rates stopped declining between 1985 and 2004, remaining about 4.6 births per a woman. However, during recent years, it gradually declined to an average of 3.3 births per woman in 2014 (a total decline of 63 percent).[16]

---

[14] Notice that the share increased also for Jewish women, but it is still the lowest percent (8.0 percent).

[15] When parents had more control of their daughters, many marriages were arranged by the parents, sometime against women's own will. A relatively high share of never-married Palestinian women was found also among Palestinian women in Gaza and the West Bank (Khawaja 2003, Table 6), as well as in other MENA countries (see Rashad at el. 2005).

[16] Okun (2013) examined the relationship between Muslim women's level of religiosity and their fertility. The fertility of more religious women has always been higher than that of less religious women, but for recent cohorts the difference was rather small. For example, among women born in the late 1960s, the gap was only 0.3 children.

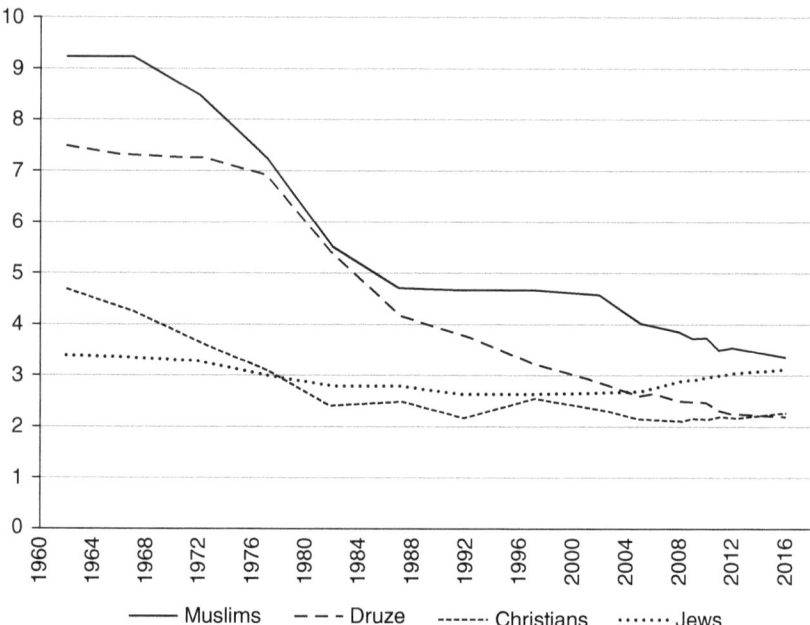

Figure 3.4 Fertility Rates by Ethno-Religious Group and Year
Source: CBS (2007), Table 3.12; (2011, 2013, 2016), Table 3.13.

In all years, the fertility rate of Christian women was the lowest among Palestinian groups, and it has sharply declined over the years. Before 1970 the fertility rate of Christian women was an average of about 4.7 births per woman; by 1980–1984 it was merely 2.4 births per woman (the lowest in the country), and since then it has fluctuated between 2.1 and 2.5.

While all Palestinian women's fertility rates declined, the reverse was happening among Jewish women. In the early years of the state, Jewish women had the lowest rate, 3.4 children on average, for example, in the early 1960s. This figure further declined to a low average of 2.6 children per woman in the 1990s, but in the last decade, Jewish women's fertility rate has been increasing so that in 2014, it was 3.1 children per woman, higher than the rates among Christian and Druze women.

Figure 3.5 presents trends in fertility rates among Arab women in selected MENA countries. Until the early 1980s, fertility rates in those countries were found to be highly homogeneous, unchanging, and extremely high. This led many scholars to consider high fertility rates to be typical to Islamic cultures (Obermeyer 1992; Courbage 1999). This conclusion was challenged in the late 1980s and early 1990s, when studies showed that fertility has been

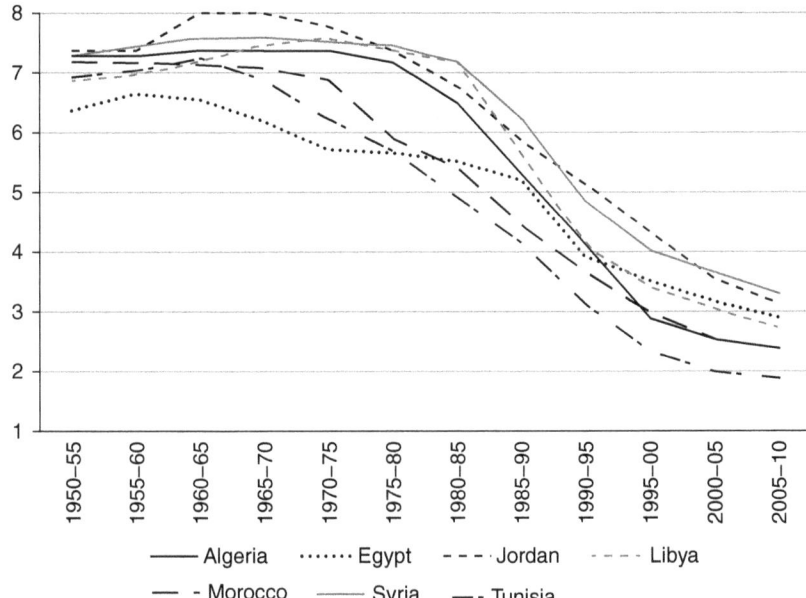

Figure 3.5 Fertility Rates for Selected MENA Countries by Year
Source: United Nations (2017).

steadily declining in MENA countries (Portugese 1998; Fargues 1989, 2000; Rashad 2000). This decline was related to explicit family planning policies introduced in these countries, higher educational attainment among women, and women's increasing participation in the labor force (Rashad 2000; D'Addato et al. 2008).

In comparison we see that the fertility rates of Muslim and Jewish women in Israel in the years 2005 to 2010 are higher than those found in MENA countries (except in Jordan and Syria where rates are somewhat higher). The lower fertility rates in most MENA countries might be explained by some differences in the social policies of the MENA countries and of Israel (Portugese 1998: Winckler 2003; D'Addato et al. 2008). Unlike Israel, the governments of most MENA countries have taken steps to encourage family-planning. In contrast, Israel's policy is pro-natalist, and large families with children are provided with financial benefits. Fertility treatments are also publicly funded. This comparison demonstrates that trends in fertility rates cannot be understood to be determined solely by cultural or religious heritage: Other factors in play must be taken into account (Kanaaneh 2002).

3.4   Summary

The data presented in this chapter show that Palestinian lives have considerably changed during the last decades. Palestinian men and women have increased their levels of education. Primary education is now universal among all groups and even secondary education has become almost universal among more recent birth cohorts. Higher education, which was rare among Muslim and Druze women as late as the 1990s, is now expanding fast among these two groups, with Muslim women surpassing their male counterparts and Druze women reaching parity with theirs. These changes have been accompanied by changes in marriage patterns. Early marriage (before the age of 19) is no longer the standard, the average age at marriage is generally rising, and higher proportions of Palestinian women have remained single longer or not married at all. Fertility rates have declined dramatically among all Palestinian groups. Yet the comparison with Jews and between the three Palestinian groups shows that tertiary education is much less common among Muslim and Druze women than among Jewish and Christian women; they also marry relatively young, and Muslim women still have, on average, more than 3.3 children.

Yet in spite of those changes and the fact that Israeli Palestinian women reside in a developed economy, they did not surpass other Arab women in MENA countries with respect to higher education or lower fertility rates.

In the next chapters, we will analyze changes in participation rates of women and their achievements in the labor market.

Appendix 3.1 *Percentage of Women Aged 18–52 without Schooling by Age Group, Birth Cohort, and Ethno-Religious Group*

Muslims

	18–24	25–31	32–38	39–45	46–52
1928–1934					86.0^a
1935–1941				67.7^a	68.6^b
1942–1948			44.8^a	46.6^b	41.2^c
1949–1955		26.3^a	16.1^b	15.7^c	16.8^d
1956–1962	7.1^a	8.6^b	3.1^c	5.1^d	5.6^e
1963–1969	2.4^b	2.3^c	1.4^d	3.7^e	
1970–1976	1.5^c	1.1^d	1.2^e		
1977–1983	0.6^d	0.8^e			
1984–1990	0.3^e				
Druze					
1928–1934					87.3^a
1935–1941				64.4^a	72.5^b
1942–1948			27.4^a	37.4^b	37.8^c
1949–1955		17^a	15.6^b	14.7^c	13.9^d
1956–1962	3.1^a	6.2^b	2.3^c	2.9^d	2.9^e
1963–1969	1.1^b	0.3^c	1.2^d	0.9^e	
1970–1976	0.9^c	1.0^d	0.0^e		
1977–1983	1.1^d	0.0^e			
1984–1990	0.0^e				
Christians					
1928–1934					24.0^a
1935–1941				12.2^a	17.7^b
1942–1948			6.1^a	6.4^b	8.6^c
1949–1955		2.1^a	2.4^b	2.5^c	2.0^d
1956–1962	1.0^a	0.8^b	0.8^c	1.3^d	0.5^e
1963–1969	0.0^b	1.9^c	0.8^d	0.0^e	
1970–1976	0.0^c	1.1^d	0.0^e		
1977–1983	0.0^d	0.0^e			
1984–1990	0.1^e				

Year of survey: ^{a} = 1979–1981; ^{b} = 1986–1988; ^{c} = 1993–1995; ^{d} = 2000–2002; ^{e} = 2007–2009.

Source: Labor Force Surveys 1979–2009.

Note: Respondents born in Israel, excluding Palestinians from the Southern District and from Jerusalem, and Druze from the Golan Heights.

Appendix 3.2 *Percentage of Women Aged 18–52 Attending At Least Secondary Education by Age Group, Birth Cohort, and Ethno-Religious Group*

Muslims

	18–24	25–31	32–38	39–45	46–52
1928–1934					1.2[a]
1935–1941				2.8[a]	2.9[b]
1942–1948			5.4[a]	4.8[b]	4.6[c]
1949–1955		11.1[a]	13.8[b]	14.5[c]	16.[d]
1956–1962	35.4[a]	33.2[b]	36.0[c]	33.6[d]	31.3[e]
1963–1969	53.3[b]	51.3[c]	53.6[d]	55.9[e]	
1970–1976	73.4[c]	69.5[d]	72.6[e]		
1977–1983	83.8[d]	84.1[e]			
1984–1990	94.1[e]				

Druze

	18–24	25–31	32–38	39–45	46–52
1928–1934					0.0[a]
1935–1941				0.9[a]	0.0[b]
1942–1948			4.5[a]	2.3[b]	2.0[c]
1949–1955		2.5[a]	5.7[b]	7.1[c]	10.0[d]
1956–1962	21.5[a]	19.5[b]	20.6[c]	22.8[d]	25.0[e]
1963–1969	42.8[b]	41.2[c]	53.0[d]	52.2[e]	
1970–1976	55.5[c]	64.4[d]	63.1[e]		
1977–1983	86.5[d]	82.4[e]			
1984–1990	98.1[e]				

Christians

	18–24	25–31	32–38	39–45	46–52
1928–1934					13.1[a]
1935–1941				27.1[a]	22.1[b]
1942–1948			38.7[a]	38.9[b]	24.6[c]
1949–1955		50.0[a]	53.6[b]	53.0[c]	54.5[d]
1956–1962	76.4[a]	78.6[b]	77.7[c]	80.0[d]	74.6[e]
1963–1969	82.3[b]	83.6[c]	82.1[d]	83.0[e]	
1970–1976	94.3[c]	93.6[d]	90.8[e]		
1977–1983	97.4[d]	98.4[e]			
1984–1990	98.3[e]				

Jews

	18–24	25–31	32–38	39–45	46–52
1928–1934					75.6[a]
1935–1941				86.2[a]	86.3[b]
1942–1948			91.1[a]	92.0[b]	93.0[c]
1949–1955		87.4[a]	88.9[b]	90.0[c]	90.6[d]
1956–1962	91.8[a]	94.0[b]	95.5[c]	95.0[d]	95.8[e]
1963–1969	98.0[b]	98.1[c]	98.2[d]	98.8[e]	
1970–1976	98.9[c]	99.2[d]	99.3[e]		
1977–1983	99.4[d]	99.3[e]			
1984–1990	99.3[e]				

Year of survey: [a] = 1979–1981; [b] = 1986–1988; [c] = 1993–1995; [d] = 2000–2002; [e] = 2007–2009.

Source: Labor Force Surveys 1979–2009.

Note: Respondents born in Israel, excluding Palestinians from the Southern District and from Jerusalem, and Druze from the Golan Heights.

Appendix 3.3 *Percentage of Women Aged 18–52 Attending Academic Education by Age Group, Birth Cohort, and Ethno-Religious Group*

Muslims

	18–24	25–31	32–38	39–45	46–52
1928–1934					0.0^a
1935–1941				0.0^a	0.0^b
1942–1948			0.5^a	0.2^b	0.5^c
1949–1955		0.6^a	0.5^b	1.1^c	2.0^d
1956–1962	1.8^a	1.6^b	2.4^c	1.9^d	3.0^e
1963–1969	4.3^b	4.2^c	4.6^d	9.1^e	
1970–1976	4.1^c	7.3^d	13.9^e		
1977–1983	10.6^d	22.3^e			
1984–1990	25.3^e				

Druze

	18–24	25–31	32–38	39–45	46–52
1928–1934					0.0^a
1935–1941				0.0^a	0.0^b
1942–1948			0.0^a	0.0^b	1.9^c
1949–1955		0.0^a	0.0^b	1.9^c	5.7^d
1956–1962	0.4^a	2.1^b	1.8^c	2.2^d	4.7^e
1963–1969	0.8^b	1.6^c	4.8^d	13.2^e	
1970–1976	1.3^c	20.1^d	14.9^e		
1977–1983	11.2^d	21.5^e			
1984–1990	19.8^e				

Christians

	18–24	25–31	32–38	39–45	46–52
1928–1934					0.9^a
1935–1941				1.5^a	0.5^b
1942–1948			3.5^a	1.1^b	4.1^c
1949–1955		4.8^a	7.8^b	3.8^c	9.2^d
1956–1962	14.6^a	8.7^b	11.4^c	14.4^d	14.9^e
1963–1969	13.5^b	19.5^c	$15.^d$	26.9^e	
1970–1976	19.4^c	32.7^d	32.8^e		
1977–1983	34.5^d	47.6^e			
1984–1990	45.1^e				

Jews

	18–24	25–31	32–38	39–45	46–52
1928–1934					13.8^a
1935–1941				19.3^a	21.9^b
1942–1948			24.8^a	29.6^b	31.5^c
1949–1955		18.6^a	22.2^b	24.1^c	28.9^d
1956–1962	10.2^a	20.1^b	20.0^c	27.6^d	31.5^e
1963–1969	11.4^b	25.4^c	32.1^d	37.7^e	
1970–1976	16.1^c	45.3^d	47.8^e		
1977–1983	21.4^d	54.7^e			
1984–1990	21.6^e				

Year of survey: [a] = 1979–1981; [b] = 1986–1988; [c] = 1993–1995; [d] = 2000–2002; [e] = 2007–2009.

Source: Labor Force Surveys 1979–2009.

Note: Respondents born in Israel, excluding Palestinians from the Southern District and from Jerusalem, and Druze from the Golan Heights.

Appendix 3.4 *Percentage of Married Women Aged 15–19, Israel and Selected MENA Countries*

Part A: Israel							
Women	1997	2005	2008	2009	2010	2011	2014
Jews	2.3	1.6	1.5	1.4	1.4	1.4	1.2
Muslims	15.6	11.2	10.2	9.3	8.8	8.2	6.6
Druze	14.4	9.2	6.8	6.2	5.6	5.0	3.5
Christians	4.5	1.8	1.2	1.1	1.0	1.0	0.7
Men							
Jews	0.3	0.0	0.2	0.4	0.4	0.4	0.5
Muslims	1.1	0.4	0.4	0.4	0.4	0.4	0.3
Druze	1.0	0.4	0.5	0.3	0.2	0.2	0.1
Christians	0.4	0.0	0.0	0.0	0.0	0.0	0.0

Source: CBS (1996), Table 2.19; (2007, 2010–2012, 2014), Table 2.20.

Part B: Selected MENA Countries					
Women	1994–95	2001–02	2004–05	2006	2012
Algeria	3.5	1.8	–	2.6 (2008)	–
Egypt	14.3	–	12.3	11.4	14.4 (2014)
Jordan	12.6	–	8.8	6.6 (2009)	6.0
Libya	0.9	–	2.4	–	–
Morocco	12.1	–	10.7	–	11.0 (2010)
Syria	–	10.9	–	–	–
Tunisia	3.0	–	2.1	–	1.2
Palestinian Authority	26.9	–	13.5	6.0	–
Men					
Algeria	0.2	0.2	–	0.1 (2008)	–
Egypt	2.1	–	0.7	–	0.2 (2014)
Jordan	1.4	–	1.0	–	0.1
Libya	0.1	–	0.5	–	–
Morocco	1.1	–	0.8	–	0.6 (2010)
Syria	–	0.2	0.0	–	–
Tunisia	0.1	–	–	–	–
Palestinian Authority	2.4	–	0.6	0.6	–

Source: UN Population Division, Fertility and Family Planning, World Marriage Data.

4 Slowly But Steadily
Muslim Women Enter the Labor Market

In this and the following chapter, we concentrate on the largest group of Palestinian women living in Israel: Muslim women who live in the northern and central parts of the country. This will be followed in Chapters 6 and 7 with labor force patterns of women from two unique Muslim groups – the Palestinian Bedouins living in the Southern District and the Palestinians in Jerusalem – who have experienced different political and social conditions and undergone different changes than the mainstream of Muslim society in Israel. Official statistics do not distinguish between Bedouin and non-Bedouin Muslims, and we therefore use geographical data as a proxy. Almost all Muslims living in the Southern District are Bedouins, whereas they constitute only a minority among Muslims living in the other five districts of Israel.

Thus, our topic in this chapter is the Muslim population of four districts (Northern, Haifa, Central, Tel Aviv) and, in addition, the small group of Muslims (about 10,000) in the Jerusalem District outside the city itself. Altogether this population numbers 875,000 people, about 80.5 percent of all Muslims in Israel (i.e. within the 1949 borders, not including the city of Jerusalem). These people are not a homogeneous group. In the past there were cultural and linguistic differences between the Muslims in the Galilee and the rest of Palestine. At the end of the 1948 war, the Triangle area (from Umm al-Fahm in the north to Kafr Qasim in the south with the exception of Tira) had not been conquered by Jewish forces but was ceded to Israel in the ceasefire agreement with Jordan in 1949 (Shlaim 1988). The trauma of the Nakba was thus felt differently in the Triangle than in the Galilee. The population of the former did not suffer from the brutality of war but did experience painful separation from family members in the rest of the Samaria Mountains region, which was now on the other side of the Green Line, as well as the loss of economic contact with that region.[1] This political separation created two socially

---

[1] Jordan and Israel drew a line that took into consideration Israel's geopolitical interests but paid little attention to the people on the ground and even split in half the Palestinian village

distinct groups (Al-Haj 2005; cf. Schölch 1983), but when the Green Line between the Triangle and the West Bank evaporated after Israel occupied the West Bank in 1967, the two groups renewed family contact and commercial ties. The Triangle area is much closer than the Galilee to the economic center of Israel. Its southern part is just east of Tel Aviv, and its northern part is not too far from the economic centers of both Tel Aviv and Haifa. The Galilee is more remote from these centers; people who live in the Western Galilee and in the Nazareth area are close to the industrial area of Haifa, but those who live in the Upper Galilee are quite far from any economic center of activity. Palestinian communities in the Galilee are more diversified than those in the Triangle in terms of ethno-religious groups. In many Galilee communities Christians and Druze live side by side with Muslims (Yonay et al. 2015). The Muslim population in the Galilee includes thousands of Bedouins – estimated at 60,000 in 2004 – some of whom were sedentarized before 1948. They live in about two dozen Bedouin villages – most of them quite small – and in some of the larger non-Bedouin communities in the area.[2] In the Central District there might be a small group of Bedouins as well, but they are not native to the area; most migrated from the south after 1948 due to the insufficient resources left for Bedouins in the Naqab (Negev) after 1948 and the ensuing conflicts among various tribes there over those resources (Marx 1967; Falah 1985, 1989b; Ben-David 1999).

4.1   Employment Trends among Muslim Women

In this section we look at some trends in Muslim women's labor force participation along with the personal and structural determinants of these trends. Our analysis is based on annual labor force surveys conducted by the CBS in Israel. We started with 1974, the first year that the official statistics listed the different groups of Palestinians – and followed these surveys until 2009 in seven-year intervals.[3] In order to be able to analyze numbers of people larger than those sampled by the CBS in each particular year, we examined the data in spans of three years, with each span beginning with the first year selected according to our intervals. We thus ended up with six time periods (1974–1976, 1979–1981, 1986–1988, 1993–1995, 2000–2002, 2007–2009). We counted as belonging to the paid labor force all those

---

of Barta'a. The name "the Triangle" itself is related to the three big towns (Nablus, Jenin, and Tulkarm) that were left on the Jordanian side of the Green Line in 1949.

[2] Due to the small size of Bedouin communities in the Galilee, the CBS does not enable us to identify those communities therefore, we cannot analyze them separately. See more in Chapter 6.

[3] The interval between the first two periods is only five years.

who reported that they had worked or had looked for work in the week before the survey was conducted. Our analysis took into account only individuals born in Israel. Due to Israel's restriction on immigration of Palestinians, almost all of those who are in Israel were born there. The Jewish population includes many immigrants; we decided to exclude them because we wanted to compare the Palestinians in Israel to Jews who grew up in the same society.

Starting with total labor force participation, the comparison between Muslim and Jewish women is reported in Figure 4.1. In 1974–1976, only 7.7 percent of Muslim women in the age bracket 18–52 belonged to the paid labor force. This is a very low rate, typical of early industrial societies, and not surprising. Only eight years earlier, the Israeli military administration governing Palestinian communities was removed, and the infrastructure of the rural villages and their ties with the Jewish economy could not change much in this short period (Pappé 2006; Bäuml 2007, 2011).

Moving across the years we see a constant rise in Muslim women's employment. However, the increase was not even. There were three big

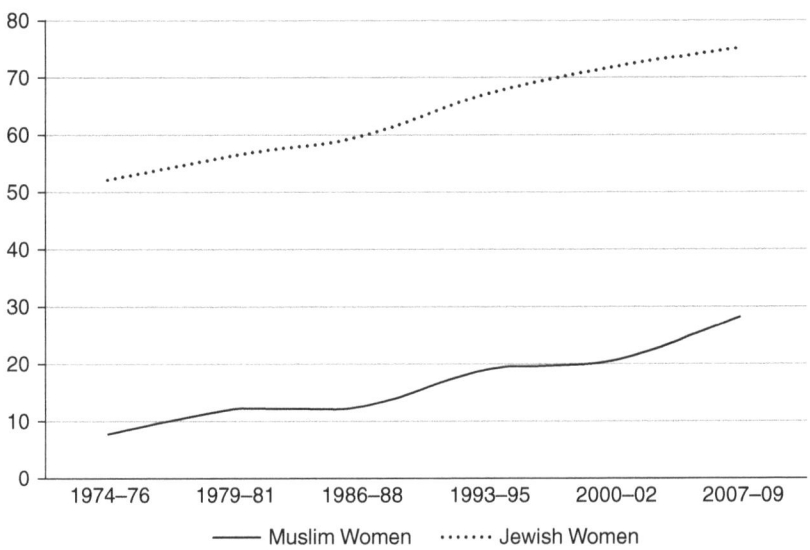

Figure 4.1 Labor Force Participation of Muslim and Jewish Women Aged 18–52
Source: Labor force Surveys 1974–2009.
Note: Respondents born in Israel, excluding Palestinians from the Southern District and from Jerusalem, and Druze from the Golan Heights.

leaps over this period: (1) a 56 percent increase (from 7.7 to 12.0 percent) from 1974–1976 to 1979–1981, which might be related to the expansion of educational opportunities due to a wider enforcement of compulsory education and the establishment of new high schools (Mazawi 1994; Al-Haj 1995; Kalekin-Fishman 2004); (2) a 51 percent increase (from 12.5 to 18.9 percent) from 1986–1988 to 1993–1995, perhaps due to the relatively large budgets channeled to Palestinian communities in those years and to the opening of more positions for Palestinians in the state administration during the Rabin (Labor) government (1992–1995; Aronoff 2000, 104; Smooha 2002); (3) a 37 percent increase (from 20.5 to 28.1 percent) from 2000–2002 to 2007–2009, possibly related to the expansion of the system of higher education and to the expansion of the public sector, which created job opportunities for highly educated Palestinian women (see Chapter 3). Overall, during the 35-year span of our study, the participation rate of Muslim women in the labor market almost quadrupled to 28.1 percent, and yet it was still hardly half of the rate of Jewish women in the labor market at the *beginning* of the period (52 percent in 1974–1976) and about a third of the rate of Jewish women in the last period (75 percent).

4.2   Patterns of Labor Force Participation by Birth Cohorts

Utilizing the pooled labor force surveys we further examined the trends in labor force participation of Muslim women as divided into *birth cohorts* and *age groups*, each spanning seven years.[4] Looking at specific cohorts sharpens our ability to capture the dynamics of long and gradual changes by comparing the different experiences of consecutive cohorts. The oldest cohort in our sample consists of Muslim women born in 1928–1934 (aged 46–52 in 1979–1981, our earliest period in the cohort analysis), and the youngest cohort consists of Muslim women born in 1984–1990 (aged 18–24 in 2007–2009, our last period). In each of our six periods, one cohort passed the upper age boundary of our analysis and another cohort entered the labor force.[5]

---

[4] A synthetic cohort follows the respondents who were born in a certain period across successive surveys. It is "synthetic" because it is not really the same people who fill in the questionnaires, but representative samples of the same real birth cohort. We excluded the 1974–1976 labor force surveys since, according to the synthetic cohort design, some of the respondents overlap with individuals included in the 1979–1981 surveys.

[5] For example, the 1928–1934 cohort included in the 1979–1981 period was 53 and older in the second survey of 1986–1988, and hence excluded from our analysis; the 1963–1969 cohort was too young in 1979–1981 and was therefore first sampled in the 1986–1988 surveys.

Table 4.1 *Labor Force Participation of Muslims and Jews Women Aged 18–52 by Birth Cohort and Age*

	18–24	25–31	32–38	39–45	46–52
Panel A: Muslim Women					
1928–1934					2.1^a
1935–1941				2.3^a	3.2^b
1942–1948			5.6^a	4.6^b	6.2^c
1949–1955		12.7^a	8.2^b	12.5^c	8.1^d
1956–1962	21.2^a	14.6^b	17.1^c	19.1^d	17.6^e
1963–1969	18.2^b	21.6^c	22.1^d	29.5^e	
1970–1976	24.1^c	25.1^d	35.2^e		
1977–1983	20.2^d	33.3^e			
1984–1990	21.3^e				
Panel B: Jewish Women (Born in Israel)					
1928–1934					63.6^a
1935–1941				69.2^a	70.4^b
1942–1948			68.5^a	75.6^b	79.9^c
1949–1955		61.0^a	66.1^b	77.5^c	78.2^d
1956–1962	45.4^a	65.0^b	74.4^c	79.3^d	80.6^e
1963–1969	45.2^b	73.2^c	78.3^d	84.5^e	
1970–1976	50.0^c	80.4^d	84.2^e		
1977–1983	52.5^d	81.4^e			
1984–1990	52.3^e				

Year of survey: ^{a} = 1979–1981; ^{b} = 1986–1988; ^{c} = 1993–1995; ^{d} = 2000–2002; ^{e}= 2007–2009.
Source: Labor force Surveys 1979–2009.
Note: Respondents born in Israel, excluding Palestinians from the Southern District and from Jerusalem, and Druze from the Golan Heights.

In order to comprehend the significance of the changes in Palestinian women's employment, it helps to begin with trends among the comparable group of Jewish women (Table 4.1, panel B). We find that the latter women's likelihood of having a paid job steadily and considerably increased from one cohort to another, and that such increases occurred in each period of their lives. For example, 61 percent of Jewish women from the 1949–1955 cohort were in the labor market when they were 25–31, compared with 81 percent of the 1977–1983 cohort at the same age. This consistent pattern was not observed among Muslim women (Table 4.1, panel A). For the Muslim women, we see very modest increases among cohorts born before 1956. The cohort of 1956–1962, which reached the labor market in the second half of the 1970s, shows a greater propensity to participate in the labor market than the previous cohort at any age group, and since then, each cohort surpasses its predecessor in LFP like the cohorts of Jewish women.

Comparing age groups at a given birth cohort, it is evident that Jewish women in each of the birth cohorts have increased their labor market participation with age. The greatest increases (from 45–50 percent to more than 65 percent) occur between very young Jewish women (18–24) and women in the next age group, 25–31 – typically the years when women finish their tertiary education and join the labor market. In the years in which higher education in Israel expanded, the rise in employment rates between these two age brackets is the largest. Jewish women's rates of employment continue to rise with age as children grow up and leave home. This relationship between higher age and increased labor market participation is typical to advanced industrial societies in which many women acquire higher education and join the labor market in increasing numbers (Goldin 1990; Huber 1991).

Muslim women fit this pattern only in recent cohorts, starting with the 1963–1969 cohort whose participation rates monotonically grew from 18 percent to 29 percent as the women got older. In the previous cohort, born 1956–1962, the youngest women were the most active in the labor market with a participation rate of 21 percent. As common in early industrial societies, some women of this cohort left the labor market as the women of this cohort got married, and therefore the rates fluctuated in the 15–19 percent range. For earlier cohorts we do not have the employment rates of the pre-marriage age (18–24), but we see that employment rates are quite low and do not change with age.

4.3   Labor Force Participation: Married and Single Women

The previous analysis demonstrates that the growing participation in the labor market of Palestinian women stems from the entrance into it of women in the older age brackets from the more recent age cohorts. This indicates an entrance of married women. In this section we further elaborate on this topic. Figure 4.2 compares the labor force participation of married and single women across time among both Muslim and Jewish women. We focus on the age bracket 25–52, because most Muslim women marry before the age of 25. Reflecting the increase of employment among older women described above, there was a significant increase of the participation of married Muslim women in the paid market from less than 3 percent in 1974–1976 to more than 26 percent in 2007–2009. Married Jewish women experienced a large and constant increase as well, but the rate of participation among them was already 54 percent in 1974–

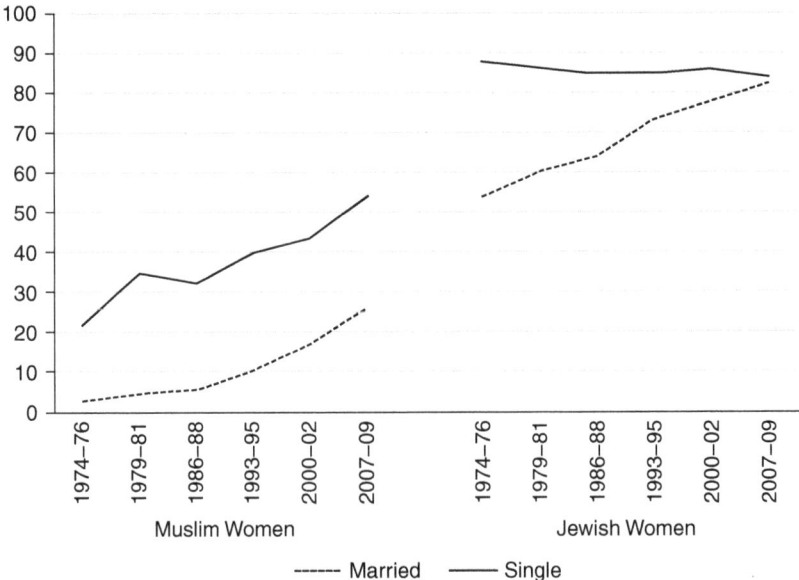

Figure 4.2 Labor Force Participation of Muslim and Jewish Women
Aged 25–52 by Marital Status and Year
Source: Labor force Surveys 1974–2009.
Note: Respondents born in Israel, excluding Palestinians from the
Southern District and from Jerusalem, and Druze from the Golan Heights.

1976, and it reached the very high rate of 82 percent at the end of the
period studied, keeping the huge gap between them and their Muslim
counterparts.

In all years, the employment rates of Muslim single women were
much higher than that of married ones. It is very uncommon among
Muslims to have a child out of marriage, an option that has become
more legitimate and common, though still limited, among Jews. Thus
Muslim single women are not limited by childcare duties and costs
and are not expected to take care of husbands' needs. Yet most single
Muslim women live with their parents and might be expected to help
with household duties and to take care of their elderly parents, tasks
that compete with paid employment. In addition, living with parents
may free some single women from the need to gain income to support
themselves, but others might be expected to contribute to the overall
household income. As women's employment has become more prevalent among Muslims and as more rewarding positions have become

available, single women's LFP rates rose from 22 to 54 percent. Still, this increase was less dramatic than that which occurred in the LFP of married women: the gap between the employment rate of single and married women decreased during the years of our study from a ratio of 8.11 to a ratio of 2.06 in 2007–2009. In comparison, among Jewish single women, who typically live on their own and usually have no children (and if they do, ordinarily only one), gainful employment is a necessity, and LFP has been constantly high at 84–88 percent. With the growing presence of married women in the labor force, the ratio of single to married women's rates decreased from 1.6 in 1974–1976 to almost parity in 2007–2009.

Who Are the Married Women Who Work? The analysis so far has shown that the main story regarding Muslim women's work outside the home is that married women, who are the large majority among women, are still for the most part not in the labor market: Only one in four is employed at any given time.[6] Why, after all the educational, economic, and cultural changes that took place in Israel in general, and in the Palestinian community in particular, are three out of four married women not employed? To answer this question, the following sections of this chapter explore the factors affecting the labor market behavior of these women. For this purpose we grouped women's characteristics into four main clusters. In the Section 4.4, we look at the relationships between human capital (measured by the highest level of education achieved) and employment. In Section 4.5, we examine the impact of family size (the number of children and their ages). In Section 4.6, we look at husbands' education (per se and in conjunction with wives' education), and in Section 4.7, we examine the relevance of place of residence. In the last section, we also discuss single women in order to understand why almost half of them were not in the labor force in 2007–2009 at the time of the last survey.

4.4   Education and Labor Force Participation

A woman's level of education is a valuable resource in the labor market. Among other things, it is a key factor in determining employment.

---

[6] We say "at any given time" to counteract the wrong assumption that Muslim women are divided into a majority that has never been employed and a small working minority. Among the 74 percent who were not employed according to the 2007–2009 surveys, many might have been employed in earlier periods of their marriage. Work histories of Palestinian women have not been studied, but when we wanted to interview, for another study, women who have stayed out of the labor market for their entire married life, they were difficult to find.

Figure 4.3 presents the rate of married Muslim women in the labor market according to the last school attended.[7] As seen from this figure, the impact of education on women's employment is enormous for both groups (Muslims and Jews), but its impact is particularly extreme in the case of Muslims. Looking at the last period 2007–2009, we see that almost three-quarters of married Muslim women with at least some academic education participated in the labor force, compared with about half of those with non-academic postsecondary education, and

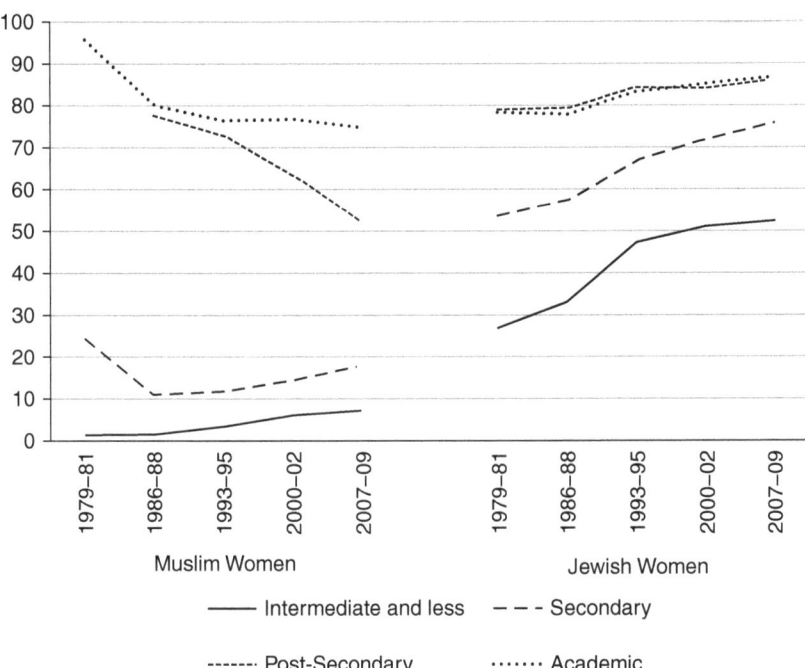

Figure 4.3 Labor Force Participation of Muslim and Jewish Married Women Aged 25–52 by Education and Year
Source: Labor force Surveys 1979–2009.
Note: Respondents born in Israel, excluding Palestinians from the Southern District and from Jerusalem, and Druze from the Golan Heights.

---

[7] We distinguished four educational levels: (1) intermediate (or lower) school; (2) secondary school; (3) postsecondary but not academic; (4) academic education (including colleges of education). The 1974–1976 data include only years of schooling; the type of school attended was not asked.

a much lower rate of 18 percent among those with only secondary education. The share of women with the lowest schooling who are employed was miniscule (less than 8 percent).

For married Jewish women, education is also very significant, but with over half of those with less than a secondary education being gainfully employed (in 2007–2009), the impact of the subsequent educational levels is necessarily smaller. Secondary education raises the LFP to 76 percent, and tertiary education brings it to 86–87 percent. Among Jewish married women in all years, academic degrees did not have extra value for entering the labor market as compared with non-academic postsecondary education, probably because of the high rates of participation of women with the latter. Over all, it is obvious that gaps in the employment rates of Muslim and Jewish women are mainly due to the huge gaps between these groups in the lower educational levels. Muslim women at these levels are hardly employed, and this includes women with secondary education, of whom more than 80 percent are not in the labor market (referring again to 2007–2009). All of which tell us that jobs for women with secondary education or less are available merely for Jewish women and hardly exist for Muslim women. We should remember that a large majority of Muslims have not continued their education beyond the secondary level, and therefore this fact is a key factor in the low LFP rate of Muslim women in general.

Another crucial key for understanding the low LFP of Muslim women is the fact that in each educational level, the share of employed women has declined over the years, save for women with a very low educational level for whom labor market participation rates have been consistently very low and have remained so over the years. At the highest (academic) educational level, in 1979–1981 almost all women with some academic education (96 percent) participated in the labor market. This extremely high rate is undoubtedly related to the fact that very few Muslim women at the time had reached this educational level, and they must have been exceptionally talented and steadfast.[8] It is nevertheless surprising that the rate of employment among Muslim women with some academic education has declined steadily over the years to about 75 percent in 2007–2009. An even stronger decline is evident among Muslim women with non-academic tertiary education, whose rates of LFP have dropped from 78 percent in 1986–1988 to 53 percent in 2007–2009. The explanation for these trends might be labor market

---

[8] For the pioneering women in specific Arab groups, see Abu-Rabia-Queder 2008 (on Bedouin women) and Naomi Weiner-Levy 2006 (on Druze). See also Sa'ar 2006.

saturation, as great numbers of Muslim women have continued their education beyond the secondary level.

This trend did not occur among married Jewish women. Their LFP rates have increased within *all* educational levels. For example, Jewish women with tertiary education (either academic or not) increased their employment share from 78–79 percent in 1979–1981 to 86–87 percent in 2007–2009. These are small gains, but they are consistent and stable, and they took place even though many more Jewish women have gained postsecondary degrees as compared with Muslim women. The fact that growing proportions of those Muslim women who invested in postsecondary and academic education are outside of the labor force seems to be a strong indication that they are the only ones who face a saturated labor market. That is, since many fewer positions in the Israeli labor market are practically available to Palestinians than to Jews, highly educated Muslim women find it more difficult to get a suitable job than equally educated Jewish women, although higher education among Muslims is less prevalent than among Jews.

4.5   Family Composition and Labor Force Participation

Since women are expected to take care of children, the number of children in the family and their ages affect married women's employment rates. The larger the number of children in the family and the younger they are, the heavier the childcare burden and the higher the barrier to labor market participation. This claim has been verified in numerous studies in various societies, but the relative impact of children on women's work outside the home has been found to differ across societies depending on the availability of social institutions that may support childcare (Gornick and Meyers 2003; Mandel and Semyonov 2006). In this section we therefore examine the size of the impact of children on employment among Muslim women over the years. We are especially interested in finding out whether the difference in LFP between women with fewer children and those with more children has decreased in more recent years. To answer this question we concentrate on women in the age bracket 25–38, the age when Muslim women are likely to have young children.[9] Figure 4.4 presents the results for married Muslim and Jewish women.

---

[9] In light of the distribution of the number of children Muslim women have, we classified the number of children into four categories: 0–2, 3, 4, and 5 and more. We had one category of 0–2 children because the number of married women with no child or with only one child was very small, especially in the early periods.

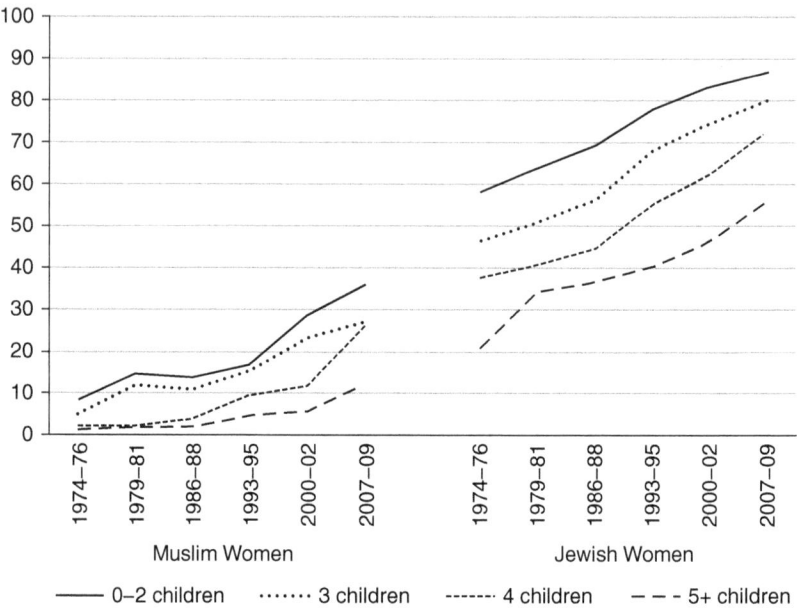

Figure 4.4 Labor Force Participation of Muslim and Jewish Married
Women Aged 25–38 by Number of Children (<15) and Year
Source: Labor force Surveys 1974–2009.
Note: Respondents born in Israel, excluding Palestinians from the
Southern District and from Jerusalem, and Druze from the Golan
Heights.

As has been found in studies conducted in many countries, each additional child heightens the barrier to women's LFP. This is true for all
years and for both Muslim and Jewish women. Reflecting the general
trends of a growing women's LFP, we can also see that for each category
of number of children, employment increases from one survey to the next
among Muslim and Jewish women alike. Yet there are some differences
between the two groups. Among Muslim women, there is a relatively high
increase from 2000–2002 to 2007–2009 in LFP among women with four
children and more. For women with three children and fewer, a significant upswing took place in the second half of the 1990s.

Comparing between Muslim and Jewish women shows that a high
number of children is less of a barrier among the latter than among the
former. This means not only that Jewish women are more likely to
participate in the labor market than Muslim women with the same number of children but also that having more children has less of an impact on

Jewish mothers' labor market participation compared to its impact on Muslim mothers.[10] The impact of children on women's LFP depends also on the children's ages. We checked this relation for all periods and found that the employment of married women, both Muslim and Jewish, with older children was significantly higher than that of women with younger children.

4.6   Husband's Education and Women's Labor Force Participation

Previous studies have shown that a husband with a high level of education is likely to enhance his wife's chances to enter the labor market. A husband's high level of education serves as a labor market resource. Highly educated husbands are more likely to have information on job vacancies, as well as knowledge on where to find jobs and how to apply for them. When job terms are negotiated, they are in a better position to provide information and moral support, which may help their wives achieve more favorable terms (Bernasco et al. 1998; Kraus 2002; Huang et al. 2009). Highly educated husbands are also more likely than less-educated ones to have progressive attitudes that support women's rights and gender equality in the public sphere and at home. Such ideological attitudes may perhaps facilitate wives' LFP, even though clearly not every man practices his ideology in his private life.[11]

In order to assess the relationships between husbands' education and their wives' employment, we took into consideration the wives' own education as well. Appendix 4.1 presents the percentage of employed women within various combinations of their husbands' and their own levels of education in various years. Starting with Muslim women with a low level of education, we see that their share in the labor market was very low, no matter what the husband's education was. We have already shown that the employment of Muslim women with secondary education was somewhat higher compared to that of Muslim women with a low level

---

[10] For example, in 2000–2002 the odds of participating in the labor market of married Muslim women with a small number of children were 2.4 times those of Muslim women with four children, and almost 5 times higher than those of Muslim women with five children and more. The comparable odds for married Jewish women with children are 1.33 and 1.80. These higher odds may indicate scarcity in childcare facilities available for Muslim Palestinians in their place of residence.

[11] Highly educated husbands may also provide an "income effect." Given their higher income on average, the pressure for an additional salary might be smaller. Yet studies have consistently found that the income effect is smaller than the positive influence of a husband's education on his wife's employment. It is possible that consumption expectations rise with education, and therefore highly educated husbands' income is not sufficient to satisfy the expected needs (Smits et al. 1996).

of education. This tendency increased when women with secondary education had a husband with tertiary education (save in 1979–1981). Women with tertiary education had the highest employment rates, and these rates further increased with the level of the husband's education. For example, in 2007–2009 almost 55 percent of Muslim women with tertiary education married to a husband with a *low* level of education were employed, compared to 62 percent of those married to husbands with *secondary* education, and 77 percent of those married to husbands with *tertiary* education.[12]

4.7   Place of Residence and Labor Force Participation

Place of residence determines the economic opportunities available for its inhabitants and as such is related to women's employment experiences. In Chapter 2 we discussed the scarce economic opportunities in Palestinian communities. We believe this is one of the major causes behind the low LFP rates of Palestinian women in Israel. The prospects of paid employment are much higher in mixed Palestinian-Jewish localities. Although most Palestinians are segregated from the Jewish majority, about 7 percent of them reside in such mixed communities (Tel Aviv-Jaffa, Haifa, Acre, Ramla, Lydda, Maalot-Tarshiha, Karmiel, and Nazareth Illit). Many Muslims who reside in the northern districts of Israel share communities with Palestinians from other ethno-religious groups (Christian and Druze), while Muslims residing in the center (the Triangle) live in homogeneous Muslim localities. The presence of Christians in a locality was found to enhance Muslim and Druze women's employment (Yonay et al. 2015). To examine the relationships between place of residence and women's employment rates we distinguished between three groups of residence: (1) mixed urban localities with Jews; (2) the north (without the mixed localities); and (3) the center (The Triangle).

Figure 4.5 presents these results. In all years, Muslim women in mixed Palestinian-Jewish localities have had much higher odds of being in the labor market, whether we compared them to Muslim women residing in the Triangle or to those residing in the northern districts of the country. In 2007–2009 almost every second married Muslim woman residing in mixed Palestinian-Jewish localities was employed, while only every fourth Muslim woman residing in the Palestinian localities in the north and center was enrolled in the labor market.

[12] Examining the experience of married Jewish women (table not presented) shows that husbands' educational achievements were a valuable resource for Jewish women as well. Whether a Jewish woman had a low, intermediate, or high level of education, her likelihood of being employed increased with the level of her husband's education.

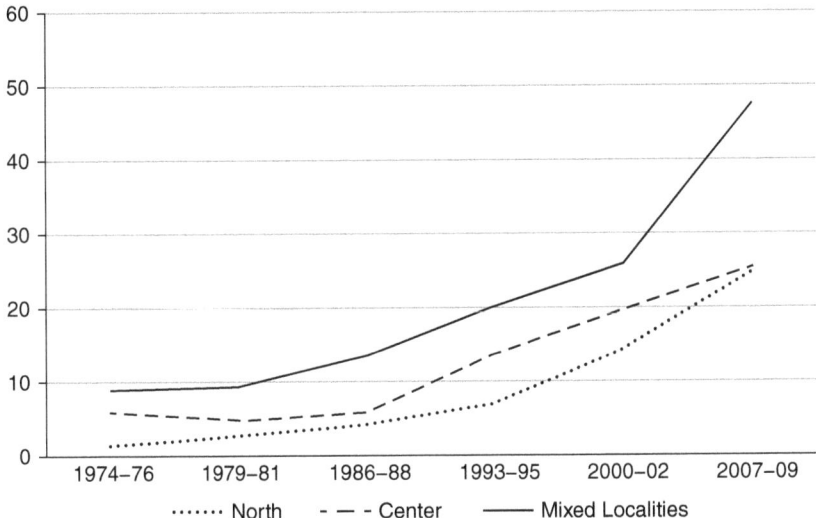

Figure 4.5 Labor Force Participation of Married Muslim Women Aged 25–52 by Place of Residence and Year
Source: Labor Force Surveys 1974–2009.
Note: Respondents born in Israel, excluding Palestinians from the Southern District and from Jerusalem, and Druze from the Golan Heights.

Comparing the employment rates of women living in the center (the Triangle) to women residing in the north shows that the employment rates of married Muslim women living in the Triangle were higher compared to those living in the north. The higher employment rates of Muslim women in the Triangle may be a result of the closeness of this region to the commercial and industrial centers of Tel Aviv and its surrounding areas. This advantage, however, disappeared in 2007–2009. An interesting result is that the LFP rate in mixed cities sharply rose from 25 to 48 percent between 2000–2002 and 2007–2009. This increase might be related to greater availability of jobs within the Jewish sector (see Chapter 5). It is also possible that during these years a greater number of Palestinians who wished to benefit from the advantages of modern cities moved to mixed cities. Since those women are also more likely to seek employment, they might be responsible to this sharp upswing.

The above descriptive analyses highlight the main factors which shape the employment of Muslim women. All these factors, however, are highly interrelated. It is therefore necessary to examine these interrelations by performing a multivariate analysis for each of the periods included in our study in order to identify their net impacts. We performed this analysis (excluding the 1974–1976 period because it did not include data on last school attended) and the results confirmed much of the information obtained in the descriptive analyses (Appendix 4.2). The multivariate analysis enabled us to find the net contribution of each factor. We found, for example, that women with secondary education married to husbands with tertiary education had 5 times higher odds of being employed compared to women with low level of education married to husbands with low level education (the reference group). The odds of Muslim women with tertiary education married to husbands with low education were almost 20 times higher than the reference group, and these odds further increased to 28 if they were married to husbands with secondary education. When husbands had tertiary education as well, the odds were astronomical: 60 times higher (all figures are for 2007–2009). These high figures further underscore the importance not only of women's education but that of their husbands as well. Following these net effects in earlier periods shows that the educational effects were even stronger then, but they are still very large in recent years.

Looking at the net effects of an additional child, we see that at the earliest period it reduced women's LFP by about 17 percent, and this figure has declined to about 10 percent in later years. The impact of having a young child has also declined over time. Net of other control variables, in 1986–1988 the odds that women with young children would participate in the labor force was 40 percent lower relative to women with older children. This figure declined over the years and in 2007–2009, the odds that women with younger children would hold a paid job was 16 percent lower relative to women with older children.

The multivariate analysis corroborates also the finding that living in mixed Palestinian-Jewish localities which have richer economic opportunities relative to homogeneously Palestinian communities increases women's employment rates. According to the multivariate analysis, the net effect of this factor was to increase Muslim women's employment in 2007–2009 by 240 percent relative to women who resided in Palestinian localities in the north. In earlier periods the size of this effect was similar. Unlike the results observed in the descriptive statistics, when all women's characteristics are taken into consideration, women residing in the Triangle did not have higher odds of being employed compared to women living in the north, and in 2007–2009 the net effect of living in the Triangle on women's LFP was even negative. We did not observe this effect in the descriptive analysis probably because it was offset by other characteristics of women in that region.

4.8   Determinants of Single Muslim Women's Employment

In this last section we look at the determinants affecting single Muslim women's employment rates. Although single women are much fewer than married women, their number is significant and they require special attention. Although they are much more likely to be gainfully employed, about half of them are not in the labor market. This is puzzling because they are not expected to take care of husbands and children, although they might be expected to help in their parents' households. Understanding the barriers to their employment may help us understand the problems that prevent other Muslim women from gaining paid employment.

Utilizing the above multivariate analysis, we estimated the net effects of women's characteristics on their employment. The results are presented in Appendix 4.3. Our analysis is of single Muslim women aged 25–52. The crucial determinant that affects single women's employment is their education. In 1979–1981, single Muslim women with secondary education had 6.4 times the chances of being employed compared to women with a low level of education, and 10.3 times the chances of being employed (compared to the latter women) when they had tertiary education. As is the case for married Muslim women, these strong effects of education on employment have declined over the years studied although they are still high.

Residing in mixed Palestinian-Jewish cities significantly increased single Muslim women's opportunities for employment as did those of married women. In 2007–2009, single Muslim women residing in mixed Palestinian-Jewish localities had 1.7 times the chances of being employed compared to single Muslim women residing in the north. Residing in the Triangle significantly increased single Muslim's women's odds of being employed by 66 percent in the first period (1979–1981) but significantly reduced these odds (like it did for married women) by about 37 percent in the last period (2007–2009). The changing impact of the residence in these two regions may indicate differences in the availability of economic opportunities in the two areas.

4.9   Summary

Our analysis shows that in spite of the significant gains in LFP of Muslim women during the 35 years of our study, their employment rates are still very low. The low rate, less than 30 percent, is very uncommon to industrial societies such as Israel. We saw that the growth in Muslim women's employment has been achieved mainly by cohort replacement, that is, recent birth cohorts with higher tendency to work entering the labor force in higher rates than earlier birth cohorts. This trend is quite recent. It started perhaps with the 1956–1962 birth cohort and became more visible in the next one (1963–1969). The trend continues with younger cohorts, but the change has not been large enough to catch up with employment rates among Jewish women. If the change continues at the current tempo, it would take several generations before Palestinian women reach the LFP rates of Jewish women. We noticed also slight evidence (for the younger birth cohorts) that the participation of Muslim women in the labor force modestly increases during their life cycle.

This finding reasserts the question that motivated our study: Why has the employment rate of Muslim women remained low and not risen faster after so many years in spite of the growing opportunities for women in an economy as developed as Israel with its extensive public and private sectors? The question is even more puzzling if we keep in mind that the Muslim women investigated in this chapter have undergone a large reduction in fertility rates and a large increase in the percentage of women with tertiary education. The various analyses performed in this chapter were conducted in an attempt to find clues to answering this question. Our results show that the main cause of low LFP of Muslim women is the lack of economic opportunities available to them.

An important finding that supports our interpretation is the change in high-school educated women's employment. In 1979–1981 Muslim women with secondary education were more likely to be employed than in 2007–2009. Almost a quarter of them were in the labor force (see, Figure 4.3). This rate demonstrates that even in the 1970s women with relatively low levels of education were interested in labor market employment. Whatever cultural norms existed did not prevent many women from seeking employment. But LFP among Muslim women with secondary education dropped to 11–12 percent in the second half of the 1980s and mid-1990s, and started to climb back only in the 2000s. It was still lower at the last period studied here (18 percent in 2007–2009) than during its 1979–1981 record. The reason behind this decrease in LFP in the 1980s and 1990s is the structural change in the textile and garment industries (see Section 5.3) where most Muslim women with low levels of education worked in the 1970s. When those industries were moved to other countries in the Far East and, following the Oslo Accord, to neighboring countries, those opportunities were not been replaced by other alternatives. These changes provide strong evidence that employment opportunities are important in explaining the low rate of Muslim women's employment.

Another piece of strong evidence is related to Muslim women with tertiary education. It is not surprising that in all years highly educated Muslim women had a very high rate of employment, even higher than that of Jewish women with comparable education during the first two periods of our study. Nevertheless, the rate of employed women among these Muslim women has declined over the years. During the 1979–1981 period, when only a small fraction of Muslim women achieved tertiary education, almost all of them were employed (95.7 percent in 1979–1981). As more Muslim women achieved this educational level, the probability of their entering the labor market declined. It is still quite high (75 percent in 2007–2009) but the trend of reduction is consistent. Even more dramatic is the reduction in employment rates among women with non-academic postsecondary education (from 78 percent in 1986–1988 to 53 in 2007–2009). As explained above, these reduction trends seem to indicate a saturated employment structure, but it looks as if this saturation affects Muslim women only. Unlike the latter, Jewish women with tertiary education – whose numbers have been much larger than those of Muslim women – have not experienced effects of such saturation and their rates of employment have continued to rise all along. We are thus left with the conclusion that only the job market available to Muslim women is saturated. This is in line with the claim that the lower participation of Muslim and Arab women in Western countries is related to the limited options they face due to discrimination against them.

Appendix 4.1 *Labor Force Participation of Muslim Women Aged 25–52 by Their and Their Husbands' Education and Year*

	1979–81	1986–88	1993–95	2000–02	2007–09
Wife with Low + Husband with Low Education	1.5	1.7	3.4	6.3	6.8
Wife with Low + Husband with Secondary Education	1.8	2.9	4.3	6.3	7.7
Wife with Low + Husband with Tertiary Education	4.4	2.8	5.8	4.5	12.5
Wife with Secondary + Husband with Low Education	18.1	8.8	9.3	13.2	18.5
Wife with Secondary + Husband with Secondary Education	33.3	9.7	11.1	12.9	16.5
Wife with Secondary + Husband with Tertiary Education	19.2	14.9	19.7	22.4	22.8
Wife with Tertiary + Husband with Low Education	62.5	57.1	60.9	54.5	54.7
Wife with Tertiary + Husband with Secondary Education	Low N	79.3	68.9	69.4	62.5
Wife with Tertiary + Husband with Tertiary Education	97.1	86.9	79.4	81.9	77.3

Source: Labor Force Surveys 1979–2009.
Note: Respondents born in Israel, excluding Palestinians from the Southern District and from Jerusalem, and Druze from the Golan Heights.
Note: low education = intermediate education and less.

Appendix 4.2 *Logistic Coefficients and Standard Errors (in parentheses) Predicting LFP of Married Muslim Women Aged 25–52 by Year*

	1979–1981		1986–1988		1993–1995		2000–2002		2007–2009	
	B/S.E.	Exp. (B)	B/S.E.	Exp. (B)	B/S.E.	Exp. (B)	B/S.E.	Exp. (B)	B/S.E.	Exp. (B)
Wife's education X husband's education										
Wife with low and husband with secondary education	0.217 (0.464)	1.24	0.408 (0.352)	1.50	0.555* (0.225)	1.74	0.097 (0.175)	1.10	0.052* (0.195)	1.05
Wife with low and husband with tertiary education	0.801 (0.541)	2.22	0.496 (0.610)	1.64	0.754* (0.367)	2.12	−0.625 (0.421)	0.53	0.644 (0.364)	1.90
Wife with secondary and husband with low education	2.278* (0.423)	9.75	1.529* (0.299)	4.61	1.175* (0.222)	3.24	0.950* (0.139)	2.59	1.207* (0.141)	3.34
Wife with secondary and husband with secondary education	2.338* (0.378)	10.36	1.713* (0.312)	5.54	1.440* (0.197)	4.22	0.813* (0.133)	2.25	1.081* (0.129)	2.95
Wife with secondary and husband with tertiary education	2.251* (0.456)	9.49	2.121* (0.363)	8.33	2.250* (0.223)	9.48	1.376* (0.160)	3.96	1.622* (0.166)	5.06
Wife with tertiary and husband with low education	4.310* (0.508)	74.41	4.648* (0.563)	104.38	4.748* (0.460)	115.32	2.798* (0.251)	16.41	2.970* (0.207)	19.48
Wife with tertiary and husband with secondary education	5.589* (0.246)	267.4	6.529* (0.608)	684.88	4.431* (0.276)	84.05	3.530* (0.181)	34.12	3.339* (0.148)	28.19

Appendix 4.2 (cont.)

	1979–1981		1986–1988		1993–1995		2000–2002		2007–2009	
	B/S.E.	Exp. (B)	B/S.E.	Exp. (B)	B/S.E.	Exp. (B)	B/S.E.	Exp. (B)	B/S.E.	Exp. (B)
Wife with tertiary and husband with tertiary education	7.638* (0.379)	2074.6	6.405* (0.403)	605.07	4.937* (0.232)	139.34	4.276* (0.164)	71.93	4.101* (0.146)	60.41
Living in the Center	0.312 (0.254)	1.36	-0.366 (0.226)	0.69	0.092 (0.133)	1.09	0.174 (0.089)	1.19	-0.200* (0.075)	0.82
Living in a mixed cities	0.741* (0.309)	2.10	1.362* (0.225)	3.91	1.445* (0.179)	4.24	1.238* (0.144)	3.44	1.224* (0.156)	3.40
Number of children under 15	-0.311* (0.070)	0.83	-0.143* (0.060)	0.87	-0.110* (0.043)	0.90	-0.150* (0.031)	0.86	-0.089* (0.027)	0.91
Having children under 5	-0.524 (0.349)	0.59	-0.508* (0.263)	0.60	-0.063 (0.166)	0.94	-0.264* (0.113)	0.76	-0.175* (0.090)	0.84
Age	0.002 (0.019)	1.00	-0.011 (0.016)	0.99	0.018 (0.011)	1.02	-0.007* (0.008)	0.99	0.004 (0.006)	1.00
Intercept	-3.648		-3.029		-4.016		-1.965		-3.190	
2 Log Likelihood	707.6		1020.9		2112.7		4149.6		5378.6	
N	3,070		3,638		4,045		4,872		5,066	
Nagelkerke R²	0.491		0.472		0.394		0.375		0.384	

Variables: The dependent variable is labor force participation, coded 1 if the woman belongs to the labor force, and 0 otherwise; the independent variables are: combinations of wives' and husbands' education (distinguishing among three levels of education (intermediary and less, secondary, tertiary); the reference group is spouses with low education), place of residence, distinguishing between those who reside in mixed localities, center, and north (the omitted category); number of children under 15, having children under 5, and age.

Source: Labor Force Surveys 1979–2009.

*: p <0.05

Note: Respondents born in Israel, excluding Palestinians from the Southern District and from Jerusalem, and Druze from the Golan Heights.

Appendix 4.3 *Logistic Coefficients and Standard Errors (in parentheses) Predicting LFP of Single Muslim Women Aged 25–52 by Year*

	1979–1981		1986–1988		1993–1995		2000–2002		2007–2009	
	B/S.E.	Exp. (B)	B/S.E.	Exp. (B)	B/S.E.	Exp. (B)	B/S.E.	Exp. (B)	B/S.E.	Exp. (B)
Secondary education	1.856* (0.645)	6.398	0.716* (0.197)	2.047	1.117* (0.145)	3.055	0.664* (0.138)	1.942	1.126* (0.151)	3.082
Tertiary education	2.337* (0.982)	10.346	2.547* (0.478)	12.768	2.935* (0.347)	18.822	2.066* (0.212)	7.895	1.855* (0.180)	6.392
Living in the center	0.508* (0.235)	1.662	-0.085 (0.172)	0.919	0.265 (0.146)	1.309	0.082 (0.137)	1.086	-0.457* (0.144)	0.633
Living in a mixed cities	-0.318 (0.599)	0.728	0.473 (0.306)	1.605	1.419* (0.268)	4.132	0.241 (0.237)	1.273	0.532* (0.230)	1.703
Age	-0.102 (0.029)	0.903	-0.011 (0.016)	0.989	-0.012 (0.013)	0.989	0.008 (0.010)	1.008	0.028* (0.010)	1.029
Intercept	2.333		-0.808		-0.619		-1.205		-1.588	
2 Log Likelihood	444.2		876.1		1319.9		1556.7		1460.6	
N	278		645		968		1,226		1,155	
Nagelkerke R^2	0.133		0.100		0.216		0.132		0.150	

Variables: The dependent variable is labor force participation, coded 1 if the woman belongs to the labor force, and 0 otherwise; the independent variables are: education (distinguishing between intermediary and less (reference category), secondary, and tertiary), place of residence, distinguishing between those who reside in mixed localities, center, and north (the omitted category), age.

Source: Labor Force Surveys 1979–2009.

*: p <0.05

Note: Respondents bcrm in Israel, excluding Palestinians from the Southern District and from Jerusalem, and Druze from the Golan Heights.

5 Limited Success
Muslim Women's Standing in the Labor Market

In the previous chapter we showed the trends of labor force participation of Muslim women in Israel. In this chapter we follow those women who are employed, and investigate their labor force characteristics. We analyze four main issues related to their work.

(1) The trends and determinants of part-time employment. The implications of part-time employment are very different from those of full-time work, and it is important to see how many women are employed in this manner and why.

(2) Commuting patterns. Studying which women work in their own communities and which have to commute to other localities may help us understand the opportunities, problems, and constraints Palestinian women face when they look for work.

(3) The occupations and segments of the economy in which these women are found. Analysis of these occupations and positions will show us which employment opportunities are actually open for Muslim Palestinians. By finding out where they work, we may also gain some clues concerning the reasons many Muslim women are not employed.

(4) The earnings attained by Muslim women. This analysis will inform us about another aspect of Muslim women's economic disadvantage.

Throughout this chapter, we compare Muslim women with Jewish women and, in some cases, with Muslim men. As in the previous chapter, we exclude the Palestinians in the Southern District (almost all of whom are Bedouins) and in East Jerusalem (who are mostly part of the West Bank society and are not Israeli citizens). In the Jewish population, we include only those born in Israel in order to avoid the complication of adding the dimension of immigration to the comparison of Jews to Palestinians.

5.1 Part-Time Employment and Women's Standing in the Labor Market

Since the 1970s the percentage of part-time workers has increased in all Western societies regardless of their economic regime. This trend was observed also in Israel from the 1950s to about 1980 (Stier and Lewin-Epstein 2000; Kraus 2002, Chapter 5; Cohen and Stier 2006). Several explanations for this increase are related to global structural economic changes. One explanation is that employers are interested in hiring a flexible labor force in order to be able to contract the number of workers during periods of recession (Negrey 1993; Tilly 1996; Blossfeld and Hakim 1997). Another line of explanation is related to the economic changes that have occurred in modern economies. The transition of the economy from manufacturing to services and the growth of public sector employment increased the demand for part-time workers (Rosenfeld and Birkelund 1995). Hence, in countries with a highly developed service sector, one finds higher proportions of part-time employees than in countries with less developed services (Lester 1996). On the supply side, around the late 1960s and early 1970s, a high increase in women's labor force participation occurred, and since women have traditionally been responsible for childcare and household duties, many of them preferred part-time work as a strategy of reconciling family duties with work in the labor market (Rosenfeld and Birkelund 1995; Tilly 1996; Blossfeld and Hakim 1997; Smith et al. 1998; Kalleberg 2000; Kraus 2002).

It is well known that part-time work is associated with lower rewards and benefits: lower hourly wages, reduced fringe benefits, fewer opportunities for job mobility, and less job security than full-time positions. Part-time workers are also less likely to have authority and autonomy than full-time workers (Golden and Appelbaum 1992; Kalleberg and Reskin 1995; Hakim 1996; Lester 1996; Gornick and Jacobs 1996; Tilly 1996; Blossfeld and Hakim 1997; Bardasi and Gornick 2000; Kalleberg 2000; Stier and Lewin-Epstein 2000; Kraus 2002; Gregory and Connolly 2008). Another cost of part-time employment might be the loss of various welfare benefits. If various policies cover part-time workers, as in Germany, France, the Netherlands, and Sweden, more workers, especially women, would choose this option than in countries where workers may lose those benefits if they work part-time (Tilly 1996; Crompton 2006; Lewis et al. 2008).

Since part-time work is much more common among women than among men, it places women in a disadvantaged economic position, affecting their status both in the labor market and in the family. For example, Stier and Lewin-Epstein observed that while "full-time employment is associated with rewards that constitute bargaining resources that affect the distribution of tasks and responsibilities within the household ... part-time involvement in market work [is] a way to maintain rather than change the traditional division of labor" (2000: 391–392).

Some women may prefer to work part time while other women would rather work full time but cannot find suitable positions. Following the human capital theory, the decision of a couple whether to specialize in a labor market career or in tasks related to childrearing and family duties is a voluntary decision within the context of the family. Women, however, are often compelled to specialize in the domestic tasks because they tend to earn less income and are often discriminated against in hiring and promotions (Hakim 1997: 42). Talking about "preference" is therefore misleading. If women had equal opportunities in the workplace, and if family duties were shared equally by both spouses, choices as to part-time work versus full-time work might be quite different (Walby 1986; Hochschild 1989).

Muslim women also face the choice between full- and part-time work, and in what follows, we look at their trend of part-time employment across years. Is part-time employment as prevalent among them as it has been among Jewish women in Israel (Kraus 2002)? How common is it in various age groups and birth cohorts? How does family composition affect part-time employment? Do Muslim women work part time because of domestic duties or due to the lack of full-time job opportunities? Labor-force surveys ask part-time workers why they do not work full time, and we used the answers that Muslim and Jewish women gave in an attempt to understand the prevalence of part-time employment among the two groups. For our analysis we defined part-time employment based on respondents' self-reports. Usually workers who reported part-time employment worked fewer than 35 hours a week.

Trends in Muslim Women's Part-Time Employment. As observed in other countries, we found that part-time work was more common among Muslim women than among Muslim men (Figure 5.1), and its frequency increased over the years with the growing share of Muslim women in the labor market. In 1974–1976 a little less than 20 percent of Muslim women worked part time, and this percentage rose to almost 40 percent in 2007–2009. The major increase occurred in the early 2000s, a period of substantial expansion of Muslim women's LFP. The share of part-time employment among Muslim men has been low (around 10 percent) and has hardly changed during the years studied. Until the mid-1990s, part-time work was more common among Jewish women than among Muslim women, but since 2000–2002 the share of part-time work has been similar for the two groups. It is evident that part-time work has remained predominantly a female phenomenon that expands with the growing LFP of women. Two out of five women, either Muslim or Jewish, participate only on a part-time basis in the labor market.

A better understanding of the changes in part-time work emerges when we look more closely into the various birth cohorts and follow their

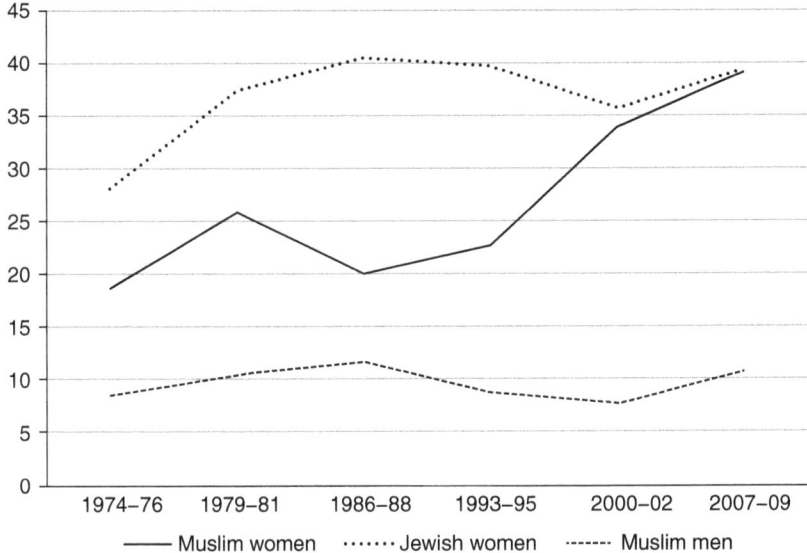

Figure 5.1 Part-Time Employment among Muslim Women and Men
and Jewish Women Aged 18–52 by Year
Source: Labor Force Surveys 1974–2009.
Note: Respondents born in Israel, excluding Palestinians from the
Southern District and from Jerusalem, and Druze from the Golan Heights.

employment patterns over the years. The results of this analysis are presented in Table 5.1. The columns of this table tell us about the changes
across different birth cohorts in each age group. From the birth cohort born
in 1963–1969, the likelihood of a Muslim woman to hold a part-time job
has increased monotonically when moving from an older birth cohort to a
more recent one. For example, following Muslim women in the age bracket
25–31, we see that 20 percent of those born in the years 1956–1962 had
part-time work at this age, and this share has increased to more than 37
percent for Muslim women born between 1970–1976. It further increased
to more than 42 percent among women in the same age bracket born in
1977–1983.

In order to ascertain whether Muslim women's probability of holding a
part-time job changes during the course of their life cycle, we inspected the
variation within cohorts (see rows in Table 5.1 for which we have at least
four observations). In contradiction to the expectation that we would find a
shift from part-time to full-time employment as employed women grow
older and have fewer childcare responsibilities, we observed that within a

Table 5.1 *Part-Time Employment of Muslim and Jewish Women
Aged 18–52 by Birth Cohort and Age Group*

	18–24	25–31	32–38	39–45	46–52
A. Muslim					
1928–1934					28.6^a
1935–1941				23.8^a	35.8^b
1942–1948			23.3^a	24.4^b	38.8^c
1949–1955		22.8^a	20.2^b	21.4^c	24.1^d
1956–1962	25.8^a	20.0^b	20.8^c	34.1^d	30.5^e
1963–1969	18.2^b	24.3^c	31.2^d	34.5^e	
1970–1976	19.1^c	37.3^d	36.2^e		
1977–1983	33.3^d	42.4^e			
1984–1990	47.9^e				
B. Jews					
1928–1934					45.0^a
1935–1941				42.9^a	43.1^b
1942–1948			43.4^a	38.4^b	40.0^c
1949–1955		38.3^a	54.5^b	39.4^c	34.6^d
1956–1962	29.7^a	40.7^b	41.4^c	37.3^d	35.9^e
1963–1969	36.0^b	37.0^c	34.6^d	34.5^e	
1970–1976	40.7^c	37.5^d	36.2^e		
1977–1983	43.3^d	37.9^e			
1984–1990	51.8^e				

Year of survey: ^{a} = 1979–1981; ^{b} = 1986–1988; ^{c} = 1993–1995; ^{d} = 2000–2002; ^{e} = 2007–2009.
Source: Labor Force Surveys 1979–2009.
Note: Respondents born in Israel, excluding Palestinians from the Southern District and from Jerusalem, and Druze from the Golan Heights.

given birth cohort, Muslim women tend to be fully employed when they are young and increase their share as part-time workers as they get older. For example, of working Muslim women born in 1963–1969, about 18 percent held part-time jobs when they were in the age bracket 18–24. Seven years later, when they were in the age bracket 25–31, part-time positions accounted for 24 percent, and by the time the women of this cohort reached the age of 39–45, more than third of them worked part-time.

We repeated the same analysis for employed Jewish women born in Israel. The results are presented in the second panel of Table 5.1. From this comparison we see that, in general, an opposite age-related trend occurred for Jewish women, although among them the changes are very small. Part-time work was more common in the older birth cohort and slightly declined when we move to the younger birth cohorts (this is the case only when those women are 32 and above). Only among the youngest age group (18–24) do we find an increase in part-time work when moving from the older to the youngest birth cohorts, probably due to the rise in the number of those who are in tertiary education and combine education with paid employment. Examining whether the probability of holding a part-time job among Jewish women changes during the course of their life cycle, we found that hardly any shift from part-time to full-time work is observed as women get older.

Part-Time Employment and Its Determinants: A Multivariate Analysis. In this section we examine the net effects of women's education and their family composition on part-time work, utilizing the logistic regression technique (see Appendix 5.1). The higher the level of women's education, the lower the probability of holding part-time work. In 2007–2009, women with tertiary education had a 55 percent lower probability of being employed part-time compared to women with the lowest level of education. Marriage increased the odds of being employed part time, but this effect has declined over the years. In 1986–1988 married Muslim women had 3.5 times the odds of working part time as compared to single Muslim women. This marriage effect declined to odds of 2.8 in 1993–1995 and 1.6 in 2000–2002. In 2007–2009 the effect of marriage on part-time employment was positive but insignificant. The declining impact of marriage may reflect the increasing legitimacy of married women's labor market participation. They are not expected, as before, to retire when they get married or to shorten their workload in order to provide for their husbands at home.[1]

Unlike in Western countries where studies found that women with large number of children, especially young ones, have higher odds of holding a part-time job (Rosenfeld and Birkelund 1995; Hakim 1996; Han and Moen 1999; Kraus 2002), this is barely the case for Muslim women (see Appendix 5.1). Net of other variables, we did not find that the number of children had a significant effect on Muslim women's part-time work. This might be related to the fact that many of the Muslim women are involuntary part-time workers, as will be shown below. Even when we looked at the effect of young children (under five), we did not find any significant effect, save for the last period (2007–2009). In this last period a higher rate of Muslim women entered the labor market; perhaps the growing numbers of these women included a greater number of women who were sensitive to the age of their children. Among Jewish women, an additional child in the

---

[1] Among Jewish women marriage increased the odds of part-time work until the mid-1990s, but in more recent years, single Jewish women had higher odds of being employed part-time (figures for Jews are not included in the Table).

household did reduce their odds of being employed part time, but having young children in the family did not have an additional impact.

Voluntary and Involuntary Part-Time Work. Workers may choose to work part time due to their own preferences and various constraints that they see as legitimate reasons for not working full time (voluntary part-time work) or alternatively because they cannot find a fitting full-time position despite their preference for full-time employment (involuntary part-time work). In the latter case, we may talk of "half a job in the sense that it is only half the job that the employee wants" (Tilly 1996: 3; cf. Kraus 2002: 104; Cohen and Stier 2006). Part-time workers in our study were asked to report their reasons for not working full time. Respondents reporting that they could not find full-time jobs were classified as "involuntary part-time workers"; respondents selecting all other options (such as "not interested," "a housewife," "incapacitated") were defined as "voluntary part-time workers." The findings suggest that, unlike Jewish women for whom part-time work results mainly from voluntary choices, for Muslim women part-time work is mainly involuntary.

The shares of involuntary part-time work are presented in Figure 5.2. We see that the incidence of reportedly involuntary part-time work among

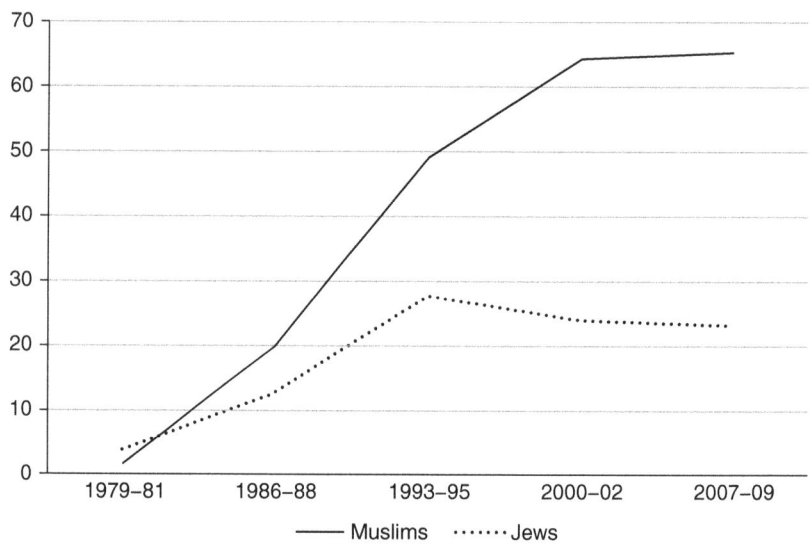

Figure 5.2 Involuntary Part-Time Work of Women Aged 25–52 by Ethno-Religious Group and Year
Source: Labor Force Surveys 1979–2009.
Note: Respondents born in Israel, excluding Palestinians from the Southern District and from Jerusalem, and Druze from the Golan Heights.

Muslim women was very low in the early years when very few women were employed and few of them worked part-time. As the share of Muslim women in the labor market rose, involuntary part-time work among them has become much more common. Most Muslim women (around 65 percent in the last two periods) holding part-time jobs reported that they worked part-time because they were not able to find a full-time position. This is true regardless of the educational level of those Muslim women. As a matter of fact, involuntary part-time work is very common among part-time teachers. Teaching is one of the most common occupations for highly educated Muslim women, and more than a third of them worked part-time. Almost all of those who worked part-time (88 percent) reported to be doing so involuntarily.[2] The very high proportion of involuntary part-time teaching demonstrates the difficulty of finding an open vacancy in Arabic schools, which is strong evidence that even highly educated Muslim women face scarce job opportunities. [3]

5.2   Trends in Local Employment and Commuting

In Chapter 2 we saw that most Palestinians live in communities that are composed of Palestinians only. This fact has created a sheltered economy, where Palestinians do not have to compete with Jews (Semyonov and Lewin-Epstein 1994; Yonay and Kraus 2001; Khattab 2003). Shops, manufacturing firms, and public and personal services are mostly, or often exclusively, staffed with Palestinians. The latter may come from neighboring communities, but local residents who know the owners and managers are usually first in line to work in the local establishments and services.

Yet as also discussed in Chapter 2, the Palestinian enclave economy is comprised of small enterprises that are likely to employ only a few workers. These enterprises are typically in peripheral industries with low margins of profits and fewer opportunities for employment mobility (Haider 1995; Yonay and Kraus 2001). Given the underdeveloped infrastructure of most Palestinian communities, the larger and more successful industries need to be relocated in industrial zones in the developed Jewish communities, forcing local workers to commute if they want to be employed in those enterprises. Hence it is no wonder that Muslim women (as well as men) do not find a sufficient number of jobs in their own places of residence and have to

---

[2] Our analysis of the distribution of part-time employment by education and occupation is not presented here and is available on request.
[3] For Jewish women, the share of involuntary part-time work was very low in 1979–1981 (4 percent) and increased until the mid-1990s; it has remained stable since then (around 25 percent).

look for employment in other localities away from their homes. But do they get good offers from outside their place of residence? This will be the main focus of our next analysis.

In a free market with equal opportunities where workers are able to choose where to work, it would be those with high human capital that would seek to broaden their work opportunities beyond the opportunities they face in their own localities, as they search for highly paid prestigious jobs (Simpson 1980, 1987). It is usually men rather than women who have a higher probability of having jobs far from home, since women are usually expected to be responsible for family duties and traveling long distances interferes with the ability to fulfill those duties (White 1977). As we will show, these predictions hold true for Jewish workers (men and women), who have a wide range of job opportunities in the dominant economy, but not for Muslim workers.

In the labor force surveys, respondents were asked to identify their workplace locality. Combining this information with information on their place of residence, we looked at whether the workplace of Muslim workers is within their place of residence or rather requires commuting to other localities. Results are presented in Figure 5.3.

Somewhat more than a third of Muslim women aged 18–52 worked outside their place of residence (36.6 percent) in the late 1970s, and this share has hardly changed along the years. Comparing these results with those of Muslim men and Jewish women we find: (1) Muslim men are much less likely than Muslim women to work in their locality of residence; around 63 to 67 percent of them commute to other localities (in 1979–1981, it was somewhat lower at 57 percent; figures not shown); (2) In 1979–1981, the share of Jewish women who commuted to work was very similar to the share of Muslim women – 34 and 37 percent, respectively – but unlike that of Muslim women, the share of Jewish women commuting to work monotonically increased, so in 2007–2009 almost half of them worked outside their communities.

Which Muslim women work outside their locality of residence? Figure 5.3 shows that it is mostly Muslim women with the lowest educational level (who comprise a high share of Muslim women, as we see in Figure 3.1) who are more likely to commute. For each of the years studied, around 45 percent of working women with low levels of education had to travel to other localities to work, while Muslim women with tertiary and secondary education were more likely to work in their own communities: only about a third of them worked outside their locality of residence. This pattern of commuting is paradoxical. Commuting is costly, and the earning potential of women with low levels of education is very low, and therefore we would expect them to work in their own

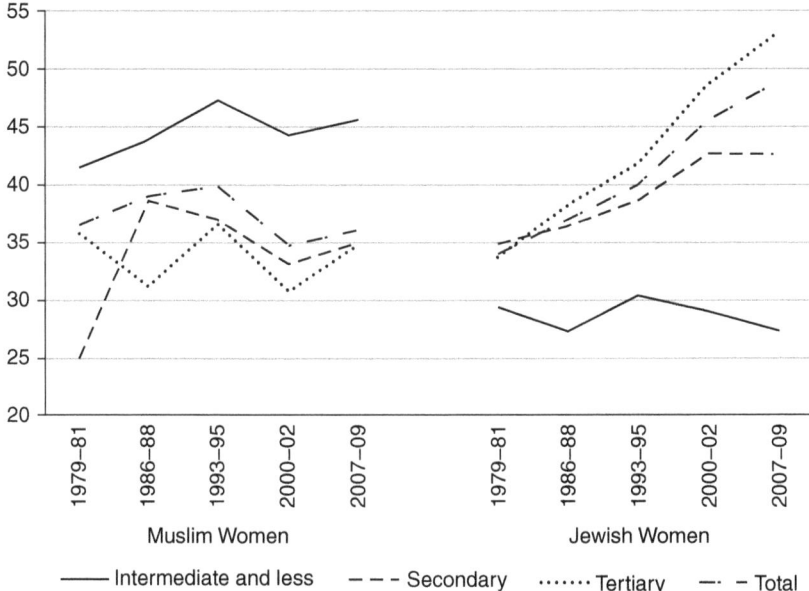

Figure 5.3 Commuting to Work of Muslim and Jewish Women Aged 18–52 by Education and Year
Source: Labor Force Surveys 1979–2009.
Note: Respondents born in Israel, excluding Palestinians from the Southern District and from Jerusalem, and Druze from the Golan Heights.

localities. This is indeed the case for Jewish women with low level of educations, around three-quarters of whom (in all years) are able to find enough jobs in their own localities so that they do not have to commute. As the education of Jewish women increases, they tend to find jobs outside their community of residence. For example, in 2007–2009, 53.2 percent of Jewish women with tertiary education did commute, compared to 34.8 percent of Muslim women at this level of education. This comparison provides more evidence regarding the meager opportunities of both less-educated and highly educated Muslim women. Palestinian communities are underdeveloped and therefore lack enough jobs suited for women with low levels of education. There are public services that cater to the local residents and provide work opportunities for women with high-level education. But if the latter want to exploit their advanced human capital to find better jobs, they would have to search for work in the dominant economy, where their nationality may constitute an obstacle in the competition with Jewish women. These findings were corroborated in a multivariate analysis predicting Muslim women's commuting (results not shown). This analysis found that Muslim women's probability of commuting in all years decreased with age and with the number of children. Dwelling in small localities with scarcer job opportunities increased Muslim women's odds of commuting to work in other localities.

5.3   Economic Sectors and Branches and Occupational Enrollment

Various jobs carry with them different economic rewards, prestige, power, and psychic income, and therefore stronger groups try to limit the access of weaker groups to the more attractive positions within the labor market. Thus while male-dominated occupations entail higher income, prestige, and power, female-dominated occupations are characterized by lack of power, low wages, and fewer opportunities for advancement (Reskin and Roos 1990; Kraus 2002; Stier and Yaish 2014).

Another important distinction in labor markets that affects workers' well-being and success is their sector of employment, distinguishing between public and private. Since we do not have information on ownership, we used type of economic activity as a proxy, using the Central Bureau of Statistics' classification. The public sector is thus defined as including all those employed in public administration, education, health, welfare, and social-work services. All other branches are defined in this book as belonging to the private sector.[4]

The public sector is not subject to the profit-maximization logic that characterizes the private sector, and it may be able to pay its workers higher wages (Mueller 2000). In current liberal democracies, it is also known to operate according to egalitarian and formal bureaucratic procedures and is subject to legal inspection. Due to such procedures, studies have found less discrimination against various deprived groups, such as women and ethnic minorities in the public sector (Lewin-Epstein and Stier 1987; DiPrete 1989; Blau and Kahn 1996; Disney and Gosling 1998; Kraus 2002; Melly 2005). The private sector is heterogeneous, and work conditions and rewards greatly vary among various firms. Political economists and students of labor markets have therefore suggested a distinction between core and periphery sectors. The core operates under conditions of long-term planning, high productivity, high profits, intensive utilization of capital, high incidence of monopoly elements, and a large degree of

---

[4] One should note that according to this definition, private schools and hospitals, for example, are defined as part of the public sector, while state-owned utilities and industries are defined as belonging to the private sector.

unionization.[5] It follows from these attributes that employment in core industries entails high wages, good working conditions, chances for advancement, and stability. By contrast, industries within the periphery are noted for their labor intensity, low productivity, intense competition, low profits, and weak unionization. Consequently, employment in peripheral branches is characterized by low wages, poor working conditions, and little chance for advancement (Doeringer and Piore, 1971; Lewin-Epstain and Stier 1987; Kraus, 1992; Yaish and Kraus 2003).

The way that female and male workers from various ethnic groups (or ethno-religious, in our case) are assorted to positions within the economic structure is therefore a major mechanism of social stratification, which has critical implications for employees' working conditions, advancement, and earnings (cf. Glass et al. 1988; Gornick and Jacobs, 1998). In what follows, we describe the location of Muslim women within the Israeli economy. We first look at their placement in the various economic sectors and then analyze their occupational structure.

Muslim Women and Economic Branch Enrollment. Based on labor force surveys, we followed the economic branches and sectors of employment of Muslim women in the last thirty years and compared them to the employment of Jewish women and Muslim men. The results are presented in Appendix 5.2, panel A. We see that in the early periods of our study it was the agricultural economic branch that was the main employment branch for Muslim women, but over the years, as the weight of this economic branch in the national economy and the labor market declined, so did Muslim women's enrollment in this economic branch. In 1974–1976, about a third of Muslim female workers – (who, we should remember, were only 7.7 percent of all women aged 18–52 at that time; Figure 4.1) – worked in agriculture. By 1979–1981, this figure declined to 26.2 percent, and it has further declined gradually to 2.5 percent in 2007–2009. The manufacturing branch became an alternative source of employment for Muslim women. While in the mid-1970s one-fifth of Muslim women worked in this branch, in the late 1980s this figure increased to more than 40 percent. The majority of Muslim women in this economic branch (around three quarters) were enrolled in sewing workshops. At that time the textile and garment industry was a mainstay of the Israeli economy, but since then its importance has declined, and during the 1990s the sewing workshops were relocated to neighboring Arab countries and the Far East, where labor has been even cheaper than in the Palestinian communities of Israel.[6] Following this

---

[5] Although unionization has declined in the neoliberal era, unions in core industries have better defended their power than in peripheral industries. This is very much the case in Israel.
[6] The sewing workshops in Druze villages have prevailed; see Chapter 8.

structural change, less than 7 percent of Muslim women worked in the manufacturing economic branch in the last period, 2007–2009.

With the increase in Muslim women's education and the declining opportunities for work in the manufacturing sector, more Muslim women found work in the public sector, mainly in education, health, and welfare services. Until the mid-1990s, somewhat more than a third of Muslim women were enrolled in this sector, and since then, their share in the public sector has increased to almost 64 percent.

A vastly significant feature of Muslim women's employment is the narrow spectrum of job positions available for them. This is evident, *inter alia*, in their high concentration in the public sector. For illustration, in the most recent period (2007–2009) we find that more than six out of ten Muslim women were employed in the public sector (63.7 percent), the majority of them in educational services (40.5 percent) and in health and welfare services (18.0 percent). At the same time, less than 44 percent of Jewish women were enrolled in the public sector (Appendix 5.2). An additional 22 percent of Muslim women were enrolled in low peripheral services, mainly in wholesale and retail trade. Unlike Jewish women, Muslim female workers are very seldom enrolled in core services. The latter account for 19.7 percent of all Jewish female workers, compared to only 4.3 percent of Muslim women, who are also grossly underrepresented in public administration. The latter provided employment to only 1.7 percent of them in 2007–2009, while 5.2 percent of Jewish employed women were occupied in this branch.[7]

The limited range of industrial branches in which Muslim women work characterizes that of Muslim men as well. Panel C of Appendix 5.2 shows, for instance, that in 2007–2009 almost every second Muslim man worked in the manufacturing (mainly in the peripheral industries) and the construction branches, in which less than a quarter of Jewish men worked (panel D). Muslim men not in these branches worked mainly in the peripheral service sectors (repair of vehicles, wholesales, or accommodation and restaurant services). Muslim men, like Muslim women, are underrepresented in the core services and in public administration. Almost 20 percent of all Jewish men worked in the former, and additional 5.4 percent in the latter, in contrast to 4.3 (in core services) and 1.2 percent (in public administration) of Muslim men.

The fact that Muslim women and men are concentrated in few economic branches is a strong indication that many positions are blocked to Palestinian workers. To document this limitation, we have further calculated the concentration index for Muslim and Jewish women and men

---

[7] Notice that, unlike for Muslim women, the share of Jewish women in our study working in the agriculture and transformative industries was very low.

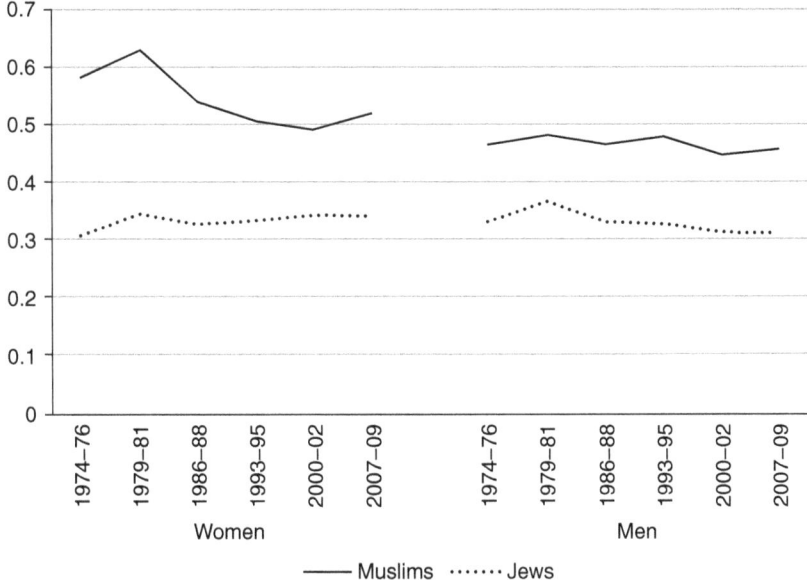

Figure 5.4 Index of Concentration on Economic Branches of Muslims and Jews Aged 18–52 by Gender and Year

across years. The indices indicate the proportion of individuals who would have to change industries to be evenly distributed across the 15 industrial sectors (Jacobs 1989). These calculations show that although Muslim women's concentration has slightly declined over the years (from 0.58 in 1974–1976 to 0.52 to 2007–2009), their concentration in all years is the highest, followed by Muslim men (0.45–0.48). The branch distribution of Jews, men and women, is much more diversified (concentration ranges from 0.30 to 0.36). See Figure 5.4.

Trends in Occupational Enrollment. Related to the changes that Muslim women have experienced with regard to their sectorial and economic branch employment, they have also experienced changes in their occupational enrollment. This is seen in Appendix 5.3. Every second working woman in the mid-1970s worked in agricultural and in manual occupations (51.9 percent), while somewhat more than a quarter (28.6 percent) were employed in associate professional and technical occupations. During the same period, Jewish women were already well established in the professional and technical occupations with almost a third enrolled in them (and an additional 3.6 percent in academic professional occupations).[8] A much lower share of Jewish women (less than 10 percent) worked in the low status manual occupations.

With the changes in the industrial composition of the Israeli economy, Muslim women's share in manual and agricultural occupations has declined over the years, and their employment in the associate professional and technical occupations has steadily risen to more than 40 percent in 2007–2009 (with an additional 1.5 percent in other high-prestige academic and managerial occupations). Large growth has also been recorded in low non-manual occupations; in clerical occupations from less than 4 percent in 1974–1976 to almost 17 percent in 2007–2009, in service occupations (travel agents, cooks, childcare workers, cosmeticians, barbers, police-women) from 10 percent to 25 percent, and in sales from 5 percent to 10 percent in the same years. In contrast to Jewish women, however, very few Muslim women have entered the high-status occupations of the academic professions (less than 2 percent, in 2007–2009) and of the managerial occupations (less than half a percent in 2007–2009); the figures for Jewish women in this period were 7.3 and 5.4 percent, respectively.[9]

The previous analysis of major occupational groups showed a shift in Muslim women's work from manual to non-manual occupations, but it did not show their distribution among specific occupations. If we move now to a more detailed classification of occupations and look at the three-digit categorization, an amazing picture emerges: More than 71 percent of all working Muslim women in 2007–2009, and only 39 percent of working Jewish women, were enrolled in *only* 12 occupations (data not shown); the most prevalent among them were teachers (36.5 percent including kinder-garten assistants), nurses (9.1 percent), clerical workers (9.6 percent), sales-women (9.0 percent), and kitchen workers (7.0 percent).

Academic Education and Occupational Enrollment. Workers invest in human capital and would like to work in occupations that fit their investment and pay off in terms of the time, effort, and money invested. One way to study social stratification is by examining to what degree members of various social groups manage to achieve this goal. For this purpose we defined all academic professionals, associate professionals, and managerial occupations as fitting workers with academic

---

[8] Our classification is based on the Israeli CBS classification of occupations (CBS 1994). Examples of academic occupations are lawyers, physicians, economists, and accountants; professional and technical occupations are technicians, teachers, social workers, nurses, and journalists.

[9] In all years the majority of the Muslim men were mostly employed in low manual occupations. The share of Muslim men employed in these occupations has declined monotonically over the years, but more than 60 percent were still enrolled in those occupations in 2007–2009 (figures not shown).

degrees. We further distinguished between teachers and the rest of these occupations. As in many other countries, teaching used to be a respected and rewarding occupation in Israel, but its standing and its pecuniary rewards have declined over the last decades (Addi-Raccah 2002 for Israel; Hargreaves 2009 for a comparative perspective). For Muslim women with academic degrees in the age bracket 25–52, a very low share has been employed in the most rewarding academic, professional, and managerial occupations, and this share has actually decreased from 23 percent in 1993–1995 to 17 percent in 2007–2009 (more than half of whom worked as nurses; table not presented).[10] Among Jewish women, their proportion, 35 percent, was much higher than that of Muslim women in 1993–1995 and increased to 41 percent in 2007–2009, in contrast to the decline among Muslim women.

What do academic Muslim women do? Not surprisingly, large numbers of them have worked as teachers. This is a phenomenon that can be observed in many countries, but there are striking differences between Muslim and Jewish women in Israel. The latter have more of a chance of being employed in better positions and are less likely to be teachers (only 37 percent in 1993–1995, declining monotonically to 23 percent in 2007–2009). Among Muslim women on the other hand, the percentage of teachers among academically educated women has been amazingly high: 58–60 percent, showing no change over the years studied. There is nothing bad in being a teacher; it is a desirable job for many Palestinian and Jewish women in Israel. Nevertheless, these figures are another indication that many positions that may fit educated women have been closed to Muslim women.

It is not only Muslim women who have had suffered from job shortage; their male counterparts have also faced a limited access to the best jobs. The share of highly educated Muslim men aged 25–52 enrolled in the highly rewarding academic, professional, and managerial occupations has been much lower than that of Jewish men, and the gap between the two groups has hardly narrowed. In 2007–2009, the respective figures were 40 percent and 60 percent. Muslim men have had to compromise on teaching, and although their share in teaching has declined (from 41 percent in 1993–1995), it was still relatively very high, 19 percent, in 2007–2009, much higher than among academic Jewish men (4 percent).

Net Effects of Ethnicity and Gender on the Occupational Enrollment of Workers with an Academic Degree. So far we presented the occupational structure of Muslims and Jews, men and women. As is well known, occupational assignments are determined by workers'

---

[10] In both 1979–1981 and 1986–1988, we had relatively few Muslim women (fewer than 130) with academic education who were enrolled in the paid market.

characteristics, such as education, age, marital status, and place of residence in addition to their ethnicity and gender affiliation. Since the various groups might differ with regard to these personal attributes, we conclude this part of the chapter with a multivariate analysis that measures the net impact, controlling for personal variables, of gender and ethno-religious group on the likelihood of working in suitable jobs (for workers aged 25–52). The results are presented in Appendix 5.4.[11]

From these results we learn that the disadvantage of academic Muslim women enrollment in the most desirable positions, which we found in the descriptive analysis, is replicated in the multivariate analysis. Among the highly educated workers, it is both gender and ethno-religious group that determined workers' occupational allocation, net of control variables. Both Jewish and Muslim women, and Muslim men, are by far less likely to be employed in academic and professional occupations compared to Jewish men. Muslim men are closest to Jewish men but still 57 percent less likely to hold such positions (in 2007–2009). Jewish women's disadvantage compared to Jewish men is not much larger than Muslim men's, with 63 percent lower odds. Highly educated Muslim women are far behind all other groups. Their net odds to be in good positions are 92 percent less of those of Jewish men.

Academic workers who do not find suitable jobs and do not give up on salaried work have to compromise on less desirable jobs. In the case of Muslim women, they also have low odds of being employed in clerical and service occupations relative to Jewish men, and the result is that many of them work as teachers. They have 41 times higher odds than Jewish men of being employed as schoolteachers (in 2007–2009), much higher than the odds observed among Jewish women (6.4 times higher than Jewish men). Educated Muslim men had 5.3 times the probability of being employed as schoolteachers than that of Jewish men, and 1.8 times the probability of working in unskilled and skilled occupations as the latter.

Net of the control variables, educated Muslim women's opportunities were less limited in the earlier years than in recent ones, but changes were very small. For academically educated Muslim women, the relative odds of entering the academic and professional occupations were 88 percent lower than Jewish men in the earliest period (1993–1995). This negative trend stands in contrast to the experience of both Muslim men and Jewish women. The latter two groups improved their likelihood of getting such positions. The improvement for Muslim men (from 70 percent of Jewish men's odds in 1993–1995 to 57 percent in 2007–2009) was stronger than that of Jewish women (from 72 to 63 percent in the same period).

---

[11] Very much the same results were obtained when analyzing the ethnic and gender effects on occupational allocation using the multinomial analysis.

5.4   Trends in Muslim Women's Earnings

In this section we add more evidence about the standing of Muslim women in the labor market, this time in terms of their earnings. We pay special attention to the following questions: (1) How are Muslim women compensated for their labor in comparison to Jewish women and to Muslim men? (2) Are Muslim women disadvantaged in their earning attainment compared to the two above groups?

The data used in this section are based on the combined labor force surveys and income surveys conducted yearly by the Israeli CBS. We had to combine these two surveys since the income survey in Israel does not identify Israeli Palestinians by religion. We start in 1998 because earlier combined data are not available. In order to get a larger number of respondents for our analysis, we combined the following years: 1998 to 2001, 2002 to 2005, and 2006 to 2008. Consistent with the previous chapters, we excluded Muslim women residing in the Southern District and in Jerusalem.[12]

Patterns of Earnings Gaps. The ratios of median monthly earnings of employees aged 25 to 52 are presented in Table 5.2. In order to see if gaps change with age, we also examined these ratios separately for two age groups, 25–38 and 39–52 (for the median monthly earnings themselves see Appendix 5.5). As expected in each period and within both age groups (see the first column), Muslim women earned much less than Jewish women, but the gap narrowed along the years from 60 to 70 percent. Comparing the earning gaps between the two age groups, we see that the earning gaps were somewhat larger among the older employees (39–52), an age at which many employees are already established in the labor market, than among the younger women. Muslim women (within the two age groups) also earned much less than their male counterparts (the second column). In the years 1998–2001, Muslim women earned only 65 percent of what Muslim men earned, and this gap has declined during the years but has remained quite high (74–76 percent). This gap was about the same in the two age groups. Among Jews the gender gap was even larger, between 63 and 68 percent, and this gap is larger for the older group than the younger (the fourth column). The Muslim-Jewish earning gap among men is much bigger than among women (the third column).

Sources of Ethno-Religious and Gender Earning Gaps: Multivariate Analysis. In this section we examine the sources of

---

[12] The income surveys comprise merely 25 percent of the labor force data, thus leaving us with too small a sample every single year for reliable analysis. The last period collapses only three years because the data for 2009 was not available for us at the time of analysis. We needed special permission from the CBS to combine these two surveys.

Table 5.2 *Gender and Ethnic Ratios of Median Monthly Earnings of Workers Aged 25–52 by Gender and Year*

Year	Women: Muslim/Jewish	Muslims: Women/Men	Men: Muslim/Jewish	Jews: Women/Men
1998–2001				
25–38	0.624	0.657	0.651	0.686
39–52	0.589	0.617	0.538	0.565
Total	0.599	0.650	0.583	0.632
2002–2005				
25–38	0.696	0.729	0.656	0.687
39–52	0.670	0.718	0.568	0.608
Total	0.687	0.741	0.605	0.652
2006–2008				
25–38	0.745	0.769	0.694	0.716
39–52	0.685	0.767	0.551	0.616
Total	0.700	0.758	0.625	0.676

Source: Combined Labor Force Survey and Income Survey 1998–2008.
Note: Respondents born in Israel, excluding Palestinians from the Southern District and from Jerusalem, and Druze from the Golan Heights.

earnings gaps between (1) Muslim and Jewish women, and (2) Muslim women and Muslim men. As common in such studies, we control for compositional differences, that is, we take into consideration differences in the characteristics of the various groups that may explain part of the gaps. For example, if one group has a higher level of education on average than another group, its higher income might be the result of this educational gap. The part of the gap that is not explained by compositional differences is explained by the differential rewards that these groups get for their various compositional characteristics.

Appendix 5.5 shows the distribution for the selected variables included in the regression equations. Starting with the comparison of Muslim and Jewish working women,[13] as expected from what we already know, Muslim women have less human capital than Jewish women. For example, whereas 64 percent of Jewish women had tertiary education in 2006–2008, the respective percentage for Muslim women was only 56 percent. Muslim women also worked 1.7 hours less per week than Jewish women, and a much higher proportion of them worked in skilled manual occupations (17.1 versus 5.9 percent, respectively). Seventy-one percent of Muslim women worked in the public sector, compared to only 43.2 percent of Jewish women.

---

[13] These distributions differ from those presented in Chapter 3 because the latter described the total population of women, whereas here we analyze working women only.

Working Muslim women differed from their male counterparts as well. They worked fewer hours per week, and they accumulated less work experience.[14] Notice, however, that the educational level of working Muslim women was higher than that of their male counterparts and they worked in very different occupations and economic sectors than Muslim men. The majority of Muslim men worked in manual jobs and in the private sector, whereas women worked in white-collar jobs in the public sector. Given these differences in human capital, labor inputs, and labor market characteristics, it is not surprising that Muslim women differed in their earnings from both Jewish women and Muslim men.

Predicting Earning Returns from Individuals' Characteristics. One way of measuring earning discrimination is to examine the differential rewards that various groups of workers get for their human capital, labor input, and labor market characteristics. These rewards are often referred to as the "conversion rates" into earnings of the resources workers bring to the labor force. This can be accomplished by running separate multivariate regression equations predicting employee earnings for four groups (Muslim/Jewish; women/men). Following are the findings of these equations as done for each of the three periods studied. The earning equations are presented in Appendix 5.6.

Comparison of the regression equations of Muslim and Jewish women reveals that the latter got higher returns than the former. Another important difference between the two groups of women is that only Jewish women are rewarded for working in the private sector while Palestinian women were rewarded for working in the public one in 1998–2001. Finally, when the regression equations for Muslim women were compared with those of Muslim men, we find that there are no significant differences for most of the compositional variables examined, including tertiary education, an additional year in the paid market, work in the public sector (save in 2002–2005 when Muslim men got higher returns than Muslim women for working in this sector), and for an additional hour worked (save in 1998–2001, when Muslim men also had an advantage retlative to Muslim women). The only exception was work in high non-manual jobs that contributed much more to Muslim men's earnings than to women's earnings. This last advantage may stem from the fact that Muslim women in this category worked mainly as schoolteachers, while Muslim men were

---

[14] The work experience gap between women and men is probably much higher than presented in Appendix 5.5 because we measured experience according to subjects' age (minus their years of education; see variables definition in Appendix 5.6). Since women's work experience suffers from more interruptions, their measured experience is more likely than men's to be overestimated.

employed in a somewhat broader spectrum of high non-manual occupations (cf. Bental et al. 2017).

Counterfactual Earnings of Muslim Women. Based on the above observations we posed four more questions: *First*, what would Muslim women's monthly earnings be if they were subject to the same processes as those of Jewish women, holding constant their personal characteristics? *Second*, what would Muslim women's monthly earnings be if they had possessed the same personal characteristics as Jewish women, holding constant their attainment process? The *third* and the *fourth* questions are the same as the first two questions but compare Muslim women to Muslim men. The answers to these four questions would tell us about the importance of Muslim women's personal characteristics, as compared with the importance of the conversion rates of these characteristics to generating Muslim women's lower earnings.

If Muslim women had the same conversion rates as Jewish women, their monthly earnings would be much higher, narrowing the gaps between them and Jewish women by 45 percent in 1998–2001, 25 percent in 2001–2005, and by 56 percent in the last period. Muslim women would also benefit, though to a lesser degree, had they possessed the same resources as Jewish women, holding constant their conversion rates. They would narrow the earnings gaps with Jewish women by 16 percent in 1998–2001, 29 percent in 2002–2005, and 16 percent in 2006–2008. The resources in which they most differed from Jewish women were education and sectorial enrollment (see Appendix 5.5).

We replicated the same analysis in regard to the gaps between Muslim women and men. Had Muslim women kept their own characteristics but been subject to the same conversion rates as Muslim men, the gender gaps would be reversed. In 1998–2001, women would get 11 percent more than men, and in the next two periods, 2002–2005 and 2006–2008, it would be much larger at 45 percent and 52 percent, respectively. The reason for this result is the fact that Muslim women have achieved more education on average than Muslim men and are more concentrated in non-manual occupations. Had Muslim women been similar to Muslim men in their education, occupational enrollment, and other compositional characteristics, holding constant their conversion rates, the earning gender gap among Muslims would have almost disappeared. This result means that the advantage that Muslim women had over their male counterparts in level of education and, consequently, in occupational enrollment was offset by men's advantage in experience and in weekly hours of work (Appendix 5.5).

5.5   Summary

In this chapter we analyzed four main issues – part-time employment, commuting, sectorial and occupational placement, and earnings. Each one of these contributed to our understanding of the general picture regarding Muslim women's labor market experience.

First, we considered part-time employment. A considerable share of Muslim women who have entered the paid labor market, almost 40 percent, held part-time work in 2007–2009. While this rate is similar to that of Jewish women, important differences emerge when we further analyzed the specifics of part-time work. Unlike Jewish women, among whom part-time rates have been quite stable, the percentage of part-time employment among Muslim women was lower in the earlier years and has steadily increased as more women have entered the labor market. This finding may indicate difficulties in finding work as more women occupy the relatively few positions open for Muslim workers in a Jewish-dominated society. This hypothesis is further corroborated by looking at the reasons given by part-time workers. Most Muslim women working part-time say that they are interested in full-time work but have not found such positions. Although the share of part-time Jewish workers was, as said above, very much like that of Muslim women, the majority did not express interest in working more hours.

The analysis of commuting patterns also adds to our understanding of the precarious standing of Muslim women in the labor force. Concentrating on Muslim women with a low level of education, we observed that they worked mostly outside their place of residence. The fact that they have to commute means that they have not found paid work in their own communities. Commuting to work is costly in time and travel expenses, and low-education jobs do not pay enough to justify commuting had alternatives existed in women's own localities. It is therefore safe to assume that Muslim women with a low level of education commute because they do not have enough opportunities in the Palestinian communities in which they live, probably because of the underdeveloped character of these places (Section 2.5). It is also quite safe to assume that had more opportunities existed in these women's communities, more women with a low level of education would join the labor force, because the costs of traveling to the workplace would be much lower.

The other side of the coin concerns Muslim women with higher education. The fact that, compared to Jewish women, many of them are employed in their own localities probably means that they were not able to find attractive jobs elsewhere. With Palestinian communities being underdeveloped, attractive jobs exist mostly in Jewish communities, where job-seeking Muslim women might be subject to discrimination.

The fact that they are employed mostly within their own communities means, first, that they have less desirable jobs, and, second, that they have few opportunities available in the better-paying jobs of big corporations and in public administration, which are found almost exclusively in Jewish communities.

This conclusion is further supported by our analysis of economic sectors and occupations. Muslims in Israel in general, and Muslim women in particular, face a very narrow job spectrum. They are under-represented in the core industries and core services, and they hardly work in state public administration. While Muslim men work in construction and in peripheral services, Muslim women have been able to find jobs in the more rewarding public sector, but have been limited to two areas only, education (catering to Palestinian pupils) and health. Consequently, Muslim women have a very slim occupational range. The majority, more than 70 percent, are enrolled in only 12 three-digit occupations (out of about 400). When looking at workers with academic education, the picture is even more troubling. Highly educated Muslim women are mainly enrolled in only two occupations: the majority work as teachers, and an additional percentage is enrolled in nursing. This is in contrast to the experience of Jewish women who are employed in a very wide spectrum of occupations. This fact indicates that many positions that fit educated women are blocked for Muslim women, as suggested at the end of the previous chapter when we discussed the declining rates of LFP among Muslim women who have acquired an academic degree.

Finally, although employed in the public sector, having a high level of education, and working in high non-manual jobs, Muslim women earn much less than Jewish women and less than their male counterparts. The multivariate analysis of earnings untangled the sources of these earning gaps. We found that the lower earnings of Muslim women stem not only from their lower inputs but also from the fact that they are less rewarded than the other groups on some of their compositional characteristics. This is an important finding by itself but it also adds to the accumulating evidence that the low rate of LFP among Muslim women is related to structural characteristics of their work. If they earn less money than Jews, then their income might not be sufficient to cover the costs of employment, and this fact may explain at least part of the employment gap between Muslim and Jewish women.

In sum, despite the increased participation of Muslim women in the labor market in Israel, they are hardly integrated into it. They have difficulties in finding employment and in entering a wide spectrum of jobs. If they do find work it is a job with relatively low economic rewards.

Appendix 5.1 *Logistic Coefficients and Standard Errors (in parentheses) Predicting Part-Time vs. Full-Time Employment of Muslim Women Aged 25–52 by Year*

	1979–1981		1986–1988		1993–1995		2000–2002		2007–2009	
	B/S.E.	Exp. (B)	B/S.E.	Exp. (B)	B/S.E.	Exp. (B)	B/S.E.	Exp. (B)	B/S.E.	Exp. (B)
Secondary education	−0.092	0.912	−0.149	0.862	−0.150	0.861	−0.516*	0.597	−0.408*	0.665
	(0.395)		(0.298)		(0.205)		(0.147)		(0.150)	
Tertiary education	−0.652	0.520	−0.245	0.782	−0.184	0.832	−0.730*	0.482	−0.805*	0.447
	(0.400)		(0.319)		(0.215)		(0.149)		(0.146)	
Married	0.535	1.708	1.272*	3.569	1.031*	2.804	0.503*	1.652	0.208	1.232
	(0.533)		(0.370)		(0.252)		(0.190)		(0.149)	
Number of children under 15	−0.141	0.869	0.029	1.029	−0.153	0.858	−0.045	0.956	−0.073	0.930
	(0.103)		(0.111)		(0.082)		(0.053)		(0.042)	
Having children under 5	0.568	1.764	−1.085	0.338	0.428	1.534	0.032	1.032	0.318*	1.374
	(0.490)		(0.688)		(0.262)		(0.160)		(0.123)	
Age	0.016	1.016	0.002	1.002	0.000	1.000	−0.030*	0.971	−0.033*	0.967
	(0.025)		(0.020)		(0.015)		(0.010)		(0.008)	
Intercept	−1.673		−1.615		−1.660		0.525		1.067	
2 Log Likelihood	330.9		459.3		931.7		1920.9		2794.3	
Over all prediction	73.6		78.1		76.9		65.9		61.6	
N	222		403		789		1,282		1,775	
R^2	0.024		0.048		0.057		0.029		0.038	

Variables: The dependent variable is part-time employment, coded 1 if the woman works part time, and 0 otherwise; the independent variables are: education (distinguishing among three levels of education, intermediary and less (the reference group), secondary, tertiary); marital status (coded 1 if ever married; 0 otherwise), number of children under 15, having children under 5, and age.

Source: Labor force Surveys 1979–2009.

★: p <0.05

Note: Respondents born in Israel, excluding Palestinians from the Southern District and from Jerusalem, and Druze from the Golan Heights.

Appendix 5.2 *Economic Branch Distribution of Muslims and Jews Age 18–52 by Gender and Year*

	1974–76	1979–81	1986–88	1993–95	2000–02	2007–09
A. Muslim Women						
Agriculture	32.4	26.2	8.8	5.5	2.9	2.5
Manufacturing	20.8	30.4	40.7	34.1	14.8	6.8
Construction	0.0	0.0	0.0	0.0	1.0	0.7
Peripheral services	8.4	6.1	10.8	10.3	22.4	22.0
Wholesale and retail trade, repair of vehicles and personal and household goods	(5.9)	(3.7)	(6.5)	(5.5)	(13.0)	(13.4)
Core services	0.2	2.7	1.9	7.3	5.3	4.3
Public Sector	38.2	35.6	37.8	42.9	53.6	63.7
Public administration	(0.9)	(0.6)	(2.2)	(2.3)	(3.8)	(1.7)
Education	(28.3)	(26.4)	(24.2)	(24.8)	(30.2)	(40.5)
Health services, welfare and social work	(7.0)	(6.9)	(7.7)	(13.3)	(16.8)	(18.0)
Total	100.0	100.0	100.0	100.0	100.0	100.0
N	544	866	1,024	1,663	2,385	2,877
B. Jewish Women						
Agriculture	3.1	2.9	2.2	1.3	0.5	0.4
Manufacturing	14.3	11.6	13.0	11.2	8.9	8.4
Construction	1.0	1.2	0.9	1.1	1.1	0.8
Peripheral services	18.7	17.8	22.7	26.1	25.9	26.8

Appendix 5.2 (cont.)

	1974–76	1979–81	1986–88	1993–95	2000–02	2007–09
Wholesale and retail trade, repair of vehicles and personal and household goods	(6.7)	(7.5)	(10.4)	(12.7)	(12.7)	(12.8)
Core services	14.5	16.2	16.1	15.6	17.6	19.7
Public Sector	48.5	50.3	45.1	44.7	46.0	43.9
Public administration	(10.3)	(10.3)	(6.9)	(5.7)	(6.3)	(5.2)
Education	(27.3)	(27.4)	(23.6)	(22.8)	(22.7)	(21.6)
Health services, welfare and social work	(8.2)	(8.5)	(9.5)	(10.7)	(11.8)	(11.8)
Total	100.0	100.0	100.0	100.0	100.0	100.0
N	16,504	20,401	26,352	33,663	36,765	39,292
C. Muslim Men						
Agriculture	12.4	12.7	10.3	6.0	4.1	3.9
Manufacturing	17.2	21.2	24.0	22.5	18.5	18.5
Construction	33.8	29.0	24.0	32.0	27.0	29.3
Peripheral services	24.0	23.3	30.0	24.8	32.3	31.8
Wholesale and retail trade, repair of vehicles and personal and household goods	(11.8)	(12.3)	(14.4)	(13.2)	(17.7)	(18.3)
Core services	1.6	1.8	1.6	2.8	3.9	4.3
Public Sector	11.0	12.0	10.1	11.9	14.2	12.2
Public administration	(2.6)	(1.8)	(1.7)	(2.4)	(2.6)	(1.2)
Education	(5.8)	(6.7)	(5.0)	(5.1)	(5.6)	(4.8)

Appendix 5.2 (*cont.*)

	1974–76	1979–81	1986–88	1993–95	2000–02	2007–09
Health services, welfare and social work	(0.8)	(1.5)	(1.8)	(2.5)	(3.4)	(3.8)
Total	100.0	100.0	100.0	100.0	100.0	100.0
N	6,748	6,544	7,560	8,127	8,552	8,699
D. Jewish Men						
Agriculture	7.8	8.4	6.6	4.5	3.2	2.3
Manufacturing	29.5	29.3	29.0	25.4	21.5	17.8
Construction	8.7	7.1	5.8	8.9	6.2	6.0
Peripheral services	25.2	25.2	27.4	31.2	33.0	35.0
Wholesale and retail trade, repair of vehicles and personal and household goods	(10.8)	(12.1)	(14.3)	(16.0)	(15.6)	(16.2)
Core services	9.1	10.5	12.7	11.7	16.4	19.3
Public Sector	19.7	19.5	18.5	18.3	19.7	19.6
Public administration	(8.9)	(8.6)	(7.2)	(6.5)	(6.5)	(5.4)
Education	(6.2)	(5.1)	(4.7)	(4.5)	(4.9)	(5.3)
Health services, welfare and social work	(2.1)	(2.3)	(2.6)	(2.5)	(3.1)	(3.0)
Total	100.0	100.0	100.0	100.0	100.0	100.0
N	19,329	22,982	30,022	36,751	37,494	38,237

Source: Labor Force Surveys 1974–2009.

Note: Respondents born in Israel, excluding Palestinians from the Southern District and from Jerusalem, and Druze from the Golan Heights.

Appendix 5.3 *Occupational Distribution of Muslim and Jewish Women Aged 18–52 by Year*

	1974–1976	1979–1981	1986–1988	1993–1995	2000–2002	2007–2009
A. Muslim Women						
Academic professionals	0.0	0.0	0.9	0.5	1.4	1.5
Associate professionals and technicians	28.6	26.3	20.4	26.0	31.2	40.1
Managers	0.0	0.0	0.0	0.0	0.5	0.4
Clericals	3.9	6.7	10.6	16.4	16.8	16.7
Sales	5.2	3.4	4.1	3.5	8.4	9.9
Service workers	10.4	7.6	16.3	17.5	26.3	25.4
Agricultural workers	15.5	3.4	2.1	3.4	1.5	0.8
Skilled manual workers	16.9	26.3	28.5	25.4	11.4	3.2
Unskilled manual workers	19.5	26.3	17.1	7.3	2.4	2.0
Total	100.0	100.0	100.0	100.0	100.0	100.0
N	554	871	1,024	1,667	2,380	2,879
B. Jewish Women						
Academic professionals	3.6	4.2	4.1	4.7	5.8	7.3
Associate professionals and technicians	32.8	33.5	29.6	28.3	28.0	27.4
Managers	0.8	0.9	2.3	2.5	5.0	5.4
Clericals	39.1	39.4	34.2	34.4	34.4	31.9
Sales	3.5	4.1	6.5	8.8	8.5	9.3
Service workers	10.9	10.3	15.9	16.6	15.8	16.4
Agricultural workers	1.8	1.9	1.2	0.5	0.4	0.2
Skilled manual workers	5.9	4.7	5.0	3.2	1.8	1.6
Unskilled manual workers	1.6	1.0	1.2	1.0	0.3	0.5
Total	100.0	100.0	100.0	100.0	100.0	100.0
N	16,839	20,401	25,766	33,651	36,655	39,203

Source: Labor Force Surveys 1974–2009.
Note: Respondents born in Israel, excluding Palestinians from the Southern District and from Jerusalem, and Druze from the Golan Heights.

Appendix 5.4 *Ethnicity and Gender Coefficients and Standard Errors (in Parentheses) Predicting Occupational Enrollment of Highly Educated Workers Aged 25–52 by Year*

	1993–1995		2000–2002		2007–2009	
	B /S.E.	Exp. (B)	B /S.E.	Exp. (B)	B /S.E.	Exp. (B)
Academic and Professional Occupations						
Muslim women	−2.147*	0.117	−2.360*	0.094	−2.556*	0.078
	(.210)		(0.072)		(0.102)	
Jewish women	−1.262*	0.283	−1.188*	0.304	−0.987*	0.373
	(0.042)		(0.036)		(0.032)	
Muslim men	−1.215*	0.297	−1.017*	0.362	−0.846*	0.429
	(0.099)		(0.072)		(0.057)	

	Teachers					
	1993–1995		2000–2002		2007–2009	
	B /S.E.	Exp. B	B /S.E.	Exp. B	B /S.E.	Exp. B
Muslim women	3.648*	38.386	3.837*	46.377	3.725*	41.456
	(0.165)		(0.115)		(0.088)	
Jewish women	2.382*	10.831	2.098*	8.152	1.863*	6.442
	(0.065)		(0.061)		(0.057)	
Muslim men	2.521*	12.444	2.228*	9.279	1.665*	5.286
	(0.103)		(0.088)		(0.088)	

	Clerical and Service Occupations					
	1993–1995		2000–2002		2007–2009	
	B /S.E.	Exp. B	B /S.E.	Exp. B	B /S.E.	Exp. B
Muslim women	−0.801*	0.449	−0.657*	0.518	−0.375*	0.687
	(0.192)		(0.135)		(0.088)	
Jewish women	0.035	1.036	0.463*	1.589	0423*	1.526
	(0.048)		(0.043)		(0.036)	
Muslim men	−0.933*	0.393	−0.432*	0.649	−0.073	0.930
	(0.142)		(0.107)		(0.084)	

	Skilled and Unskilled Occupations					
	1993–1995		2000–2002		2007–2009	
	B /S.E.	Exp. B	B /S.E.	Exp. B	B /S.E.	Exp. B
Muslim women	−2.922*	0.075	−3.673*	0.025	−2.688*	0.068
	(0.250)		(0.863)		(0.443)	
Jewish women	−1.822*	0.162	−2.356*	0.095	−1.917*	0.147
	(0.119)		(0.158)		(0.125)	
Muslim men	−0.169*	0.845	0.055	1.056	0.566*	1.761
	(0.160)		(0.143)		(0.120)	

Variables: The dependent variables in our analysis are four occupational groups (coded 1 when the individual is affiliated with them and 0 otherwise). The four occupational groups are: (1) professionals (including academic professionals, associate professionals, technicians, and managers but not teachers), (2) teachers, (3) clerical and service workers, (4) manual workers. The control variables are: place of residence, distinguishing between those who reside in mixed localities (the omitted category), center and north; age of the respondent; marital status; and years completed in academic education. The effect of ethnicity and gender are introduced by creating four groups of workers (Muslim women, Jewish women, Muslim men, Jewish men (the reference group)).

Source: Labor Force Surveys 1993–2009.

*: p <0.05

Note: Respondents born in Israel, excluding Palestinians from the Southern District and from Jerusalem, and Druze from the Golan Heights.

Appendix 5.5 *Distribution and Means of Selected Variables among Muslim and Jewish Employees Aged 25–52 by Gender and Year*

	Muslim Women			Jewish women			Muslim men			Jewish men		
	1998–2001	2002–2005	2006–2008	1998–2001	2002–2005	2006–2008	1998–2001	2002–2005	2006–2008	1998–2001	2002–2005	2006–2008
Median monthly earnings (NIS)												
25–38	2,656.8	2,988.5	3,292.1	4,257.6	4,292.0	4,417.6	4,038.0	4,098.5	4,279.9	6,202.2	6,243.2	6,168.4
39–52	2,933.0	3,479.5	3,666.6	4,979.1	5,186.7	5,352.6	4,750.0	4,845.8	4,778.7	8,816.6	8,520.4	8,678.9
Total (25–52)	2,700.6	3,186.0	3,334.1	4,504.9	4,633.7	4,755.9	4,154.6	4,297.0	4,397.2	7,121.3	7,101.2	7,026.7
Human capital and labor inputs												
Intermediate and less	27.4	22.0	16.0	2.5	1.7	1.1	37.2	33.8	29.7	4.5	3.0	2.0
Secondary	31.9	30.2	28.3	43.1	39.6	34.6	45.3	45.0	47.7	47.6	44.5	40.6
Tertiary	40.7	47.8	55.7	54.4	58.7	64.3	17.5	21.2	22.6	47.9	52.5	57.4
Total	(100.0)	(100.0)	(100.0)	(100.0)	(100.0)	(100.0)	(100.0)	(100.0)	(100.0)	(100.0)	(100.0)	(100.0)
Weekly work hours	32.9	30.6	31.9	33.9	34.4	33.6	44.5	44.0	45.5	45.4	44.8	44.2
Years in labor force	17.2	17.7	17.6	17.6	17.9	17.9	19.8	19.5	20.0	18.0	18.2	17.9

Appendix 5.5 (*cont.*)

	Muslim Women			Jewish women			Muslim men			Jewish men		
	1998–2001	2002–2005	2006–2008	1998–2001	2002–2005	2006–2008	1998–2001	2002–2005	2006–2008	1998–2001	2002–2005	2006–2008
Labor market characteristics												
High non-manual	37.5	41.3	48.3	40.4	41.0	42.3	15.3	16.4	14.2	41.6	43.2	45.3
Low non-manual	31.5	33.0	34.6	53.1	52.7	51.8	4.0	12.8	13.7	26.5	26.8	27.6
Manual (skilled and unskilled)	31.0	25.7	17.1	6.5	6.3	5.9	80.7	70.8	72.1	31.9	30.0	27.1
Total	(100.0)	(100.0)	(100.0)	(100.0)	(100.0)	(100.0)	(100.0)	(100.0)	(100.0)	(100.0)	(100.0)	(100.0)
Public sector percentage	63.5	68.8	71.0	45.5	45.5	43.2	16.7	16.5	13.9	17.6	18.1	17.3
N	285	397	321	4,861	5,775	4,487	1,117	1,106	913	4,761	5,490	4,169

Source: Combined Labor Force Survey and Income Survey 1998–2008.
Note: Respondents born in Israel, excluding Palestinians from the Southern District and from Jerusalem, and Druze from the Golan Heights.

Appendix 5.6 Regression Coefficients and Standard Errors (in parentheses) Predicting Monthly Earnings among Muslim and Jewish Employees Aged 25–52 by Gender and Year

	1998–2001				2002–2005				2006–2008			
	Muslim women	Jewish women	Muslim men	Jewish men	Muslim Women	Jewish women	Muslim men	Jewish men	Muslim Women	Jewish women	Muslim men	Jewish men
Secondary	604.2* (251.9)	585.8 (356.4)	761.1* (155.5)	1,786.1* (471.9)	97.4 (754.3)	506.3 (362.0)	541.8* (208.8)	1,211.7* (515.3)	153.3 (342.0)	510.3 (629.4)	304.5 (210.3)	881.9 (751.7)
Tertiary	2,207.5* (359.1)	2,784.1* (373.9)	2,465.6* (295.9)	5,682.5* (507.0)	1,986.9* (944.4)	2,501.8* (373.7)	1,756.7* (351.8)	4,923.5* (541.4)	1,634.0* (413.0)	2,508.6* (642.6)	1,113.8* (323.7)	4,710.4* (773.0)
Weekly hours	48.2* (7.3)	124.5* (4.4)	74.5* (8.1)	88.9* (7.1)	68.9* (17.7)	127.8* (3.7)	69.5* (8.4)	116.1* (6.5)	74.3* (8.7)	126.8* (5.0)	59.3* (10.1)	97.8* (7.6)
Single	-244.5 (162.8)	-477.4* (147.5)	-70.5 (210.1)	-1,544.5* (258.4)	-625.3 (481.6)	-788.4* (125.4)	-556.4* (266.9)	-1,748.2* (238.6)	-611.3* (193.3)	-770.4* (179.9)	-644.2* (275.4)	-1,405* (285.9)
Experience	164.9* (44.3)	311.0* (29.5)	211.6* (44.1)	523.7* (55.8)	186.0 (114.2)	240.9* (25.4)	91.3 (60.1)	510.5* (53.1)	124.6* (47.8)	297.8* (36.3)	81.5 (63.6)	696.9* (65.1)
Experience squared	-2.87* (1.09)	-5.96* (0.76)	-3.31* (0.98)	-8.67* (1.40)	-3.42 (2.99)	-3.96* (0.64)	-0.99 (1.36)	-9.21* (1.29)	-2.04 (1.22)	-5.60* (0.93)	-1.05 (1.41)	-13.16 (1.60)
High non-manual	993.6* (358.7)	3,193.1* (256.6)	2,081.9* (300.5)	4,252.8* (256.3)	1,428.1* (761.7)	3,110.5* (219.0)	2,734.9* (354.9)	4,307.7* (240.2)	1,056.9* (413.2)	3,302.1* (309.5)	3,225.7* (363.7)	4,929.7* (285.8)
Low non-manual	-106.8 (246.9)	1,079.4* (226.3)	242.4 (196.2)	836.1* (247.1)	-112.7 (684.2)	1,105.0* (194.6)	448.8 (260.0)	1,072.3* (232.3)	207.1 (317.1)	920.6* (279.2)	376.5 (255.9)	1,023.0* (282.0)
Public sector	395.9* (197.2)	-1,494.8* (114.4)	631.1* (239.0)	-1610.7* (242.2)	124.8 (581.4)	-1,364.8* (98.8)	1025.7* (293.7)	-1,653.2* (224.8)	399.5 (227.3)	-1,631.2* (137.7)	283.5 (313.9)	-2,004.5* (274.9)

Appendix 5.6 (cont.)

	1998–2001				2002–2005				2006–2008			
	Muslim women	Jewish women	Muslim men	Jewish men	Muslim Women	Jewish women	Muslim men	Jewish men	Muslim Women	Jewish women	Muslim men	Jewish men
Intercept	-1,797.5*	-4,744.0*	2,242.3*	-5,702.3*	-1,761.2	-4,258*	-491.5	-6,156.4*	-1,786.3*	-4,263.4*	346.0	-7,118.8*
	(528)	(447.1)	(613.8)	(737.5)	(1,336.5)	(428.1)	(773.7)	(745.5)	(548.0)	(709.7)	(860.6)	(994.9)
R^2	.556	.314	.342	.288	.143	.344	.283	.294	.442	.274	.255	.295

Variables: The dependent variable is the mean monthly earnings from current job adjusted to the 2000 consumer price index. The independent variables included: Marital status (dummy variable, coded 1 for single women, 0 for those ever-married including divorced and widowed women); education (distinguishing between intermediate and less, the reference category, secondary, and tertiary); experience (age minus years of schooling minus five); hours (number of hours worked during the last week); occupational enrollment, distinguishing among three broad groups (high non-manual (workers in academic, professional and managerial occupations); low non-manual (clerical and service workers); manual workers, the reference group); employment sector (coded 1 for those employed in the public sector and 0 for those in the private sector).

Source: Combined Labor Force Survey and Income Survey 1998–2008.

*: p <0.05

Note: Respondents born in Israel, excluding Palestinians from the Southern District and from Jerusalem, and Druze from the Golan Heights.

6 Far and Isolated
Bedouin Women in the Naqab

6.1 Introduction: The History and Current Features of Bedouin Society in Israel

Pastoralism based on movement through grazing areas and farming in fixed settlements have long been two forms of subsistence economy in various parts of the world. These two types of agricultural production have created different social organizations that have interacted with each other in various ways. In the history of the MENA region, this distinction has been embodied in two distinct social groups: *fellaheen* ("farmers" in Arabic) and Bedouins,[1] the nomadic tribes that subsist on pastoral production in all the countries of the region. Modern studies of nomadic societies in general, and of the MENA region Bedouins in particular, have shown that romantic ideas of nomadic people as freely roaming the land in search of available grazing areas is extremely inaccurate. Nomadic peoples move in specific territories, where they recognize, struggle over, and solve disputes about land rights; circulate among fixed locations of encampments according to the season; and rely upon occasional farming where and when the conditions allow it (Marx 1978; Swidler 1980; Abu-Rabia 2001; Kressel 2003).

Our analysis of Palestinian women's employment depends on understanding that the Bedouins live under different circumstances than the other Palestinians analyzed in the previous two chapters.[2] They are recognized by themselves and by other Arabs (in Israel and elsewhere in the MENA region) as a separate group with their own social organization and distinct cultural patterns (Jakubowska 1992). Like all social groups, the Bedouins are also not a homogeneous group; important distinctions exist among them. Their culture, like any culture, constantly changes and adapts

---

[1] "Bedouin" can be both singular and plural, but we prefer to use "Bedouins" for the plural. The Naqab is the Arabic name of what Hebrew speakers call the Negev. The names are clearly related. We prefer the Arabic word because we are writing about Arab residents of the area.

[2] As we will explain below, some of the women included in the data analyzed in Chapters 4 and 5 are also Bedouins.

to new developments. Social processes that have occurred among the non-Bedouin Muslim Palestinians in Israel might not have taken place in Bedouin society or might have taken place differently (Abu-Saad 2005). This chapter examines the place of women's employment in the Bedouin society in Israel. In analyzing women's status among Bedouins, we must take into account that the Israeli state has treated the Bedouins differently than it has other Muslims. In what follows, we describe the history of the Bedouins and the general features of their society at present, but we begin with the problem of estimating the size of this group.

How Many Bedouins Live in Israel? Unlike religious affiliations, which are recorded by the state, there is no official registration of Bedouins in Israel, and therefore there are no official statistics about their numbers. Yet it is known that in the Naqab, all the native Arabs are Bedouins. The Israeli CBS counts the number of citizens in each district and registers their religion, and thus we know the number of Muslims in the Southern District, which might be used as a proxy for the number of Bedouins in the Naqab.[3] This equation is not totally accurate: Some non-Bedouin Muslims from more northern regions did move to the south, especially to Beer-Sheba (one of Israel's largest cities and the economic center of the south) and to Eilat (where the tourist industry attracts many workers from the north). But the number of Muslims in these two cities is small, and therefore it is safe to assume that almost all of the 211,200 Muslims counted in the Southern District in 2012 were Bedouins.[4] There are some Bedouins in the northern areas of Israel, but it is difficult to estimate their number because official statistics do not allow us to separate them from other Muslims. These Bedouins were included in our analyses in Chapters 4 and 5.[5]

---

[3] According to the Statistical Abstract of Israel (CBS 2013, Table 2.19), the number of Muslims in the northern part of the Southern District (the Ashkelon subdistrict) is only 900. In the Beer-Sheba subdistrict, which covers the whole area of the Naqab, there were 210,300 Muslims.

[4] Due to a shortage of teachers in Bedouin communities, some non-Bedouin Palestinians from other regions might have moved to these communities, but we assume that their number is small.

[5] Marx (1967) cites reports that recorded that there were 16,000 Bedouins in the Naqab and 7,000 in the Galilee in 1960. In Falah's articles (1985, 37; 1989b, 72), the number of Galilee Bedouins reported is sometimes above half of the number of the Naqab Bedouins, and sometimes just below a half. In 1999, Ben-David estimated the number of Bedouins in the Naqab, the north (Galilee), and the center at 110,000, 50,000 and 10,000, respectively (1999). In 2013 an Israeli army officer told a Knesset committee that there were about 200,000 Bedouins in the south and 100,000 in the Galilee. According to all the above figures, the Bedouins in the north are about a third of the Bedouin population in Israel. This is a substantial number that should be remembered when we discuss the Muslims who live in the north and center.

Bedouin History of the Naqab. During the Ottoman period, when there were no international boundaries in the region, the Bedouins migrated from the Syrian Desert to the north of Israel (Galilee) and from the Arabian and the Sinai peninsulas to the Naqab (Marx 1967; Falah 1985; Tarrow 2008). They also changed their way of life from a nomadic to a semi-nomadic life style as many of them began to cultivate the land, and growing crops became one of their major economic activities together with keeping livestock (Marx 1967; Falah 1983, 1985; Abu-Saad 2005).

During the British Mandate, many Bedouins, especially in the Galilee, parted from the traditional semi-pastoral way of living and settled in permanent communities (Falah 1983). We did not find estimates of their number. At the end of the Mandate, the number of the Bedouins in the Naqab ranged between 60,000 and 90,000 (Boneh 1983, 47–48; Dinero 2010, 3).[6] Due to their geographical and socio-political distinctiveness, the Bedouins did not participate in the Palestinian struggle against the colonial British government or the Jewish settlers. Exploiting the resulting rift between Bedouins and other Palestinians as well as some intertribal conflicts among Bedouins, the Jewish leadership managed to gain the cooperation of several Bedouin tribes. This cooperation may have prevented their expulsion from the newly established Israeli state, especially in the north. In the Naqab, only 11,000 Bedouins remained; the rest moved, or were expelled to Jordan (to the West Bank and southern Jordan), to the Gaza Strip, and to the Sinai Peninsula (Boneh 1983; Jakubowska 1992; Yiftachel 2003, 31; Tarrow 2008, 139).[7]

During the early years of the state, movement between Sinai, the Naqab, and Jordan was still possible though illegal, and some Bedouins moved in and out. Some were forced out by Israel in the years after the 1948 war. Jakubowska, for example, argues that Israel forced Bedouins out as late as 1959 (1992, 88; see also Falah 1985; Abu-Saad 2005). Only in 1953 did the Bedouins who remained in the Naqab started to get Israeli citizenship officially (Boneh 1983; 1952 according to Jakubowska 1992, 89). The state concentrated all of these Bedouins in one area ("the Seyag"[8]) in order to free the rest of the Naqab for the state's own ends (Falah 1989b, 78; Yiftachel 2003, 31; Tarrow 2008, 139–40; Dinero 2010, 3).[9] These

[6] Falah (1989b, 78) provides an estimate of more than 70,000, based on Schwartz (1959, 158). Abu-Rabia-Queder and Arar put the number at 75,000 (2011, 357); Tarrow offers a wide range of 60,000 to 100,000 (2008, 139).

[7] Boneh (1983) refers to this movement as entirely voluntary out of Bedouins' fear of Jewish soldiers or their wish not to be under Israeli rule. Other writers talk about forced expulsion.

[8] The area in the northeastern part of the Naqab, between Beer-Sheba, Dimona, and Arad, is about 1,000 km², one-tenth the area that the Bedouins had lived in before.

[9] Most of the Bedouins were moved to this Seyag area from much more fertile lands in the western part of the Naqab.

included establishing Jewish communities in order to reinforce Jewish claims over the land in which very few Jews – or none – had lived prior to 1948 (Abu-Saad 2005), establishing military bases, and engaging in mineral extraction. Like all other Palestinians, the Bedouins in this closed area were subjected to the military administration (see Section 2.2). For a population in which pastoralism was a major economic branch, limits on movements were even more restrictive than for other Palestinians (Jakubowska 1992; Meir 1997; Yiftachel 2003; Dinero 2004; Abu-Saad 2005; Tarrow 2008). The concentration of Bedouins in one area also created questions about land rights. Part of the land in this area belonged to one tribe that used to live there. The rest belonged to Bedouins who had moved or were pushed out of Israel; this land was seized by the state according to Israeli law. The state then leased it to the landless Bedouins and also gave them permits to graze in areas outside the closed territory, according to available grazing areas, needs, and officials' discretion. Creating this dependence thus enabled the state to control the Bedouin population and interfere in its life (Falah 1985; Yiftachel 2003; Abu-Saad 2005).

The Unrecognized Villages. The state has never developed housing or employment sources within the restricted Seyag area. The Bedouins therefore established small villages there, without state-authorized development plans and without the state's help or intervention. There are about 45 such small villages that have never been recognized by the state as authorized communities, and the state has therefore refused to provide these communities an infrastructure or elementary services (Falah 1985; Shamir 1996; Medzini 1998; Yiftachel 2003; Swirski and Hasson 2005; Swirski 2008). In these unrecognized villages Bedouins are forbidden to build any permanent buildings or to pave roads. Since these communities do not exist from the state's point of view, the national utility companies cannot supply water pipes or connect those localities to the electricity grid, and the residents have to bring in water in containers and use their own generators. Only the most basic services are provided, and that is often only following long legal and public campaigns and following juridical rulings. Bedouins in these unrecognized villages, which are not identified on any map, have no valid home address, cannot vote in elections and cannot be elected to local government. They thus have no local administration of their own (Swirski and Hasson 2005, 6; see also Abu-Saad 2005, 2008; Tarrow 2008; Kanaaneh 2010: 45).

The State-Planned Towns. During the mid-1960s, a new state policy emerged. It was decided to relocate the Bedouins again, this time into state-planned towns (Kressel 2003, 72; Abu-Saad 2005; Meir and

Baskind 2006, 76). The stated goal was to modernize the Bedouins and to provide them with public services, but another hidden goal of relocation was evidently to weaken the Bedouins' efforts to reclaim their lands and to stop their unplanned settlement activities (Abu Saad 2003, 104; see also Khazanov, 1998; Yiftachel 2003; Abu-Saad 2008).[10] Seven such towns were established (Falah 1989b, 86).[11] These state-planned towns have "evolved quickly into pockets of deprivation, unemployment, dependency, crime and social tension" (Yiftachel 2003, 35; see also Falah 1985; Meir 1997; Medzini 1998; Lithwick 2002, 2003; Abu Saad 2008; Tarrow 2008). Abu-Saad emphasizes the contrast with the towns built in the area for the Jewish population:

> The [Bedouin] towns were designed as dormitory towns ... Aside from the provided basic services (water, electricity, telephone hook-up, schools, and clinics) the towns lacked the essential characteristics of urbanization. Unlike the neighboring urban settlements in the Jewish sector, the Bedouin towns had no internal sources of employment, nor did they have internal or external basic transportation networks to facilitate access to work in other towns. The Bedouin towns also lacked banks, post offices, sewage systems, public libraries, and recreational and cultural centers (2003, 105).

Dinero argues that despite all the problems, "living in the towns *does* have its benefits." In his study of one town he found that "residents who have resettled [in that town] are in many ways better off socially and economically than their family and friends in the neighboring *pezurah* [diaspora]" (2010, 35). Yet he argues that the advantages are not strong enough to attract more people to these towns.

About half of the Bedouins (about 100,000 people) have remained in the unrecognized villages (Tarrow 2008).[12] Most of those who moved to

---

[10] State efforts and pressures on nomadic peoples to settle down are not unique to Israel and are often rife with tension and conflicts due to the comprehensive changes involved in sedentarization. In Israel the conflict is intensified by the national and religious gaps between the state and the nomadic people (Fallah 1989b, Law-Yone 2003; Kressel 2003, ch.1).

[11] The seven planned towns are (in order of founding): Tel As-Sabi (Tel-Sheva; 13,500 people; established 1968), Rahat (41,000, est. 1972) Ar'arat an-Naqab (12,500, est. 1981); Kuseife (16,000, est. 1982), Shaquib al-Salam (Segev-Shalom, 6,800, est. 1984), Hura (10,000, est. 1989), and Lakiya (8,000, est. 1990).

[12] Ben-David (1999) estimates the number of those who lived in the scattered "unrecognized" villages at 57,000 out of 110,000, about 52 percent of Naqab Bedouins in 1999. Abu-Rabia (2000, 84) puts their percentage at 40 percent, while Kressel puts the figure at 57 percent (2003, 72). Jakubowska (1992, 91) cites an improbable proportion of 90 percent who lived in just five settlements in the late 1980s. According to an official site of the Ministry of Agriculture and Rural Development, the number of residents in the planned towns in 2012 was 129,571, and in the unrecognized villages 76,749 (MARD 2016). The figures are hard to calculate because the population of the latter is surveyed only in the census, and there were large changes between the last two censuses (1995 and 2008). The state is in a prolonged and bitter struggle with the Bedouin community, and

the towns originated from the lower rung in the Bedouin social order, the fellaheen (farmers). The fellaheen Bedouin were sharecropper tenants with no formal land ownership rights who lived for generations under the protection of the "true Bedouins," the traditionally more prestigious group. To improve their low social standing many of the fellaheen were willing to settle in the new towns as a way of breaking the centuries-old patronage of the true Bedouins and their dependence on the latter. That is also why most of those considered to be true Bedouins declined to be relocated to these new established localities and refused to officially give up their claims to get back the land taken by the state (Kressel 2003, 72; Yiftachel 2003, 35; Meir and Baskind 2006, 76–77; Tarrow 2008).

Since the early 2000s, 11 Bedouin villages were established or recognized by the state in an attempt to resolve the conflict of the state with the Bedouins, but the Bedouins demand recognition of several dozens of other villages in the area. According to the statistics provided by the state, in 2012 only about a tenth of the Bedouins outside the planned towns lived in those recognized villages (MARD 2016). The regional councils, which are responsible for educational and social services for the recognized villages, have been administered by officials appointed by the Ministry of the Interior rather than by elected representatives. This is usually a temporary measure taken under exceptional circumstances, but in the case of the Bedouin regional councils, it has been extended since their establishment in 2004.

Educational Facilities. The first schools for Bedouins were established during the mandatory period (1921–1948), but very few Bedouin boys and no girls were enrolled in them (Abu-Saad 1991). Following the changes in the Bedouin way of life and the need for formal education as a resource for employment, the demand for education has increased. Nevertheless, despite the fact that compulsory education was introduced in Israel in 1949, it was only twenty years later (in 1968) that the Bedouins were provided schools (Abu-Rabia-Queder 2006; Tarrow 2008; Dinero 2010). The state did not give the Bedouins the option of having separate classrooms for girls and boys, as was done for the ultra-orthodox Jews, and therefore girls were not sent to school during those years. Although this violated the law, the state did not make enough of an effort to solve the problem. Below, we will examine the gradual entrance of Bedouin girls into state schools, but it is widely acknowledged that the educational system is still lacking and unsatisfactory. Elementary schools have been established in

therefore the figures provided by government agencies are not necessarily the most reliable.

the state-planned Bedouin towns, but these schools have a very poor infrastructure, lack qualified teachers, and have overcrowded class-rooms (Abu-Saad 1995, 1996; Lithwick 2003; Tarrow 2008; Dinero 2010). Facilities for pupils with special needs hardly exist and parents need to take legal measures to secure them (Tarrow 2008; Dinero 2010). It was not until the late 1970s that two high schools were established in two of the new towns (Abu-Rabia-Queder 2006), and a special high school for girls was opened only recently in order to overcome conservative parents' reluctance to send girls to co-ed schools (Tarrow 2008, 149).

The situation is much worse in the unrecognized villages. Pupils do not only suffer from a shortage of schools, but the schools that exist are often housed in shacks with no electricity or running water, and they serve children only through the elementary and intermediate levels. Children have to travel large distances to study in high schools, and adequate transportation is not provided (Abu-Rabia-Queder 2006; Tarrow 2008).[13] It is no wonder that Bedouin children have the highest dropout rate and the lowest achievement scores in the country (Abu-Saad 1991, 1995; Tarrow 2008; Abu-Bader and Gottlieb 2009).

Employment Options. The major economic source of the Bedouins in the Naqab before 1948 was herding, but farming was common as well (Abu-Saad 2005). In Israel, both herding and farming have decreased considerably. The state has confiscated most of the Bedouins' land, forcing many of them to leave their traditional work. Many men looked instead for work in construction and industry in the emerging Jewish towns in the area. As elsewhere in Israel, the newly established state was eager to settle Jews in the areas where Palestinians used to live, in order to secure its claim to those areas. This policy had even more far-reaching consequences in the Naqab. There were extremely few Jewish settlements in that vast area, and its political future in the 1950s seemed still open (Abu-Saad 2005). The state therefore built several new Jewish (develop-ment) towns and made special efforts to settle new Jewish immigrants there, although the latter were quite reluctant to live far from the densely populated and economically prosperous center of Israel. To avoid Jews' flight from the Naqab, state policies aimed at providing employment for the Jewish population, and the state therefore subsidized the establish-ment of industrial zones near the Jewish towns and encouraged large factories to move to the Naqab.

---

[13] Jewish children in small rural communities also have to travel to regional schools, but school buses are scheduled to reach all communities. The small unrecognized villages do not enjoy this "luxury," and high school students often have to walk long distances to reach the road where they can catch public transportation.

The planning of the new Bedouin towns did not include industrial zones, and no attempt has been made to lure industry there (Yiftachel 2003). Without work in their own communities, Bedouin men have found work in low-paying, low-skill manual jobs in the Jewish sector. Many of them work as drivers, construction workers, or as agricultural laborers in the Jewish settlements (Dinero 2010). Some of the Bedouins have opened their own small businesses (grocery stores, garages, etc.). Somewhat larger businesses have been established in the heavy machinery branch that has become a niche for Bedouin men (Ginat 1998; Dinero 2004). These businesses have provided some employment to Bedouin men and still men from the planned Bedouin towns have always had very high unemployment rates (Meir 1997, 9).[14]

Very few statistical analyses have been conducted on the Bedouins in the unrecognized villages. The labor force surveys interview only the residents in the seven planned Bedouin towns, and although people from the unrecognized villages comprise about half of the Bedouins in the south, they are not included in these surveys.[15] We can only imagine with high level of certainty (based on the elaborate study of Abu-Bader and Gottlieb 2008, 2009) that the economic opportunities and the occupational standing of Bedouins in the unrecognized villages are much worse than those of the Bedouins in the Bedouin towns.

Bedouin Women. Changes in the Bedouin way of life totally changed the social status of Bedouin women (Meir 1997; Dinero 1997; Abu-Rabia-Queder 2008). Although the lives of all Bedouins have changed following the establishment of Israel and the declining role of herding, the most crucial change was the relocation of about half of all Bedouins to the new, planned towns. Sedentarization may appear to some readers to mean modernization, a process that brings nomads closer to modern culture, but the influence of this process on women is more complicated. In the semi-nomadic life, women took part in the process of agricultural production. Settling in one of the state-planned towns has meant reliance on wage labor, and as in the

---

[14] Our argument that state development policies in the Naqab have targeted the Jewish communities built during the 1950s and 1960s does not imply that the development of those Jewish towns was successful. This was obviously far from the truth. Most development towns have remained poor and underdeveloped with lacking social services, inferior education, and insufficient employment sources (Yiftachel and Meir 1998; Yiftachel 2000). Motzafi-Haller (2012) artfully describes the austere hardships with which the residents of one development town in the Naqab (Yeroham) deal. Yet even the meager resources allocated to such towns are much larger than those channeled to the Bedouin towns.

[15] The decision not to survey these communities might be a political or symbolic way of denying them recognition even by the state's statistical bureau, or it may signify indifference to the fortune of the residents of these communities who do not interest the policymakers anyway.

first stage of the industrial revolution in Europe, men became wage earners while women were limited to the domestic duties of home and childcare. Men thus gained more economic control over women. Men also more strictly enforced rules of women's modesty and restrictions on women's movement, because the town is a public space, in contrast to the smaller villages where all residents belonged to the same clan (Meir 1997; Fenster 1999; Meir and Baskind 2006, 82; Marteu 2005). Yet life in the Bedouin towns had some advantages for women. Urban men spend most of the day out of the house, leaving women a higher degree of freedom and control on domestic issues. Furthermore, in the towns large numbers of women lived closer to each other than previously in the unrecognized villages, and this proximity gave them new possibilities to share knowledge and to rethink their status as women (Lewando-Hundt 1984; Abu-Rabia-Queder 2007).

Previous studies of the Bedouin planned towns showed that the economic activity of Bedouin women in the labor market was extremely low (Meir and Baskind 2006, 80). Employment options for Bedouin women with secondary or lower levels of education have been meager. The industrial zones in Jewish cities and towns and the mineral industry are located far from the Bedouin towns and have therefore provided almost no jobs for Bedouin women. Bedouin women enrolled in the labor market were engaged in minor domestic production or local market activities, like sales in their home stores or craft work such as traditional weaving (Meir 1997; Abu-Bader and Gottlieb 2009). For women with a higher level of education, teaching has been the main option (Abu-Bader and Gottlieb 2009, 36). It has always been the first occupation highly educated women enter into when the salaried employment of women began to be accepted. As such employment becomes more common, women move to other occupations as well; among Bedouin women this expansion is yet to occur.

Before embarking on our analysis some methodological remarks are required. The analysis in this chapter is based on two data sets. One data set is the labor force surveys used in our previous analyses. As mentioned above, these surveys include only Bedouins from the towns; this means that they exclude about half of the Bedouin people in the Naqab who live in unrecognized villages. In order to get some information on the latter, we used the last Israeli census data, from 2008. For this population, therefore, we have one point of time only.

In analyzing the labor force surveys, we collapse three years together at each time period in order to increase our sample size. We start our analysis with the first surveys which include a number of Bedouin towns (1995–1997)[16], and add two more time periods (2001–2003 and 2007–2009) so as to follow the trends over the relatively short time for which we have data.

[16] The Israeli labor force surveys have covered Bedouins only since the early 1990s, and at that time only one Bedouin town (Rahat) was included in the survey. It was only in the mid-1990s that the Israeli CBS labor force surveys included more Bedouin towns.

We analyze data regarding the residents of the seven planned Bedouin towns, and deal with the Bedouins from the villages in the south (the unrecognized villages) after, in the last section of this chapter. We start our analysis with some descriptive information on personal demographic characteristics such as age distribution, marriage, and fertility rates, and continue with a description of educational achievements over the years. As we have shown in previous chapters, personal demographic characteristics have bearing on women's labor market behavior, which will be analyzed in the following sections. Throughout our analysis, our results will be compared to Muslims from the northern and the central regions analyzed in Chapters 4 and 5 (for matters of simplicity we will refer to them in what follows as "Other Muslims"[17]).

6.2   Characteristics of Bedouin Women in the Bedouin Towns, 1995–2009

Bedouin women marry earlier than Other Muslim women. For example, in 2007–2009 42 percent of Bedouin women in the 18–23 age bracket were already married, a percentage almost twice as high as among Other Muslim women in the same age bracket (21 percent). Given this fact, it is not surprising that they have more children compared to Other Muslim women. In fact, Bedouin women are the group with the highest birth rates in Israel. According to the CBS, in 1997 Bedouin women (including both those in the planned towns and the unrecognized villages) gave birth to 9.7 children on average, and although this birth rate has declined over the years to an average of 5.7 children per woman in 2009 (a substantive decline of more than 40 percent in just 12 years), it has remained stable since then. The fertility of Muslim women in other districts is much lower. In the Central District, where fertility is the highest among those other districts, the fertility in 1997 and 2009 was 4.56 and 3.63, respectively.

Due to their high fertility rates, Bedouin women are, on average, younger than Other Muslim women in Israel, who are themselves on the average younger than Jewish women. In 2007–2009, for example, we found that more than 58 percent of Bedouin women were in the two youngest age groups (18–24 and 25–31) while only 48 percent of Other Muslim women were in these two age groups. Very few (only 19 percent) Bedouin women were in the two oldest age groups (39–45 and 46–52), a much lower share than among the Other Muslim women (30 percent).

---

[17] We remind the readers that the "Other Muslim women" group includes Bedouin women in the northern districts who could not be identified as Bedouin in our data.

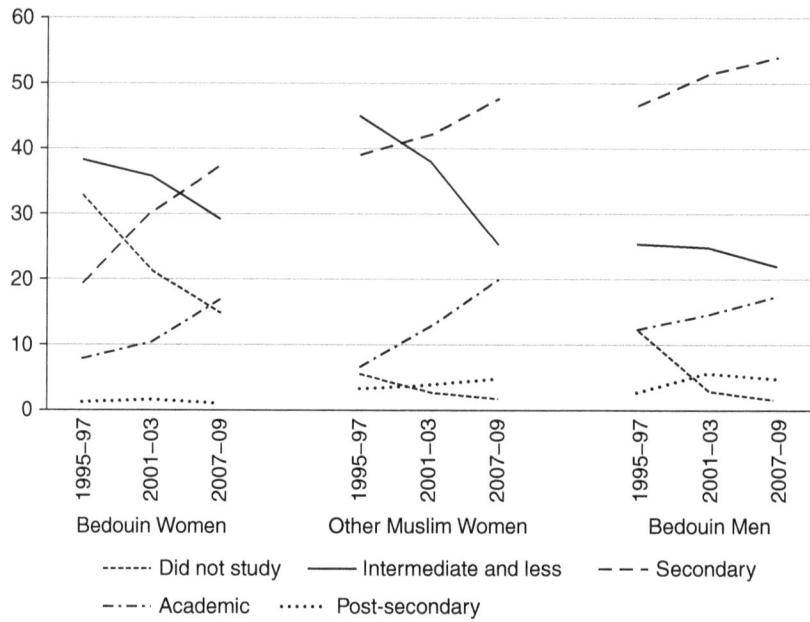

Figure 6.1 Highest School Attended of Muslims Aged 18–52 in
Bedouin Towns and Other Muslims by Gender and Year
Source: Labor Force Surveys 1995–2009.
Note: All Muslims excluding Jerusalem (unrecognized Bedouin villages
are not included in the LFS).

Given the poor educational opportunities in the planned Bedouin
towns as described above, it is no wonder that the educational achievements of Bedouins from these towns are very low. Nevertheless, Bedouin
men and Bedouin women have improved their educational achievements
over time. Based on the labor force surveys, we found that in 1995–1997
about a third of Bedouin women (aged 18–52) did not attend any school.
This percentage has declined since then, but in 2007–2009, 15.1 percent
of Bedouin women in the seven towns still had no schooling (Figure 6.1).
This is eight times higher than among Other Muslim women in Israel (less
than 2 percent with no schooling in the respective period).

Inspecting the other educational levels, we see that Bedouin women
have monotonically increased their share in secondary education from
19.5 percent in 1995–1997 to 37.5 percent in 2007–2009, an increase
that has occurred mainly through cohort replacement (figures not
shown). Bedouin women also doubled their attendance in tertiary

education; in 1995–1997 only 9.3 percent had some sort of tertiary education (postsecondary and academic); by 2007–2009, this share had increased to 18.1 percent. In spite of the dramatic improvements in Bedouin women's tertiary education, their educational achievements are still lower than those of Other Muslim women in Israel (around 25 percent).

The striking increase in Bedouin women's education is also seen in their years of schooling. They have increased their education monotonically from a very low mean of 6.1 years in 1995–1997 to 9.1 in 2007–2009, but their educational attainment is still 2.1 years lower than that of Other Muslim women in the respective years. Until 1968, it was mainly Bedouin boys who were sent to school. In all years studied, the educational achievements of Bedouin men have been much higher than those of Bedouin women. For example, in 2007–2009, 15.1 percent of Bedouin women and only 1.7 percent of men had not attended school. Hence in all years, the mean years of schooling of Bedouin men are much higher than those of Bedouin women. In 1995–1997, men had on average 9.7 years of schooling, and women, merely 6.1, a gap of 3.6 years. Although this educational gap between men and women has declined over the years, in 2007–2009, it was still quite large, 2.2 years (11.3 and 8.9 years, respectively).

6.3   Labor Force Participation of Women in the Bedouin Towns

Given the lack of or extremely deficient services provided by the state, the non-existent or limited infrastructure in the Bedouin communities, the distance from industrial centers and the lack of public transportation, and – perhaps most important and closely related to the above issues – the low educational attainments of Bedouin women, one would not be surprised to see that Bedouin women's labor force participation is extremely low. The high fertility rate among these women also hinders their employment, but one should remember that a high fertility rate is also an outcome of low LFP rates and not only a cause thereof.

In 2007–2009 only one-fifth of Bedouin women aged 18–52 were employed. This is twice as much as only twelve years earlier (9.3 percent in 1995–1997) but still much less than among the Other Muslim women in Israel (about 28 percent, see Figure 4.1). Nevertheless the gap between Bedouin women and the Other Muslim women has narrowed over the years. In 1995–1997, the odds of Other Muslim women being enrolled in the labor market were twice as high as those of Bedouin women in the Southern District, but by 2007–2009, these odds were only 1.37 as high.[18] In the same years the rate of Bedouin men participating in the labor market declined from 78 percent in 1995–1997 to 65 percent in 2007–2009. This last LFP rate is 13 percent lower than among Other Muslims men in the same year. The gap in men's employment between Other Muslim men and Bedouin men is a phenomenon that did not occur in the previous two periods, and it might reflect the lack of work opportunities in the south, which affects both men and women.

Who are the Bedouin women who work? In the rest of this section, we further elaborate our analysis and examine the characteristics of Bedouin women in the labor market. We look at how Bedouin women's employment is related to age, marital status, education, and number of children. Here again as in previous chapters we start with a descriptive analysis and end with a multivariate analysis.

Age and Labor Force Participation. Although Bedouin women in all age groups have increased their employment rates during the years, a massive monotonic increase was found among Bedouin women in the age bracket 32–38 from 3.1 percent in 1995–1997 to 26.2 percent in 2007–2009, while the older group's (women 39–45) rate has risen more moderately but still tripled from 4.9 to 15.3 percent. The LFP of women in the age bracket 25–31 rose as well but only during the last years of our study (from 15.0 percent in 1995–1997 to almost 30 percent in 2007–2009). Bedouin women older than 45, in contrast, were hardly employed. This was true in the early years of our study and has not changed during the years. Another interesting observation is that in the age group 25–31 Bedouin women almost reached parity with Other Muslim women in 2007–2009 (see Figure 6.2). This is in line with our earlier observation that the gap between the two Muslim subpopulations has narrowed during the years, indicating that Bedouin women are slowly closing the gap with mainstream Muslim society in Israel, at least in terms of employment rates.

Marriage and Labor Force Participation. Throughout the years of our study the share of single women in the labor market has been higher than the share of married women and hovered around 25 percent. Yet the gap between single and married women has substantially declined over the years because married women tripled their share in the labor market from 5.0 percent in 1995–1997 to 18.6 in 2007–2009. This is still a low figure but the large increase during such a short time demonstrates a fast process of change.

---

[18] In 1995–1997, 18.7 percent of the Other Muslim women and 9.3 percent of the Bedouin women were employed. In 2007–2009 the respective figures were 27.8 and 20.3 percent, respectively.

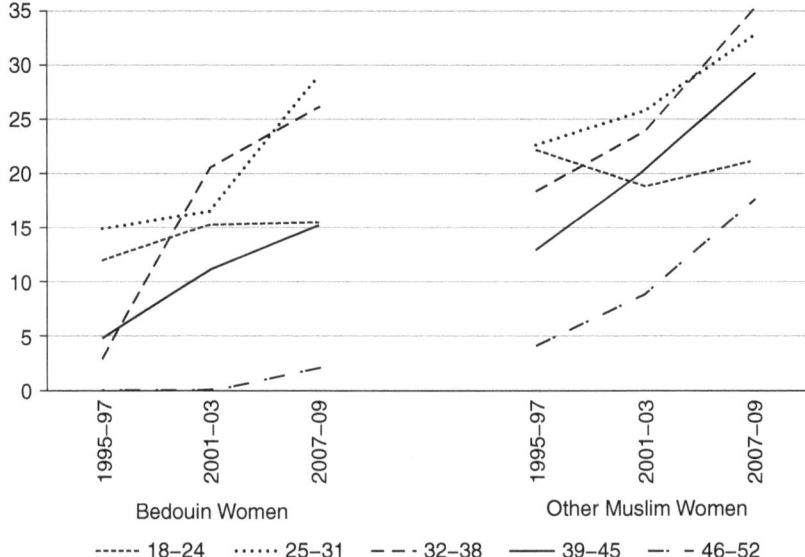

Figure 6.2 Labor Force Participation of Muslim Women Aged 18–52 in Bedouin Towns and Other Muslim Women by Age Group and Year
Source: Labor Force Surveys 1995–2009.
Note: All Muslims excluding Jerusalem (unrecognized Bedouin villages are not included in the LFS).

Education and Labor Force Participation. We now turn to women's educational attainment and their employment. We include in this analysis only women aged 25–52. We already saw that educational achievements were a major factor in increasing Muslim women's employment (Chapter 4). This is true for Bedouin women as well. Figure 6.3 presents the LFP rates of Bedouin women with different levels of education. It shows that the relationship between educational achievement and women's LFP is hardly linear. It is mostly Bedouin women with tertiary education who have been significantly present in the labor market. Starting with a high rate of 77 percent in 1995–1997, their LFP rate climbed to 83 percent in 2007–2009. Their share in employment was not different from that of the Other Muslim women in the northern and central regions during the first period, but by the last period under study it was by 10 percent higher. We should remember, however, that tertiary education is much more widespread among Muslim women in the north and the center than among Bedouins. As we explained in Chapter 4, in those areas, good positions that were open to Palestinian women,

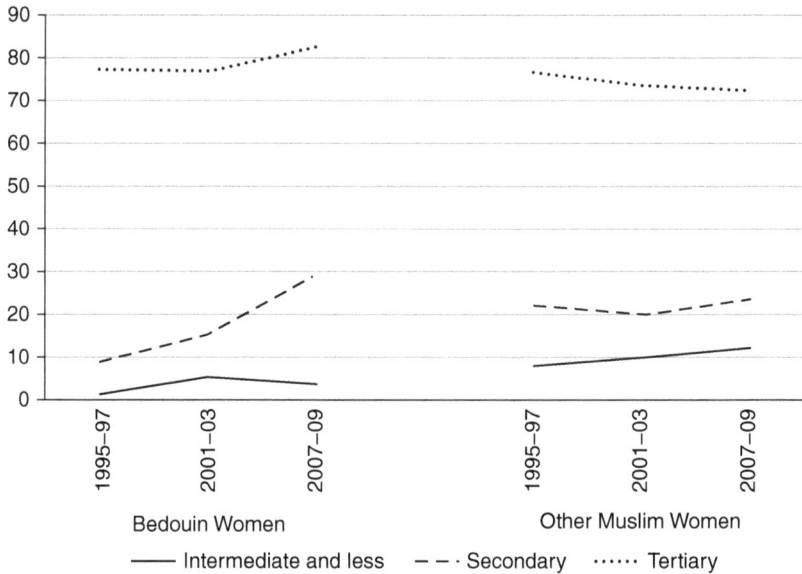

Figure 6.3 Labor Force Participation of Muslim Women Aged 25–52 in Bedouin Towns and Other Muslim Women by Education and Year
Source: Labor Force Surveys 1995–2009.
Note: All Muslims excluding Jerusalem (unrecognized Bedouin villages are not included in the LFS).

especially in the public sector, have been saturated with the growing number of highly educated women. Among the Bedouins of the south, the number of such highly educated women is still low, so women who reach such an educational level still have a sufficient number of positions open to them.[19]

Among Bedouin women with secondary education, a significant change has begun recently, with their rate in the labor market doubling from 15.4 percent in 2001–2003 to almost 30 percent in 2007–2009, just six years later. This rate is larger than that of Muslim women with the same level of education in the north and the center (but much smaller than that of Jewish women with the same level of education; see Chapter 4). This advantage of

---

[19] In fact, many Palestinians from the north and the center who do not find work as teachers close to their own communities, or who prefer to live at a distance from the extended family, work as teachers in Bedouin towns in the south (Abu-Rabia 2000, 90). They can do this because there are not enough local teachers, and therefore there are still enough open positions.

Bedouin over Other Muslim women might also be related to the fact that in the Bedouin communities of the south women with academic degrees have available suitable jobs and do not compete with women with secondary education over lower-level positions as they do in Palestinian communities in the other regions (Yonay and Kraus 2013). In contrast to the change among women with high-school education, no change was observed among women with the lowest educational level. In 2007–2009, fewer than 4 percent of these women, who still constitute 44 percent of Bedouin women, were employed, even less than in 2001–2003 (5.4 percent). This is also less than the LFP rate of Other Muslim women with a low level of education, 12.6 percent of whom were employed in 2007–2009.

A multivariate analysis reaffirms the above findings and gives us the size of the net influences of each factor (Appendix 6.1). As among other Muslim women in Israel, human capital measured by women's educational level is the most important determinant of Bedouin women's employment. For example, in 2007–2009 Bedouin women with tertiary education had 132 times the odds of participating in the labor market than Bedouin women with intermediate or lower levels of education, while women with secondary education had just 9.6 times the odds of the women with low levels of education. The effects of education were less in the previous period (2001–2003) than in 2007–2009. This is in contrast to the declining effect of education among Other Muslim women in the north and the center (Chapter 4). This finding is in line with the explanation we have suggested regarding the saturation of opportunities available for highly educated Muslims in the north and the center, a saturation not yet reached in the south.

As found in the descriptive part, being single increases Bedouin women's probability of being employed. This impact was enormous in the first period under consideration, and shrank a great deal by the second, but even then single women had 7.6 times the probability of being employed than married women. The multivariate analysis included a control for the number of children and their ages, variables not included in the descriptive analysis. Surprisingly, the number of children had a significant effect on Bedouin women's employment *only* in 2001–2003 (an additional child reduced Bedouin women's employment by 16 percent) but did not have a significant effect in 2007–2009. Having at least one young child did not have any impact in either period. Having children, especially young ones, do affect Other Muslim women's LFP, thus raising the question why these variables had no effect on Bedouin women in the planned towns (except for the number of children in 2001–2003). It is possible that this outcome is the result of the low variance of LFP, education, and fertility among Bedouin women.

In sum, although the labor force participation of women from the Bedouin towns is still considerably lower than among Other Muslim women in Israel, there are some signs that they are closing the gap. Education is expanding, and employment is becoming much more prevalent among Bedouin women with secondary education and among married women. Given the age structure of Bedouin society, cohort replacement might be expected to help close the gap in the coming years. It should be remembered, however, that the achievements of Muslim women in the more northern districts still leave much room for improvement. The aspiration should be for faster increases in LFP rates of all Muslim women in Israel.

6.4   Characteristics of Bedouin Women's Employment

In this section we present some general descriptive statistics on the labor force standing of employed Bedouin women (aged 18–52). In order to include more working women in our analysis we collapsed the data into the following periods: 1995–2001, 2002–2005, and 2006–2009. We start with the distribution of sectors and economic branches among Bedouin women and men and compare them to those of Other Muslim workers in Israel (Appendix 6.2). We observe that a very high percentage of Bedouin women worked in the public sector (85.1 percent in 2006–2009), mainly in the educational services (67.2 percent), and a relatively lower rate worked in the health and welfare services (13.2 percent). Inspecting these trends over the years we see very little change. In 1995–2001, a somewhat larger percentage worked in education (73.9 percent), and smaller percentage in health and welfare services (6.8 percent), indicating the entrance of Bedouin women to additional occupations, but the change is modest.

Comparing the respective industrial enrollment of Bedouin women to that of the Other Muslim women we find that Bedouin women were occupied in an even more limited range of economic branches than their counterparts who lived north of the Naqab. For example, in 2006–2009, we find that despite the limited economic opportunities of the Other Muslims, they had a higher share of workers in manufacturing, peripheral services, and health and welfare services than women in the Bedouin towns. The fact that Bedouin women are rarely employed in the private sector indicates the very limited range of positions available to them, a fact that is a major cause of their low LFP.

Bedouin men and women work in completely different economic branches. Many of the Bedouin men, around 36.2 percent, worked in 2006–2009 in the manufacturing and construction economic sectors, and an additional 33.3 percent are enrolled in peripheral services. A relatively low share of men is enrolled in the public sector. Like Bedouin women, Bedouin men are also more limited in their employment choices than Other Muslim men. One explanation for the narrow range of opportunities of Bedouin women and men is that Bedouins in the south face more barriers in the labor market than Other Muslims – either because of stronger prejudices and negative attitudes toward them or because of the weakness of their own communities in terms of local economy and deficient public services, or as a result of both of these factors.

The limited job opportunities of Bedouin women are further demonstrated when examining their occupational enrollment. In 1995–2001 a vast majority of working women in the Bedouin towns (63 percent) worked as teachers, and although this percentage has declined, nearly one out of two working Bedouin women still worked as a teacher in 2007–2009 (46 percent), by about 15 percent more than among Other Muslim women (Appendix 6.3). This dependence on teaching further demonstrates our previous claim about the extremely limited employment opportunities for Bedouin women. The decline in the reliance upon teaching jobs has been achieved through the increasing entrance of Bedouin women into low prestige service occupations. In 1995–2001, 17.3 percent of these women were enrolled in these services, and this rate more than doubled in 2006–2009 (37.7 percent). The most prevalent among these service occupations was that of children's caregiver.

When comparing the occupational distribution of Bedouin women to that of Other Muslim women in Israel (Appendix 6.3), we see that the latter have a higher share of workers as nurses, clerical workers, and saleswomen, occupations in which Bedouin women are hardly present. Some examples may demonstrate this situation: (1) There were almost no Bedouin nurses in our sample (only two women worked as nurses in 1995–2001, and one in 2002–2005). Among Other Muslim women, 189 were nurses in 2006–2009 (5.2 percent). (2) While more than 16 percent of Other Muslim women worked in clerical occupations, only 6.2 percent of Bedouin women were enrolled in such occupations. (3) Perhaps most revealing is the low presence of Bedouin women in sales occupations. From zero in 1995–2001, the fraction of Bedouin women in these occupations rose to a miniscule 0.3 percent, much lower than the 9.3 percent among Other Muslim women. The low numbers of Bedouin women in the above occupations is related to the weakness of the Bedouin economy and to the depth of segregation in the south. In the northern and central districts many Jews shop in neighboring Palestinian communities, and although many Jewish employers avoid employing Palestinians, other Jewish employers do hire them as salespersons, clerks, secretaries etc. In the south, the practice of shopping in Palestinian (Bedouin) towns is less common, there are fewer employment opportunities in the towns themselves, and Jewish economic centers are few and far from the Bedouin towns.

The opportunities for Bedouin men are also meager. In the second part of Appendix 6.3, we see that in all years, the majority of Bedouin men worked in skilled and unskilled manual occupations and in agriculture, so that the rate of employed men in these occupations has remained high – two-thirds in 1995–2001 and 60.1 percent in 2006–2009. Among these workers many worked in construction (12 percent in 2006–2009) and as drivers (15.6 percent in 2006–2009). The presence of Bedouin men in high white-collar occupations (academic, professional, managerial) has hardly changed (19.5 percent in 1995–2001 and 20.2 percent in 2006–2009). Of this category teaching is the major occupation, accounting for about 43 percent of all high-prestige workers in 1995–2001, and for more than half in the last two periods. The occupational structure of the Naqab Bedouin and Other Muslim men is quite similar, but the Bedouin men in white-collar occupations have been more concentrated in teaching, and those in blue-collar occupations have been more concentrated in agricultural work. The differences are not large and may reflect the economic structure of the south in general, and the open positions for Palestinians in particular.

In the last section of our analysis of working women in Bedouin towns we look at how many of them work part-time. We see that the rate of part-time workers is very low, much lower than among Other Muslim women. For example in 2006–2009, about 24.5 percent of Bedouin working women worked part-time, compared to 38 percent among Other Muslim women. When Bedouin women were asked for the reasons why they worked part-time, three-quarters reported that they had not been able to find a full-time position.[20]

6.5   The Work Experience of Bedouin Women in the Unrecognized Villages

In the following section, we present some data on Bedouin Muslim women who reside in dozens of small villages, the so-called unrecognized villages, although 11 of them were recognized (or newly established to replace others) since 2004. Since this population is not included in the Israeli labor surveys, our analysis is based on the last Israeli census conducted in 2008.[21]

We start with a demographic description of Bedouin women in the age bracket 18–52. Like the women in the Bedouin towns, Bedouin women

---

[20] We do not examine the earnings of Bedouin women because both the combined income surveys and labor force surveys and census data include samples too small for reliable statistical inference.

[21] According to our inquiry with the CBS, the newly recognized villages are not yet included in the labor force survey sampling schemes.

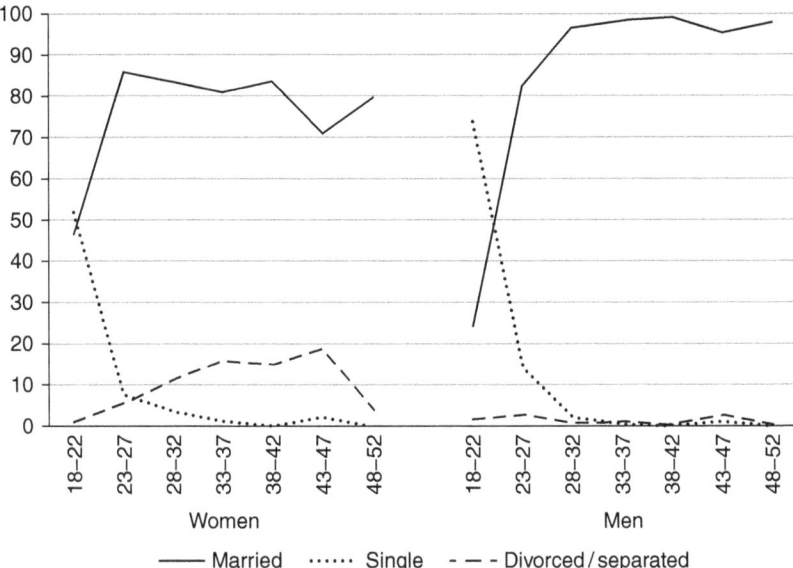

Figure 6.4 Marital Status of Bedouins in Unrecognized Villages by
Gender and Age Group, 2008
Source: 2008 Census.
Note: Only Muslims from the Southern District who do not live in the
seven planned towns.

from the unrecognized villages are on average quite young. Their majority
(60 percent) is in the age bracket of 18–32, and only about 14 percent
belong to the older age groups of 43–52. Most of them marry at a
relatively young age (Figure 6.4), so almost half (47 percent) of those in
the age bracket 18–22 are already married, a somewhat higher share than
among women in the Bedouin towns (about 42 percent; not presented).

   Among the older age groups we notice that a relatively high proportion of
women are divorced (this is not the case for women in the planned towns).
Among women aged 33–47 the divorce rates hover between 15 and almost
19 percent. This high rate of divorce might be related to the fact that
polygyny still exists among Bedouins, especially among those who have
refused to move to the towns. Since polygyny is against the law in Israel, it
is possible that many of these "divorced women" declare themselves to be
divorced (or separated) only when asked in the census about their marital
status, although they are considered as wives according to Muslim law, and
still live with their husbands. This speculation needs to be corroborated.
Bedouin men residing in unrecognized villages marry at somewhat older ages
than their brides, and by the age of 23–27, almost 83 percent of them are
married; when they reach the age of 28–32, almost all are married. During

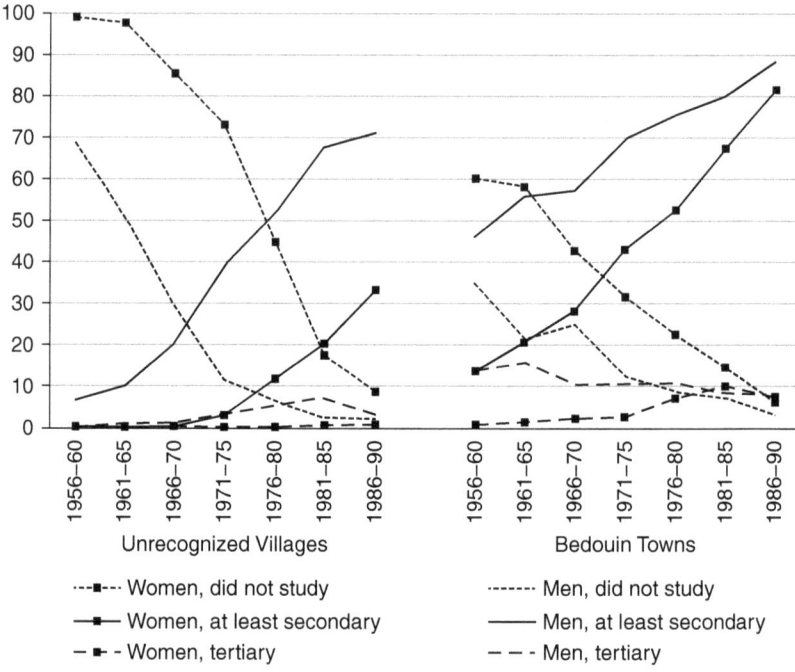

Figure 6.5 Highest School Attended of Bedouin Men and Women
Aged 18–52 in Unrecognized Villages and in Bedouin Towns by Birth
Years, 2008
Source: 2008 Census.
Note: Only Muslims from the Southern District.

their life course, they remain married and hardly divorce. The gap in divorce
rates between Bedouin women and men supports our hypothesis that the
high divorce rate of women does not reflect an actual separation of spouses.

Given the young age of women at marriage, it is not surprising to find a
very high birth rate among Bedouin women in unrecognized villages.
More than 40 percent of Bedouin women at the age of 28–32 have already
given birth to five or more children, which is very much the same as
among women in Bedouin towns, but when women in the villages reach
the 33–37 age bracket, the percentage of women who have had this
number of children climbs to 72 percent, while the respective figure for
women in Bedouin towns is 10 percent lower.

Educational attainment among Bedouin women in unrecognized villages is the lowest in Israel. Practically no woman born in the years
1956–1960 and 1961–1965 attended any school (Figure 6.5). School
attendance was still low for women born in 1971–1975 (only about 27

percent attended any level of schooling), but since then we notice a considerable increase in women's school attendance. Among women born in 1981–1985, the rate of school attendance increased to 82 percent, and it climbed still further among women born in 1986–1990 (to 91.4 percent). Despite this improvement in school attendance among Bedouin women in the unrecognized villages, according to the 2008 census, there were still Bedouin women younger than 52 who had not had any schooling, in spite of the Compulsory Education Law, which was enacted almost 60 years earlier in 1949.

Very few of the women who attended primary and intermediate schools have attended secondary education. Among those born in 1981–1985, about a fifth attended the secondary level, and this share increased to 33 percent among women born in 1986–1990. No significant number of the Bedouin women in unrecognized villages had attended tertiary education.[22] Figure 6.5 shows that the educational achievements of women in the planned Bedouin towns are much higher than those of Bedouin women from the unrecognized villages. Of the youngest cohort (born 1986–1990), for instance, only 33 percent of women from the unrecognized villages attended at least secondary schooling, while 81.5 percent of those from the Bedouin towns did so.

In all years Bedouin men in the unrecognized villages had by far higher school attendance than Bedouin women. This gender gap is similar to that which used to exist among Other Muslims but was reversed in favor of women (see Chapter 3). This gap has also considerably narrowed in the Bedouin planned towns but is still significant there.

Finally we inspect the labor force participation of Bedouin women in the unrecognized localities. Here we encounter a puzzle. As explained in Chapter 4, our definition of belonging to the labor force includes, in addition to those actually employed, those people who are unemployed but actively seek employment. Among other groups of Palestinian and Jewish women and men, the percentage of such unemployed workers was quite low (including women in the Bedouin towns, among whom only 3 percent of all women aged 18–52 were unemployed), but among Bedouin women in the unrecognized villages, 10.4 percent of all women said that they were seeking employment, and only 0.4 percent were actually employed. We checked the data and also consulted the professional staff at the CBS, and these figures were validated. This result is quite strange. The unemployment rate was also relatively high among Bedouin men (35 percent of those aged 18–52 compared to 28 percent who were employed), and this held true within each of the age groups. This is much

---

[22] Only among the youngest cohorts (those born after 1981) do we find a small fraction (less than one percent) of women who attended tertiary education.

higher than the rate of 8 percent unemployed Bedouin men in the Bedouin towns (out of all men aged 18–52), but still a possibly valid datum given the poor employment condition of this group.[23]

6.6   Summary

Bedouin women in the Naqab suffer from multiple marginalization: as women, as part of the disadvantaged Palestinian minority in Israel, as part of an ex-nomadic group which has had to adjust to life in permanent settlements, as members of a Palestinian group that has had harsher conflicts with the Jewish state than the other Palestinians over territorial claims, and as part of the population in the Naqab, an economically lesser developed region of Israel.

Bedouin women marry young and have high fertility rates and relatively lower levels of education than Other Muslim women in Israel. Consequently they also have very low employment rates. The poor conditions of the schools, the resulting low educational achievements, the lack of employment opportunities close to home, the distance from potential employment, as well as discrimination and low wages for working in the Jewish sector are strong enough reasons to explain the low labor force participation of women in Bedouin towns. In the unrecognized villages, the same factors are even harsher reducing women's LFP there to a negligible level.

Although women in Bedouin towns have increased their employment rates, they have very slim occupational opportunities. It is only highly educated women who can become schoolteachers; other women lack other opportunities. Since the Bedouin culture is quite different from that of other Muslims and considered more conservative in terms of gender relations, many writers attribute the lower achievements of Bedouin women to it. As we emphasized at the outset of our research, our approach is different. We look for the political-economic conditions that preserve traditional cultures or push them to change. The Bedouins in the south of Israel have been kept at the margins of Israeli society. They were removed from their lands, neglected by the state, and enticed into dead-end towns. Rather than helping them to overcome the hardship of sedentarization, the state has fought against them and has made little effort to advance their communities and to provide them with sources of livelihood. Living in the economic periphery of Israel where employment is a problem even to the members of the Jewish majority, the Bedouin women's chances of advancing their education and their employment have been the lowest among all groups of Palestinians in Israel. The recent rise in educational achievements and employment shows that the potential is there if opportunities are offered.

---

[23] Among the men, 37.2 percent were out of the labor force, similar to the 34.6 figure of men in the state-planned towns in 2007–2009.

Appendix 6.1 *Logistic Coefficients and Standard Errors (in parentheses) Predicting LFP of Bedouin Women Aged 25–52 by Year*

	2001–2003		2007–2009	
	B/S.E.	EXP. (B)	B/S.E.	EXP. (B)
Secondary education	1.061*	2.890	2.259*	9.573
	(0.367)		(0.303)	
Tertiary education	4.354*	77.779	4.886*	132.4
	(0.373)		(0.360)	
Family composition				
Single	2.852*	17.329	2.030*	7.618
	(0.540)		(0.440)	
Number of children	−0.175*	0.840	−0.051	0.950
under 15	(0.089)		(0.063)	
Have children under 5	0.478	1.613	0.348	1.417
	(0.493)		(0.372)	
Age	0.013	1.013	0.020	1.020
	(0.026)		(0.022)	
Intercept	−3.437		−4.162	
N	1,002		682	
2 Log likelihood	344.1		554.9	
Nagelkerke R^2	0.540		0.545	

Variables: The dependent variable is labor force participation, coded 1 if the woman belongs to the labor force, and 0 otherwise; the independent variables are: education (distinguishing among three levels of education (intermediary and less (the referenced group), secondary, tertiary); family status (single is coded 1; ever-married is coded 0); number of children under 15, having children under 5, and age.
Source: Labor force Surveys 1995–2009.
*: $p < 0.05$
Note: All Muslims excluding Jerusalem (unrecognized Bedouin villages are not included in the LFS).

Appendix 6.2 *Economic Branch Distribution of Muslims Aged 18–52 in Bedouin Towns and Other Muslims by Gender and Year*

	1995–2001	2002–2005	2006–2009	2006–2009
		Bedouin Women		Other Muslim Women
Agriculture	5.6	4.2	2.4	2.3
Manufacturing	2.6	3.2	2.1	6.9
Construction	0.0	0.0	0.0	0.0
Peripheral services	3.1	4.8	5.5	22.0
Wholesale and retail trade, repair of vehicles and personal and household goods	(1.2)	(3.2)	(0.7)	(13.9)
Core services	3.1	2.1	4.9	4.4
Public Sector	85.6	85.7	85.1	64.4
Public administration	(4.1)	(5.5)	(1.9)	(2.3)
Education	(73.9)	(68.1)	(67.2)	(41.9)
Health services and welfare and social work	(6.8)	(9.5)	(13.2)	(18.2)
Total	100.0	100.0	100.0	100.0
N	161	189	287	3,623
		Bedouin Men		Other Muslim Men
Agriculture	8.2	7.6	8.3	3.9
Manufacturing	14.2	15.3	13.5	18.5
Construction	25.1	24.0	22.7	30.3
Peripheral services	31.6	28.9	33.3	31.9
Wholesale and retail trade, repair of vehicles and personal and household goods	(12.4)	(10.8)	(15.0)	(18.2)
Core services	5.3	5.7	6.2	4.4
Public sector	15.6	18.5	16.0	11.0
Public administration	(3.2)	(3.8)	(1.9)	(1.4)
Education	(9.8)	(12.0)	(13.2)	(4.8)
Health services and welfare and social work	(2.6)	(2.7)	(0.9)	(3.7)
Total	100.0	100.0	100.0	100.0
N	1,140	892	1,045	11,245

Source: Labor force Surveys 1995–2009.
Note: All Muslims excluding Jerusalem (unrecognized Bedouin villages are not included in the LFS).

Appendix 6.3 *Occupational Distribution of Muslims Aged 18–52 in Bedouin Towns and Other Muslims by Gender and Year*

	Bedouin Women			Other Muslim Women
	1995–01	2002–05	2006–09	2006–09
Academic professionals	0.0	1.6	0.3	1.9
Associate professionals and technicians	66.7	43.4	48.8	40.0
Teachers in secondary education	(6.2)	(2.3)	(3.1)	(4.0)
Teachers in intermediate and primary schools	(56.8)	(39.2)	(42.9)	(27.5)
Nurses	(1.2)	(0.5)	(0.0)	(5.2)
Managers	1.2	0.5	1.4	0.7
Clericals	5.5	4.2	6.2	16.2
Sales workers	0.0	0.5	0.3	9.3
Service workers	17.3	41.8	37.7	25.3
Housemaids	(2.5)	(3.7)	(6.6)	(6.9)
Childcare and kindergarten assistants	(8.6)	(27.0)	(22.5)	(6.5)
Kitchen workers, domestic cleaners and helper	(6.2)	(9.0)	(5.9)	(8.6)
Agriculture workers	5.6	4.2	4.8	2.6
Skilled manual workers	3.0	1.1	0.0	3.0
Unskilled manual workers	0.6	2.6	0.4	1.0
Total	100.0	100.0	100.0	100.0
N	162	189	289	3,627

	Bedouin Men			Other Muslim Men
Academic professionals	4.2	3.5	2.6	3.4
Associate professionals and technicians	10.6	12.6	14.7	7.6
Teachers in secondary schools	(2.9)	(3.3)	(3.0)	(1.3)
Teachers in primary and intermediate schools	(5.5)	(7.3)	(9.7)	(2.4)
Mangers	4.7	3.3	2.9	2.0
Clericals	3.6	3.9	1.8	3.7
Sales workers	2.2	3.9	6.0	8.8
Service workers	8.1	10.2	12.0	11.8
Kitchen workers, domestic cleaners, and helpers	(6.3)	(8.0)	(7.9)	(6.9)
Agriculture workers	7.7	6.3	10.5	5.5
Skilled workers	48.0	48.4	44.0	50.8
Locksmith workers and welders	(3.0)	(4.5)	(4.4)	(4.7)
Builders	(8.6)	(5.9)	(7.4)	(12.0)
Construction operators	(8.2)	(10.0)	(4.6)	(2.5)
Drivers	(15.8)	(16.3)	(15.6)	(7.4)

Appendix 6.3 (*cont.*)

	Bedouin Men			Other Muslim Men
Unskilled workers	11.0	7.9	5.6	6.5
Total	100.0	100.0	100.0	100.0
N	1,141	892	1,051	11,346

Source: Labor force Surveys 1995–2009.

Note: All Muslims excluding Jerusalem (unrecognized Bedouin villages are not included in the LFS). Included are occupations in which at least 3 percent of women or of men were enrolled. in at least one period.

7 Residents But Not Citizens
The Annexed Muslim Women of Jerusalem

7.1 The Setting

Jerusalem's Unique Past. As a sacred place for three monotheistic religions – Judaism, Christianity, and Islam – Jerusalem has deep symbolic and political importance (Abu-Odeh 1992; Albin 1997; Klein 2004; Mourad 2008; Peters 2008; Robson 2011). The modernization of the city started in the late Ottoman period, when the District of Jerusalem was carved out of the province of Syria and modern planning and facilities were introduced to the city. When Britain established its rule over Palestine in 1920 (and was given the League of Nation's Mandate in 1922), Jerusalem became the center of government and drew many Jewish immigrants and Palestinian villagers. Both Palestinians and Jews built new neighborhoods, maintaining the ethno-religious dividing line between the two national communities (Albin 1997; Nassar 2008; Tamari 2003).

According to the UN partition decision of November 1947, Jerusalem (including the adjacent town of Bethlehem) was supposed to become a neutral zone (Corpus Separatum) administered by the UN (Cattan 1981; Quigley 1996; Choshen 2002; Lapidoth 2002). Following the 1948 war, the city was divided into two parts: the Western side and the Mount Scopus enclave became part of Israel, and the eastern part, including the Old Quarter with its sacred sites, was annexed to Jordan as part of what is recognized today as the West Bank. Jews who lived in the Old Quarter were taken as prisoners of war and were eventually expelled to Israel, while the Palestinian residents of Palestinian neighborhoods on the western side (e.g. Baq'ah, Qatamon, Musrara, and Talbiya) were forced out of Israel. Israel expanded West Jerusalem and included in its jurisdiction 39 of the neighboring Palestinian villages (e.g. Ein Karim, Deir Yasin, Lifta, El-Maliha), whose residents were also forced out of Israel. One village, Beit Safafa, was also divided; its northern side became part of the Jewish West Jerusalem, and its southern part remained part of the Jordanian West Bank (Mattar 1983; Said 1995; Quigley 1996; Albin 1997; Tamari 1999, 2003; Cohen 2007).

Jerusalem was declared the capital of Israel only in December 1949 in response to the UN General Assembly's decision earlier that month to reaffirm the international status of the city.[1] Due to the UN decision, very few countries have recognized Jerusalem as Israel's capital, and almost all the international embassies in Israel are located in Tel Aviv (Cattan 1981; Quigley 1996). Many Israeli government offices have also remained in the Tel Aviv area, which as the economic and cultural hub of Israel drew many more people than West Jerusalem. Meanwhile Jordan – whose annexation of the whole West Bank was also not recognized internationally – declared East Jerusalem as its second capital (after Amman) and took control of its holy places. The religious importance of Jerusalem and its central location in the West Bank turned the Jordanian part of the city into the commercial, administrative, and cultural heart of the West Bank, but still it was overshadowed by the fast-developing Amman (Klein 2001; Cohen 2007; Katz 2008).

A Divided Society in a Unified City. During the 1967 war, the whole West Bank was conquered by Israel, and East Jerusalem came under Israeli rule. While most of the West Bank (as well as the Gaza Strip and the Golan Heights) was put under a military administration that persists to this day, a few weeks after the war ended, Israel annexed the Jordanian part of Jerusalem (including the Old Quarter) and 28 villages in the city's immediate vicinity, and put them all under the jurisdiction of the Jerusalem municipality. The municipal boundaries of Jerusalem thus expanded from 44 square kilometers (West Jerusalem was 38 square kilometers, and East Jerusalem was only 6 square kilometers) to 108, and later to 123 (Albin 1997; Klein 2001, 19; cf. Choshen 2002).[2]

The status of Jerusalem has become a bone of contention between Israel and the international community. The latter considers any area behind the Green Line as part of the occupied West Bank, and Israel's annexation of East Jerusalem and the adjacent villages is considered a grave violation of international law (Quigley 1996; Albin 1997; Imseis 2000). Within Israeli politics, however, the unification of the

---

[1] It was preceded by a declaration of the Palestinian leadership in September 1948 of Jerusalem as the capital of a Palestinian state, but the state has never come to life (Cohen 2007, 27).

[2] See map of Jerusalem at the end of this chapter. Some areas annexed to Jerusalem were taken from Bethlehem and Beit Jalla, two towns south of Jerusalem (Klein 2001, 19). The term "annexation" is used by many scholars writing on Jerusalem, but Lustick argues that Israel has carefully avoided this term and in fact did not enact any explicit law annexing East Jerusalem and surrounding villages to Israel. The de facto annexation was achieved by administrative maneuvers that allowed the state to expand its jurisdiction to any area under its control (Lustick 2008).

city and the exclusive sovereignty of Israel over it have become principles that no mainstream politician dares challenge (Lustick 1996,
2008; Albin 1997).[3]

The illegitimacy of the annexation has been aggravated by the denial of
full citizenship to the population that had lived in the area until 1967.
These people were granted permanent residency but not citizenship
(Halabi 1997; Rempel 1997).[4] Because of this residency, Palestinian
Jerusalemites have had the right to live and work in Israel without needing
special permits, unlike their compatriots in the rest of the West Bank.
They are also entitled to all the social services that citizens get, including
health insurance and social security (Halabi 1997; Tamari 2003). What is
then the significance of their legal status as non-citizens?

There are two areas in which this status has severe implications.
First, as non-citizens, Palestinian Jerusalemites cannot take part in
shaping Israel's future by participating in its national elections
(Halabi 1997). Officially the Palestinian residents of Jerusalem may
apply for citizenship, and a few of them have actually done so, but the
majority resists such application because it means recognition of the
Israeli annexation of East Jerusalem and its vicinity (Yiftachel and
Yacobi 2003; Tamari 2003; Ju'beh 2007). It is also doubtful whether
this population could actually exercise their right to citizenship. Those
who have applied have encountered bureaucratic obstacles that have
made obtaining citizenship difficult and rare. In any case, the situation
in which Israel is the sovereign but the residents are not its citizens has
been convenient for Israeli governments, which have done nothing to
change it (Albin 1997; Halabi 1997; Rempel 1997; Cheshin et al.
1999; Yiftachel and Yacobi 2002; Tamari 2003; Hasson 2010).[5]

---

[3] Israeli discourse looks upon the artificially created current municipal boundaries of
Jerusalem as part of the historically meaningful and religiously sacred location for Jews.
Within this discourse, even remote villages or towns that had never been part of Jerusalem
before1967 are considered to be integral parts of the city. The senselessness of this
position is evident (Abu-Odeh 1992; Lustick 1996; Albin 1997, 129).

[4] Official residency was actually denied to about 30,000 Palestinian Jerusalemites who were
not at home during the census Israel conducted a short time after the 1967 war. These
people were, however, entitled to return to their homes; some of them were eventually
accorded residency, but many have not received such status to this day, and their position
in the city has remained precarious (United Nations 2013, 6).

[5] Lustick (2008) claims that in fact there is no legal obligation to grant citizenship to the
Palestinian residents of Jerusalem because the city was not officially annexed (cf. Halabi
1997; Rempel 1997). Residents may apply for citizenship (as any other person in the world
may), and a few actually get it according to the state's discretion. According to Hasson's
article in the daily *Haaretz*, the number of applicants started to rise in the 2000s, and
during the first decade of the twenty-first century 3,374 Palestinian residents were granted
citizenship. This is still just a bit more than 1 percent of the Palestinian population in
Jerusalem (Hasson 2010).

The second dire implication of not being citizens is that unlike citizenship, residency might be easily revoked (Rempel 1997). According to Israeli law, a resident's permanent residency is subject to revocation when living abroad for more than seven years (United Nation 2013, 9). In recent years, in an attempt to curtail the number of Palestinians in Jerusalem, Israel started to apply the same revocation policy even toward Palestinian Jerusalemites who reside in the West Bank.[6] Thus permanent residents from Jerusalem who work in the city and conduct their businesses there, may lose their Israeli residency IDs if they move to their spouse's home outside Jerusalem or build their homes on cheaper land outside the city's boundaries (Halabi 1997).[7]

Due to the importance Israel ascribes to the percentage of Jews in Jerusalem, it has built new neighborhoods for Jews only throughout the city, and especially beyond the Green Line, where it was especially important for Israel to assert its sovereignty (Mattar 1983; Musallam 1996; Albin 1997; Kaminker 1997; Rempel 1997; Klein 2001; Tamari 2003). In 2013, the total population of Jerusalem amounted to 822,600 inhabitants, of which 293,900 are Palestinians (12,000 Christians[8], and the rest Muslims), almost all of whom live beyond the Green Line. Except for a few foreigners, the rest, about half a million, are Jews (CBS 2014, Table 2.20). The official statistics in Israel do not distinguish between residents of West Jerusalem (within the Green Line) and of the area annexed by Israel east of the Green line. However, unofficial statistics from 2009 estimate the total population of municipal Jerusalem beyond the Green Line to be 466,600 inhabitants, of which about 40 percent (about 187,000) were Jews, and 60 percent (280,000) were Palestinians (Choshen and Korach 2011).

Divided Education in a Unified City. According to Israeli law, Palestinian residents of Jerusalem, regardless of citizenship, are supposedly subject to the same educational policies as Palestinian citizens in

---

[6] Approximately 14,000 Palestinians from Jerusalem have lost their status as permanent residents of Israel from 1967 to 2014 – more than a half of them in 2005–2014 (B'Tselem 2013).

[7] The revocation of permanent residency when people live outside Israel makes sense when these people are immigrants who received this status after moving to Israel and living in it. It is less reasonable when it involves indigenous people born in Jerusalem to families who have lived there for generations. One should also remember that immigrant Jews get citizenship immediately upon arrival according to the Law of Return, so revocation of residency is relevant only for non-Jews (B'Tselem 2013).

[8] The low number of Christians in Jerusalem is the result of a continuous emigration of Christians who, given their church affiliation and connections with large Christian Palestinian communities in many countries, could better benefit from their human capital abroad than in the conflict-ridden Jerusalem (Tsimhoni 1993; Robson 2011).

other regions of the country. Yet forcing Israeli education on thousands of Palestinian children in Jerusalem was not successful. Beyond the resistance to teaching their children according to Israeli ideologies, parents wanted to keep the road open to higher education and employment in Arab countries. Prior to 1967, Palestinians in Jerusalem had close ties with educational, economic, and cultural institutions in the West Bank, Jordan, and the rest of the Arab world, places where Israeli matriculation diplomas were not recognized. The local population was interested in maintaining the Jordanian educational programs that led to Arab-recognized certificates, and therefore sent their children to private schools (including those run by the Waqf, the communal Muslim organization) where Jordanian curricula were used and Jordanian standard examinations were taken. As the number of pupils in the public schools plummeted, the Israeli government gave up and agreed that public schools would also teach according to the Jordanian curricula, with the addition of Hebrew classes, and that students would take the same standard examinations as all high school students in the West Bank (Manna 1997; Cohen 2007, 131–132). Following the Oslo Accords, the Jordanian curricula were replaced in the West Bank and Gaza Strip by those of the Palestinian Authority, and Palestinian schools in Jerusalem followed suit (Manna 1997; Klein 2005, 60).[9]

Israeli authorities have, however, remained responsible for building schools and for their administration. The Ministry of Education is responsible for funding, but municipal authorities administer the actual operation of schools and, hence, control the distribution of resources among the schools in the municipality. In Jerusalem, the exclusion of Palestinians from local politics has seriously hampered the provision of appropriate educational services. Although they are about a third of the population in Jerusalem, Palestinians have no representation in the City Council (Tamari 2003; Klein 2005; Ju'beh 2007), and consequently they receive a smaller piece of the municipal cake. In the mid-1990s, the Palestinian neighborhoods of Jerusalem got only 6–7 percent of the city budget (Manna 1997, 21; cf. Albin 1997, 136; Margalit 2001; Siniora 2001).

Thus, city officials have not paid attention to the needs of the Palestinian population, and their school system has suffered from severe neglect and very low budgets (Manna 1997; Khan 2001; Reiter 2003). There is a large shortage of day-care facilities and classrooms. For example, in 2012 there was a shortage of 1,100 classrooms for Palestinian children, and this shortage has further increased in the following years

---

[9] Israeli authorities have censored both the Jordanian and the Palestinian curricula in an attempt to eliminate materials considered anti-Jewish, anti-Israeli, or subversive.

(Alyan et al. 2012b, 7). The classrooms are extremely overcrowded, and thousands of students attend unsuitable classrooms, some of which are placed in residential buildings, and some of which are attended in double shifts in order to accommodate the large number of students.

The attainments of Palestinian children are unavoidably affected by these stark conditions. This can be seen, for example, from the very high dropout rates for Palestinian children. According to the official statistics of the Jerusalem Education Administration, substantial dropping out begins as early as the first grade and increases thereafter. Two percent of the children do not attend first grade, and 40 percent do not reach the last year of high school (Alyan et al. 2012b). "The average dropout rate among the Arab sector in Israel for grades 7th to 12th is 6.2 percent, and 4.2 percent among the Jewish sector in Israel, while in East Jerusalem it reached 17.3 percent" (ibid., 16). Such a staggering rate is undoubtedly the outcome of neglect by the city government, which has no political incentive to remedy the educational crisis. It also reflects the weakness of the local Palestinian community due to Israel's continuing efforts to curb Palestinian organization in a city that Israel wants to control alone (Musallam 1996; Cheshin et al. 1999).

Israel's decision to withdraw its own educational curricula and high school matriculation exams affect higher education as well. Most Palestinian high school graduates in Jerusalem have continued their education either in Arabic institutions of higher education in Jerusalem itself or in such institutions in the West Bank and Jordan (Reiter 2003). Very few students have obtained the Israeli matriculation diploma required for entering Israeli colleges and universities. Moreover, students attain only a low level of Hebrew: Their teachers have for the most part not graduated from Israeli institutions and are not exposed to Hebrew at home. Consequently, even if they are interested in studying at Israeli higher education institutions, high school graduates find it very difficult to be accepted by these institutions (Alyan et al. 2012a). Writing in 2003, Reiter quotes the number of Palestinian Jerusalemites who study at the Hebrew University of Jerusalem – the oldest and one of the largest universities in Israel –as only 50, a negligible number that indicates that the Palestinian population of Jerusalem does not benefit from its proximity to this prestigious institution (Reiter 2003, 190). At the same time, Israeli authorities do not recognize degrees issued by Palestinian institutions, so in order to be hired by Israeli workplaces, the graduates of such institutions must add Israeli certificates, which require additional courses and additional examinations. Professionals who have studied in Jordan or other countries – mostly medicine and the paramedical professions – are also required to pass Israeli exams before getting their licenses.[10]

The Economy in the Shadow of a National Struggle. Political economists and economic sociologists argue that power relations and political maneuvering affect the labor market and the structure of economic activity. In Jerusalem, one does not need theory to see how the city's economy and the economic status of its Palestinians vacillate according to the political events related to the Palestinian-Israeli conflict (Abu-Saud 2007). This assertion will be evident in the following chronicle of political economic circumstances.

Before Israeli Annexation. Until 1967, East Jerusalem was the center of the West Bank, located in the middle of the area and halfway between Hebron (al-Khalil) and Nablus. As the religious center and pilgrimage destination for believers of the three monotheistic religions, the city enjoyed moderate prosperity. Yet the Jordanian Hashemite regime was more interested in developing Amman as the economic and political heart of the kingdom, and was not interested in making Jerusalem its competitor. The city therefore did not develop much during the Hashemite rule (Romann 1978; Katz 2008).

Under Israeli Rule. Following the 1967 war, the economic standing of the local population improved as Jerusalem became a center of commerce between Israel and the West bank and, indirectly, the Arab world. The number of tourists grew and included many Israelis and Jews. The development of Jewish neighborhoods in the annexed areas violated the rights of the Palestinian residents but also created employment opportunities and led to economic growth that benefited Palestinians, not only Jews (Romann 1978;Romann and Weingrod 1991; Albin 1997; Siniora 2001; Cohen 2007).

In terms of employment, the annexation of East Jerusalem and its surrounding opened the Israeli labor market to those who unwillingly became permanent residents of Israel. Other residents of the West Bank also entered the Israeli labor market, but they depended on the good will of Israeli policy-makers and officials for special licenses and permits.[11] Jerusalemites (according to the new municipal boundaries) had

---

[10] Due to such difficulties there are some indications that recently some Palestinian high school graduates prefer studying in Israeli higher education institutions. There is no research yet on this topic but see Hasson 2012a, 2012b.

[11] In the years right after 1967, employment in Israel was open to Palestinians from the West Bank and the Gaza Strip, but later Israel started to regulate the entrance of these workers according to both security considerations and employment needs (Shenhav and Berda 2009).

the right to work everywhere (Romann 1978; Romann and Weingrod 1991; Siniora 2001). However, highly educated Palestinians in Jerusalem have been especially limited in the Israeli labor market since their educational credentials were not accepted as valid. Moreover, these Jerusalemites could not rely on municipal employment, as did the Palestinians within Green-Line Israel. Many highly educated women and men among the latter have been absorbed in public services that cater to the local population. In Jerusalem, due to the practical exclusion of Palestinians from the municipal politics, these services have remained limited and have not provided sufficient employment opportunities for these highly educated workers. According to Margalit (2001), for example, only five educational psychologists and ten community workers served the Palestinian communities in Jerusalem, compared to 75 and 135, respectively, who served the Jewish communities.

The First Intifada (1987–1991). Since 1987 the intensification of the national Palestinian struggle and the violent clashes between Palestinians and Jews have created new barriers to economic possibilities for the former. During the First Intifada – the civilian uprising of the Palestinians in the West Bank and the Gaza Strip – the Israeli government limited movement between the occupied territories and Israel (including Jerusalem), thus disrupting the role of East Jerusalem as a center of interaction for Palestinians from the West Bank (Abu-Saud 2007; Albin 1997).

The Establishment of the Palestinian Authority and Beginning of the Peace Process (1993–2000). The 1993 Oslo Accords between Israelis and Palestinians opened new economic possibilities but terrorist attacks by Palestinian opponents of these accords led to a proliferation of Israeli military checkpoints and other restrictions on movements from the West Bank to Israel (Musallam 1996; Siniora 2001; Cohen 2007). The Oslo process also weakened Jerusalem's central standing in the West Bank. As the Palestinian Authority established its headquarters in Ramallah, only a few miles north of Jerusalem, and as Israel – with an eye fixed on the negotiations over the city's future – started to monitor more strictly the presence of non-resident Palestinians in Jerusalem, the center of political, economic, and cultural activities of the West Bank gravitated to Ramallah (Siniora 2001; Cohen 2007; Ju'beh 2007).

Israel's attempt to bolster its claims on Jerusalem led to revocations of permanent residency of those Palestinian Jerusalemites who did not actually live in the city. Contrary to Israel's intentions, this policy actually increased the number of Palestinians living in Jerusalem, as many permanent residents who had moved to suburban areas outside of the city returned to Jerusalem so as not to lose this status. This inward migration crowded the Palestinian neighborhoods, overloaded the under-financed municipal services in these neighborhoods, and increased the jam-packing of classrooms (Alyan et al. 2012b).

The Second Intifada (2000–2005) and the Separation Barriers (2002 to Present). The economic situation of Jerusalem's Palestinians has become much worse with the Second Intifada, as the cycle of violence escalated and Israel resorted to harsher measures and heavier limitations on movement between Jerusalem and the West Bank (Abu-Saud 2007; Ju'beh 2007). The most devastating measure was the construction of the "separation barrier" beginning in 2002. According to the Israeli government, the barrier – a system of walls and electronic fences – was supposed to defend Israeli citizens from Palestinian terrorists, but many of its parts are located well within the West Bank, separating dozens of Palestinian villages west of the barrier from the West Bank urban centers east of it, and separating other villages from their own lands. Because some Jewish settlements are located deep in the West Bank, the barrier is not a straight line which runs along the Green Line, but rather a convoluted line with many enclaves, making it (when completed) 700 kilometers long. Nowhere along its course is the barrier more meandering than in and around Jerusalem, where many Jewish neighborhoods and nearby West Bank Jewish settlements are located close to Palestinian towns and villages. The plan to include, "west" of the barriers, as many Jewish settlers as possible, and as few Palestinians as possible, has created 142 kilometers of separation walls that cut right through Palestinian neighborhoods in Jerusalem and separate the city from villages outside it (OCHA 2011).

The separation barrier severely hinders the access of Palestinians from the West Bank to Jerusalem, damaging the position of Jerusalem even more than before. The separation barrier not only separates the West Bank from Jerusalem but also separates about 80,000 permanent residents in eight Palestinian neighborhoods east of the barrier from the rest of the city, in which most of the administrative, commercial, educational, and cultural institutions are located and where most workplaces are found. The permanent residents who live east of the barrier may cross to the other side but they have to do so at checkpoints, which are few, necessitating long detours and hours spent standing in long lines. The separation barrier interferes with the lives of Palestinian Jerusalemites. It makes it harder for those on one side of the wall to go to schools – primary, secondary, and postsecondary – on the other side. Going to a doctor or a lawyer, or to city hall for a license, have become long and tedious missions. In neighborhoods that are "on the wrong side" of the wall, the city has neglected to provide services (Savitch and Garb 2006; Abu-Saud

2007; Cohen 2007; Sabella 2007; Alyan et al. 2012a, 3; Alyan et al. 2012b). Women's employment has suffered most. When working mothers have to wait several hours to cross the barrier, in addition to their regular working and transportation time, it may make employment impossible or unprofitable. If it is difficult to predict when fathers might return from work, mothers might have to stay at home. The lack of municipal services in some neighborhoods means fewer employment opportunities for women there.

The Employment of Palestinian Women in Jerusalem. There are very few exceptional studies on the socioeconomic situation of the Palestinian residents of Jerusalem. In an early study more than 20 years ago, Ashkenasi found that many college-educated Palestinian Jerusalemites were unemployed or underpaid (Ashkenasi 1992, 85–6). The more recent regime of road blocks, checkpoints, and separation barriers must have worsened economic conditions and hampered employment. A recent study found that the majority of the Palestinian population in Jerusalem is poor. Seventy-eight percent of adults and 84 percent of the children live below the Israeli poverty line; these figures are higher today than in 2006, when the respective figures were 64 and 73 percent, respectively (Alyan et al. 2012a, 1). Poverty in both years was related to high rates of unemployment among Palestinian men in Jerusalem.

How is women's employment affected by the circumstances described in the previous pages? This is an issue that has never been researched. Almost all studies conducted by Israeli sociologists have not separated Palestinian women residing in Israel proper from those who live in Jerusalem. But the Palestinian women in Jerusalem face unique conditions. Their economic, cultural, and political ties with Palestinian society in the West Bank are deeper than their ties with the Palestinian society formed in Israel after 1948. They lack citizenship status, which Palestinian women in Israel proper have – but they have, at least formally, freedom of movement and of employment in Israel that other West Bank residents lack. They are part of the largest city in Israel, which has a large concentration of government agencies, NGOs, religious institutions, and tourist attractions, but they belong to a group that has restricted access to the services and opportunities available to the Jewish residents. They live on the frontline of the Palestinian-Jewish confrontation and suffer more severely the economic consequences of this conflict. Studying the pattern of employment of Muslim women in Jerusalem would enable us to understand how women's employment is influenced by political and economic circumstances.

We start our analysis with a descriptive section on Muslim Jerusalemite women, in which we study the trends of family composition, educational attainment, labor force participation, and occupational enrollment and its correlates. As in previous chapters, we conclude with a multivariate analysis, which predicts these women's labor force participation rates. We base our analysis on both labor force surveys (1974–2009) and the censuses of 1995 and 2008 conducted by the Israeli CBS.[12] Our target population is Muslim women who reside in Jerusalem. The share of Christians in Jerusalem is very low, only around 2 percent, and insufficient for statistical analysis.

Throughout our analysis we compared our target population to two other Muslim groups: (1) Muslim women living in mixed Palestinian-Jewish cities in Israel (Haifa, Tel Aviv-Jaffa, Acre, Lydda, Ramla). As ethno-religiously heterogeneous urban communities, these five cities share this diversity with Jerusalem, and therefore we thought that comparison is appropriate; (2) The major group of Muslim women in Israel – those who live in the villages and towns of the Galilee and the Triangle. In several of the following analyses we also compared Muslim women in Jerusalem with their male counterparts in the city and with Jewish women in Israel.

Two words of caution are necessary. First, the data on Muslims in Jerusalem include all those who identified themselves as Muslim in the labor surveys and censuses, and live in Jerusalem. Among them there are less than two percent who belong to the Muslim population of Israel *within* the Green Line.[13] They are included in our analysis because we cannot identify them and exclude them, but they are too few to change our results. A second warning is that due to changing political conditions

---

[12] An additional data set available is the Palestinian Social Survey for East Jerusalem conducted in the years 2005 and 2010 by the Palestinian Central Bureau of Statistics. Since the results obtained from these surveys were very similar to the information obtained from the data provided by the Israeli CBS, and in order to facilitate the comparison with Muslim residents of large cities in Israel, we use here the Israeli data only. The similarity between the Israeli and the Palestinian data supports the reliability of both data sets.

[13] There are two groups of such people. First, those who reside (or originated in) the Israeli part of Beit Safafa, a divided village which became part of West Jerusalem after 1949, and those who have come to live in the city from Palestinian communities in Israel within the Green Line, often for reasons of employment (Manna 1997; Weingrod and Manna 1998). According to official statistics, only 2 percent of Palestinians in Jerusalem are Israeli citizens, and this number includes, in addition to the above two groups, the few Palestinians from the annexed parts of Jerusalem who applied for and got citizenship. The share of Muslims in Jerusalem who came from the Palestinian population within Israel proper is therefore even lower than two percent. Manna (1997) writes that there were about 2,000 Palestinians who moved from communities inside Israel to Jerusalem. His monograph tells of problems they encountered due to differences between them and the native Palestinian Jerusalemites in addition to the problems due to exclusion from Jewish society.

the population in Jerusalem has been unstable, as many Palestinians move away or back according to the level of violent clashes, the difficulties in crossing the checkpoints, and the degree of the threat of having one's permanent residency revoked. Some differences in various socioeconomic measures that we found while comparing various time periods may partially be explained by differences in the populations included in the study in each period.

7.2   Characteristics of Muslim Women in Jerusalem

Marital Patterns and Fertility. Jerusalemite Muslim women exhibit different family patterns than Palestinian women in Israel. They marry at a younger age – 19.8 on average (in 2007–2009), which is 1.5 year younger than Israeli Muslim women and 2.6 years younger than Muslim brides from the mixed Palestinian-Jewish cities. While the two Israeli reference groups of Muslim women began to marry at a later age mainly in the last decade (especially so in the mixed localities), this was not the experience of women from Jerusalem who have continued to marry at a young age without a significant change over the years studied (Figure 7.1).[14]

Muslim men in Jerusalem marry at a much older age than the women, so that their average age at marriage is pretty much the same as among the Muslim men in Israel. As a result, the age gap between brides and grooms is highest in Jerusalem. For example, in 2007–2009 Muslim grooms living in Jerusalem were 5.5 years older than their brides, compared with 4 years older among the major Muslim group in Israel, and 3 years older among Muslims living in the mixed cities.

Figure 7.2 presents the fertility rates of Muslim women residing in Jerusalem. The general trend is of stability in 1996–2004 (rates around 4.5) and a steady decline from 2006, reaching 3.2 in 2014, a decline of about 22 percent in the last eight years. This decline was much smaller than that observed among Muslim women in the rest of the West Bank (33 percent) and a bit larger than that among Muslim women in Israel (16 percent). Since 2008, Muslim women in Jerusalem have had higher fertility rates than even women from the generally more rural area of the West Bank. In 2014, while the fertility rate of Muslim women from

---

[14] We use here labor force surveys in which the question asked is about the age of "current marriage." In Chapter 3 we used published data from the Central Bureau of Statistics' yearbook based on the question about "age at first marriage," which was included in censuses. Due to low rates of divorce and remarriage, there is not much difference in the average of the two measures, as is evident in the young age of "current marriage" among women in Jerusalem. Yet the older average age in the five mixed cities might be due to a relatively large number of people who remarried at an older age.

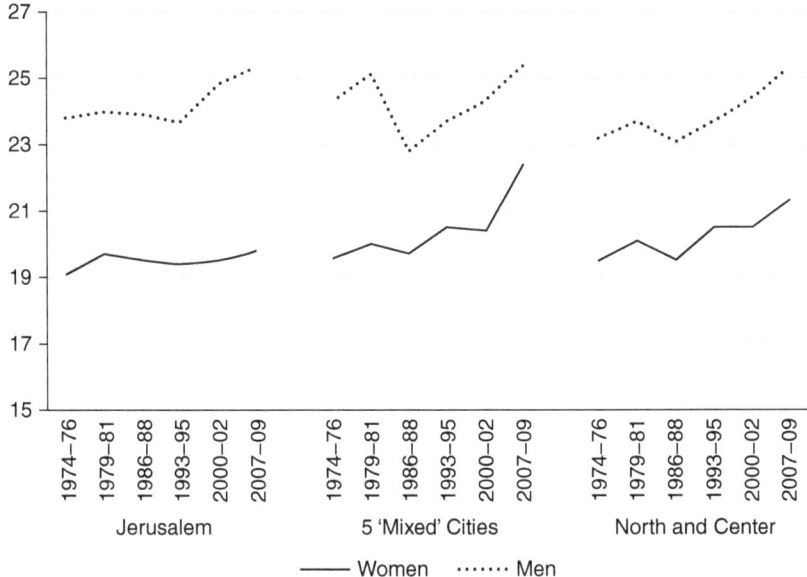

Figure 7.1 Mean Age of Current Marriage of Muslims in Jerusalem and
Selected Groups Aged 18–52 by Gender and Year
Source: Labor force Surveys 1974–2009.
Note: Only Muslims from the north, the center, and Jerusalem.

Jerusalem was on average 3.2 children per a woman, the rate for all
Muslims in Israel was 3.35 and for Palestinians in the West Bank (of
whom about 97 percent are Muslim) 2.8 (CBS 1998, 2000, 2002, 2003,
2004, 2009 2012; Index Mundi 2015)

Educational Attainment. In spite of their young age at marriage and
high fertility rates, the share of Muslim women who have attended academic institutions (including teacher colleges) was higher in all years
among Muslim women from Jerusalem than among Muslim women in
Israel including the more urban ones residing in mixed cities (Figure 7.3).
The percentage of Muslim Jerusalemite women attending tertiary level
institutions increased steadily from 7.6 percent in 1979–1981 to 28.4
percent in 2000–2002. By that time, the parallel figures between the two
Israeli groups of Muslim women did not reach 15 percent. In the recent
period (2007–2009) Jerusalemite Muslim women maintained their
advantage, but the gap between them and the Muslim women in Israel
has become much smaller as the latter have sharply increased their tertiary
education (to 23.5–26.7 percent), while it has declined among Muslim

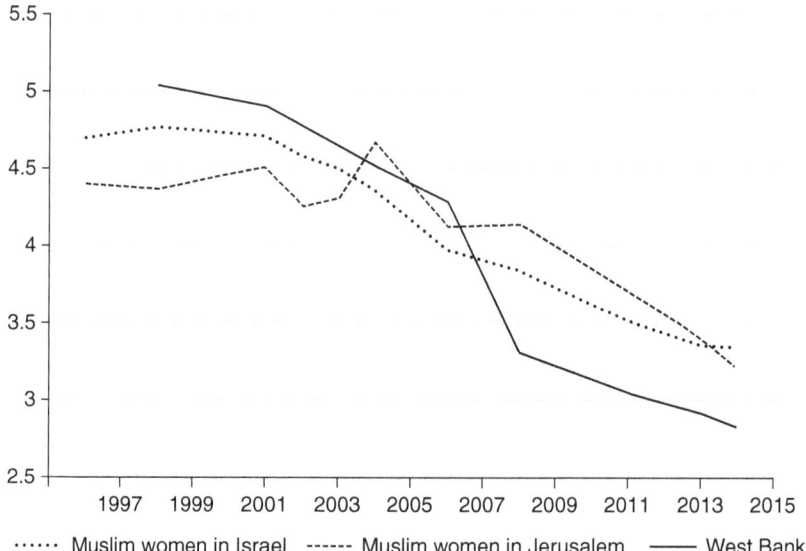

Figure 7.2 Fertility Rates of Muslim Women in Jerusalem and Selected Groups by Year
Source: CBS (1998, 2000, 2002–2005), Table 3.10; CBS (2009, 2012), Table 3.12; CBS (2016), Table 3.13; www.indexmundi.com.

women in Jerusalem. Given the continuation of expansion in tertiary education among Muslim women in Israel from about about 14 percent in 2000–2002 to more than 23 percent, the drop of 1.5 percent for Jerusalemite Muslim women indicates the possible emergence of new obstacles for tertiary education among Palestinians in Jerusalem. This is also evident in a drop in tertiary education attendance among Muslim men in Jerusalem from 28.5 to 21.9 percent in the respective years (not shown in the figure). Decreasing tertiary education rates in Jerusalem are probably related to problems in higher education during the second Intifada (2000–2005).

The share of Muslim women with at least secondary education in 1979–1981 was similar in Jerusalem and the five mixed cities and lower among other Muslim women in Israel. This share was tripled among the Muslim women in Jerusalem – from 23 percent in 1979–1981 to 67 percent in 2007–2009, and from 25 to 78 percent for Muslim women in the five mixed cities during the same timespan. The latter thus gained an advantage over the women in Jerusalem. The upswing was even more impressive for the major group of Muslim women in Israel, who started

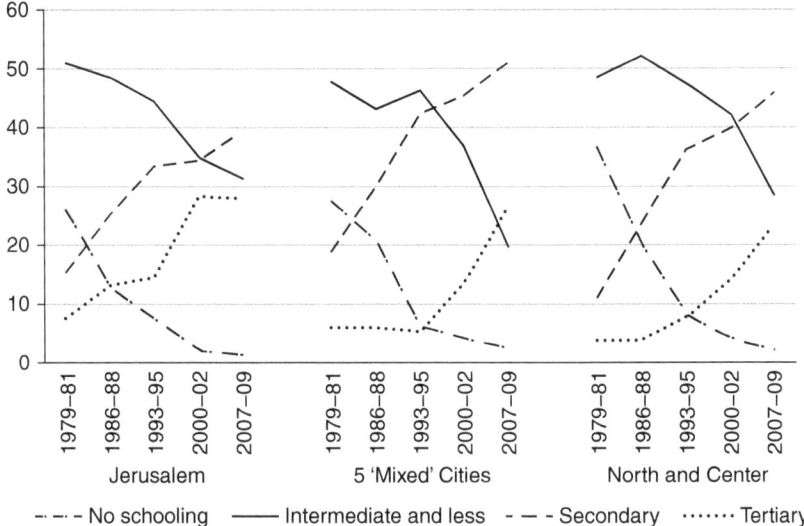

Figure 7.3 Highest School Attended of Muslims Women Aged 18–52 in Jerusalem and Selected Groups by Year
Source: Labor force Surveys 1979–2009.
Note: Only Muslims from the north, the center, and Jerusalem.

with a level of 15 percent in 1979–1981 and passed Jerusalemite women by 2 percent in 2007–2009. These trends indicate that the rise in education among Jerusalemite women has stopped.

Finally, examining the educational gender gaps between Muslim women and men in Jerusalem (figures not shown), we see that in the earlier period a high share of Muslim women, about a quarter, did not have any schooling at all, whereas for the men school attendance was nearly universal. As the school attendance of Muslim women became more common, they started to close the educational gap with their male counterparts. Looking at the percentages of men and women having at least secondary education, women almost reached parity with men in 1993–1995 (48 and 52 percent) and passed the men in the next two periods (67 and 65 percent in 2007–2009). In tertiary education, women reached parity with men in 2000–2002 (28.4 and 28.5 percent). In that period non-academic tertiary education became much more prevalent than before, and since this was true for men more than for women (9.5 and 4.3 percent, respectively; figures not shown), women achieved an advantage in the academic track (24.1 and 19.0 percent). As we said before, compared to 2000–2002 the figures for 2007–2009 are lower for both sexes in both academic and non-academic postsecondary education. The consistency of this downward pattern in Jerusalem, and the fact that it is unique to Jerusalem – among no other groups did we find declining rates of education – suggests that the exceptional political problems in the city have impeded the efforts of individual Palestinians to advance their education. The separation barrier is undoubtedly one of the biggest obstacles interrupting normal life in Jerusalem including the educational plans of Palestinian Jerusalemites.

7.3   Labor Force Participation of Muslim Women in Jerusalem

Early marriage and high fertility rates are supposed to depress the labor force participation of Muslim women in Jerusalem, but their relatively broad exposure to academic education should encourage participation. What then was their actual labor force behavior? Figure 7.4 presents the LFP

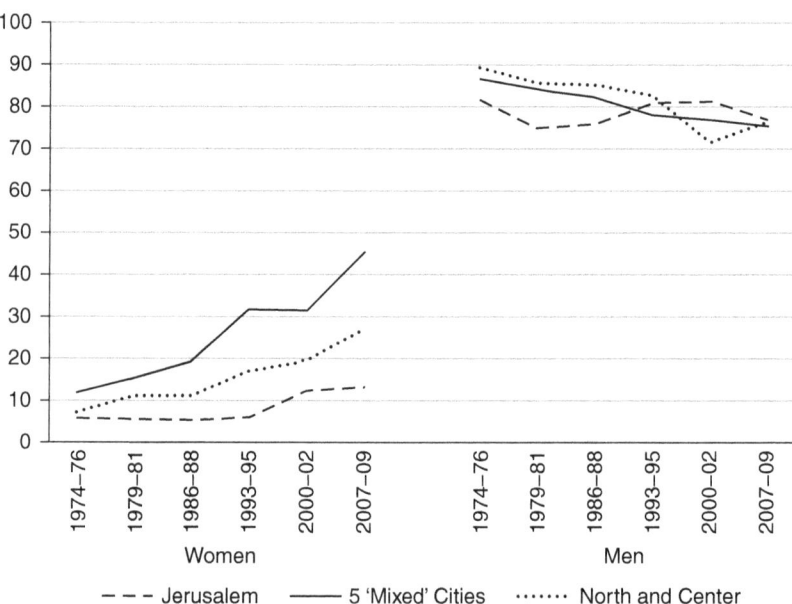

Figure 7.4 Labor Force Participation of Muslims in Jerusalem and Selected Groups Aged 18–52 by Gender and Year
Source: Labor force Surveys 1974–2009.
Note: Only Muslims from the north, the center, and Jerusalem.

rates of Muslim women residing in Jerusalem in comparison to other Israeli Muslim women. It is quite evident that the former's high educational achievements have not been sufficient to draw them into the labor market. Until 1993–1995 the percentage of employed women was small and stable (5.5–6.3 percent). It was doubled in 2000–2002 to 12.7 percent but then hardly changed by 2007–2009 (13.3 percent).

This experience of Muslim women in Jerusalem is very different from that of Muslim women in Israel within the Green Line. If we compare the Jerusalemite Muslim women to the major group of Muslim women in Israel (residing in the north and the center) we notice that they had similar rates of employment in the mid-1970s (6 and 7.5 percent, respectively), but while nothing has changed in the labor patterns of the Jerusalemites until 2000, the Muslim women in Israel have steadily raised their LFP to 27 percent, double the rate of the women in Jerusalem (in 2007–2009). The employment gaps are more striking if we compare Muslim women from Jerusalem with urban Muslim women who live, like them, in ethno-religiously heterogeneous mixed cities. Muslim women in these five cities have been much more likely to be employed than those in the rest of Israel and in Jerusalem. At the end of the period we studied, 45 percent of them were employed, 3.4 times more than among Muslim Jerusalemite women.

Muslim men residing in Jerusalem have much the same rate of employment as Israeli Muslim men, whether living in a mixed Palestinian-Jewish locality or elsewhere in the north and center. Yet unemployment rates among the Jerusalemites are relatively very high and have increased during the years. A sharp increase in their unemployment has occurred since 2000 (more than 12 percent of unemployment).[15]

Education and Employment. The relationship between education and labor force participation is presented in Figure 7.5. What we observe is quite glum even among the most educated Muslim women. In all years, Muslim women in Jerusalem with a low level of education have stayed at home and have not taken part in the labor market. At most, 2.3 percent were gainfully employed over the years. Among Muslim women with secondary education, about a tenth are employed, and this rate has not changed at all during the period studied. As we showed in Chapter 4, the majority of Muslim women without a tertiary education in Israel are not

---

[15] Unemployed workers are included in labor force participation rates reported in our analyses. We did not present unemployment data earlier because it was very low and similar in the groups we compared. In this case, however, it is very high and limited to Palestinian men only. For women, unemployment figures are almost always low – and hover between 1 to 2 percent, probably because women who do not find a job are likely to consider themselves as housewives and not as unemployed.

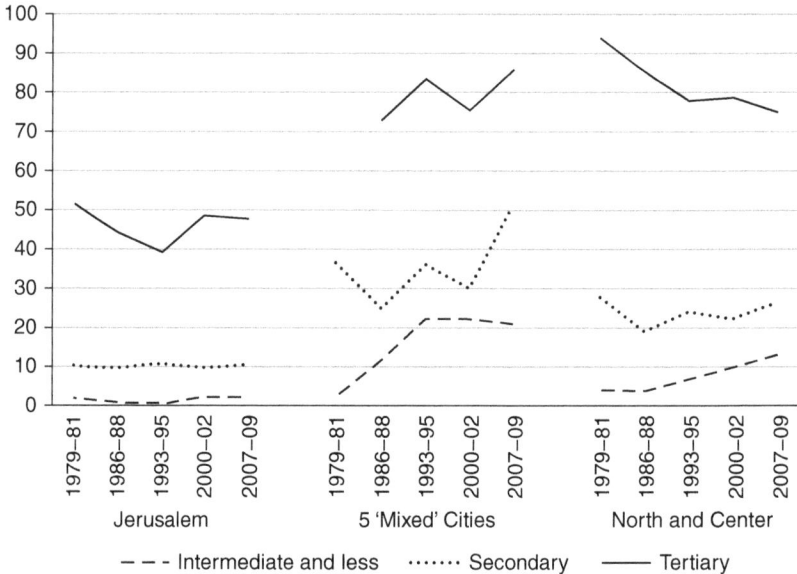

Figure 7.5 Labor force Participation of Muslim Women in Jerusalem
and Selected Groups Aged 25–52 by Education and Year
Source: Labor force Surveys 1979–2009.
Note: Only Muslims from the north, the center, and Jerusalem.

in the labor force. Nevertheless, the labor force participation rates of the
latter women are much higher than those of the Jerusalemites. Among the
population of Muslim women in Israel proper who have less than a
secondary education, 13 percent were employed in 2007–2009, and
among those with at least some high school education the rate was
double, 26 percent. Among the urban Muslim women in the five cities,
the respective shares were 21 and 51 percent.

The highest share of enrollment in the labor market of Muslim
women in Jerusalem is observed, as expected, among women with
tertiary education, but even among those highly educated women less
than 52 percent took part in the labor market. The figures have fluctuated during the years without a discernable trend, in contrast to
declining participation among highly educated Muslim women in
Israel. This decline notwithstanding, the rate of participation was
56 percent higher among Muslim women in the north and center (75
percent), and 79 percent higher among those in mixed cities
(85.5 percent).

Marital Status and Labor Force Participation. As among other groups of Muslim women, Muslim single women in Jerusalem are much more likely to be employed than married women. Until 2000–2002 the latter hardly worked outside the home, and only in the last two periods of our study we found 9–10 percent of married women in the labor force (figures not shown). While similar patterns are found among Muslim women in Israel, the odds of single to married women to be in the labor market are much lower among the Israeli Muslim women. In 2007–2009, single women in Jerusalem had 2.2 higher odds of being in the labor market compared to married women, a ratio higher than the ratio for Muslim women in Israel residing in the northern and central districts (1.40) and in the mixed cities (ratio of 1.16).

We conclude this section with a multivariate analysis to predict the labor force participation of Muslim women in Jerusalem. To this end we ran five logistic regressions, one for each of the periods studied, in which the dependent variable is whether the woman was enrolled in the labor market. The results corroborate the observations made above in the descriptive analysis (Appendix 7.1).

In sum, fewer Muslim women in Jerusalem are involved in the labor force than could be expected based on their educational achievements. The rates are also lower than one would expect from a major city like Jerusalem with its large tourist industry, numerous NGOs and religious institutions, and expanded public services (Albin 1997, 133; Margalit 2001). These lower rates might be explained by early marriage and high fertility, but we suspect that the causality may be reversed: Due to lesser employment opportunities, women may marry at a young age and have many children. Support for this might be found in the fact that upward trends were reversed in the 2000s after the second Intifada had erupted and following the construction of the separation barrier that greatly obstructed the economic, cultural, and educational activities of Palestinians. The fact that Muslim women in Israel have continued to increase their rate of entering the labor market while such progress has stalled in Jerusalem indicates that external factors are involved. The restrictions of movement and the decline of the Palestinian economy in the city seem to offer reasonable explanations for the low LFP of women. A deteriorating educational system is also a factor that may greatly affect women's involvement. The City of Jerusalem does not provide enough primary schools, and one may suspect that municipal day-care institutions are also in great shortage. For women with children this is a crucial factor that may further delay their employment. More insight might be gained by analyzing the employment patterns of those women who did join the labor market, a task we take up in the next section.

7.4   Employment Characteristics and Earnings of Muslim Women in Jerusalem

In this part of our analysis, we present the labor characteristics and the economic branch and occupational enrollment of Muslim women in Jerusalem. Because the number of gainfully employed women was low and the sample size in labor force surveys was too small to enable elaborate statistical analysis, this last section is based on the censuses conducted by the Israeli CBS in 1995 and 2008. The data show that 93 percent of the employed Muslim women in Jerusalem worked full-time in 2008. This is much more than among Muslim women in Israel, among whom almost two-fifths worked part-time, and is related to the low share of employment among Muslim women in Jerusalem. Ninety-two percent of those women worked within the city borders. The respective figure for Muslim women in the north and the center who worked in their place of residence was much smaller, 64 percent in 2007–2009. Among men the picture is similar: 80 percent of men in Jerusalem worked in the city itself, much more than the 30 percent of Muslim men in Israel who worked in the municipality they lived in. The low commuting rates of Jerusalemites are related to the fact that Jerusalem is a big city and is quite far from other major employment sources in Israel.

A relatively larger number among the Muslim women in Jerusalem as compared with Muslim women in Israel worked through contracting agencies. The figure for Jerusalem was 8 percent only, but this is twice as much as for Muslim women residing in the five mixed cities and Muslim women residing in the north and the center, about 4 percent. A similar gap is found among men: 7.5 percent of male Muslims in Jerusalem worked through a contracting agency, compared with 4 percent of Muslim men in Israel. These figures might be related to the difficulties of Palestinians in Jerusalem in finding employment. In Jerusalem the walls between Palestinians and Jews, both physical and social, are higher and less penetrable than within Israel, making it more difficult for Palestinians to find work directly in workplaces run by Jews.

The employment opportunities of Muslim Palestinian women in Jerusalem are, like those open to Bedouin women (Chapter 6), even more limited than those of the Muslim women in the center and the north who, as we saw in Chapter 5, are much more restricted than those of Jewish women. This is evident in the narrow sectorial and economic branch enrollment of Muslim women in Jerusalem (Appendix 7.2). A large majority of the women worked in the public sector, three out of four in 1995, and 81 percent in 2008. Within this sector hardly any Muslim woman (less than 2 percent) has gotten a job in public administration, a major source of employment in Jerusalem, where the Knesset, the Supreme Court, government ministries, and many state agencies are located. These institutions provided employment to more than 12 percent of Jewish women in Jerusalem, showing the employment potential of this economic branch (figure not shown in the table). Like the Muslim women in Israel, the majority of Muslim women in Jerusalem worked in 2008 in the educational services (53 percent) and health and welfare services (22 percent). But whereas these two economic branches provided work for 42 percent of employed women in the five mixed cities, and for 58 percent of those living in the north and the center, in Jerusalem these two branches accounted for 75.5 percent of women's employment. This high concentration is probably the outcome of blocked employment in other economic branches.

The concentration of Muslim women in Jerusalem in education and health services means that they are very dependent on the public sector. In Israel, in the five mixed Palestinian-Jewish cities women worked equally in both sectors (public and private), whereas among those living in Palestinian communities in the north and the center, the private sector accounted only for 36 percent, reflecting the underdeveloped economy in these communities. The share of the private sector is the lowest among Muslim women residing in Jerusalem. Merely 19 percent of them worked in the private sector in 2008. This is a surprising finding. Jerusalem used to be an economic hub of the West Bank and many businesses catered to the tourist industry. One could have expected more women to work in family businesses as saleswomen or in clerical occupations. The Palestinian economy, however, has been severely hurt by the events described above.

Whereas almost all women were employed in the public sector, 85 percent of Muslim men in Jerusalem worked in the private sector, most of them in peripheral economic branches such as personal services (e.g. retail trade, hotels, restaurants, and transportation) and in the construction sectors. Only 11 percent of the men worked in the manufacturing economic sector – a decline from 19.4 percent in 1995 – a relatively low figure compared to almost 20 percent of Muslim men residing in the five mixed cities and in the north and the center (figures not shown in the table). All the above is another indication of the economic structure of Jerusalem, where services are dominant and industry is limited.

Let us move to the occupational enrollment of Muslim women in Jerusalem. From Appendix 7.3 we learn once more of their extremely limited job enrollment as almost 70 percent of them are enrolled in merely four occupations (in the most-detailed three-digit classification). The most common occupation was schoolteacher, with a little more than

two-fifths of the women enrolled in this category in 1995, and almost half
(48.1 percent) in 2008. Many of those teachers taught in intermediate
and lower levels. In 2008, the other three occupations were as follows: 6.1
percent of the women in Jerusalem worked as secretaries, 8.6 as personal
care workers in institutions and private homes, and 6.8 percent as cleaners and kitchen helpers. Muslim women have been highly segregated
from their men counterparts: In 2008 about three out of four Muslim men
residing in Jerusalem worked as service workers or as skilled, semi-skilled,
and unskilled manual workers. Many of these workers were drivers (12.6
percent), cleaners and kitchen helpers (10.5 percent), and construction
workers (5.6 percent).

The narrow occupational range applies to Muslim women with academic degrees as well. Looking at women in the age bracket 25–52 (not
shown in the table), we observe that more than 70 percent of them were
schoolteachers (60 percent teachers in intermediate and lower levels and
10 percent in secondary schools). The remainder was distributed as
follows: 3.5 percent social workers, 4.3 percent in nursing, and almost 2
percent as pharmacists. Thirteen percent of academic women worked in
the low non-manual occupations as clerical workers.

Jerusalemite Muslim men with academic education were enrolled in a
broader spectrum of occupations than their female counterparts.
Although many were teachers (about 17 percent), many others worked
as medical doctors (6.6 percent), lawyers (4.6 percent), dentists (2 percent), and pharmacists. Nevertheless almost 40 percent of them worked
in occupations which do not fit their educational investment, including
salesmen (4.1 percent), drivers (5.7 percent), and cleaners and kitchen
workers (2.5 percent).

Earnings of Muslim Women in Jerusalem. We used the 2008 census
data to investigate the earnings of Muslim women living in Jerusalem. We
restricted our analysis to Muslim women and men enrolled in the labor
market in the age bracket 25–52. The monthly earnings of Muslim
women in Jerusalem were very similar in 2008 to those of the Muslim
women in Israel proper (not including Bedouin women from the
Southern District): about 5,100 NIS per month.[16] These earnings were
about 67 percent of what Jewish women earned (see Appendix 7.4).
Gender gaps were much lower among Muslims residing in Jerusalem

---

[16] In November 2008, the exchange rate was 3.78 shekels (NIS) per 1 American dollar. In
the examination of earnings we compared Muslim women in Jerusalem with the two
Israeli groups of Muslim women combined due to the technical necessities of the
statistical analysis.

compared to the gender earning gaps among the other Palestinians residing in Israel within the Green Line.

Earnings Attainment: A Multivariate Analysis. In this section we analyze the earnings attainment of Muslim women and men residing in Jerusalem and compare this earning attainment process to the experience of Jewish women born in Israel. We found that the above groups differed not only with respect to their earnings but also with respect to their demographic personal characteristics, human capital, and labor input. Jewish women worked more hours per week, and a higher share among them worked in the private sector, while Muslim women from Jerusalem had a higher share of workers with tertiary education, and a higher share of them were enrolled in high non-manual jobs compared to Jewish women (Appendix 7.5).

The higher monthly earnings of Muslim men residing in Jerusalem compared to Muslim women are associated with their advantage in work experience and labor input. They have accumulated about 20 years of seniority, which is about 2.7 years more than women. On average they worked 43 hours per a week, 11 hours more than their female counterparts. On the other hand, Muslim women had higher educational achievements; a higher share among them was enrolled in high non-manual jobs, and a higher share among them worked in the public sector.

We now examine the relative success with which Jerusalemite women may convert various compositional characteristics into earnings in comparison to their male counterparts and to Jewish women. This we accomplished by running separate multivariate regression equations predicting mean earnings.[17] The regression equations for the three groups are presented in Appendix 7.6.

Comparing the regression coefficients obtained for Muslim women in Jerusalem with those obtained for Jewish women reveals several significant differences. Jewish women enjoyed higher earning returns for each of the variables included in the regression. That is, each additional year of experience in the labor force is expected to raise their monthly earnings by 436 NIS, compared with 167 NIS accrued to Muslim women for each additional year of experience.

---

[17] Before conducting this analysis we tested whether the regression equations significantly differed among the three groups. We first compared the earning processes of Jerusalemite Muslim women and Jewish women by running two models. (1) We regressed the dependent variable on the independent variables and on a dummy variable representing Jewish women in Israel; and (2) we added to the above regression interaction terms between each of the independent variables and the above dummy variable. Using the F-test, we found that the interaction terms significantly increased the explained variance and concluded that the two groups of women experienced different earning attainment processes. We repeated the same procedure with Muslim women and men in Jerusalem and reached a similar conclusion that the two sexes experienced different processes.

Every added hour of work yields 182 NIS for Jewish women and merely 73 NIS for Muslim women in Jerusalem. The net earning returns to the highest educational level achieved are also greater for Jewish women, 3,474 NIS, substantially more than the 2,724 premium that Muslim women in Jerusalem can expect for their tertiary education. Jewish employed women enrolled in high non-manual occupations are expected to raise their monthly earnings by 4,642 NIS, again much more than what Muslim women in Jerusalem get (2,260 NIS). All women, Muslim and Jews, pay an earnings penalty for working in the public sector, but the Muslim women from Jerusalem pay the lowest penalty, 768 NIS, while the penalty paid by Jewish women is much higher, 2,678 NIS.

Comparison of the regression equations of Muslim women residing in Jerusalem and their male counterparts reveals that Muslim men working in high non-manual occupations are expected to raise their monthly earnings by 3,299 NIS, 1,040 NIS more than their women counterparts. While Muslim women are significantly penalized for working in the public sector (see above), Muslim men are rewarded by 560 NIS for working in that sector. Muslim women, however, get higher returns than men for the highest educational level, 2,724 and 1,451 NIS, respectively. Every added hour of work yields an expected monthly rise in earnings of 72 NIS for Muslim women and only 51 NIS for men.

Counterfactual Earnings of Muslim Women. As in Chapter 5, we posed four more questions based on the above observations: *First*, what would monthly earnings of Muslim women in Jerusalem be if they were subject to the same processes as those of Jewish women (in Israel), holding constant their personal characteristics? *Second*, what would the monthly earnings of those Muslim women be if they had possessed the same personal characteristics as Jewish women, holding constant their attainment process? The *third* and the *fourth* questions are the same as the first two questions but compare Muslim women in Jerusalem to their male counterparts in the city. The answers to these four questions would tell us about the importance of Muslim women's personal characteristics, as compared with the importance of the conversion rates of these characteristics to generating Muslim women's lower earnings.

If Muslim women in Jerusalem had the same conversion rates as Jewish women, their monthly earnings would be much higher (NIS 6248), narrowing the gaps between them and Jewish women by 43 percent. Had Muslim women in Jerusalem possessed the same resources as Jewish women, holding constant their conversion rates, they would earn slightly less (NIS 213) than what they actually earned. This is related to the fact that in Jerusalem it is mostly the highly educated Muslim women who have the opportunity to work, whereas among Jews, almost all women have the chance to enter the labor market.

As we did when we analyzed earning gaps among Muslim women and men in the north and center, we replicated the above analysis in regard to the gender gaps among Muslims in Jerusalem. Had Muslim women kept their own characteristics but been subject to the same conversion rates as Muslim men, the gender gaps would be reversed and women would get NIS 7,029, almost 20 percent more than men. Had Muslim women in Jerusalem been similar to Muslim men in their education, occupational enrollment, and other compositional characteristics, holding constant their conversion rates, their earnings would be much lower (NIS 3,893), more than doubling the earning gender gap among Jerusalemite Muslims.

Thus we see that Muslim women residing in Jerusalem are economically discriminated against in the labor market not only relative to Jewish women but compared to their male counterparts as well, as their success in converting their various compositional characteristics into earnings is inferior to that of the other two groups.

7.5   Summary

In Chapters 4 and 5, we saw that Muslim women in Israel are highly disadvantaged with respect to labor force participation and labor force achievements. In the previous chapter we encountered a specific group of Muslim women, the Bedouin women in the south, who were much more disadvantaged than the mainstream Muslim society in Israel. We attributed their worse conditions, *inter alia*, to their geographical isolation and distance from Jewish communities and economic centers, to their constant struggle against the government, and to their neglect by the state, especially in communities that are not even recognized by the government as legitimate communities.

Jerusalem's Muslim women seem to be subject to opposite forces: They live in the largest city in Israel, in a center of government, tourism, and religions, and at a point of encounter between the West Bank and Israel, and between the south and the north of the West Bank. Jerusalem has a glorious past not only in ancient times but also in modern times with Ottoman renovations in the nineteenth century and British prosperity in the twentieth. The division of the city in 1948 placed it under the shadow of Amman and Tel Aviv, but it continued to be a central city both in Jordan and in Israel. The unification and enlargement of the city after 1967 invigorated it economically. Israel poured huge budgets into developing the city and turned it into a busy metropolitan center. One could expect that with so much activity, the employment rates of Muslim women would be higher than in less developed urban communities.

Yet this is not the case. In spite of the seemingly favorable conditions in Jerusalem, the employment rates of Muslim women have been very low even compared to the low labor force participation rates of Muslim women elsewhere in Israel. This is especially evident when we look at LFP rates of women with higher education: About half of them do not participate in the labor market. We believe that the special circumstances under which Palestinians in Jerusalem live account for the reduced labor market participation of women. Three major factors were mentioned in the first part of this chapter and we discuss them briefly again here.

The first factor is the weak position of Palestinians in the municipality of Jerusalem. Being run by Palestinians and catering to Arabic speakers, local authorities in Palestinian communities in Israel (within the 1949 borders) employ many male and female Palestinians including many women in professional well-paying positions. In the five mixed cities in Israel, the majority of the population and the powerful local politicians are Jewish, but Palestinians take part in the local politics and may gain some power which may be translated into positions in the municipality and into more services for the Palestinian population. In Jerusalem the story is different. Although numerically Palestinians are a stronger minority in Jerusalem than in any of the five other ethno-religiously heterogeneous cities, politically they have less power because they do not take part in municipal elections. As a result the services provided for the Palestinians are much fewer and smaller, and even the school system provides less employment due to overcrowded classes and to the too high school dropout rate. Palestinians in Jerusalem have less political clout for securing employment within the municipality, and thus what should have been a major potential source of employment provides relatively much fewer positions to Muslim women as compared to other municipalities in which they live in Israel.

The second major factor is the neglect of Palestinians by the state, given its focus on encouraging Jews to settle in Jerusalem. Israel has used its augmented power and resources to enlarge and advance the Jewish population of Jerusalem, and rather than sharing the fruits of development with Palestinians, has tried to limit their number, implicitly encouraging them to leave and slowing their economic development. In Jerusalem Palestinians are also less likely to find employment in state bureaucracies, a major employment option for Jewish women and men.

The third factor is that being on the front line of the Israeli-Palestinian conflict has hurt the Palestinians in Jerusalem even further. The construction of the separation wall was a major blow, the ramifications of which are still well felt throughout all the Palestinian neighborhoods of Jerusalem. Arab Jerusalem used to be an economic hub where West Bank merchants, politicians, artists, and activists met. The city provided various services to the whole West Bank and was a place where dozens of NGOs operated. Since the first Intifada, movement into Jerusalem from the West Bank has become more difficult, and hardships have increased even at the time of the Oslo Accords, as well as later during the second Intifada. The separation barrier has cut off several neighborhoods of Jerusalem from the rest of the city, making the search for jobs more difficult. The impact of these restrictions is evident in the stagnation and decline in educational achievements and employment. These negative trends indicate that structural conditions are at fault. Other indications are the very narrow occupational and economic enrollment of those Jerusalem Muslim women who have entered the labor market. Muslim women are blocked in many occupations. The very low earnings and the disadvantage in converting their personal resources into earnings might be considered as further structural impediments that keep women away from employment.

Thus in spite of the central location of Jerusalem – economically, politically, and religiously – Muslim women in Jerusalem share a similar vulnerability with the isolated Bedouin women of the south. Both groups have to wage a tough struggle to defend what they have. Whereas the Bedouins in the south lag behind other Palestinians in their educational achievements, the Palestinians in Jerusalem are educated but do not have the certificates required by the Israeli labor market. While the Bedouins live in isolated distant communities, in Jerusalem isolation and distance were artificially created. Neighborhoods that used to be a few minutes away from each other are now separated by walls, and towns that were close suburbs of Jerusalem are now practically disconnected.

Appendix 7.1 *Logistic Coefficients and Standard Errors (in parentheses) Predicting LFP of Muslim Women Aged 18–52 in Jerusalem by Year*

	1979–1981		1986–1988		1993–1995		2000–2002		2007–2009	
	B/S.E.	Exp. (B)	B/S.E.	Exp. (B)	B/S.E.	Exp. (B)	B/S.E.	Exp. (B)	B/S.E.	Exp. (B)
Secondary education	0.894*	2.444	2.184*	8.880	1.428*	4.169	1.313*	3.718	0.546*	1.727
	(0.476)		(0.534)		(0.351)		(0.307)		(0.272)	
Tertiary education	3.442*	31.234	3.992*	54.138	2.768*	15.926	2.996*	20.011	2.567*	13.033
	(0.440)		(0.537)		(0.371)		(0.285)		(0.249)	
Single	−0.001	0.999	1.753*	5.774	0.636*	1.889	0.224	1.252	0.394	1.482
	(0.416)		(0.553)		(0.320)		(0.246)		(0.260)	
Number of Children (under 15)	−0.550*	0.577	−0.444*	0.641	−0.714*	0.489	−0.526*	0.591	−0.447*	0.639
	(0.120)		(0.194)		(0.136)		(0.083)		(0.086)	
Age 18–24	−0.497	0.608	−1.670*	0.188	−1.854*	0.157	−1.969*	0.140	−2.417*	0.089
	(0.690)		(0.772)		(0.422)		(0.371)		(0.384)	
Age 25–31	0.863	2.369	0.504	1.655	−0.208	0.812	−0.396	0.673	0.038	1.038
	(0.675)		(0.777)		(0.406)		(0.352)		(0.320)	
Age 32–38	1.456*	4.288	1.775	5.901	0.727	2.068	0.341	1.407	0.619	1.858
	(0.703)		(0.834)		(0.431)		(0.372)		(0.333)	
Age 39–45	−16.889	0.000	2.180*	8.847	−0.054	0.948	0.450	1.568	−0.085	0.919
	(2519.47)		(0.805)		(0.516)		(0.361)		(0.346)	
Constant	−3.061		−5.546		−2.965		−2.606		−2.409	
−2Log likelihood	258.9		308.3		522.9		866.7		964.0	
N	1,308		1,165		1,546		1,611		1,740	
Nagelkerke R²	0.425		0.475		0.321		0.371		0.375	

Variables: The dependent variable is labor force participation, coded 1 if the woman belongs to the labor force, and 0 otherwise; the independent variables are: education (distinguishing between intermediary and less (the omitted group), secondary, and tertiary education), marital status (single women were coded 1, 0 otherwise), number of children under 15, and women's age group (the omitted group 46–52).

Source: Labor Force surveys 1979–2009.

*: p <0.05

Note: Only Muslim women in Jerusalem.

Appendix 7.2 *Economic Branch Distribution of Muslims in Jerusalem and Selected Groups Aged 18–52 by Gender and Year*

	Women				Men	
	Jerusalem		5 Mixed Cities	North & Center	Jerusalem	
	1995	2008	2008	2008	1995	2008
Agriculture	0.2	0.0	0.0	1.8	1.2	0.9
Manufacturing	5.7	2.4	5.7	5.5	19.4	11.1
Construction	2.4	0.0	0.0	0.8	20.3	16.3
Peripheral services	10.3	8.9	30.7	17.0	38.5	48.6
Wholesale and retail trade, repair of vehicles and personal and household goods	(5.5)	(3.6)	(18.8)	(11.1)	(18.5)	(22.5)
Accommodation services and restaurants	(3.1)	(1.6)	(6.1)	(2.3)	(11.4)	(12.4)
Transport, storage and communication	(1.7)	(1.4)	(2.9)	(1.9)	(8.6)	(13.4)
Core services	4.4	7.7	15.2	9.3	4.3	7.8
Total Private sector	24.3	19.0	51.6	36.4	83.7	84.7
Public Sector	75.7	81.0	48.4	63.6	16.3	15.3
Public administration services	(2.0)	(1.7)	(2.0)	(4.2)	(1.0)	(1.4)
Educational services	(46.9)	(53.1)	(23.7)	(42.6)	(5.1)	(4.3)
Health services; welfare and social work services	(22.4)	(22.4)	(17.9)	(15.5)	(4.9)	(5.2)
Total	100.0	(00.0	100.0	100.0	100.0	100.0
N	544	1025	755	4,990	4,592	5,928

Source: 1995 and 2008 Censuses.
Note: Only Muslims from the north, the center, and Jerusalem.

Appendix 7.3 *Occupational Distribution of Muslims in Jerusalem Aged 18–52 by Gender and Year*

	Women		Men	
	1995	2008	1995	2008
Academic professionals	6.0	5.3	3.5	4.2
Associate professionals and technicians	50.8	53.7	6.0	4.7
Teachers in secondary and post-secondary school	(13.7)	(5.6)	(1.5)	(0.5)
Teachers in primary school	(27.5)	(42.5)	(1.7)	(2.2)
Nurses	(5.1)	(0.0)	(0.5)	(0.0)
Managers	1.1	1.4	0.9	2.1
Clericals and salespeople	18.6	15.5	13.4	14.3
Secretary	(8.1)	(6.1)	(0.2)	(0.1)
Saleswomen	(2.5)	(1.4)	(7.5)	(7.2)
Service workers	7.2	13.6	5.8	7.5
Institution and home-based personal care workers	(2.8)	(8.6)	(0.2)	(0.8)
Agriculture workers	0.0	0.0	0.0	0.0
Skilled workers	7.0	1.1	45.8	45.0
Electrical machines and fitters	(0.4)	(0.1)	(2.6)	(3.0)
Builders	(0.0)	(0.0)	(1.7)	(5.6)
Cab drivers	(0.0)	(0.0)	(2.3)	(3.7)
Truck and semi-trailer drivers	(0.0)	(0.0)	(1.6)	(4.6)
Other drivers	(0.1)	(0.1)	(5.3)	(4.3)
Unskilled workers	9.3	9.4	24.7	22.2
Kitchen workers and cleaners	(6.0)	(6.8)	(7.5)	(10.5)
Unskilled construction workers	(0.9)	(0.0)	(6.6)	(1.1)
Total	100.0	100.0	100	100
N	531	1,036	4,529	5,845

Source: 1995 and 2008 Censuses.
Note: Only Muslim women from Jerusalem; Occupations with at least 3 percent Muslim men or women in them for at least one year.

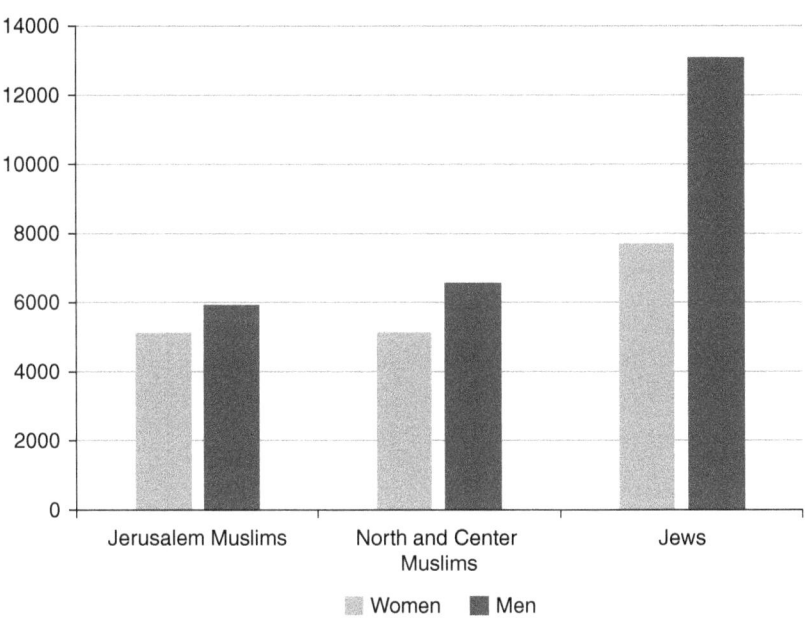

Women ▒ Men ■

Appendix 7.4 Mean Gross Monthly Earnings in NIS of Muslim Workers Aged 25–52 in Jerusalem and Selected Groups by Gender, 2008
Source: 2008 Census.
Note: Only Muslims from the north, the center, and Jerusalem.

Appendix 7.5 *Mean and Standard Deviation (in parentheses) for Selected Variables of Muslim Workers and Jewish Women Aged 25–52 in Jerusalem by Gender, 2008*

	Muslims in Jerusalem		Jews in Israel
	Women	Men	Women
Married	64.70	88.57	72.92
Education:			
Intermediate or less	16.48	52.66	4.04
Secondary	12.92	24.78	38.04
Tertiary	70.60	22.56	57.56
Experience	16.94	19.64	17.07
	(8.46)	(8.30)	(8.43)
Experience squared	358.75	454.84	362.85
	(321.62)	(357.48)	(320.78)
Hours worked	32.37	43.36	36.59
	(9.59)	(9.83)	(11.52)
Occupational affiliation:			
High non-manual	62.98	12.76	45.69
Low non-manual	26.69	19.9	49.32
Skilled workers	10.33	67.2	4.99
Public sector	81.92	18.05	49.89
N	813	3,551	69,741

Source: 2008 Census.
Note: Only Muslims in Jerusalem and all Jewish women born in Israel.

Appendix 7.6 *Regression Coefficients and Standard Errors (in parentheses) Predicting Gross Monthly Earnings for Muslim Workers in Jerusalem and Jewish Women Aged 25–52 by Gender, 2008*

	Muslims in Jerusalem		Jews in Israel
	Women	Men	Women
Single	−294.9	−634.3*	−620.0*
	(220.0)	(232.4)	(49.0)
Secondary education	854.8*	520.7*	413.9*
	(408.1)	(169.5)	(108.0)
Tertiary education	2724.4*	1451.2*	3474.1*
	(300.9)	(220.8)	(100.9)
Experience	166.9*	171.4*	436.3*
	(50.6)	(38.8)	(11.5)
Experience squared	−1.513	−2.817*	−7.119*
	(1.337)	(0.872)	(0.303)
High non-manual occupations	2259.1*	3298.9*	4642.6*
	(508.1)	(267.1)	(108.2)
Low non-manual occupations	704.3	340.6*	1714.7*
	(428.9)	(170.0)	(100.6)
Public sector	−768.2*	560.1*	−2678.2*
	(310.8)	(193.0)	(46.6)
Hours worked	72.8*	51.2*	182.3*
	(11.00)	(3.955)	(1.90)
Constant	−2718.2	−18.575*	−7970.8
R^2	0.266	0.131	0.296

Variables: The dependent variable is gross monthly earnings, measured in Israeli new shekels (NIS); the independent variables are: education (distinguishing between intermediary and lower (the reference group), secondary, and tertiary work experience (age minus years of schooling minus five) and its square, occupational allocation (distinguishing between high non-manual, low non-manual, and manual workers (the reference group)), employment sector (coded 1 if public and 0 if private), hours worked, and marital status (coded 1 if single, 0 if ever-married).
Source: 2008 Census.
*: $p < 0.05$
Note: Only Muslims in Jerusalem and all Jewish women born in Israel.

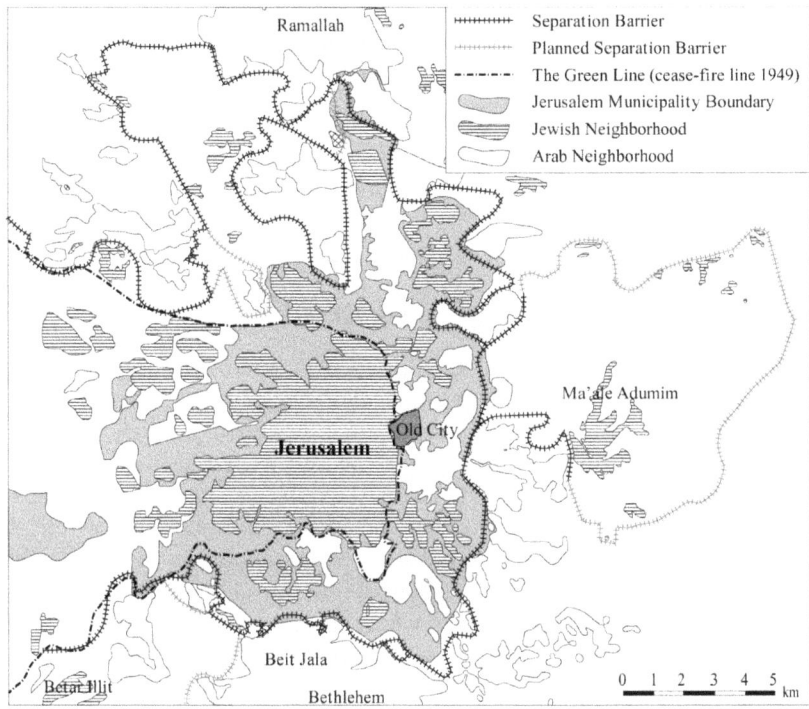

Jerusalem and Its Surroundings
Source: Created by Noga Yoselevich, Department of Geography and
Environmental Studies, University of Haifa

8   The "Favorite Minority"?
Druze Women in the Labor Market

8.1   Historical, Political, and Social Background

In this chapter we turn to another group of women who are Arab and Palestinian, although in Israeli discourse their status as such is questioned or denied: Druze women. The Druze[1] are members of a religious group which emerged in Egypt in the eleventh century as an offshoot of Islam, and although today it is widely considered to be a separate religion, some still consider it an Islamic sect. This movement had many followers all over the Middle East, but due to fierce persecutions against them the only communities that have endured were in the Aleppo area, in the Damascus area, and in Mount Lebanon, from where they expanded to the northern parts of Palestine (today Israel and Jordan) in the seventeenth century (Firro 1992; Parsons 2000).

Our decision to refer to this group as Arab and Palestinian was not a simple matter. As Arabic-speakers, there should be no question as to their ethnic identity as Arabs; and as members of an indigenous group that has lived in Palestine/Israel for centuries before the Zionist settlement, there should be no problem in calling them Palestinians. Nevertheless, the identity of this group is controversial among its members, as well as in the eyes of the other ethno-religious groups in Israel. Following we explain how this situation developed, but we must emphasize at the outset that we are not party to this controversy. We treat this group as Arab and as Palestinian based on their language and location.[2]

In the last centuries, relationships between the Druze and the Christians and Muslims in the Greater Syria area have varied depending, *inter alia*, on ties of the various groups with the Ottomans as well as on European interventions and on the politics of national emergence (Firro

---

[1] Some writers use "Druzes" in plural (e.g. Firro 1999), but in most texts "Druze" is both singular and plural.
[2] Many Israelis, including many Druze, would consider our decision wrong, but an alternative distinguishing the Druze from the Palestinians would alienate others of those involved. See Hassan 1992.

178

1999; Parsons 2000). In Syria and Lebanon, most Druze participated in the national movements while competing Druze factions in Mandatory Palestine chose conflicting directions: Some chose to take part in the Palestinian national movement and others preferred Druze particularism – the idea that Druze ethnicity and identity make them distinct from other Arabs. This conflict was part of a power struggle among Druze leaders over control of the Druze community. Zionist leaders allied with those Druze who favored particularism.[3] When the Israeli state was established in 1948, the internal struggle among Druze factions continued, but now the state could use its resources to strengthen those Druze who did not see themselves as part of the Palestinian nation (see Chapter 2). As Firro notes, "the [state's] policy aimed at weaning [the Druze] away from the larger Palestinian Arab community by fostering 'Druze particularism'" (Firro 2001, 41; cf. Frisch 1993; Gelber 1995; Hajjar 1996; Parsons 2000). The state recognized the Druze as belonging to a separate "nationality" and since the mid 1950s identified them in this way on their Israeli identity cards and in the official Population Registry. As in the case of other religions under the state, Druze religious institutions were given the authority to administer marriage, divorce, and burial, thus enhancing the power of the religious leadership within the Druze community.[4]

Among the Palestinian groups in Israel, the Druze have been singled out as "the most loyal group" and, as such, have been granted special treatment by the state (Karayanni 2007, 364). Two major institutional measures have solidified the exceptional status of the Druze – the separation of schools, and the military draft. First, as explained in Chapter 3, a special educational subsystem was created especially for them with separate curricula that emphasize Druze heritage and play down their ties to Muslims. Thus while Muslims and Christians in Israel share the same school system, the relatively small Druze group has its own system (Kanaaneh, 2002, 140–141).[5] Perhaps the second measure has been more consequential: the military draft. Other Palestinians are exempted from mandatory service in the Israeli army, although some may ask to be recruited. In contrast, in1956 Israeli government officials and Druze

---

[3] See Gelber 1995, Parsons 2000, and Zeedan 2015 on the developing relations between Jewish officials and Druze local leaders during the Mandatory period and on their negotiations during the 1948 war.
[4] According to Gelber (1995, 242–243), although the Druze were subject to the same military government of the occupied Palestinian communities as other Palestinians, they got some privileges due to their cooperation with Jewish forces. They were allowed to keep their arms and were allowed to establish their own courts soon after the Galilee was conquered by Israel in the summer of 1948.
[5] In Palestinian communities in which Druze live with Christians and Muslims, this separation of the educational systems weakens the integration of the community (Badran 2012).

leaders agreed upon mandatory conscription of all Druze men except for those who were initiated into the religious scripts and principles (Hassan 1992; Frisch 1993; Hajjar 1996; Firro 2001; Hassan 2001; Kanaaneh 2009; Zeedan 2015).[6] Unlike Jewish women, Druze women have not been required to join the army, and cannot be recruited even if they want to (Hajjar 1996). The military is a central institution in Israeli society, and service in it carries practical and symbolic benefits. Military service provides occupational training in many fields and enables Druze men to enter the social networks of Jews, a practice that may help them find jobs. Many employers view military service as a sign of general aptitude and may prefer Druze who served in the army over other Israeli Palestinians who have not. Military service also opens the way to careers in related occupations and branches such as security, police, and corrections (Hassan 1992; Firro 2001, 48; Hassan 2001; Kanaaneh 2009). Another advantage of military service is the economic benefits that veterans get. Such benefits often provide young people with start-up funding for academic studies or for opening a small business of their own.

Serving in the army, however, has more than just economic implications. By serving in the army Druze men join the Jewish populace in its prolonged and deep conflict with the Palestinians in the Occupied Territories, and with other Arab nations. Druze soldiers, who are often put at the front of the conflict, are viewed as betraying their Arab heritage not only by the Palestinians in the Occupied Territories but also by Palestinian citizens in Israel who are their neighbors in many communities in the Galilee. By serving in the army Druze men might also be influenced by the values, aspirations, and attitudes of their Jewish comrades in arms. Such service may thus facilitate ties between Druze and Jews. Many Jewish and Druze leaders refer to the military service of the Druze as the "blood pact" between the two ethno-religious groups, and Druze leaders try to cash in on such rhetoric to elicit more funding and state projects for their communities. Many of these communities were added to the state's list of preferred "development areas" qualified for increased state assistance for industrial development. Yet due to their limited

---

[6] The Druze scripts and doctrines are taught only to those who declare, when reaching maturity, that they are willing to live properly according to the rules of the Druze faith. They are called *uqqal* ("the wise ones," "the initiated"), which is often translated as "religious," creating a false impression that those who do not take such a step are not religious. Those others, the *juhhal* ("the ignorant," "the uninitiated"), are not initiated to the Druze doctrine and they are less strict in their ways of life, but they are not necessarily "unreligious" (Firro 1999, 14–15).

political power, Druze communities receive far less support than the Jewish communities (Hajjar 1996, 4; cf. Hassan 1992, 2001).

Over all, the emphasis on the Jewish character of the state has kept the Druze as outsiders who in spite of their contribution to the Jewish cause have not been fully admitted to the Israeli collective (Yiftachel and Segal 1998). Their similarity in appearance, language, and life-style to other Palestinians brings many Jews to discriminate against them as with other Palestinians. Distinguishing the Druze from other Palestinians fails when these groups live together. More than a tenth of the Druze live as a minority in the same municipalities as Muslim and Christian Palestinians and suffer like their neighbors from the pro-Jewish bias of state policies, including confiscation of land (Yiftachel and Segal 1998; Firro 1999).[7] In localities in which Druze are the majority, they have also suffered from land confiscation as much as the other Palestinian communities in Israel, because the establishment of new Jewish settlements has always been the primary state interest.

The Druze' efforts to maintain their separate identity bears upon gender relations within the community because of their perception of traditional norms as part of the Druze special "way of life" (Firro 1999; Hassan 2001; Weiner-Levy 2006, 2009, 2011; Brek 2011).[8] A conspic-uous example has to do with marriage: Druze are religiously allowed to marry only people born as Druze. Interfaith marriage is uncommon in Israel in general, but non-Druze may marry converts from other religions. Druze may not, since there is no conversion to the Druze faith. Marrying an outsider brings about expulsion from the community. With every change feared as a step toward assimilation, demands to change the status of women might be thought to threaten the group's identity. At the same time, military service exposes young Druze men to the dominant Jewish culture, an experience that might affect the attitudes and views of the Druze.

In this chapter, we inspect how the patterns of Druze life as well as the special relations with the Jewish state shape the employment patterns of Druze women. We compare Druze women with Muslim women on the basis of the labor force surveys that we used in previous chapters as well.

---

[7] This figure is based on our calculation from data on all 17 communities in which the Druze live in Israel.

[8] It should be emphasized that we are not proposing a cultural explanation. On the contrary, the emphasis on tradition is part of the political choice of certain Druze leaders to separate the Druze in Israel from other Palestinians and to align themselves with the Israeli state (Hajjar 1996; Hassan 2001). The way the Druze in the Golan Heights express their ethnic affiliation is very different (see Hajjar 1996, 5; 2001, fn33, 326).

To rule out the possibility that differences between Druze and Muslim women are due to different economic opportunities, we compare Druze women only to the Muslim women who live in the same area as they do. The Druze population, which numbered 110,300 in 2013 (CBS 2015, Tables 2.2 and 2.15),[9] resides in 17 communities: Most of them (11) are populated almost exclusively (95–100 percent) by Druze; in three localities, they constitute a large majority (58–77 percent), and in three other municipalities, they are a sizable minority (14–31 percent) living side by side with Muslims and Christian Palestinians but not with Jews. All the Druze communities are in the north, but they are concentrated in three subdistricts, Acre and Kinneret in the Northern District, and the Haifa subdistrict of the Haifa District. The first two subdistricts are far from the economic center of Israel and are relatively poor. The socioeconomic ranking of the Druze municipalities by the CBS is 3 or 4 (on a scale of 1 to 10, where 1 is the lowest), similar to the ranking of other Palestinian communities and lower than the ranking of most Jewish ones.[10]

Before embarking on our empirical analysis, let us recall some basic information on the education and family patterns of Druze women which we presented in Chapter 3. Although Druze women have experienced a large increase in their educational attainments, their achievements are still relatively low. In 2007–2009, only 71 percent attended at least secondary education, a rate much lower than among Jewish and Christian women, and slightly lower than among Muslim women (Figure 3.2b). In the same period, a fifth of Druze women (19.7 percent) attended academic education. This is similar to the share of Muslim women (20.3 percent), but much lower than the share of Christian women and Jewish women (Figure 3.2c). Druze women have also experienced major changes in their family composition. Their average age at first marriage increased from 19 in 1970 to 22.9 in 2014 (CSB 2016, Table 3.6), and a rising share of them remained single (Table 3.1). Most consequentially, Druze women have experienced a striking decline in fertility rates from an average 7.25 births per a woman in 1970–1974 to 2.2 births in 2014 (Figure 3.4).

8.2   Labor Force Participation and Its Determinants

We start with a description of the trends of Druze women's labor force participation within age groups and across years, and then analyze the

---

[9] Not including the Druze in the Golan Heights, who are included in Israeli official statistics but are Syrian citizens according to international law and their own identification (Mara'i and Halabi 1992; Sheleff 1994; Maoz 1994).

[10] The index is composed of 16 separate indicators that can be grouped into four dimensions: demography, standard of living, education, and employment.

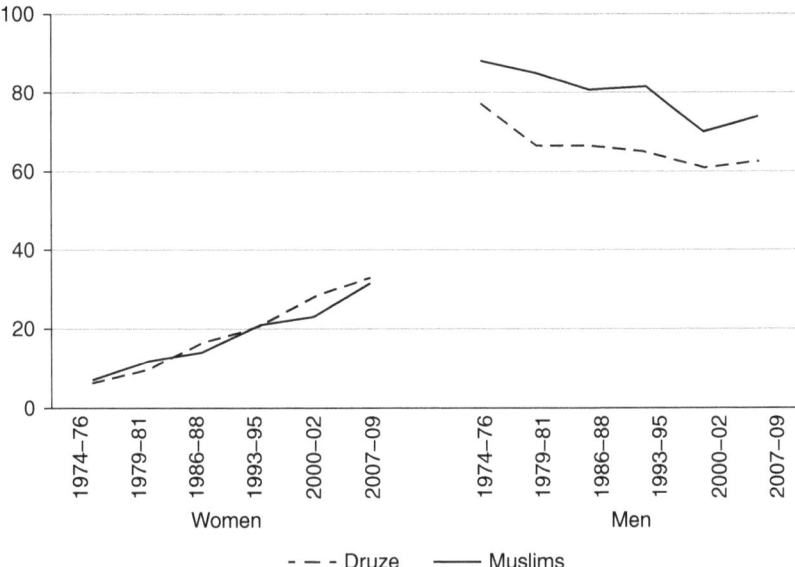

Figure 8.1 Labor Force Participation of Druze and Muslims Aged
18–52 by Gender and Year
Source: Labor Force Surveys 1974–2009.
Note: Only Druze (excluding the Golan Heights) and Muslims residing
in the subdistricts where the Druze live.

determinants of this LFP. We follow in Section 8.3 with an examination
of part-time versus full-time employment and an analysis of the variables
that affect these types of employment. Next, we consider commuting
patterns as well as the industrial and occupational enrollment of Druze
women. Lastly, we analyze Druze women's earnings attainments.

Druze women have substantially increased their labor force participation from 5.1 percent in 1974–1976 to almost 33 percent in 2007–2009.
This is more than the rate of Muslim women reported in previous chapters but similar to that of Muslim women living in the same subdistricts as
the Druze (31.4 percent; Figure 8.1).

Unlike women's increasing LFP, Druze men's labor participation
rates have sharply declined during the same time. In the mid-1970s
almost 80 percent of Druze men were employed, while in 2007–2009
merely 64 percent of them were enrolled in the labor market, a rate
much lower than that of Muslim men residing in the same subdistricts.
A part of this decline might be related to Druze men's slight increased

enrollment in mandatory and career military service. In 1995–2001, almost 29 percent of Druze men were enrolled in the military; in 2002–2009, this share increased to 33 percent.[11]

Examining labor force participation and age, we see that Druze women within the two older age groups have monotonically increased their rate in the labor market. Women aged 25–38 increased their rate from a very low level (2.2 percent) to almost 40 percent in 2007–2009, and women aged 39–52 increased it from almost nil to 28.6 percent. Among the youngest women (aged 18–24), rates also increased (from 12.7 to almost 35 percent in 2000–2002) but dropped to 28 percent during the last period under study. One reason for this decline could be that these women increasingly attended tertiary education, which delays their entrance into the labor market. Until the early 1990s women in the youngest age group had the highest share in the labor market, but in 2007–2009 women aged 25–38 surpassed the younger age group (results not presented). This trend is typical in modernizing societies when women invest in postsecondary education and then join the labor force in large numbers. In what follows, we analyze the relationship between labor force participation and various personal demographic characteristics of Druze women, beginning with education.

Excluding the youngest women (aged 18–24), many of whom are still engaged in academic studies, Figure 8.2 shows the LFP rates of Druze women with different levels of education. As expected, the higher the level of education, the higher the labor force participation. As among other Palestinian groups – women who have attended tertiary education are much more likely to be employed than women with a lower level of education. In 2000–2002 as many as 86 percent of Druze women with at least some tertiary education were enrolled in the labor market, and although this share declined to 78 percent in 2007–2009, it is still at a very high level. The LFP of Druze women with at least some secondary education was much lower in all periods: About 20 percent until 2000–2002, but increasing to almost a third in the last period under study. The LFP of Druze women without secondary education has been very low,

---

[11] Until 2011, the Israeli Central Bureau of Statistics' definition of (civilian) labor force participation did not include in the labor force individuals enrolled in the Israeli army either as drafted or career soldiers. The CBS asked those individuals who did not participate in the civilian labor force why they were not employed, and one of the answers individuals might have chosen is "military service." The age distribution in military service among Druze men in the years 2002–2009 was 33 percent in the ages 18–24 (this age group includes men doing mandatory service); 10.9 in the ages 25–31; 8.9 in the ages 32–38; and 5.2 percent in the ages 39–44. After the age of 45 hardly any Druze man is enrolled in military service.

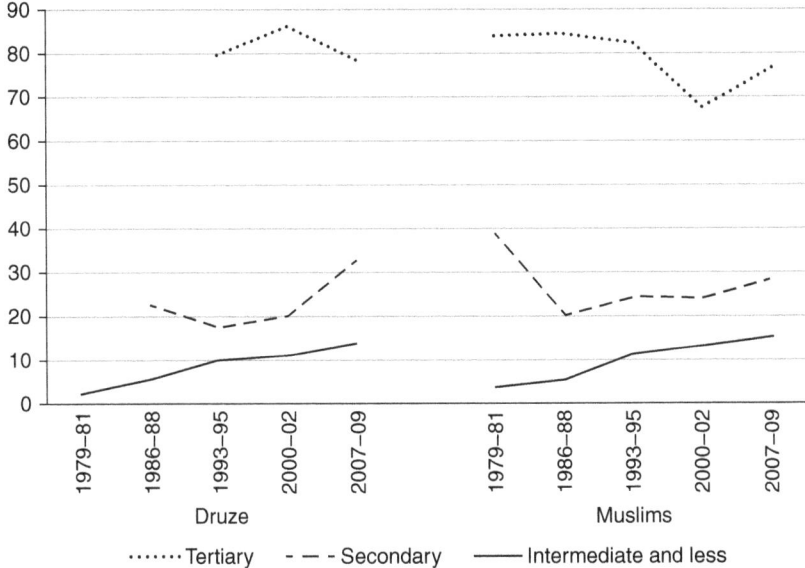

Figure 8.2 Labor Force Participation of Druze and Muslim Women
Aged 25–52 by Education and Year
Source: Labor Force Surveys 1979–2009.
Note: Only Druze (excluding the Golan Heights) and Muslims residing
in the subdistricts where the Druze live.

but rose to a significant level of 14 percent by 2007–2009. A comparison
of Druze and Muslim women (in the same subdistricts) with the same
level of education reveals small and inconsistent differences.

As among other Palestinian groups in Israel, single Druze women have
higher odds of being employed than married women (including widowed
and divorced women), but the gap between single and married women
has shrunk with time as more and more married Druze women started to
work outside their homes. Thus, in 1986–1988 single Druze women had
10 times the probability of being employed compared to married women.
By 2000–2002 this ratio declined to 1.8, and in 2007–2009 it was 1.2.

We next examine the interrelations between women's characteristics and
LFP by performing a multivariate analysis for each of the periods included in
our study in order to identify their net impacts (we started with the 1993–
1995 period since in the earlier years very few Druze women were
employed). We repeated our analysis for Muslim women residing in
the same subdistricts as the Druze women. The results confirmed much
of the information obtained in the descriptive analyses (Appendix 8.1).

The multivariate analysis enables us to find the net contribution of each factor. We find, for example, that in 2007–2009 Druze women with secondary education had 3.6 times higher odds of being employed compared to women with a low level of education (the reference group). The odds of Druze women with tertiary education were 34 times higher than the reference group. Following these net effects in earlier periods shows that the educational effects were even stronger then, but they are still very large in recent years.

Looking at the net effects of an additional child, we see that in all years studied it had no impact on Druze women's LFP while reducing that of Muslim women. Net of other control variables, in 1993–1995 and in 2000–2002 the odds of Druze women with *young* children to participate in the labor force was about 50 percent lower relative to women with older children. This effect disappeared in the last period. This was not the case of Muslim women for whom having a young child was an obstacle for employment both in 2000–2002 and in 2007–2009. The fact that number of children and their ages played a bigger role in Muslim women's employment than in Druze women's employment may result from wider availability of child care facilities for Druze communities relative to Muslim ones (in the same subdistricts). The difference in impact of young children on employment between Druze and Muslim women may also be related to the fact that more Druze than Muslim women work in their own localities as will be seen in the next section. When women have to commute, the presence of children is a bigger obstacle for mothers' employment, and Druze working mothers suffer less than Muslim mothers from this problem.

8.3   Employment Characteristics and Earnings of Druze Women

In the second part of our analysis, we examine the labor market standing of those Druze women enrolled in it. As in previous chapters, we are interested in documenting trends of part-time employment, commuting, industrial and occupational enrollment, and earning achievements. Data about these trends help us understand the situation of Druze women in the labor market and how it has changed along time.

Part-Time Employment. Part-time employment is more common among Druze women than among Druze men.[12] In the early years, when the share of Druze women in the labor market was still very low,

---

[12] Our definition of part-time employment is based on respondents' self-report; see Section 5.1.

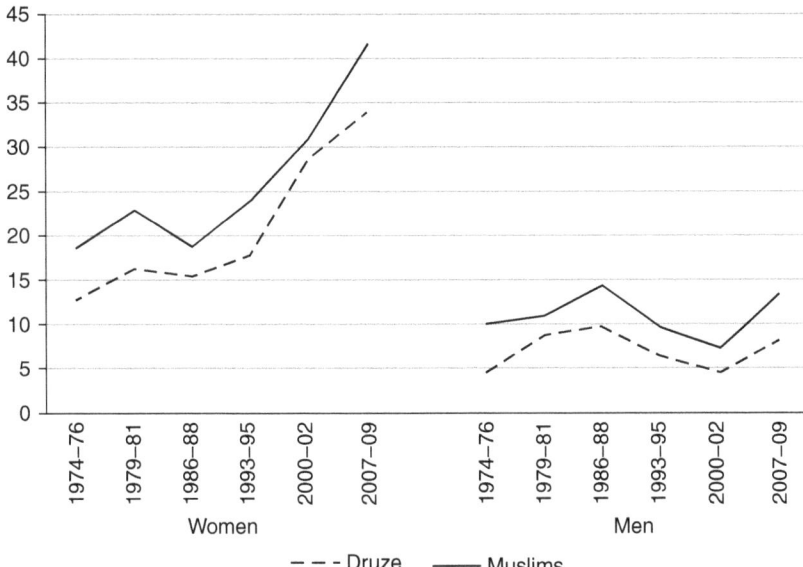

Figure 8.3 Part-Time Employment of Druze and Muslim Workers
Aged 18–52 by Gender and Year
Source: Labor Force Surveys 1974–2009.
Note: Only Druze (excluding the Golan Heights) and Muslims residing
in the subdistricts where the Druze live.

most of them were fully employed. As their share in employment increased, so did their share of part-time work. Thus, in 1974–1976 only 12.8 percent of the employed Druze women worked part time, and this likelihood increased monotonically to 33.9 in 2007–2009 (Figure 8.3). The fact that many women who join the labor market work part time is part of a pattern we observed among Muslim and Jewish women (Figure 5.1) and is common in other countries as well (Stier and Lewin-Epstein 2000, 390). Comparing Druze women with the Muslim women who reside in the same subdistricts (and face roughly the same labor market opportunities and constraints) reveals that Druze women are less likely to work part-time than their Muslim neighbors. This gap was the highest in recent years, when 42 percent of Muslim women in the labor market worked part time, 10 percent higher than among Druze women. Although part-time employment of both Druze men and Muslim men is low in all years, the share of part-time work is also higher among Muslim men than among Druze men. The fact that more Druze women and men work full-time than Muslims may indicate more job availability for Druze than for Muslims.

As the readers may remember, women who work part-time were asked about the reasons for working part time. The incidence of "voluntary" part-time work among Druze women was very low. Most of the Druze women holding part-time work reported that they worked part time because they had not been able to find full-time work (71 percent in 2000–2002; 65 percent in 2007–2009). Similar distribution of reasons for part-time employment were reported by Muslim women residing in the same subdistricts as the Druze, and also by the larger Muslim population analyzed in Chapter 5 (Figure 5.2). Both Muslim and Druze women are very different from Jewish women, among whom "voluntary" part-time work has been much more prevalent.

Commuting. From Figure 8.4 we see that in all years studied Druze women had a relatively high probability of working in their own localities of residence, but commuting is gradually becoming more frequent, rising from about 20 percent at the beginning of the studied period to 28 percent at the end. However, even the high commuting rate in the last period is lower than that of Muslim women workers in the same subdistricts. Among the latter at least a third commuted to their workplace. Among men there were no significant differences between Druze and Muslims in the same regions with two-thirds of the two groups employed outside their localities of residence.

The gaps in commuting between Druze and Muslim women are consistent when we examine specific subgroups. Single women and young women (aged 18–24) are much more likely to commute than married and older women, but among Muslim women, commuting is more frequent in all categories. Blue-collar women workers much more often than white-collar workers have to seek employment outside the locality, but in both categories Druze women are more likely to find employment at their residence community. Of Druze women in (skilled and unskilled) manual occupations, 56 percent had to commute (in 2007–2009), a high figure but below that of Muslim women who are manual workers, among whom almost three-quarters worked outside their locality of residence. Most Druze teachers – as many as 90 percent – found work in their communities, while a quarter of Muslim teachers worked in other municipalities than their own. These differences demonstrate that Druze communities have more employment opportunities both in industry for women with lower education and in social services for women with higher education.

Industrial and Occupational Enrollment. We showed in Chapter 5 that Muslim women in Israel have been enrolled in very few occupational groups and industrial braches, and in Chapters 6 and 7 we saw that

Bedouin women in the south and Muslim women in Jerusalem have been even more restricted in the diversity of their work. In this chapter, we examine the diversity of Druze women's employment venues. As in our previous analyses, we rely on the labor force surveys performed in the last 30 years, but we focus our presentation here on the last period (2007–2009), distinguishing between six broad economic branches and then further went into more detailed classifications (two- or three-digit economic classification).

Appendix 8.2 shows that Druze women were also concentrated in very limited economic sectors. The majority (51.5 percent) worked in the public sector, about 70 percent of them in education. In addition; almost a quarter of Druze women worked in peripheral services (24.7 percent), mainly in retail and sales. An additional 15.4 percent worked in the manufacturing sector, especially in the garment industry and in food production.

A comparison between Druze and Muslim women in the same subdistricts shows some similarity but also interesting differences. More than 85 percent of Druze women are concentrated, like Muslim women, in three economic branches (public social services, the manufacturing sector, and peripheral services) and in the same specific branches within these sectors. But a higher share of Druze women than Muslim women work in the manufacturing sector (15.4 and 9.6 percent, respectively), and a lower share of Druze women work in health and welfare services (9.1 percent and 18.8 percent, respectively). These differences may reflect different economic opportunities that the two groups have in specific communities or differential connections to the social networks operative in various economic branches.

It is also interesting to inspect the economic enrollment of Druze men which is quite different from that of Muslim men residing in the same subdistricts. Almost all of the Druze men (91.8 percent) are concentrated in merely three broad economic sectors: the manufacturing and construction sectors (40.3 percent), peripheral services (32.4 percent), and the public sector (20.4 present). Their distribution within each of these sectors is much broader than that of Druze women. For example, Druze men who are enrolled in the peripheral services are occupied in almost all of the economic branches in this broad category. A public social service which attracts Druze men is "order and safety"– mostly work as policemen, security workers, and jail wardens. This branch is open to Druze men due to their mandatory military service. None of the Druze women or the Muslim men in the same regions enters work in this economic branch (figures not shown).

While the share of employed Druze women rose from 5 to 33 percent during the period of our study, the industrial branches in which they are enrolled have also changed considerably over the years. Their high

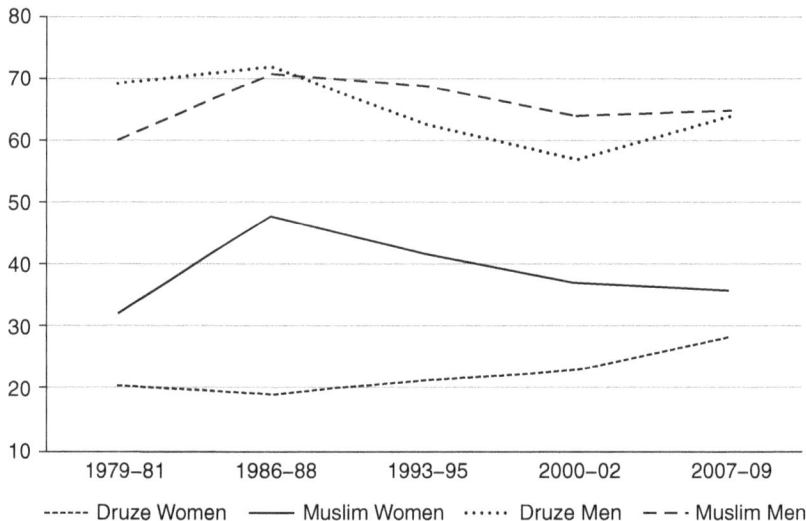

Figure 8.4 Commuting to Work of Druze and Muslim Workers Aged
18–52 by Gender and Year
Source: Labor Force Surveys 1979–2009.
Note: Only Druze (excluding the Golan Heights) and Muslims residing
in the subdistricts where the Druze live.

enrollment in the manufacturing sector, which was between 57 and 72
percent until 2000, dropped to half of that in 2000–2002 (29 percent),
and was cut to half again by 2007–2009 (15 percent). Agriculture, which
still accounted for more than 10 percent of Druze women's employment
in the mid-1970s, now provides employment for a negligible number.
With the decline of Druze women's employment in both the manufacturing and the agricultural sectors, we find an increase in two other branches:
peripheral services and the public sector. Until the late 1980s very few
Druze women were involved in peripheral services but since then the
importance of this sector for their employment has risen constantly,
with the majority of women in this sector entering retail trade and sale
activities. Druze women have also increased their rate in the public sector,
especially in health and welfare services (from 2.1 percent in 1974 to 9.1
percent in 2007–2009) and in education (from 27.7 percent to almost 36
percent, respectively).

Together with the rising labor force participation of Druze women and the
changes in the economic branches in which they work, we find changes in
their occupational enrollment (Appendix 8.3): (1) The decline in the share

of Druze women in the manufacturing and agricultural sectors is reflected in a sharp decline in their rate in skilled and unskilled manual occupations from 65–70 percent in the mid-1970s and the 1980s to 16 percent in the last period studied. (2) The increased rate of Druze women in the peripheral services is reflected in a large rise in the rate of those in low non-manual occupations, including clerical, sales, and personal service occupations. Until 2000 about 20 percent of working Druze women were enrolled in this broad occupational group (only 10 percent in 1979–1981), but their rate rose to more than 30 percent in 2000–2002, and in the most recent period (2007–2009) it climbed to more than half of the employed Druze women. About half of these women are in service occupations (25.6 percent) and the rest are divided between clerical jobs and sales. (3) The increasing share of Druze women in the public sector was reflected in their increasing share in professional and technical occupations. Druze women tripled their share in this occupational group from 11 percent in 1974–1976 to more than 30 percent in 2007–2009, but only 2 percent of working Druze women penetrated the occupational glass ceiling of academic profession occupations, and only a fraction of 1 percent are managers.

Druze women, like other Palestinian women in Israel, are employed in a very limited range of occupations. Referring to three-digit occupations in 2007–2009, we find that more than a third of Druze women (36.6 percent) are engaged in teaching jobs (28.7 percent as teachers, and 7.9 as kindergarten assistants). Three other occupations account for almost another third of Druze women: saleswomen (12.5 percent), clerical workers (11.7 percent), and skilled workers in the garment industry (7.7 percent).

Overall there is a great similarity of occupational enrollment between Druze and Muslim women on the three-digit classification (table not shown). According to the index of dissimilarity between Druze and Muslim women, only 15.4 percent of the women in one group would have to change their occupational enrollment in order to equalize these two occupational distributions. Nevertheless there are some interesting differences : (1) the rate of Druze women enrolled in (qualified and unqualified) nursing (3.8 percent) is much lower than among Muslim women (10.5 percent); (2) Muslim women have a larger presence in clerical jobs than Druze women, although the gap is not large (15.2 and 11.7 percent, respectively); (3) a much larger rate of Druze women work as saleswomen compared to Muslim women: 14.2 and 6.9 percent, respectively; (4) Druze women also have an advantage in skilled manual occupations, mainly due to the fact that almost 8 percent of Druze women in the labor market are employed as skilled dressmakers, an occupation in which hardly any Muslim woman is employed. Druze men also have limited occupational options. Forty-five percent of them work in skilled and unskilled manual occupations, an additional 24 percent in service jobs (mainly in security jobs and as policemen), and very few in high white-collar occupations.

Occupational Enrollment of Workers with a High Level of Education. In 1993–1995 less than 4 percent of Druze women in the work age (25–52) had attended an academic institution. Seven years later, the percentage was over 16 percent, and in 2007–2009 it was close to a fifth. Due to the importance of higher education for women's employment, we examine in more detail the occupational enrollment of Druze women with academic education and compare it to that of Muslim women with the same level of education who live in the same regions (figures not shown). We learn that highly educated Druze and Muslim women are employed in very few occupational categories. The positive news is that the majority, almost 75 percent, work in occupations that do fit their educational achievements in high non-manual occupations. A closer look at the numbers tells us that Druze women are much more concentrated than Muslim women in teaching and are hardly present in other occupations. Highly educated Muslim women, in contrast, also show significant presence in nursing. Academically educated Druze women who are not in teaching work mostly in non-academic occupations: 13.6 percent in clerical positions (similar to the rate of academically educated Muslim women in such positions) and in the services, mostly as kindergarten assistants (6.1 percent). The fact that there is no significant number of Druze women in nursing is telling and requires an explanation. Since this niche is open to Muslim women, discrimination by Jewish managers is unlikely to be the explanation. There is a constant demand for nurses in all areas of the country, and hence the lack of Druze nurses may reflect their own preferences rather than an external constraint.

A look at the occupational enrollment of highly educated Druze men tells us that although they enter a wider range of occupations relative to their female counterparts, they have a lesser chance than women of working in education-fitting high non-manual occupations. More than half of the highly educated Druze men do not have fitting occupational opportunities and are enrolled in the low prestige service occupations, mainly as policemen and other security workers (about a third). It is possible, however, that rather than being pushed toward non-academic positions due to a lack of open academic positions, many Druze policemen and wardens completed academic training as part of their service in the police and the prison system. Both of these institutions attract recruits by providing them with an academic education, thus improving the quality of their personnel.

Earnings. We end this chapter with a look into the earnings of Druze women. To this end we use the 2008 census data.[13] We restricted our analysis to Druze women and men in the age bracket 25–52, who participated in the labor market as employees. Druze women's median earnings in 2008 were NIS 3,226 per month, and their median hourly earnings were NIS 31.4. Muslim women from the same subdistricts earned NIS 300 per month more (NIS 3,528 per month) and by NIS 0.75 more per hour (32.2 per hour). Druze men earned much more. Their median gross monthly earnings were NIS 6,685 per month, and NIS 34.8 per hour, while Muslim men (in the same geographical area) earned much less – only NIS 5,085 per month and NIS 29.2 per hour. The gender and ethno-religious gaps might be due to differences in the composition of each group and their human capital, but the high earnings of Druze men stand out as far above those of Druze women. In 2008 Druze women earned only 48 percent of what their male counterparts earned, while Muslim women earned 69 percent of what their male counterparts did. To figure out the causes of the above gaps we move as usual to a multivariate analysis.

Multivariate Analysis. In order to understand the earnings gaps and to see how Druze are rewarded for their human capital relative to Muslims in the same subdistricts, we ran four multivariate regression equations predicting gross monthly earnings for Druze women, Druze men, Muslim women, and Muslim men (from the same subdistricts). The results are presented in Appendix 8.4. The return rate to holding a tertiary certificate for Druze women was NIS 2,881, and to finishing high school NIS 761. Being enrolled in high non-manual occupations (compared to Druze women enrolled in manual occupations) increases Druze women's monthly earnings by NIS 2,448. An additional year of experience in the labor market increases Druze women's monthly earnings by NIS 353, and an additional working hour increases their monthly earnings by NIS 83. Working in the public sector does not have a significant effect on Druze women's earnings compared to working in the private sector. When comparing these figures with those of Muslim women,[14] we found that the Druze and Muslim women received similar rewards for their labor market characteristics, except for labor force experience for which Druze women got significantly higher returns compared to Muslim women. Another difference between the two groups of women is that being single significantly decreased Muslim women's earnings but not those of Druze women.

---

[13] We used here the census data since the number of female Druze workers in the combined labor force survey and income survey was too small to allow a statistical analysis.

[14] Using the z-test for equality of regression coefficients (Paternoster et al. 1998).

Based on the above observations we posed two more questions. First we asked: What would Druze women's earnings be, holding constant their compositional characteristics had they been treated as Muslim women (that is, had the impact of each independent variable been the same as experienced by Muslim women)? The second question is the same but with regard to the gender gap: What would Druze women's earnings be holding constant their compositional characteristics had they been treated as Druze men?[15] A comparison of the answers to these questions is likely to be informative as regarding the treatment of Druze women in the labor market. If Druze women had the same conversion potential as Muslim women (that is, had they received the same rewards for the independent variables as Muslim women), their monthly earnings would slightly decrease (8.6 percent), but if they had the same conversion potential as their male counterparts, they would increase their earnings by more than 60 percent. This tells us that Druze women are not treated differently with respect to earnings than Muslim women living in the area, but they are considerably disadvantaged compared to their male counterparts. Druze men receive much more generous economic rewards in the labor market.

8.4   Summary

The changes in Druze women's lives have been similar to those that transpired in the lives of the Muslim women in Israel in general, and those who live next to them in the same or in nearby communities in particular. According to several measures, it seems that Druze women lagged a bit behind Muslim women in their areas in the past, but have more recently closed the gap and even surpassed the Muslims. However, overall the patterns of labor force participation are similar for the two groups. Both started from very low rates (5–6 percent) in the mid-1970s and advanced gradually to a bit more than 30 percent at the end of the first decade of the twenty-first century.

As among Muslim women, Druze women with tertiary education are much more likely to be employed, but women with a lower level of education also increased their LFP with time. Increasing LFP rates are also observed for married women and for women with children, and the pace of the change has been quite similar for the two ethno-religious groups. Nevertheless, the number of children and their ages are less of an obstacle for Druze women.

---

[15] We asked similar questions regarding the earnings gap between Muslim and Jewish women and the gap between Muslim women and men. We use here the same logic of inquiry. See Section 5.4.

The rise of LFP among Druze women is accompanied, as among Muslim women, by a rising rate of part-time employment, but Druze women have been more likely to work full time compared to Muslim women in their region. Part-time employment among Palestinians in Israel is related to shortage of job opportunities, and the majority of both Druze and Muslim women with part-time positions reported that they preferred full-time work but did not find full-time jobs. The fact that fewer Druze women work part time may thus be interpreted as a sign that the supply of jobs is greater for Druze than for Muslims. This conclusion is supported by the fact that Druze women, and especially those with higher education, are much more likely to find jobs in their own locality of residence compared with Muslim women. The differences between the two groups are large, which seems to indicate that Druze communities have more economic opportunities than Muslim communities. As among Muslim women, it is mostly Druze women who are enrolled in low status occupations who work outside their community of residence, but even among them fewer women than Muslim women have to commute in order to find employment.

Druze women, like the groups of Muslim women we wrote about in previous chapters, are concentrated in very few economic branches. Almost 85 percent of Druze women are concentrated in only three broad economic sectors (social services, the manufacturing sector, and the peripheral service sector). This distribution is very similar to that of Muslim women in the same regions. Seventy percent of highly educated Druze women are teachers. The fact that teaching is the main occupation of educated women is hardly surprising, but among the Druze the magnitude of this concentration is extraordinary, compared with 57 percent among Muslim women in the same areas, which by itself was more than twice higher than among Jews (23 percent). The similarity of Druze and Muslim women is seen also in their earnings. Although Muslim women get on average NIS 300 more than Druze, this low gap is mainly explained by different characteristics of the two groups.

Given that social control of women among the Druze is tighter than among Muslims (Hassan 2001), the fact that the two groups of women share similar employment patterns, and Druze women even have slight advantages in several indicators (a smaller percentage of part-time work, fewer women commuting to work, a somewhat higher rate of employment among married women) might be interpreted as a sign that economic conditions are more important for LFP than culture. Druze communities are better treated by the Israeli government, and the Druze have better relations as a group with the dominant Jewish group (Hassan 1992, 2001). These advantages are translated to more economic resources and hence more employment opportunities than in Muslim communities.

Druze men have an earnings advantage over Muslim men, a gap that is reflected in a large gap between Druze men and Druze women. Most of this gender gap is a result of the higher returns Druze men get for their human capital and personal and work characteristics. This advantage might be related to the better ties with members of the dominant Jewish group that Druze men acquire during their military service. It may also be the outcome of relatively good salaries paid to Druze men in security-related jobs. In any case, it is related to the status of the Druze in Israel as the preferred minority. If this interpretation is correct, then the question is why women do not enjoy this status. Clearly, they do not serve in the army and this may reduce their ties and familiarity with Jewish society (cf. Hajjar 1996). It is also possible that they benefit less from the ties between Druze and Jews because most of them live in villages and towns far from the employment centers of Haifa and Tel Aviv, and unlike the men they cannot commute far due to childcare duties. The availability of work within the community enables women to find employment, but in the poor and less developed rural communities, earnings are more limited.

Appendix 8.1 *Logistic Coefficients and Standard Errors (in parentheses) Predicting LFP of Druze and Muslim Women Aged 25–52 by Year*

	1993–1995		2000–2002		2007–2009	
			Druze			
	B/S.E.	Exp. (B)	B/S.E.	Exp. (B)	B/S.E.)	Exp. (B)
Secondary education	1.546*	4.691	1.448*	4.428	1.291*	3.636
	(0.365)		(0.256)		(0.208)	
Tertiary education	4.424*	83.465	3.906*	49.707	3.531*	34.164
	(0.506)		(0.328)		(0.277)	
Single	2.220*	9.207	2.263*	9.611	2.027*	7.428
	(0.439)		(0.327)		(0.292)	
Number of Children under 15	−0.105	0.900	−0.023	0.977	0.130	1.139
	(0.123)		(0.087)		(0.085)	
Having children under 5	−0.685*	0.504	−0.749*	0.473	−0.108	0.898
	(0.308)		(0.303)		(0.244)	
Age	−0.036	0.965	−0.055*	(0.946)	0.021	1.022
	(0.021)		(0.018)		(0.014)	
Constant	−1.353		0.043		3.251	
−2Log likelihood	441.4		650.3		868.6	
N	805		898		888	
Nagelkerke R^2	0.430		0.476		0.369	
			Muslims			
	B (S.E)	Exp. (B)	B (S.E)	Exp. (B)	B (S.E)	Exp. (B)
Secondary education	1.189*	3.284	0.791*	2.207	1.124*	3.079
	(0.169)		(0.133)		(0.123)	
Tertiary education	4.223*	68.265	2.879*	17.802	3.413*	30.342
	(0.325)		(0.176)		(0.157)	
Single	1.542*	4.675	1.083*	2.955	1.284*	3.610
	(0.227)		(0.179)		(0.100)	
Number of Children under 15	−0.246*	0.782	−0.111*	0.895	−0.098*	0.907
	(0.006)		(0.050)		(0.047)	
Having children under 5	−0.037	1.038	−0.410*	0.664	−0.248*	0.784
	(0.244)		(0.170)		(0.120)	
Age	−0.014	0.986	−0.018*	(0.946)	0.013	1.013
	(0.012)		(0.009)		(0.009)	
Constant	−1.694		−1.207		−2.384	
−2Log likelihood	1299.6		2092.9		255.7	
N	1,954		2,446		2,589	
Nagelkerke R^2	0.355		0.284		0.355	

Variables: The dependent variable is labor force participation, coded 1 if the woman belongs to the labor force, and 0 otherwise; the independent variables are: education (distinguishing between intermediary and less (the reference group), secondary, and tertiary education), marital status (single women were coded 1, 0 otherwise), number of children under 15, having children under 5, and age.

Source: Labor Force Surveys 1993–2009.

*: p <0.05

Note: Only Druze (excluding the Golan Heights) and Muslims residing in the subdistricts where the Druze live.

Appendix 8.2 *Economic Branch Distribution of Druze and Muslims Aged 18–52 by Gender, 2007–2009*

	Women		Men	
	Druze	Muslim	Druze	Muslim
Agriculture	1.7	2.7	3.3	4.0
Manufacturing	15.4	9.6	24.6	20.2
Manufacturing of food products	(4.4)	(5.0)	(1.6)	(3.6)
Manufacturing of wearing apparel	(6.4)	(1.2)	(0.7)	(0.6)
Construction	0.0	0.0	15.7	27.9
Peripheral services	24.7	19.4	32.4	30.8
Wholesale and retail trade, repair of vehicles and personal and household goods	(15.9)	(11.1)	(12.9)	(18.5)
Retail sale	(13.9)	(8.4)	(5.6)	(7.5)
Accommodation services and restaurant	(4.3)	(4.0)	(4.5)	(5.8)
Core services	6.7	5.3	3.6	4.1
Public sector	51.5	63.0	20.4	13.0
Public administration	(2.3)	(1.9)	(13.6)	(1.4)
State public order and security activities			(11.9)	
Education	(35.8)	(38.2)	(3.2)	(5.1)
Health services and welfare and social work	(9.1)	(18.8)	(2.3)	(3.2)
Total	100.0	100.0	100.0	100.0
N	397	1,119	853	2,999

Source: Labor force Surveys 2007–2009.

Note: Only Druze (excluding the Golan Heights) and Muslims residing in the subdistricts where the Druze live.

Appendix 8.3 *Occupational Distribution of Druze and Muslim Women Aged 18–52 by Year*

	1974–1976	1979–1981	1986–1988	1993–1995	2000–2002	2007–2009
Druze						
Academic professionals	0.0	0.0	0.0	0.4	0.0	2.0
Associate professionals and technicians	10.9	23.1	10.3	17.9	39.8	30.5
Managers	0.0	0.0	0.0	0.0	0.8	0.3
Clerical occupations	0.0	1.3	6.3	7.1	14.1	11.7
Sales	0.0	1.3	2.3	2.9	6.3	14.2
Service workers	19.6	6.4	10.3	12.1	11.8	25.6
Agriculture workers	4.3	2.6	0.0	0.4	0.0	0.0
Skilled manual workers	54.3	59.0	63.8	48.3	20.4	10.7
Unskilled workers	10.9	6.4	6.9	10.8	6.8	5.1
Total	100.0	100.0	100.0	100.0	100.0	100.0
N	46	78	174	240	382	394
Muslims						
Academic professionals	0.0	0.9	0.8	0.3	0.8	2.7
Associate professionals and technicians	10.9	9.3	8.8	19.9	23.5	35.2
Managers	0.0	2.5	3.5	0.3	0.4	0.5
Clerical occupations	3.4	6.2	6.0	14.4	15.5	15.2
Sales	2.6	2.5	4.8	3.1	6.3	6.9
Service workers	21.3	23.9	25.4	20.4	27.9	28.8
Agriculture workers	9.3	4.8	3.3	0.7	2.1	1.1
Skilled manual workers	35.0	33.6	35.1	31.2	17.5	4.2
Unskilled workers	21.7	16.3	12.5	9.7	6.0	5.4
Total	100.0	100.0	100.0	100.0	100.0	100.0
N	742	645	800	613	933	1,115

Source: Labor Force Surveys 1974–2009.
Note: Only Druze (excluding the Golan Heights) and Muslims residing in the subdistricts where the Druze live.

Appendix 8.4 *Regression Coefficients and Standard Errors (in parentheses) Predicting Gross Monthly Earnings of Druze and Muslim Workers Aged 25–52 by Gender, 2008*

	Druze Women	Muslim Women	Druze Men	Muslim men
Single	60.6	−0.285*	−1070.2*	−524.8*
	(252.7)	(146.4)	(475.2)	(183)
Secondary education	760.7*	406.7*	1291.6*	887.5*
	(355.0)	(201.3)	(405.0)	(139)
Tertiary education	2881.1*	2453.5*	3259.0*	2297.8*
	(409.2)	(245.8)	(498.1)	(111.9)
Experience	353.0*	232.8*	332.5*	256.7*
	(50.8)	(30.2)	(86.0)	(34.1)
Experience squared	−6.106*	−3.467*	−5.527*	−4.036*
	(1.326)	(0.783)	(1.997)	(0.764)
High non-manual occupations	2448.5*	2134.4*	3222.0*	2891*
	(420.8)	(266.6)	(477.7)	(230.1)
Low non-manual occupations	214.1	96.0	−86.5	436.9*
	(305.1)	(207.3)	(364.5)	(157.4)
Public sector	226.7	−57.8	−192.2	902.7*
	(283)	(62.5)	(361.9)	(184.1)
Hours worked	83.2*	95.6*	76.4*	70.6*
	(9.6)	(5.5)	(13.0)	(5.43)
Constant	−4450.5*	−3505.7*	−2456.7*	−1944.0
R^2	0.423	0.382	0.183	0.226

Variables: The dependent variable is gross monthly earnings and the independent variables are: Education (distinguishing between intermediate and lower (the reference group), secondary, and tertiary), work experience (age minus years of schooling minus five) and its square, occupational allocation (distinguishing between high non-manual, low non-manual, and manual workers (the reference group)), employment sector (the public sector is coded 1, and the private sector 0), hours worked in the last week, marital status (single is coded 1; otherwise coded 0).
Source: 2008 Census.
*: $p < 0.05$
Note: Only Druze (excluding the Golan Heights) and Muslims residing in the subdistricts where the Druze live.

9 The Half-Full Glass
Christian Women in the Labor Market

9.1 Background

In our last chapter we analyze the labor-market situation of Palestinian Christian women.[1] Like all ethno-religious groups in Israel, Palestinian Christians are officially defined by their religion. Unlike the Druze, however, most Christian Palestinians do not base their identity on religion but rather identify as Palestinian; throughout the twentieth century members of this group made prominent contributions to the Palestinian national movement (Haiduc-Dale 2015).[2] Christian Palestinians belong to about a dozen denominations: The Greek Orthodox make up the largest of these, followed by Greek Catholics and Roman Catholics. Smaller groups are the Maronites, Anglicans, Protestants (of various churches), and Copts (Kanaaneh, 2002, 139; Robson 2011). Together, all these groups number about 123,900 persons (additional 11,900 reside in the annexed parts of Jerusalem and its vicinity). This population is concentrated in the Northern District of Israel where 89,500 of them live, many in large villages and towns, and the District of Haifa, where additional 16,200 live, mostly in the city of Haifa itself (CBS 2013, Tables 2.19 and 2.20). The rest (7,400) live in the Tel Aviv area (mostly in Jaffa, Lydda, and Ramla).

Christian communities thrived in Palestine/Israel since the early days of the Christian Church but from the Arab conquest of the country in the seventh century until the end of the Ottoman period (with the exception of the Crusaders period) they lived under a Muslim regime, and Arabic became their native language (McGahern 2011). The cultural and social divergence of Muslims and Druze from Christians in Palestine might be tracked back to the European intrusion into Ottoman Palestine in the nineteenth century. At that time new commercial cities were developed along the coast of Palestine to deal with the expanding trade with Europe.

---

[1] Parts of the introduction for this chapter were used in Yonay et al. 2015.
[2] See Robson 2011 for a different view. Robson argues that the British policies facilitated the politicization of Christianity, and consequently "Muslim leaders began to use the new sectarian political structures of the mandate state to garner support for a nationalist movement increasingly deploying Islamist rhetoric and organization" (2011, 2).

These cities attracted many Christian and Jewish merchants from inland cities in Palestine and from other provinces of the Ottoman Empire (Schölch 1982; Sabella 1996; Kimmerling and Migdal 2003; Robson 2011). The expanding activity of Christian churches in Palestine and the influx of Christian pilgrims in the same period also benefited Christian Palestinians who were favored by Christian institutions as providers of various services and accommodations. Church schools, still prominent within Palestinian society to this day, were first built during the nineteenth century as a result of this activity (Schölch 1982; Tsimhoni 2001; Robson 2011).[3]

The replacement of a Muslim empire (Ottoman) by a Christian one (British) after World War I augmented the Christians' advantage over Muslims and they "experienced unprecedented security and prosperity during the 30-year British mandate" (Tsimhoni 2001). Tsimhoni explains that even at the beginning of the British rule, "the majority of Palestinian Christians had become urbanized, whereas the majority of the Muslims remained rural throughout the mandatory period and until the 1960s. Christians formed a significant portion of the Palestinian urban middle class; they had higher and Westernized education, smaller households, and a lower birthrate than the Muslims." Christians in Palestine/Israel have therefore "remained not only a religious group, but also a distinct social, economical (sic), and cultural one" (Tsimhoni 2001, 33). Robson (2011) argues, however, that the gaps between religious groups in Mandatory Palestine were not a mere consequence of socioeconomic differences. She attributes this fact also to a conscious policy of the colonial rulers to introduce "an inflexible sectarianism as a major organizing principle of the new state" (2011, 1).

During the Nakba of 1948, the large urban Palestinian centers in what is today Israel were destroyed, and the residents of such large cities as Jaffa, Haifa, and Jerusalem were expelled from Israel (Sabella 1996; Khalidi 2006; Pappé 2006; Robson 2011).[4] Thus, the Christian Palestinians who remained under Israeli control were mostly from the

---

[3] Muslims were accepted by church schools, but since all such schools were located in villages where Christians lived, the schools were practically inaccessible for many Muslim boys from far away villages. Notice that although Christians were overrepresented in the commercial and urban middle class of Palestine, Christian elites did not see themselves as a distinct social stratum than the Muslim elite. According to Robson (2011), both Christian and Muslim elites saw themselves as the leading elite responsible for developing and modernizing Palestine.

[4] Pressure from the Vatican and fear of the Christian world may have prevented the expulsion of Nazareth residents during the Nakba (Kimmerling and Migdal 2003, n. 500) and caused Israel to allow some Christian refugees to return from Lebanon to their villages (ibid., 181), but this was the exception rather than the rule.

rural areas of the Galilee.[5] Yet, according to the 1961 census, by that year Christians already enjoyed a higher status and larger income than Muslims at that time, and relatively higher proportions of Christian women were employed (15 percent compared to almost 10 percent among Muslim women; see Yonay and Kraus 2017). Subsequent studies have documented the advantage of Christian Palestinians over Muslim ones, and their improved education and occupational status not only relative to Muslim and Druze but also relative to Mizrahi Jews (Shavit 1989; Kraus and Yonay 2000; Khattab 2002; cf. Sa'ar 1998). Christian women have different demographic patterns than Muslims and Druze, as we showed in Chapter 3. A quick reminder: Christian women marry, on average, when they are 3.9 years older than Muslim women (Figure 3.3); they have, on average, 1.08 fewer children than Muslim women (Figure 3.4); their average level of education is higher: Almost 40 percent of Christian women in 2007–2009 have acquired an academic degree, double the rate among Muslim women (Figure 3.2C).

The recent socioeconomic advantages of Christian Palestinians may have been supported by two factors. First, although Muslim and Christian Palestinians were equally devastated during the Nakba (Sabella 1996; Robson 2011), the Christians were able to restore their community organizations more quickly due to support by European churches. Compared with "the total collapse of the Muslim structure and hierarchy in Palestine" and the virtual isolation of Israeli Muslims from other Muslim communities, this advantage of Christian Palestinians facilitated their "ascendancy within Palestinian Politics in Israel" (Pappé 2006, 155–156). Secondly, at least according to some writers, the Israeli state favored Christians over Muslims. Pappé, for instance, claims that the state was able, with partial success, "to drive a wedge between Christians and Muslims by presenting and treating the Christians as more loyal to the Jewish State" (ibid., 155). Peled (2001) attributes the preferential treatment of Christian Palestinians relative to Muslims to Israel's wish to maintain its reputation in Europe and elsewhere in the Christian world and to the involvement of the Ministry of Foreign Affairs in protecting their interests.

Given their demographic characteristics, and especially their low fertility rates and high investment in education, one would expect Christian women to enter the labor market in large numbers and to develop professional careers. In the following analyses we ask whether these expectations have been met.

---

[5] On the social characteristics of refugees and those who remained in Israel, see Mazawi 1994; Hasan 2005.

9.2   Labor Force Participation

As in previous chapters we use labor force surveys to examine Christian women's labor force participation.[6] In this chapter our main comparison group is Jewish women who live in the Northern and Haifa districts where most Christian Palestinians live. As may be expected given the relative high educational achievements of Christian women and their low fertility rates, and the fact that many of them reside in large urban localities, their labor force participation is much higher compared to other Israeli Palestinian women (Muslim, Druze) but much lower in comparison to Jewish women (Figure 9.1).

In 1974–1976 only one in five Christian women (19.5 percent) participated in the labor market. This share increased monotonically over the years, so that in 2000–2002 almost every second Christian woman (49.3 percent) was in the labor market. The monotonous rise has slowed down

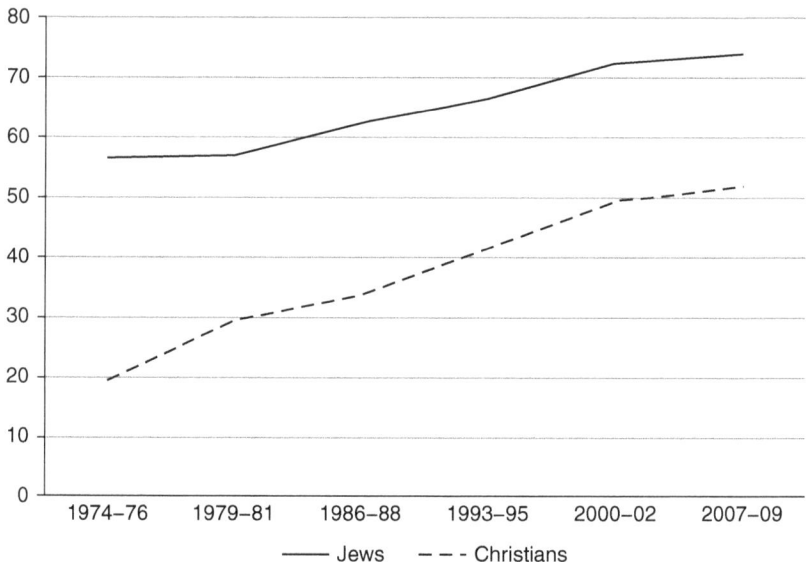

Figure 9.1 Labor Force Participation of Christian and Jewish Women Aged 18–52 by Year
Source: Labor Force Surveys 1974–2009.
Note: Only Christian women (excluding Jerusalem) and Jewish women from the Northern and Haifa districts.

---

[6] Christian Palestinians residing in Jerusalem are excluded for the reasons explained in Chapter 7.

as the level of employment has not changed much over the next seven years (51.8 percent in 2007–2009). At the end of our research period Christian women had not reached the rate of employment achieved by Jewish women at the beginning of our research period (56.5 percent in 1974–1976). Jewish women (who live in the same areas as the Christian women) have meanwhile increased their LFP rate (to almost 74 percent), and thus Christian women still lag far behind these Jewish women (Figure 9.1).[7]

Using the same synthetic cohort analysis used in Chapter 4 (see Table 4.1)[8], we see (Appendix 9.1) that Christian women's increases in the labor market result from two processes: cohort replacement and growing involvement in paid labor as women grow older. Cohort replacement is seen by comparing various generations (cohort groups) at the same stage of their lives. For example, at the age of 25–31, almost 25 percent of the women born in 1942–1948 were in the labor market, compared to 41 percent of those born 14 years later (1956–1962), and almost 64 percent of those born in 1977–1983. This is not true for the 18–24 age group, because in recent cohorts many more women spend time on tertiary education. The second process is that within each birth cohort more Christian women seek employment as they get older, do not have to take care of young children, and are freed from many of their family duties. This is mainly true, however, for women born after 1956. Looking at the patterns of Christian women born in 1963–1969, we see that 39 percent of them were in the labor market when they were 18–24 years old. Seven years later, when they were 25–31 and had probably finished their education, their share in the labor market increased by almost 10 percent (to 48.9 percent) and remained about the same (50.7 percent) when they became 32–38. Yet when these women reached the age 39–45, their share in the labor market further increased to almost 60 percent. By the age 46–52, however, the LFP rate of Christian women goes down. Like other Palestinian women, Christian women leave the labor market at a relative young age, a trend not observed among Jewish women.

What are the factors that determine Palestinian Christian women's participation in the labor force? To answer this question we first examined the gross effects of women's personal characteristics on their employment and then ran a multivariate analysis to reveal the net effects of those characteristics.

---

[7] The share of Christian men in the labor force declined monotonically from almost 90 percent in 1974–1976 to slightly more than 80 percent in 2007–2009 (not shown in figure).

[8] Since more Christian women entered the labor market earlier than other Palestinian women, we started this analysis with the 1974–1976 labor force surveys and not with the 1979–1981 surveys as in Table 4.1.

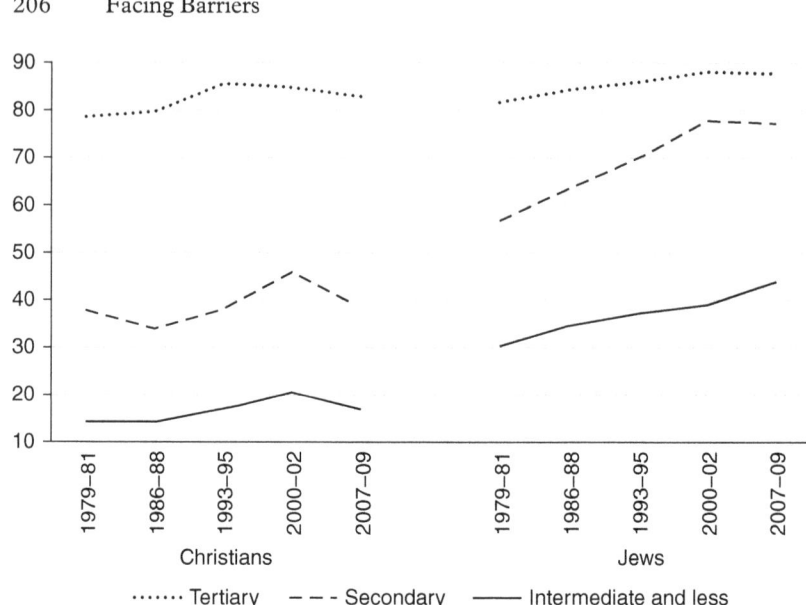

Figure 9.2 Labor Force Participation of Christian and Jewish Women
Aged 25–52 by Education and Year
Source: Labor Force Surveys 1979–2009.
Note: Only Christian women (excluding Jerusalem) and Jewish women
from the Northern and Haifa districts.

Education and Labor Force Participation. The higher Christian
women's level of education, the higher their odds of being enrolled in
the labor force, and this holds true for all years (Figure 9.2); 83.1 percent
of Christian women in the age bracket 25–52 who attended a tertiary
education were enrolled in the labor force in 2007–2009. The odds of
Christian women who attended a secondary education being employed
are about half of those attended tertiary education, and the odds of
women with the lowest level of education are about half of those with at
least some secondary education. LFP rates of Christian women within
each level of education have not changed much during the years, while
Jewish women increased their LFP rates at all education levels.
Consequently large gaps between Christian and Jewish women (residing
in Northern and Haifa districts) were formed, especially among those
with elementary education (16.9 and 43.9 percent, respectively) and
secondary education (38.5 and 77.5 percent, respectively). Among
women with at least some tertiary education the gap was small but
consistent.

Locality and Labor Force Participation. Another factor that might affect women's employment is the character of the locality in which they live. To inspect the importance of this factor we divided the Christian women into two groups: Those who reside in mixed Palestinian-Jewish towns or cities, and those who reside in communities composed of Palestinian inhabitants only.[9] Compared to the latter, the mixed cities have superior infrastructures and much better economic and occupational opportunities. These facts may explain why in all years Christian Palestinian women in these cities were much more likely to participate in the labor force than those in exclusively Palestinian communities (70 and 50 percent, respectively, in 2007–2009; figures not shown).[10] More interesting results are obtained when comparing the odds of labor force participation within educational levels in the two types of communities. Figure 9.3 shows that among Christian Palestinian women with the

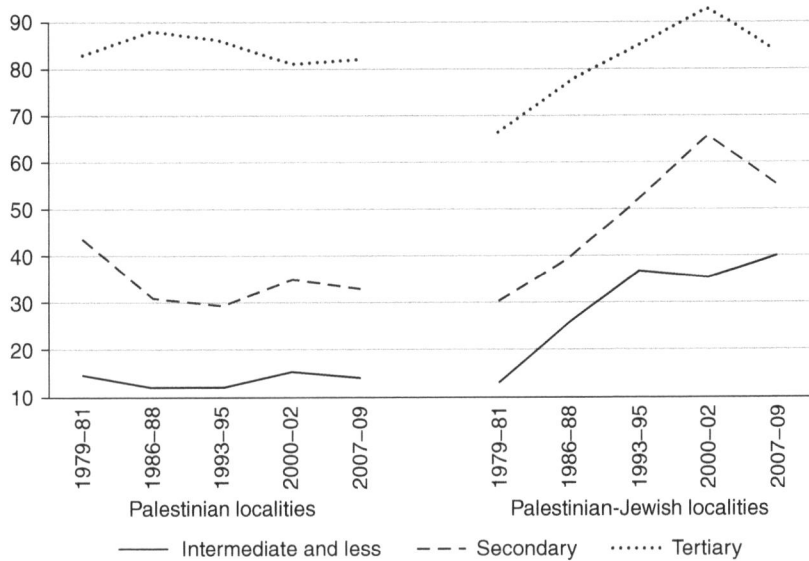

Figure 9.3 Labor Force Participation of Christian Women Aged 25–52 by Education, Locality, and Year
Source: Labor Force Surveys 1979–2009.
Note: Only Christian women (excluding Jerusalem)

---

[9] The mixed cities are Acre, Haifa, Jaffa, Ma'alot-Tarshiha, Lydda, Ramla, and Nazareth Illit.
[10] Those gaps hold true for all other years as well, save for 1979–1981 when no difference was observed.

lowest level of education (elementary and less), the gap between mixed cities and exclusively Palestinian communities is much larger: 40 and 14 percent in 2007–2009, respectively, for example. The gap was also quite large among those who attended secondary education (55 and 33 percent in the same period), while among women with tertiary education there is no difference (83.7 and 82.1 percent). These figures demonstrate the importance of the opportunity structure in generating jobs especially for women with a relatively low level of education. Here we see once more that rural Palestinian communities suffer from poor development. Highly educated women work in public services in their own communities, while women with a lower level of education do not have enough places of work due to the paucity of economic enterprises in Palestinian communities.

Marital Status and Employment. In the early years of our study employment of married Christian women was, as among Muslim and Druze women, quite rare; still, about an eighth of these women (12.1 percent in 1974–1976) worked outside the home. Among single women, employment was already quite common at that time, and about a third (34.6 percent) of these women were employed. A few years later, in 1979– 1981, more than half were in the labor market and this LFP has hardly changed since then. Meanwhile married women joined the labor market in growing numbers. Their labor force participation rates increased monotonically, and in the last period of our study it slightly surpassed the LFP rate of single women (52.8 and 49.4 percent, respectively). A similar development occurred among Jewish women.

Determinants of Christian Women's Employment: Multivariate Analysis. The above descriptive analysis highlights the main trends of Christian women's participation in the labor market and their correlations with education, marital status, and locality of residence. In this section we further examine the net effects of these compositional characteristics on Christian women's labor force participation in each of the five survey periods. To this end we regressed the dependent variable – whether a Christian Palestinian woman was in the labor force – on women's education, marital status, number of children under 15, having young children under 5, and residing in mixed Palestinian-Jewish localities as opposed to homogenous Palestinian localities.

The results are presented in Appendix 9.2. Once more we see that education is the key variable affecting women's employment. In all years women with tertiary education had the highest odds of being part of the labor force net of other variables. In 2007–2009, for instance, Christian women with tertiary education had 21 times the odds of being in the labor market compared to women with a low level of education.[11] Family composition also had an impact on Christian women's employment. Being single increased women's employment in all years but its influence has decreased over the years as found in the descriptive analysis. Thus while in 1979–1981 single women had almost 7.2 times the odds of being in the labor market compared to married women, this high ratio has declined monotonically over the years to a figure of 1.7 in 2000–2002, and by 2007–2009 there was no significant effect on employment for being married or not. Having children has been a significant constraint on the ability of Christian women to work outside the home but the effects of children has not been consistent. Each additional child under 15 reduced Christian women's odds of being employed by 19–30 percent, but in two periods (1979–1981 and 1993–1995), this effect was not significant. Net of other control variables, the odds of women with young children (under age five) to participate in the labor force were much lower than those of women with older children only in 1986–1988 and 1993–1995 (by 53 and 41 percent, respectively) but in the other periods the effect of this variable was not significant. The fact that the number of children and their ages do not have a consistent impact might be explained by the small number of children that Christian women have. The fact that having young children had no effect on women's employment in the last two decades may also suggest that Christian communities have enough day care facilities to enable mothers of toddlers to seek paid work.

Another important determinant affecting Christian women's employment is locality of residence. Since the mid-1980s Christian women in Palestinian-Jewish cities had, net of all other characteristics, higher odds of having paid employment relative to those living in Palestinian-only localities. This effect grew constantly from 1986–1988 to 2000–2002, indicating the relative advantage of the Jewish labor market (in mixed cities) over that available in Palestinian communities. In the last period this effect declined significantly but women in mixed cities still had 1.83 times the odds of being employed compared to the women in Palestinian communities.

Net Effect of Christian Affiliation on LFP. Finally, controlling for all individual characteristics (level of education, family composition, locality of residence) we see that Christian women have had in all periods a 60–70 percent lower probability of being in the labor force relative to Jewish women who live in the same areas (Northern and Haifa districts). This

---

[11] In all years, save 1979–1981, the effect of tertiary education on women's labor force participation was much larger than in 2007–2009.

finding reiterates the findings reported in Figure 9.1, but this time, since we controlled for education, family composition, and location we believe that the inferior employment of Christian women relative to Jewish women is the outcome of the less developed economy in their places of residence and blocked employment opportunities due to the preference of Jews in the Israeli economy.

9.3   Employment Characteristics and Earnings of Christian Women

After describing the trends of employment among Palestinian Christian women, we move to describe the pattern of employment and achievements of those women who are employed. With regard to the sector of employment (Appendix 9.3), we see that about half (45–55 percent) of both Christian and Jewish women (living in the northern districts of the country) were enrolled in the public sector in all periods except for the last one, with a somewhat bigger rate of Christian women in the last four periods. By 2007–2009 the two groups diverged with a rise in the rate of Christian women in the public sector to 61 percent, while that of Jewish women remained just below 45 percent.

A look at the changes in the economic branches in which Christian women are employed shows that they have increased their rates in the public sector, in wholesale and retail trade (peripheral services), and (to a smaller extent) in real estate and business services (core services), while their representation in the manufacturing sector has sharply declined from more than 25 percent in the mid-1970s to 15.2 percent in 1993–1995, and to 4.3 percent in 2007–2009. This decline is related to the fact that most of the textile manufactures where many of these women had worked have been shut down (the same misfortune that beset Muslim women, as we discussed in Section 5.3). Agriculture has completely ceased to provide Christian women with employment; in the beginning of the period 4.3 percent of Christian women were enrolled in the agricultural branch, but since the mid-1980s only a negligible number of Christian women have found work in it. Comparing Christian and Jewish women in the last period, we found that the latter have higher probabilities to be enrolled in the less rewarding branches, the manufacturing branch and peripheral services. The reason might be the scarcity of these branches in the towns and villages where the Christian women live, which is the cause of the lower labor force participation of Christian women with lower education.

Major differences are observed when comparing Christian women to their male counterparts (Appendix 9.3, panel C). First, a much smaller share of Christian men works in the public sector. A high percentage of Christian men have been employed in construction, wholesale and retail trade, repair of vehicles, and personal goods, as well as in the manufacturing sector. In 2007–2009 these economic branches accounted for more than half of all Christian men in the labor force. Thus while most Christian men are employed in the private sector, they are limited to peripheral branches.

We further examined Christian women's economic enrollment in 2007–2009 by separating them according to their locality of residence, and as expected, we found that Christian women who live in mixed Palestinian-Jewish cities were employed in a much wider spectrum of economic branches than those who live in purely Palestinian communities. Among the latter almost 72 percent are employed in social services, with core services and peripheral services accounting for an additional 22 percent of the women. In mixed localities, only 44 percent of Christian women are employed in the public sector. The other services (core and periphery) account for almost half of the women. This wider dispersion further supports our earlier observation that in mixed localities women have more options. An indicative difference is the rate of women in public administration: less than 1 percent of those living in mixed localities are enrolled in this branch, compared with more than 7 percent of those from Palestinian communities. This difference shows that in mixed localities Palestinians find it more difficult to enter good jobs because they have to compete with Jews over these positions.

The limited job options that Christian women face, especially in the Palestinian localities, is also reflected in their occupational distribution. Appendix 9.4 presents the distribution of major occupational groups, as well as a more refined distribution (two-digit classification). We included only occupations in which at least 4 percent of Christian women were enrolled at least at one point of time. The findings show that the majority of Christian women were concentrated in high white-collar occupations. Almost every second Christian woman in the mid 1970s (1974–1976) worked in associate professional and technical occupations (46.3 percent), most of them as schoolteachers. A negligible number of women worked in academic professional occupations (1.6 percent). Almost a quarter of Christian women (23.9 percent) worked in skilled and unskilled manual occupations, many of them in the garment industry. An additional 25.0 percent worked in low non-manual occupations such as clerical, sales, and service workers.

As time passed, the share of school teachers declined from 35.4 percent in 1974–1976 to 23.8 percent in 2007–2009, and the share working in skilled and unskilled manual occupations declined from 23.9 percent in the beginning of the period to merely 2.1 percent in 2007–2009. The occupations in which Christian women have increased their presence are academic professional occupations (from 1.6 to 5.6 percent), and the clerical (from 11.2 to 23.3 percent) and sales occupations (from 4.8 to 10.9 percent). Comparing Christian women's occupational enrollment with Jewish women's (residing in the Northern and Haifa districts) reveals that at the beginning of the period, Jewish women had a smaller probability of being enrolled in manual occupations and higher odds of being enrolled in clerical jobs. In the course of time, however, the occupational enrollment of these two groups has become similar, although Jewish women had a small advantage in managerial and clerical occupations.

Christian men have worked in different occupations than their female counterparts all along the period studied (Appendix 9.4, panel C). In 1974–1976 more than 70 percent of Christian men were enrolled in manual jobs (including agriculture), whereas only about a quarter (26.6 percent) of women were employed in such work. The very large rate of Christian men in manual occupations shrank over the years but in 2007–2009 almost half (48 percent) of them were still engaged in manual work. Christian women in contrast have left this kind of work, and merely 2.1 percent of them had manual jobs in 2007–2009. Thus, while 46.4 percent of Christian women worked in high non-manual occupations in 2007–2009, only 21.2 percent of Christian men did so.

In order to compare the occupational affiliation of women with similar educational levels we focus on women who attended tertiary education, who are the most likely to be employed. We look at the data of 2007–2009 and as in previous analyses look only at the occupations of Jewish women who live in the same areas as the Christians (Northern and Haifa districts). The results are presented in the first two columns of Appendix 9.5. The majority of Christian women (60 percent) were associate professionals and technicians, mostly teachers (almost 42 percent) and nurses and other paramedical occupations (12.1 percent). Some Christian women have entered academic professions (9.5 percent), most of them as lawyers (6.4 percent). Very few have entered managerial occupations (1.6 percent), while almost a quarter of the women with higher education worked in the less-prestigious clerical and sales occupations. The rate of Jewish women enrolled in clerical and sales occupation was even higher (31.2 percent), but at the same time they had a much higher share enrolled in managerial occupations (6.3 percent) and in academic professions (12.4 percent). These figures indicate that Jewish women have been favored in more prestigious occupations.

The last three columns in Appendix 9.5 compare the occupational distribution of Christian women who live in mixed Palestinian-Jewish cities with those living in exclusively Palestinian localities, and with Jewish women from the same mixed cities. Comparing first the two Christian groups, we see that although the occupational distributions of both are very much the same, nevertheless some significant differences between them exist. Higher rates of Christian women in the Palestinian-only localities are enrolled in the relatively high-status occupations of teaching, nursing, and paramedical occupations. Women residing in the mixed Palestinian-Jewish localities have entered a much broader range of occupations than those residing in the exclusively Palestinian localities, including high and low white-collar occupations as well as service occupations. This is the result of much higher LFP rates among women with at least some secondary education in the mixed cities (54.3 percent) compared to those from Palestinian localities (31.8 percent; Figure 9.3). The last figure indicates the lack of employment opportunities for women with a low level of education in Palestinian villages and towns.

A comparison of the occupational distribution of Christian and Jewish women in mixed cities reveals that Jewish women had a much higher probability of being enrolled in high prestige occupations. Almost 20 percent of Jewish women worked as academic professionals (mostly as engineers, architects, and social science workers) and as managers, almost three times the rate of Christian women in these positions. The latter worked mainly as lawyers, and very few of them held managerial jobs (0.4 percent, compared to 6 percent among Jewish women) or worked as engineers and architects (0.8 and 3.5 percent, respectively); in social science occupations the number of Christian women was negligible. A higher rate of Christian women worked in service occupations (22.3 percent), almost double the rate of service work among Jewish women living in the same cities. The comparison thus shows that Christian women who reside in mixed Palestinian-Jewish localities have a broader range of occupational opportunities compared with Christian women living in exclusively Palestinian localities, but compared with Jewish women in the same mixed cities, they have less success in entering occupations that carry more prestige and better wages and benefits.

Part-time employment. Using respondents' self-reports we examined part-time employment among Christians. As among other groups of

Palestinians and Jews, part-time work is much more common among Christian women than among Christian men. Similar to the trend among Muslim women (see Chapter 5), the share of part-time workers among Christian women has increased over the years together with their growing presence in the labor market. In 1974–1976 somewhat less than 18 percent of Christian women worked part–time, and this percentage increased monotonically to almost 39 percent in 2007–2009. The share of part-time employment among Christian men was low (around 10 percent) and has hardly changed during the years studied. In comparing Christian and Jewish women, we see that until the mid-1990s part-time work was more common among Jewish women (living in the same areas as Christians) than among Christian women, but since 2000–2002 the share of part-time work in the two groups is similar (39 percent for Christian women, and 41 for Jewish women).

Examining the reasons given by workers for not working full-time, we see that in all years a larger rate of Christian women than Jewish women reported that they worked part-time because they had not found full-time positions (involuntary part-time work; Figure 9.4). In both groups involuntary part-

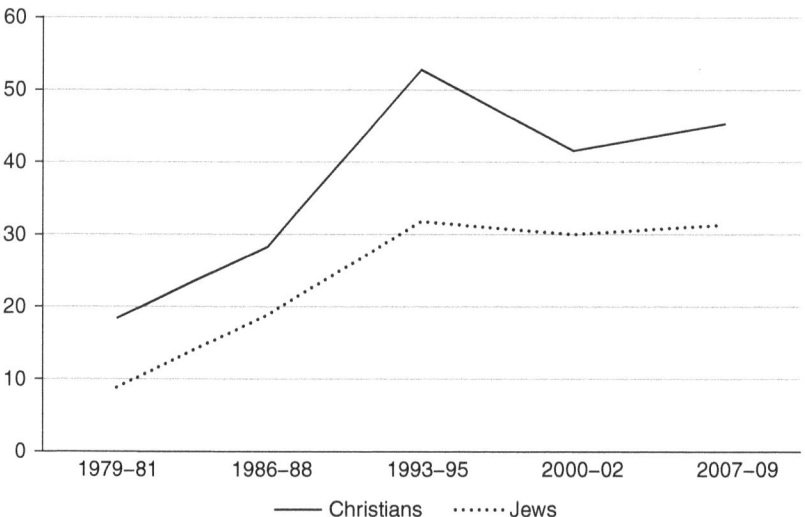

Figure 9.4 Involuntary Part-Time Work of Christian and Jewish Women Aged 18–52 by Year
Source: Labor Force Surveys 1979–2009.
Note: Only Christian women (excluding Jerusalem) and Jewish women from the Northern and Haifa districts.

time work has increased from 1979–1981 to 1993–1995 and then stabilized, but among Jewish women it stayed around 30 percent, while among Christian women it reached more than 45 percent in 2007–2009. This figure is still less than among Muslim women, which was around 65 percent in 2007–2009 (Figure 5.2). These findings indicate that like other Palestinian women, Christian women also find it more difficult than Jewish women to find jobs, but their difficulty is not as severe as among Muslim women.

Earnings. In the last section of our analysis we investigate the earnings of Christian women (aged 25–52). The data used in this section is based on the 2008 Census. The median monthly earnings of Christian women in 2008 were NIS 4,175 (while the average earnings were 5,364), less by 10 percent than the monthly earnings of Jewish women in the districts where Christians live. These earning gaps are much smaller than those between Jewish women and Muslim women (Appendix 5.5). The median earnings for Christian men were NIS 5,676, 19 percent less than the NIS 6,994 that Jewish men who live in the same districts got.

The lower earnings of Christian women compared to Jewish women may stem either from differences in human capital and labor investment or from differences in returns on personal and labor characteristics. Christian women work fewer hours (33 hours) per week than Jewish women (36 hours; partly because they do not find more work) and are more likely to work in the public sector (64 percent) than the latter (47 percent). Nevertheless Christian women have a higher share of workers with tertiary education (68 percent vs. 52 percent among Jewish women), and a higher share of them are enrolled in high non-manual jobs compared to Jewish women (53 and 40.5 percent, respectively). Both groups have accumulated very similar years of experience in the labor market (12.4 years for Christians, and 12.7 for Jews).

In order to examine the relative success with which Christian women and Jewish women convert their various compositional characteristics into earnings, we ran two separate regression equations predicting monthly earnings (Appendix 9.6, first and second columns). A comparison of the two regression equations reveals that Jewish women get NIS 1,021 more than Christian women for working in high non-manual jobs, but pay a higher "penalty"' for working in the public sector than Christian women (that is, the earnings gap between the private and the public sector is larger among Jewish women than among Christian women by NIS 1,583).[12]

---

[12] To test whether those differences are significant we used the z-test proposed by Paternoster et al. 1998.

Finally we estimated the counterfactual earnings of Christian women had they had the compositional resources of Jewish women, holding constant their earnings attainment process. The result is that they would have increased their average earnings by merely NIS 238 (from 5,364 to 5,601). Had they been subject to the same attainment process as Jewish women and holding their compositional character-istics, they would have increased their earnings by 10 percent (to NIS 5,908).

The gender gap between Christian men and women is considerably greater than the ethno-religious differences. Christian women earn on average about 72 percent of what their male counterparts earn, a gender gap smaller than that experienced by Jewish women. Christian men work 13 hours per week more than their female counterparts and have more labor force experience (14.0 and 12.4, respectively); almost half of them (48.5 percent) are enrolled in skilled manual occupations, while only 5.4 percent of women work in those occupa-tions, and they are also much more likely to be employed in the private sector (83.2 percent, compared with 36.1 of the Christian women). At the same time Christian women have a higher share of workers with tertiary education (68 and 43 percent, respectively), and a higher share of them are enrolled in high non-manual jobs (53.3 and 26.1 percent, respectively).

In order to examine the relative success with which Christian women and men convert these various compositional characteristics into earnings, we ran two separate regression equations predicting monthly earnings. Comparing the regression equations reveals some significant differences (using again the same z-test). Christian men enjoy higher returns for both secondary and tertiary education, getting NIS 1,306 for secondary education and 3,112 for tertiary education, while Christian women get practically no returns for secondary educa-tion and only NIS 1,778 for tertiary education. Both groups are rewarded for working in high non-manual occupations but Christian men get significantly NIS 935 more. Christian women get by NIS 22 more for an additional working hour (Appendix 9.6, first and third columns).

At the last stage of this comparison we estimated the counterfactual earnings of Christian women had they had the compositional resources of their male counterparts holding their earnings attainment process. The result is that their earnings would have hardly changed (their pre-dicted earnings would be NIS 5,183, while their actual mean earnings were NIS 5,364). A very different earnings prediction is obtained when holding constant Christian women's compositional characteristics but subjecting them to the same earnings attainment processes as their male counterparts. In this case they would have increased their earnings by 42.6 percent to NIS 7,652 per month.

9.4   Summary

This chapter provided a profile of the particular standing of Christian women in the labor market. Christian women marry, on the average, when they are older, compared to other Palestinian women, and have fewer children than the latter and than Jewish women. Academic education is much more prevalent among Christian women than among Druze and Muslim women, and only slightly less prevalent than among Jewish women. Given these facts, it is no wonder that Christian women's participation in the labor market is significantly higher than that of Druze and Muslim women. Yet in contrast to what one might predict based on the above facts, the share of Christian women in the labor market is much lower compared to that of Jewish women. To rule out the possibility that this difference results from the fewer opportunities available in the areas where most Christian Palestinians live, we compared Christian women only to Jewish women who live in the same districts as they do, and still, large gaps in LFP remain between these ethno-religious groups. This disadvantaged position of Christian women did not disappear when controlling for the differences between the two groups in personal and compositional characteristics. Evidence that the lower LFP of Christian women is related to difficulties in finding appropriate jobs might be found in the reasons given by part-time workers for their reduced employment. About half of the Christian women explained that they could not find full-time work.

Like all other Palestinian women in the labor market, the majority of Christian women find work mainly in the public sector, while Jewish women have many more opportunities in the private sector. Christian women have had more success than other Palestinian women in entering prestigious jobs, but there are still many occupations in which their presence is much lower compared to Jewish women. For example, among Jewish women with tertiary education 6.6 percent are either engineers, or architects, or social science workers. The respective figure for Christian women is 0.4 percent only. Concerning earnings, Christian women earn a somewhat lower income than Jewish women but much higher than those of other Palestinian women. The disadvantage relative to Jewish women stems mainly from the lower returns they receive for their resources, a fact that is usually interpreted as discrimination.

Our findings thus show that Christian women are much more integrated in the Israeli labor market than other Palestinian women. Their improved standing is related to their lower fertility rates and educational achievements. But even these women face barriers that keep them lagging behind the achievements of Jewish women. We relate this disadvantage to state policies that invest less in Palestinian communities, as well as to a systematic preference for Jews for most prestigious positions as illustrated by the lower rates of highly educated Christian women in mixed localities employed in such prestigious job relative to Jewish women in the same cities.

Appendix 9.1 *Labor Force Participation of Christian Women Aged 18–52 by Age Group and Birth Cohort*

Women	18–24	25–31	32–38	39–45	46–52
					9.2^a
1928–1934				11.7^a	10.3^b
1935–1941			13.1^a	21.3^b	17.9^c
1942–1948		24.6^a	30.4^b	24.5^c	26.5^d
1949–1955	28.4^a	33.4^b	31.2^c	39.2^d	38.2^e
1956–1962	38.3^b	41.3^c	44.1^d	54.4^e	39.4^f
1963–1969	39.2^c	48.9^d	50.7^e	59.9^f	
1970–1976	40.7^d	63.8^e	58.2^f		
1977–1983	38.4^e	63.9^f			
1984–1990	35.0^f				

Year of survey: a = 1974–1976; b = 1979–1981; c = 1986–1988; d = 1993–1995; e = 2000–2002; f = 2007–2009.
Source: Labor Force Surveys 1974–2009.
Note: Only Christian women (excluding Jerusalem).

Appendix 9.2 Logistic Coefficients and Standard Errors (in parentheses) Predicting LFP of Christian Palestinian Women Aged 25–52 by Year

	1979–1981		1986–1988		1993–1995		2000–2002		2007–2009	
	B/S.E.	Exp. (B)	B/S.E.	Exp. (B)	B/S.E.	Exp. (B)	B/S.E.	Exp. (B)	B/S.E.	Exp. (B)
Secondary education	1.762*	5.824	1.330*	3.782	1.032*	2.806	1.351*	3.862	1.065*	2.901
	(0.196)		(0.187)		(0.174)		(0.195)		(0.260)	
Tertiary education	3.069*	21.512	3.700*	40.456	3.411*	30.289	3.337*	28.133	3.035*	20.793
	(0.334)		(0.288)		(0.227)		(0.231)		(0.278)	
Mixed Palestinian-Jewish localities	-0.335	0.716	0.526*	1.692	0.853*	2.348	1.262*	3.532	0.605*	1.831
	(0.187)		(0.174)		(0.155)		(0.158)		(0.164)	
Single	1.978*	7.227	1.111*	3.036	1.065*	2.901	0.558*	1.747	-0.056	0.946
	(0.279)		(0.247)		(0.226)		(0.238)		(0.264)	
Number of children under 15	-0.078	0.925	-0.355*	0.701	-0.045	0.956	-0.257*	0.773	-0.206*	0.814
	(0.078)		(0.078)		(0.070)		(0.070)		(0.070)	
Having children under 5	-0.218	0.804	-0.746*	0.474	-0.535*	0.586	-0.216	0.806	-0.186	0.830
	(0.252)		(0.233)		(0.222)		(0.199)		(0.197)	
Age	-0.017	0.983	-0.035*	0.965	-0.019	0.981	-0.017	0.983	-0.010	0.990
	(0.013)		(0.013)		(0.012)		(0.012)		(0.012)	
Intercept	-1.442		-0.293		-1.092		-0.932		-0.935	
2 Log likelihood	953.7		1129.9		1178.6		1266.0		1213.5	
N	1,152		1,332		1,226		1,246		1,128	
Nagelkerke R2	0.377		0.441		0.437		0.412		0.346	

Variables: The dependent variable is labor force participation, coded 1 if the woman belongs to the labor force, and 0 otherwise; the independent variables are: education (distinguishing between intermediary and less (the omitted group), secondary, and tertiary education), marital status (single women were coded 1, 0 otherwise), number of children under 15, having young children under 5, age, and residence in mixed Palestinian-Jewish localities (coded 1) as opposed to homogenous Palestinian localities (coded 0).

Source: Labor Force Surveys 1979–2009.
*: p <0.05
Note: Only Christian women (excluding Jerusalem).

Appendix 9.3 *Economic Branch Distribution of Christians and Jews Aged 18–52 by Gender and Year*

	1974–1976	1979–1981	1986–1988	1993–1995	2000–2002	2007–2009
A. Christian women						
Agriculture	4.3	3.2	0.0	0.3	0.2	0.0
Manufacturing	25.5	23.3	22.5	15.2	7.7	4.3
Construction	1.3	0.8	0.2	1.2	2.0	0.5
Peripheral services	10.9	13.3	15.8	20.9	19.5	21.0
Wholesale and retail trade, repair of vehicles and personal and household goods	(5.9)	(9.1)	(10.3)	(12.6)	(15.2)	(13.1)
Core services	3.5	9.8	13.0	10.0	12.1	13.4
Real estate, renting and business activities	(2.7)	(4.8)	(5.7)	(6.3)	(8.8)	(11.0)
Public sector	54.5	48.8	48.5	52.4	55.0	60.8
Public administration	(1.6)	(3.2)	(2.5)	(3.6)	(3.6)	(4.6)
Education	(38.4)	(32.5)	(27.1)	(30.6)	(28.6)	(35.1)
Health services and welfare and social work	(12.9)	(10.7)	(14.9)	(13.8)	(18.2)	(18.2)
Total	100.0	100.0	100.0	100.0	100.0	100.0
N	372	497	630	748	911	887
B. Jewish women						
Agriculture	4.3	3.7	2.6	1.5	0.5	0.3
Manufacturing	12.7	10.3	13.0	12.2	11.9	12.1
Construction	1.5	1.1	0.8	1.3	1.2	0.8
Peripheral services	24.3	20.2	23.4	25.0	26.3	28.8
Wholesale and retail trade, repair of vehicles and personal and household goods	(6.4)	(7.4)	(10.4)	(11.8)	(13.5)	(14.1)
Core services	9.8	11.4	14.7	11.4	12.1	13.3
Real estate, renting and business activities	(5.1)	(6.5)	(8.3)	(7.0)	(8.1)	(9.8)
Public sector	47.5	53.3	45.5	48.6	47.9	44.7
Public administration	(7.1)	(9.2)	(5.1)	(4.6)	(4.8)	(5.3)
Education	(31.5)	(31.5)	(25.6)	(27.0)	(25.1)	(22.9)
Health services and welfare and social work	(7.5)	(9.5)	(9.9)	(11.9)	(13.5)	(12.8
Total	100.0	100.0	100.0	100.0	100.0	100.0
N	2,593	3,676	4,410	5,261	5,805	5,720

Appendix 9.3 (*cont.*)

	1974–1976	1979–1981	1986–1988	1993–1995	2000–2002	2007–2009
C. Christian men						
Agriculture	5.2	4.1	2.6	1.7	2.2	2.1
Manufacturing	21.8	22.0	22.4	19.4	18.6	13.7
Construction	27.4	26.7	23.3	23.5	17.0	18.8
Peripheral services	28.9	25.4	31.0	29.4	34.9	37.6
Wholesale and retail trade, repair of vehicles and personal and household goods	(17.6)	(18.0)	(19.9)	(21.0)	(22.6)	(18.7)
Core services	2.6	4.0	2.9	9.2	8,2	10.2
Real estate, renting and business activities	(1.3)	(2.5)	(1.8)	(7.2)	(6.4)	(9.0)
Public sector	14.1	17.8	17.8	16.8	19.1	17.6
Public administration	(4.0)	(4.3)	(3.6)	(3.3)	(3.4)	(2.5)
Education	(6.8)	(8.1)	(7.3)	(6.0)	(5.2)	(5.3)
Health services and welfare and social work	(1.9)	(3.4)	(4.3)	(4.4)	(6.7)	(5.4)
Total	100.0	100.0	100.0	100.0	100.0	100.0
N	1,801	1,365	1,680	1,423	1,380	1,361

Source: Labor Force Surveys 1974–2009.
Note: Only Christians (excluding Jerusalem) and Jewish women from the Northern and Haifa districts.

Appendix 9.4 *Occupational Distribution of Christians and Jews Aged 18–52 by Gender and Year*

	1974–1976	1979–1981	1986–1988	1993–1995	2000–2002	2007–2009
A. Christian Women						
Academic professionals	1.6	1.4	1.0	1.9	6.1	5.6
Associate professionals and technicians	46.3	34.3	32.6	34.6	34.8	39.8
Primary school teachers	(35.4)	(25.5)	(17.6)	(23.1)	(17.9)	(23.8)
Nurses and other paramedical	(8.0)	(5.9)	(9.0)	(4.8)	(6.4)	(7.7)
Managers	0.5	0.4	0.3	1.9	1.3	1.0
Clericals	11.2	21.2	28.7	24.0	29.1	23.3
Sales	4.8	6.7	5.4	8.0	8.2	10.9
Service workers	9.0	10.2	12.2	15.2	15.4	17.3
Agriculture workers	2.7	1.2	0.4	0.0	0.1	0.0
Skilled workers	19.4	21.0	16.2	11.1	3.1	1.8
Spinning, weaving workers	(6.1)	(3.4)	(1.0)	(0.1)	(0.0)	(0.0)
Tailors, dressmakers	(12.2)	(16.0)	(14.3)	(7.6)	(2.1)	(0.8)
Unskilled workers	4.5	3.6	3.2	3.3	1.9	0.3
Total	100.0	100.0	100.0	100.0	100.0	100.0
N	376	495	631	749	912	887
B. Jewish Women						
Academic professionals	2.6	3.8	3.8	3.6	5.6	6.6
Associate professionals and technicians	37.3	37.7	30.5	33.1	28.5	25.9
Primary school teachers	(18.1)	(16.5)	(14.4)	(15.1)	(13.1)	(11.2)
Nurses and other paramedical	(8.9)	(8.8)	(4.9)	(5.6)	(4.1)	(3.9)
Managers	0.5	0.7	1.8	1.9	3.7	4.7
Clericals	32.6	35.9	33.7	31.8	32.6	30.9
Sales	4.1	4.0	7.0	8.5	10.7	11.1
Service workers	13.5	10.5	16.5	16.3	15.7	17.4
Agriculture workers	2.3	2.1	1.2	0.6	0.3	0.2
Skilled workers	4.6	4.0	4.2	2.9	2.2	2.2
Unskilled workers	2.5	1.3	1.3	1.3	0.7	0.9
Total	100.0	100.0	100.0	100.0	100.0	100.0
N	2,628	3,676	4,390	5,271	5,798	5,710
C. Christian Men						
Academic professionals	0.8	1.5	2.7	5.5	7.9	7.0
Associate professionals and technicians	8.5	12.1	10.6	9.8	10.5	12.4
Managers	0.8	1.7	3.8	2.5	3.9	1.8
Clericals	5.5	5.7	6.7	6.7	6.1	5.2
Sales	6.7	6.7	8.5	10.9	9.6	11.2
Service workers	6.3	5.0	8.1	7.2	10.1	14.7
Agriculture workers	5.0	3.8	2.4	1.1	2.0	1.6

Appendix 9.4 *(cont.)*

	1974–1976	1979–1981	1986–1988	1993–1995	2000–2002	2007–2009
Skilled workers	60.7	55.3	50.9	52.5	45.0	41.8
Unskilled workers	5.7	8.2	6.3	3.9	4.9	4.3
Total	100.0	100.0	100.0	100.0	100.0	100.0
N	1,808	1,367	1,684	1,425	1,380	1,357

Source: Labor Force Surveys 1974–2009.
Note: Only Christians (excluding Jerusalem) and Jewish women from the Northern and Haifa districts.

Appendix 9.5 *Occupational Distribution of Christian and Jewish Women Aged 25–52 by Education and Locality, 2007–2009*

	Tertiary education		All levels of education		
	Christian	Jewish	Christian		Jewish
			Palestinian localities	Mixed localities	Mixed localities
Academic professionals	9.5	12.4	6.4	6.5	13.9
Engineers and architects	(0.4)	(3.4)	(0.0	(0.8)	(3.5)
Jurist	(6.4)	(1.4)	(4.6)	(4.2)	(1.6)
Social science workers	(0.0)	(3.2)	(0.0)	(0.0)	(3.5)
Associate professional and technicians	60.4	42.0	47.1	36.2	29.0
Teacher in secondary and post-secondary	(5.2)	(5.9)	(4.1)	(3.1)	(3.5)
Teachers in primary and kindergarten	(36.7)	(18.9)	(29.1)	(23.4)	(11.0)
Nurses and other paramedical professions	(12.1)	(7.0)	(9.9)	(4.6)	(3.9)
Managers	1.6	6.3	1.6	0.4	6.0
Clericals	18.0	25.7	22.0	24.6	28.6
Sales	5.0	5.5	8.0	8.5	8.8
Service workers	4.8	6.6	12.3	22.3	12.0
Farm workers	0.0	0.1	0.0	0.0	0.1
Skilled and unskilled workers	0.7	1.3	2.5	1.6	1.7
Total	100.0	100.0	100.0	100.0	100.0
N	505	2,892	486	260	1,274

Source: Labor Force Surveys 2007–2009.
Note: Only Christian women (excluding Jerusalem) and Jewish women from the Northern and Haifa districts.

Appendix 9.6 *Regression Coefficients and Standard Errors (in parentheses) Predicting Monthly Earnings of Christian and Jewish Workers Aged 25–52 by Gender, 2008*

	Women		Men	
	Christians	Jews	Christians	Jews
Residing in mixed	146.0	270.2*	97.2	716.0*
localities	(189.1)	(91.0)	(266.9)	(168.1)
Secondary education	−23.850	199.16	1306.4*	1516.8*
	(425.2)	(241.9)	(346.2)	(334.2)
Tertiary education	1777.9*	2280.1 *	3111.9 *	5576.3*
	(409.3)	(249.1)	(406.5)	(0.059)
Weekly hours of work	92.76*	116.36*	70.90*	115.5*
	(7.897)	(3.523)	(8.537)	(5.96)
Experience	389.05*	415.07*	448.0*	794.5*
	(53.5)	(33.57)	(72.4)	(67.74)
Experience squared	−10.94*	−9.288*	−8.699*	−14.57*
	(2.015)	(1.225)	(2.422)	(2.336)
High non-manual	2227.7*	3248.28*	3162*	4941.8*
occupations	(380.4)	(195.8)	(300.8)	(209.8)
Low non-manual	460.8	909.38*	424.2	738.5*
occupations	(410.4)	(177.37)	(292.0)	(198.1)
Work in public sector	−181.28	−1764.08*	−385.7	−3213.1*
	(206.93)	(91.23)	(341.9)	(193.3)
Intercept	−2938.1*	−3981.2*	−2695.4*	−7683.8*
	(621.9)	(350.1)	(699.4)	(546.5)
R^2	0.259	0.303	0.226	0.338

Variables: The dependent variable is gross monthly earnings, measured in Israeli New Shekels; the independent variables included: education (distinguishing between intermediate and less, the reference category, secondary, and tertiary); experience (age minus years of schooling minus five); hours (number of hours worked during the last week); occupational enrollment, distinguishing among three broad groups (high non-manual; low non-manual; manual workers, the reference group); employment sector (coded 1 for those employed in the public sector and 0 for those in the private sector); locality of residence (mixed Palestinian-Jewish localities are coded 1, 0 otherwise).
Sources: 2008 Census.
*: $p < 0.05$
Note: Only Christians (excluding Jerusalem) and Jews from the Northern and Haifa districts.

10   Conclusion
The Politics of Employment in an Ethnocracy

10.1   The Puzzle of Palestinian Women's Employment

This book was motivated by the wish to understand the forces behind the low rate of labor force participation of Israeli Palestinian women and their very poor achievements in terms of occupations and income in the Israeli labor market. Unlike many earlier researchers who implicitly or explicitly accepted this situation as a straightforward outcome of the roles assigned to women in Arab and Muslim societies, we saw this situation as a puzzle requiring a solution. The fact that rates of female labor force participation in the Arab societies around Israel have also been low relative to other regions in the world was brought by those early researchers as evidence that the situation of Israeli Palestinian women is related to the status of women in Arab societies in general and not related to local conditions in Israel. For us this fact was not part of the solution but, on the contrary, a fact that made our problem even more puzzling because the Israel economy is much more developed than that of the Arab and Muslim countries around it, and the service sector – which is especially important in providing adequate employment for women – has always been larger than usual for Israel's level of economic development. Given these auspicious conditions for women's labor, we wondered why the presence of Palestinian women in Israel's labor market is not much higher than that of women in the other Arab and Muslim countries of the MENA region, and recently even lower than in a few of those countries. Why, we therefore asked, are Jewish Israeli women who live under the same macroeconomic conditions and under the same legal and institutional arrangements as Palestinian women (at least formally), three times more likely to be gainfully employed than the latter?

To add another complicating fact to our puzzle, we would remind the readers that about half of those Jewish women are Mizrahi women, that is, they are the daughters and granddaughters of Jews who had lived in MENA countries just a generation or two ago (Dahan-Kalev 2001;

Motzafi-Haller 2001; Shenhav 2006). Although Jewish culture might have been different from that of the Muslims around them, ideas about gender relations were similar among Jews and non-Jews. Several decades after their immigration, Mizrahi Jews are still a disadvantaged group relative to Ashkenazi Jews who were originally from European countries, and yet Mizrahi women are not less likely than Ashkenazi women to be in the labor market, and taking into consideration their lower education and other variables, are even more active in the market than the Ashkenaziot (Yonay and Kraus 2017). The change in the status of Mizrahi women strengthens the enigmatic nature of our puzzle: Why has labor force participation changed much more slowly and why has it reached a much lower level among all Palestinian women than among Mizrahi women?

Moreover, another component that added to our bewilderment regarding Palestinian women's low LFP is the revolutionary changes that Palestinian women in Israel have undergone during the last decades. The rocky relationship with the Jewish majority notwithstanding, the life of all Palestinian citizens in Israel has changed radically due to their connections with the Jewish society (Rouhana 1997; Rabinowitz and Abu-Baker 2008). Gender relations have also been greatly transformed. The educational achievements of Palestinian women increased quite impressively. Secondary education has become almost universal, and sizeable and growing proportions of Palestinian women have acquired college education. Almost all colleges and universities are located in Jewish environments and Palestinian students are exposed to the dominant Jewish culture and to the academic content typical to Western higher-education institutions. Palestinians are attuned to radio and TV from neighboring Arab societies, but they also follow news and entertainment on Israeli channels that are produced by Jews for Jewish spectators. Demographically, Palestinian women marry at an older age and have much fewer children than their mothers. Lower fertility clearly demonstrates that Palestinian women take active measures to change basic patterns such as family planning. Women have also become more active politically, especially on the municipal level and in many civil society movements, establishing women's organizations for Palestinians and cooperating with the Jewish feminist movement (Abu-Baker 1998; Herzog 2004a, 2004b, 2005; Erdreich 2006, 2008; Herzog and Yahia-Younis. 2007; Daoud 2009; Abu-Rabia-Queder and Weiner-Levy 2013).

As discussed in our first chapter, common explanations for the low share of Palestinian women who work outside their homes refer to Arab cultural heritage and to the religious characteristics of Islam as key factors inhibiting Palestinian women's activities in the public sphere, including income-producing activity. This explanation may seem attractive because it resonates with what we know about clothing and movement limitations common among many segments of Arab and Muslim societies in Israel, in the MENA region, and among Arab and Muslim immigrants in Western countries. Thus, for example, a textbook on the economics of gender explains that women in MENA countries exhibit very low labor force participation rates "because of cultural attitudes and practices that prohibit women from public activities. Inhibiting factors included early marriage and female seclusion. Women in theses cultures are expected to concentrate time and effort on their families" (Jacobsen 2007, 360).

Why do we find such explanations lacking? There is no point in denying the importance of cultural constructions in shaping people's thoughts and channeling their decisions and behavior. Nor should one underestimate the precarious status of women in most, if not all, Muslim societies including the Arab countries.

Although it may seem compelling to attribute variance in behavior among ethnic groups to cultural differences, it is theoretically problematic. Culture is indeed basic to human behavior, but it is not an immutable monolithic entity that keeps behavior constant. On the contrary, culture is dynamic and changes, *inter alia*, in response to economic pressures, opportunities, and political circumstances (Weber 1958; Durkheim 1984; Sewell 1992; Lamont and Small 2008; Sa'ar 2017). The emphasis on women's chastity and modesty in the Muslim world as an explanation for women's exclusion from the public sphere ignores the fact that women were totally excluded from many public forums and from spheres of power in many patriarchal societies throughout the world – not long ago in European society as well – and they changed, partially, in the course of time due to various economic and political conditions.

There are rival explanations for the changing position of women in industrialized societies. Changes in the nature of work, the development of the service economy, the invention of new household technologies, and the decline of men's salaries have been offered as structural explanations for the growing entrance of women into labor markets. Demands of women for equal participation and notions of human rights have also been offered as ideological causes of the same process. Public demands and economic necessities are processed in the political system to produce specific outcomes, and the policies that channel women's decisions regarding paid employment thus depend also on the structure of the polity and on particular historical alignments of various political players. Hence advanced capitalist societies greatly differ in their social welfare and gender policies (Esping-Andersen 1990, 1996; Lewis 1992; Misra et al. 2007; Lewis et al. 2008). The situation of women in developing countries is also determined by specific economic resources and structures and the position of countries in the world system (Boserup 1970; Benería 1982; Tinker 1990; Pearson 1992). In Chapter 1 we reviewed the comparative literature that showed how under specific political alignments particular economic conditions in MENA countries lead to diverse outcomes in regard to women's position in general, and labor force participation in particular (Shami et al. 1990; Kandiyoti 1991b; Moghadam 1998, 2003; Charrad 2001, 2011; Karshenas and Moghadam 2001; Ross 2008).

This book joins the above body of scholarly work but whereas most studies in this direction compared countries, we looked at the politico-economic forces impinging on ethnic communities within one particular society. We wondered how the status of Palestinians in Israel shaped the economic participation of Palestinian women in general, and we looked at the specific Palestinian subgroups to see how their location and relations with the state affected the employment of women from those subgroups. Each of the last four chapters dealt with a specific group of Palestinians – Bedouins in the south, Muslims in Jerusalem (as officially defined by Israel), Druze, and Christians – with the previous two chapters describing employment patterns of the major group of Muslim Palestinians who live in the north and center of Israel. Emerging from all these finding is a large and complex picture, in which many details are similar but some parameters are different. This picture is summarily presented in Table 10.1 where some trends of labor force characteristics are followed.[1] In the next section we emphasize 11 major patterns of findings that in our view are the most relevant for deciphering the puzzle this book grappled with. Each of these patterns is a clue to the solution, which is perhaps not inclusive for solving the puzzle of Palestinian women's low employment, but taken together we believe that these clues support our thesis about the importance of economic opportunities, structural circumstances, and state policies in shaping Palestinians women's labor force behavior.

---

[1] We added one more period (2010–2011) to this summarizing table to make the picture more up to date. We could not add more years because since 2012 the Central Labor of Statistics changed the sampling technique and some definitions of the LFS. Because of these changes, the data since 2012 are not comparable to the earlier data (for more information, see CBS, N.D.).

Table 10.1 *Selected Characteristics of Israeli Women by Ethno-Religious Group and Year*

	1974–1976	1979–1981	1986–1988	1993–1995	2000–2002	2007–2009	2010–2011
Attendance of academic institutions (including teachers college, %), women aged 18–52							
Muslims, north and center	N.A.	3.5	4.1	6.0	11.9	20.3	23.3
Druze	N.A.	1.3	2.7	3.7	16.4	19.7	17.1
Christians	N.A.	9.9	11.7	20.5	29.9	39.4	40.5
Jews	N.A.	28.0	29.4	31.7	38.4	45.4	47.2
Labor force participation (%), women aged 18–52							
Muslims							
North and center	7.7	12.0	12.5	18.9	20.5	28.1	28.8
Jerusalem	6.0	5.9	5.5	6.3	12.7	13.3	15.0
Bedouins in towns	N.A.	N.A.	N.A.	9.5	15.0	20.3	18.9
				(1995–1997)	(2001–2003)		
Druze	5.1	8.7	15.7	19.9	28.2	32.8	29.9
Christians	19.5	29.3	33.6	41.6	49.3	51.8	55.9
Jews	52.2	56.5	59.8	67.2	71.9	75.2	75.9
Labor force participation (%) by last school attended, married women aged 25–52							
A. Muslims, north and center							
Low education	N.A.	1.6	1.7	3.5	6.3	7.3	7.6
Secondary education	N.A.	24.3	11.1	12.0	14.5	18.2	16.4
Tertiary education	N.A.	95.7	80.4	76.6	76.8	74.8	70.0
B. Jews							
Low education	N.A.	27.1	33.2	47.3	51.1	52.5	54.9
Secondary education	N.A.	53.9	57.4	66.8	72.0	75.9	77.6
Tertiary education	N.A.	78.3	78.0	83.2	85.3	86.8	87.5

Table 10.1 (cont.)

	1974–1976	1979–1981	1986–1988	1993–1995	2000–2002	2007–2009	2010–2011
Part-time employment (%) and its involuntary share (%), women aged 18–52							
A. Muslims, north and center							
Part-time	18.6	25.8	20.0	21.8	34.0	39.1	35.7
Involuntary	N.A.	1.9	20.0	49.0	64.3	65.3	68.9
B. Bedouins in Towns							
Part-time	N.A.	N.A.	N.A.	18.0	21.8	21.9	24.2
				(1995–2001)	(2002–2005)	(2006–2009)	
C. Druze							
Part-time	12.8	16.2	15.4	17.8	28.7	33.9	28.9
Involuntary	N.A.	N.A.	28.6	54.5	71.1	65.3	73.5
D. Christians							
Part-time	17.5	23.3	22.2	26.6	39.0	38.5	33.2
Involuntary	N.A.	18.5	28.4	52.2	41.5	45.2	49.3
E. Jews							
Part-time	28.2	37.4	40.5	39.7	35.7	39.4	42.6
Involuntary	N.A.	4.0	12.7	27.7	24.0	23.1	20.9

Table 10.1 (cont.)

	1974–1976	1979–1981	1986–1988	1993–1995	2000–2002	2007–2009	2010–2011
A. Muslims, north and center		Commuting (%), women aged 18–52					
Total		36.6	39.0	39.9	34.7	36.1	35.4
By education							
Low		41.5	43.9	47.3	44.3	45.6	49.2
Secondary		25.1	38.6	37.0	33.1	35.0	32.0
Tertiary		35.7	31.2	36.6	30.8	34.8	36.0–
B. Jews							
Total		34.0	37.0	40.0	45.6	48.9	49.1
By education							
Low		29.4	27.3	30.4	29.0	27.4	38.0
Secondary		34.9	36.4	38.7	42.7	42.6	42.4
Tertiary		33.8	38.3	41.8	48.7	53.2	57.0

Median monthly earnings (NIS), women aged 25–52 (2008)

Muslims North	Muslims Center	Muslims Jerusalem	Muslims 5 mixed cities	Druze	Christians	Jews
3,627	3,806	3,618	3,027	3,214.5	4,175	5,521

Source: Labor Force Surveys 1979–2011, 2008 Census.

10.2   Clues to the Solution of the Puzzle of Low Labor Force Experience among Palestinian Women

Clue 1: Declining Labor Force Participation of Palestinian Women with Tertiary Education. Palestinian women with tertiary education have always been much more active in the labor market than those who have not continued their studies. This is not surprising. Acquiring higher education is expensive. It is not free as in most European countries, and tuition rose significantly from the 1970s to the 1990s. It is also especially demanding for Palestinians who for the first time in their lives have to study in Hebrew. Moreover, universities and colleges are located in Jewish towns, and the majority of students and almost all lecturers and administrative personnel are Jewish. The Palestinian students often face discrimination, exclusion, and alienation in this environment. Due to the cost and difficulties they face we can assume that Palestinian women who pursue such education plan to work after their graduation.

This expectation was fully supported during the first periods analyzed in our study and yet the percentage of women with this level of education who are employed has declined over the years. Among Druze and Christian women the decline is only in recent years and quite small, but among Muslim women (married) the percentage of employment among those with tertiary education goes down continuously from more than 95 percent in 1979–1981 to below 75 percent in 2007–2009. This unexpected trend is probably related to the fact that many more women gain higher education, leading to growing competition between them for jobs that are scarce. While this is probably the case, the contrast to Jewish women is telling. Participation rates of Jewish women with tertiary education have continued to climb throughout the period regardless of ever-growing college attendance. The fact that highly educated Jewish women find jobs, while Palestinian women seem to meet difficulties in securing employment supports our thesis that low employment rates among Palestinian women is due to lack of available positions rather than due to cultural preferences.

Clue 2: Very Low Labor Force Participation of Women with Secondary Education. The core of low employment among all Palestinian women is observed among women with less than tertiary education. Among all the differentiated Palestinian groups the gap between women with at least some tertiary education and those who lack it is huge. Among Muslim women with secondary education, employment fluctuated between 18.5 and 23 percent. Among Druze women it was quite low for most of the time, and only in 2000–2002 did it start to go up quite fast, surpassing the 30 percent in 2007–2009. Among Christian women, the rates of participation were higher but dropped at the beginning of the period studied from the upper 30s to the lower 30s, rose gradually to 46 percent by 2000, and then dropped again to less than 40 percent. The low figures that characterize even the Christian women without tertiary education contrast the much higher participation rates among Jewish women, rising from 54 to 75 percent during the years covered in our study.

The huge gap between Palestinians and Jews in this level of education means that the focus of the search for a solution to our puzzle must be on finding why so many women with secondary education are not employed. The importance of this question is magnified by the size of this group. Although the number of Palestinian women with tertiary education has substantially grown during the years, about 80 percent of both Muslim and Druze women (aged 18–52), and 60 percent among Christian women, still had not reached beyond high school in 2007–2009. Is it possible that women who do not continue their studies are more traditional than those who continue to tertiary education and therefore fewer of them are interested in salaried work?

Logically this explanation is possible, yet we think that an alternative explanation, the lack of enough suitable job opportunities, is more important for understanding this pattern of low employment. An important support for this interpretation is a fact mentioned already several times in this book. During the late 1970s and through the 1980s many Palestinian women with a low level of education worked in small textile and garment factories established in many Palestinian villages, relying upon the cheap labor those women provided. This employment venue disappeared in later years when employers found cheaper labor in neighboring Arab countries and East Asia. Since then no other industries have been established in Palestinian localities, and commuting to industrial zones in Jewish areas was not a viable option, especially not for mothers, because the low salaries paid to women with low level of education is apparently not a sufficient incentive for those women who would also have to pay for transportation and child care. Additional support for this explanation is further elaborated in the next clue.

Clue 3: An Anomalous Commuting Pattern. Commuting is expensive in terms of money and time. Therefore it is more common among women with more human capital who are interested in maximizing the return on their investment (White 1977; Simpson 1980, 1987). Whereas this is indeed the case for Jewish women, Muslim women deviate from this pattern, and commuting is more common among those with lower education relative to those with tertiary education. In 2007–2009, for instance, 46 percent of the women with intermediate education and less worked outside the municipalities in which they lived, while only 36 percent of those with at least some tertiary education traveled to another municipality to work. This pattern reflects the lack of enough jobs for women with low education as a result of the lack of industrial and commercial development in Palestinian localities. It may also reflect the difficulties of Palestinian women with higher education to enter better jobs in the Jewish sector. This lack of job opportunities for women with low and high level of education is further supported in the next two clues.

Clue 4: Higher Rates of Participation in Mixed Palestinian-Jewish Cities. Palestinian women who live in mixed localities are much more active in the labor market than those who live in homogeneous Palestinian localities. For example, in 2007–2009 almost every second married Muslim woman residing in a mixed community was enrolled in a paying job, compared to only one out of four Muslim women residing in Palestinian localities. Christian women dwelling in mixed cities had 1.8 times higher chances to be employed compared to Christian women residing in purely Palestinian communities.[2]

As we said above, shortage of jobs in Palestinian localities was especially felt by women with a low level of education, and we may highlight this claim by comparing the employment of women at this level of education in the mixed cities where more jobs are available for women with all levels of education with that in the Palestinian towns. Among Muslim women with intermediate and less education in those mixed cities 21 percent had a job, compared to only 13 percent in Palestinian communities; among women with secondary education the gap was even bigger: 51.5 and 26 percent, respectively. Among Christian women with intermediate and less education the gap was also very big, 40 and 14 percent, and among Christian with secondary education the respective figures were 55 and 33 percent.

Clue 5: A Narrow Range of Industrial and Occupational Enrollment. Throughout our book we documented the limited industrial and occupational distribution of Palestinian women. With minor differences this finding was discovered among all the Palestinian subgroups. Much smaller shares of Palestinian women were employed in the private sector relative to Jewish women, and in the public sector they depended mostly on public services within their own communities (either Palestinian municipalities or in Palestinian neighborhoods in mixed cities).

---

[2] Druze women do not live in mixed Palestinian-Jewish cities.

The reasons Palestinian women are underrepresented in the private sector are related to the nature of the Palestinian economy in Israel and the discrimination and exclusion from the Jewish-owned economy. The Palestinian economy is small and limited; it is composed mostly of small firms in competitive markets, and work prospects are thus both few and not attractive. Jewish-owned firms are almost always far from Palestinian communities and require commuting. A more intimidating obstacle is the attitudes of Jewish owners and managers. Prejudice, hostility, and fear of strife among workers cause many of them to avoid hiring Palestinian workers in general, to limit their hiring to lower positions in which they do not supervise Jewish employees, and to offer them smaller salaries. Those who *do* find jobs in the private sector usually enter peripheral service industries which are prominent among Palestinian businesses.

In terms of occupations we found that large segments of Muslim, Druze, and Christian women in the labor force are enrolled in merely 2 to 3 percent of the 400 or so occupations included in the three-digit classification of occupations in the Israeli economy. This narrowness is more glaring when we examine women with an academic degree. Unlike Jewish women, Palestinian women with such a degree hardly enter academic professional occupations such as medical doctors, lawyers, and economists and are mainly employed as teachers, social workers, and administrators in Palestinian communities.

There is only one exception of a public service branch that serves the whole population and employs many Palestinians, women and men. This is the health services in which many Palestinians are employed as physicians (mostly men; see Keshet et al. 2015), nurses (both genders; see Popper-Giveon et al. 2015), pharmacists (also both genders), and other paramedical occupations. The exceptional openness of medical services attracts the attention of researchers and of lay people who seem astonished at what appears to be egalitarian employment for Palestinians, but this very astonishment underlines how few other channels are open to Palestinians with good education.

Clue 6: Involuntary Part-Time Employment. The share of part-time workers increased among women from all the Palestinian groups as well as among Jewish women as more women entered the paid market, but while in the past all Palestinian women were less inclined to work part time than Jewish women, in the last period (2007–2009) 39 percent of Muslim, Christian, *and* Jewish women worked part time, and only among Druze women was the share a bit smaller (34 percent).

More important is the reasons given by women for this form of employment. Strong evidence supporting our thesis that job scarcity is the major cause of low FLFP among Arab Palestinian women is the reason those women who work part time give when asked to explain their partial employment. In this regard Jewish women greatly differ from all Palestinian women. For the former part-time work is mostly *voluntary*, whereas for the latter, part-time work was *typically involuntary*, that is, they preferred full-time work but had to compromise on partial employment because they could not find a full-time position. The unavailability of a full-time job was given as a reason for their part-time employment by almost two-thirds of female Muslim (in the north and center) and Druze workers, compared to less than a quarter of the Jewish female workers. Among Christian part-time female workers, only 45 percent said they had been interested in a full-time job, indicating that they encounter somewhat fewer difficulties in finding work than Muslim and Druze women, and yet, it shows that they too meet more difficulties than Jewish women.

The difficulties of part-time female workers to secure more work is an important clue for solving our puzzle because it explains also the fact that many women remain out of the labor force. If even those who are employed and who have accumulated job experience find it hard to find work, it implies that those who are not employed would find it even harder to find suitable positions. If some potential workers find only a part-time job away from their towns, the salary might be too small to compensate for the costs. A part-time position in town might be good, but with so many women employed part time and not finding more work, it seems that such positions are also in shortage.

Clue 7: "Druze Particularism." At the outset of our work we reasoned that the situation of subgroups of Palestinian women must be analyzed separately in order to show how different political, economic, and socio-geographic conditions affect the employment of women; the changes in employment of Druze women is a clear example of this.

Druze women and Muslim women (living in the same areas as the Druze) shared similar statuses within their societies with both groups of women almost totally absent from the labor market in the mid 1970s. Only 5 percent of Druze women, and six of Muslim women, were gainfully employed in 1974–1976. Both groups of women have experienced radical changes in their lives since then, and expansion of paid employment was among these changes. Their patterns of employment are quite similar also at the end of our study but there are several indications that Druze women surpassed Muslim women in the level of participation. First of all, a gap of 5 percent developed in their participation rates, with 33 percent of Druze women and only 28 percent of the Muslim women belonging to the labor force in 2007–2009. The former have even a bigger advantage over Muslim women among women who attended secondary education, who, as explained above, are the key for understanding Palestinian women's low LFP (33 and 18 percent, respectively). Another advantage of Druze women is the fact that fewer of them work part time: only 34 percent, compared to 41.5 percent of Muslim women who live in the same sub-districts as the Druze.

These gaps can hardly be explained by cultural differences between the two Palestinian groups since both groups share many similar cultural attributes. The Druze even tend to maintain their traditional customs more strictly than Muslims. Many of them reside in remote and homogeneous communities, and their religious leadership is more involved in monitoring daily life due to its wish to preserve the group's separate identity. Given this adherence to the Druze tradition, how can we explain the small but significant advantage that Druze women have relative to Muslim women in terms of employment?

The answer to this question is related to the special relations between the Druze community and the state. The Druze have been more involved in the main political parties, including those in governing coalitions, and have thus established better ties with state officials and ministers. Druze leaders demanded state aid to their communities in return for the military service of Druze men, and this service might have also facilitated Druze-owned businesses. Druze men's careers in the security services and the army might have also contributed to more favorable economic conditions in Druze towns and villages. An indication of these favorable conditions is the fact that in all years studied, Druze women had by far a higher probability to work within their places of residence. For example, merely one quarter of Druze women in 2007–2009 commuted to work, by about nine percent less than Muslim women in the same geographical regions. Many of the Druze women that worked in their own localities were able to find jobs in the private sector in the manufacturing economic branch, an option that is quite rare in other Palestinian communities. The case of textile factories may demonstrate how better ties with the state enhance the employment conditions of Druze women. While most such factories were closed in Muslim villages during the 1990s, those in Druze localities have survived, and in 2007–2009 about 8 percent of Druze women still worked in the textile industry. How have they survived? It turns out that many of them produce army uniforms, a sheltered market in which good relationships with the state are advantageous and the competition with foreign producers does not exist.

Clue 8: Neglected and Harassed by the State: The Case of the Bedouins. Employment of Bedouin women in the Naqab is another example of the importance of the state and its treatment of specific minority groups, but in contrast to the Druze, the Bedouin example exemplifies the adverse impact of the state. Due to their nomadic past, Bedouins have had harsher conflicts with the Jewish state than the other Palestinians over territorial claims. Since 1948 the state has been preoccupied with moving the Bedouins from place to place, using their lands to settle Jews, controlling their movement, and fighting their efforts to sustain themselves in the poor villages they established after they lost their lands. Citizenship was granted to Bedouins only in the 1950s, and proper education even later. As part of its attempt to keep the Bedouins within as narrow a space as possible, the state established new towns and enticed the Bedouins to move into them without really developing viable economies in those towns. Punishing those who refused to move to the new towns, the state provided only minimal services – often after long public and legal campaigns – to the so-called unrecognized villages and carefully monitored their attempts to provide for themselves.

This background is crucial to understanding why much fewer Bedouin women have been enrolled in the paid labor market. The gap was very big among older cohorts and narrowed among younger generations. Among women aged 42–47, only 5.4 percent of the Bedouins participated in the labor market in 2007–2009, compared with 26 percent of Muslims in the north and center. Among the younger women aged 36–41, the gap is smaller but still quite big: 23 and 33 percent, respectively. It is only among women in their late 20s (24–29 years old) that the gap almost disappears. The situation of Bedouin women in unrecognized villages is even worse. According to the official statistics, only a tenth were identified as being in the labor force, but almost all of them were classified as unemployed.

Clue 9: Political Exclusion and Blocked Movement: The Employment of the Women in Jerusalem. The adverse impact of the state is manifest also in the case of women in Jerusalem, although the causes of this are very different from those of the Bedouin women. In contrast to the peripheral location and neglect of Bedouins, Jerusalem is not merely a central city; it is the very center. It is the largest city in Israel, a sacred city for three religions, the heart of government and politics, and a connecting point between Israel and the West Bank and between the Hebron area and Ramallah and Nablus. These characteristics seem very favorable for women's employment, and the personal attributes of Jerusalemite women are also conducive to such employment: Muslim women's fertility in Jerusalem was (until 2003) lower than that of Muslims in Israel and in the rest of the West Bank, and their level of education has been higher relative to all groups of Muslim women in

Israel; 24 percent of them have attended academic institutions in 2007–2009 (about 4–5 percent more than Muslim women in the north and center).

In spite of this encouraging background labor force participation rates of Muslim women in Jerusalem have always been much lower than those of Muslim women in mixed cities, and even below those of less developed and more peripheral purely Palestinian localities in the north and center of Israel. In 1974–1976 only six percent of Muslim women were employed, and this figure remained stable until the mid-1990s, while it rose from 12 to 32 percent among Muslim women in the Israeli mixed cities. In the 2000s the rate of employment of women in Jerusalem was doubled to around 13 percent, less than a third of the rate of women's participation in Israeli mixed Palestinian-Jewish cities, and about half the rate of women in Palestinian localities. This rate is lower also than the LFP among women in Jordan and the West Bank, where 20 and 22 percent, respectively, participated in the paid market in 2008 (ILO 2014). Whereas rates among other Muslim groups rose quite sharply during the 2000s (by about 40 percent from 2000–2002 to 2007–2009), among Jerusalemite women it rose by less than 5 percent. Unlike other Palestinian groups, in Jerusalem low employment rates have characterized women with tertiary education. Only about a half of those women were gainfully employed during the whole period analyzed.

What explains the low participation of Jerusalemite women? We think that there are three major political forces. First, in spite of annexation, Israel did not really treat the Palestinians in Jerusalem as equal residents of the city. They did not receive citizenship and the state allowed them to conduct all educational programs according to the Jordanian (and later Palestinian) curricula. Schools have to teach Hebrew, but the level of Hebrew studied is very basic, and in addition, their educational certificates are not recognized by Israeli employers, including the state. These facts hinder the conversion of the human capital of all Palestinians in Jerusalem to paid employment.

Second, since they do not recognize the annexation of East Jerusalem, the Palestinian residents do not participate in the municipal politics of Jerusalem. They do not run for office and do not vote in the municipal elections, and therefore have no political representation. Probably due to this exclusion, the social services provided for the Palestinian residents of Jerusalem are fewer and smaller than those serving Jewish residents, and hence they offer much fewer employment options for Palestinian women.

A third cause is the barriers to movement between the West Bank and Jerusalem and within Jerusalem itself due to the violent resistance of Palestinians in the West Bank (including its parts within the municipal boundaries of Jerusalem) to the Israeli occupation. Roadblocks started to multiply during the First Intifada, continued to increase through the Oslo peace process, and further multiplied during the Second Intifada. The roadblocks damaged Jerusalem's ability to serve as the commercial, political, and cultural center of the West bank, and Ramallah took up much of the activity previously conducted in Jerusalem. The Separation Wall inside Jerusalem also damaged the economic viability of the Palestinian parts of the city and limited women's possibility of reconciling market employment with family duties. This situation may explain why female employment has stagnated since 2000–2002, and why the education level stopped rising and even dropped a bit during the first decade of the twenty-first century. This stagnation in employment and higher education might have influenced women's fertility. Women in Jerusalem who used to have the lowest fertility among Muslim Palestinians (in Israel and the West Bank) now have the highest fertility except for the Bedouin women.

Clue 10: The Puzzle of Christian Women's Employment. The status of Christian women deserves special attention in our attempt to understand the forces behind Palestinian women's employment. Christian Palestinians changed their family structure most drastically, and they have much fewer children per woman than Muslim women, and their education is on average much higher than that of Muslim women. Consequently many more Christian women than Muslim work outside their homes. These findings fit the common pattern of women's employment worldwide. Yet when compared to *Jewish* women, the employment pattern of Christian women poses a puzzle. Their educational achievements are only slightly lower than those of Jewish women – 13.2 and 13.9 years of education on average, respectively, in 2007–2009 – and since the 1980's they have *fewer* children than Jewish women. Fertility rates in 2012 were 2.17 for Christian Palestinians, and 3.04 for Jews. And yet Christian Palestinian women's employment rate (slightly more than 50 percent in 2007–2009) is considerably lower than that of *Jewish* women residing in the same districts (about 74 percent). Christian women's lower odds of being gainfully employed do not disappear even after controlling for personal and family characteristics of Christian and Jewish women. Net of compositional differences, being Christian still lowers women's odds to enter the labor force. Furthermore, as in the case of Muslim and Druze women, Christian women are also concentrated in the public sector, and are hardly offered jobs in the private sector. The fact that they participate in labor markets less than could be expected from their demographic characteristics and human capital is, in our view, another indication of the closure of the dominant Jewish economy to Palestinian workers regardless of their religion.

Clue 11: Discrimination in Work Remuneration. Women's decision to work outside their home is based to a large extent on the costs of such employment in terms of paid care for children or paid help in housekeeping duties. When two groups are similar in their tastes and preferences but one group gets a higher income for the same job or is preferred in the hiring for better jobs, that also carry higher remuneration, women belonging to that group would be more likely to pursue paid employment. The situation of Jewish and Palestinian women might be such a case.

Palestinian women earn far less than Jewish women. Muslim and Druze women earn on average about two-thirds of what Jewish women earn, while the gap between Jewish and Christian women is considerably lower. The earning gap is especially high in the private sector but is also substantive in the public sector. Those differences do not stem from the fact that female Palestinian employees have less education. On the contrary, because Palestinian women with less than tertiary education are much less likely to be employed in comparison to Jewish women with non-academic education, the Palestinian women in the labor force have a higher level of education relative to female Jewish employees. The main reason for their low earnings is that they are paid much less for their labor investments compared to Jewish women. Would they be treated in the paid market as Jewish women, they would highly increase their earnings.

The low returns on human capital stems from two distinct mechanisms. First, as we saw already in Clue 5, Palestinian women are employed in a very limited range of occupations and are grossly underrepresented in many economic branches. A major reason for this narrow range is that Palestinian women face obstacles in being hired in good occupations that carry more prestige and better wages and benefits. The case of Palestinian women in mixed localities best exemplifies such hiring discrimination. Christian women in mixed cities compete with Jewish women over high-status jobs in the public sector, but due to discrimination against Palestinians they are much less likely to win this competition. When, in contrast, they pursue good positions in homogenous Palestinian localities, they are not impeded by competition with Jewish women and are hired for good positions. Consequently, less than 1 percent of Christian women living in mixed localities are enrolled in public administration, compared with more than 7 percent of those living in Palestinian communities. The second mechanism is direct discrimination in salary setting. Palestinian women, as well as men, get lower wages than Jews for the same jobs. We could not verify this kind of discrimination in our study but there are numerous indications for its existence. It is typical to remuneration of minority members in many countries, and it is also an expected outcome of discrimination in hiring: when workers are blocked from many positions because of their national, ethnic, or gender affiliation, they have to compromise on lower income for jobs which are offered to them.

Our study shows that for whatever reason Palestinian women get substantially lower returns on their human capital, and this fact is an additional crucial clue in explaining Palestinian women's low participation in the labor market. With higher wages offered we would expect more Palestinian women to join the labor force.

10.3   Concluding Remarks and Future Prospects

Where do all these clues lead us? As we acknowledged before, none of these clues is enough to reach a definite conclusion, but the accumulation of evidence about the situation of various groups of Palestinian women and the small but significant differences among them do seem to make a certain interpretation more plausible than another. All together they make the view that "Arab culture" and/or "Islam" are the main cause for the extremely low presence of Palestinian women in the Israeli labor market less plausible by presenting a picture of limited employment opportunities and of exploiting the few opportunities when available. This picture offers an alternative explanation for the low involvement of Palestinian women in the labor force which better fits theories and findings regarding women's LFP in other parts of the world and which does not require us to make special assumptions about the uniqueness of "Arab (or Muslim) culture."

Again we want to repeat and emphasize that our insistence on the central role of available employment positions is not intended to deny the power of cultural components to shape concrete patterns and to affect the specific ways social institutions evolve. Our target was more modestly to reject a certain way of using "Arab culture" or "Islam" as an ultimate explanation that resorts to culture as a catch-all entity that explains a certain behavioral pattern as a constant feature of certain groups that can be removed only by fundamentally changing that group, rather than explaining how certain employment patterns are formed by the interaction between human agents and structural conditions (Sewell 1992; Sa'ar 2007, 2017).

The insistence on the crucial importance of opportunity structure and the cautious approach to cultural accounts are not merely an academic issue. The identification of the main causes of the weak position of Palestinian women in the labor market is important also for constructing appropriate policies for integrating more women into the labor force. If culture and religion are the paramount causes, then it might be inferred that nothing can be done to encourage Palestinian women to join the labor market unless traditional patriarchal Arab culture is abandoned. This popular belief puts the burden on Palestinian women, demanding them to wage a cultural struggle within their society rather than requiring the state to create the economic conditions to facilitate their employment. The Jewish majority group and the state are perceived, according to this view, as the benevolent actors who bring Western egalitarian culture to liberate Palestinian women from Palestinian men (cf. Abu-Lughod 2002).

Our study, in contrast, highlights the negative role of the state and of the Jewish majority in narrowing the range of employment positions open to Palestinian women. As the clues listed above suggest, the fragile achievements of Palestinian women in the labor market are the outcome of their position in a society that discriminates against them in almost all aspects of social life. Palestinians are seen as strangers in their own land and are perceived by most Jewish Israelis as not really belonging to the Israeli nation. Women in Israel have had major accomplishments in making laws and constructing policies that advanced women's equality, but due to the marginalization of Palestinians, Palestinian women have benefited from these achievements much less than Jewish women. At least until recently, the state was not concerned with the low rates of employment among Palestinian women and did not search for ways to pull them into the labor market. Only recently has the state become concerned with the economic costs of not using the female labor force and placed the goal of increasing Palestinian women's employment on the national agenda. State officials often refer to traditional culture and Islam as the main impediment to the prospects of achieving this goal, and our analysis may convince them that this is not the major obstacle; that if jobs would be open and accessible to more Palestinian women, the latter would take advantage of those opportunities and join the labor force.

This lesson might be relevant also for European countries that are worried about the low labor force participation of women of Arab or Muslim origin. The European discourse is preoccupied with Muslim culture, the status of women within Muslim societies, and with the hijabs and veils that Muslim women wear. Our analysis implies that rather than fighting cultural wars and regulating women's clothing, governments should encourage integration and improve Muslim women's position by providing them more attractive employment opportunities. Reaching out to Muslim women and investing in their professional and occupational training, fighting discrimination against them, and providing them with childcare services that fit their specific needs will advance their employment and integration more than "educational" programs that seek to turn them into people they are not.

References

Abdel-Malek, Kamal, and David C. Jacobson (eds.). 1999. *Israeli Palestinian Identities in History and Literature*. New York: St. Martin's.

Abdo, Nahla, and Nira Yuval-Davis. 1995. "Palestine, Israel, and Zionist Settler Project." In Daiva Stasiulis and Nira Yuval-Davis (eds.), *Unsettling Settler Societies: Articulations of Gender, Race, Ethnicity and Class*, 291–322. London: Sage.

Abou-Tabickh, Lilian. 2010. "Women Masked Migration: Palestinian Women Explain Their Move upon Marriage." In Rhoda A. Kanaaneh and Isis Nusair (eds.), *Displaced at Home: Ethnicity and Gender among Palestinians in Israel*, ch. 11, 189–205. Albany: State University of New York.

Abu-Bader, Suleiman, and Daniel Gottlieb. 2008. "Education, Employment and Poverty among Bedouin Arabs in Southern Israel." *Hagar: Studies in Culture, Polity and Identity* 8(2): 121–135.

Abu-Bader, Suleiman, and Daniel Gottlieb. 2009. *Poverty, Education and Employment in the Arab-Bedouin Society: A Comparative View*. Working Paper 98, Jerusalem: Research and Planning Administration, The National Insurance Institute and the Van Leer Institute, Jerusalem.

Abu-Baker, Khawla. 1998. *Rocky Road: Arab Women as Political Leaders in Israel*. Raanana: The Institute for Israeli Arab Studies.

Abu-Lughod, Lila (ed.). 1998. *Remaking Women: Feminism and Modernity in the Middle East*. Princeton: Princeton University Press.

2002. "Do Muslim Women Really Need Saving? Anthropological Reflections on Cultural Relativism and Its Others." *American Anthropologist* 104(3): 783–790.

Abu-Odeh, Adnan. 1992. "Two Capitals in an Undivided Jerusalem." *Foreign Affairs* 71(2): 183–188.

Abu-Rabia, Aref. 2000. "Employment and Unemployment among the Negev Bedouin." *Nomadic People* 4(2): 84–93.

2001. *A Bedouin Century: Education and Development among the Negev Tribes in the 20th Century*. New York: Berghahn.

Abu-Rabia-Queder, Sarab. 2006. "Between Tradition and Modernization: Understanding the Problem of Female Bedouin Dropouts." *British Journal of Sociology of Education* 27(1): 3–17.

2007. "The Activism of Bedouin Women: Social and Political Resistance." *Hagar: Studies in Culture, Polity and Identity* 7(2): 67–84.

2008. *Excluded and Loved: Educated Bedouin Women's Life Stories*. Jerusalem: Magnes (in Hebrew).

Abu-Rabia-Queder, Sarab, and Khaled Arar. 2011. "Gender and Higher Education in Different National Spaces: Female Palestinian Students Attending Israeli and Jordanian Universities." *Compare* 41(3): 353–370.

Abu-Rabia-Queder, Sarab, and Naomi Weiner-Levy. 2013. "Between Local and Foreign Structures: Exploring the Agency of Palestinian Women in Israel." *Social Politics: International Studies in Gender, State & Society* 20(1): 88–108.

Abu-Saad, Ismael. 1991. "Towards an Understanding of Minority Education in Israel: The Case of the Bedouin Arabs of the Negev." *Comparative Education* 27(2): 235–242.

  1995. "Bedouin Arab Education in the Context of Radical Social Change: What Is the Future?" *Compare* 25(2): 149–160.

  1996. "Provision of Public Educational Services and Access to Higher Education among the Negev Bedouin Arabs in Israel." *Journal of Education Policy* 11(5): 527–541.

  2003. "Bedouin Arabs in Israel between the Hammer and the Anvil: Education as a Foundation for Survival and Development." In Duane Champagne and Ismael Abu-Saad (eds.), *The Future of Indigenous People: Strategies for Survival and Development*, 103–120. Los Angeles: UCLA American Indian Studies Center.

  2004a. "Palestinian Education in Israel: The Legacy of the Military Government." *Holy Land Studies* 5(1): 21–56.

  2004b. "Separate and Unequal: The Role of the State Educational System in Maintaining the Subordination of Israel's Palestinian Arab Citizens." *Social Identities* 10(1): 101–127.

  2005. "Forced Sedentarisation, Land Rights and Indigenous Resistance: The Palestinian Bedouin in the Negev." In Nur Masalha (ed.), *Catastrophe Remembered: Palestine, Israel and the Internal Refugees*, 113–142. London: Zed.

  2006. State-Controlled Education and Identity Formation among the Palestinian Arab Minority in Israel." *American Behavioral Scientist* 49(8): 1085–1100.

  2008. "Spatial Transformation and Indigenous Resistance: The Urbanization of the Palestinian Bedouin in Southern Israel." *American Behavioral Scientist* 51(12): 1713–1754.

Abu-Saud, Azzam. 2007. "Closure and Separation and Their Impact on East Jerusalem's Economic Sector." *Palestine Israel Journal of Politics, Economics and Culture* 14(1): 105–113.

Aburaiya, Issam. 2004. "The 1996 Split of the Islamic Movement in Israel: Between the Holy Text and Israeli-Palestinian Context." *International Journal of Politics, Culture and Society* 17(3): 439–455.

Aburaya, Issam, and Hisham Abu-Raiya. 2012. "On the Connection between Islamic Sacred Texts and Muslims' Political Conduct: The Israeli Dominant Elites' Conceptions." *Middle East Journal of Culture and Communication* 5(2): 101–115.

ACRI. 2013a. "To Establish an Arab School in Nazareth." www.acri.org.il/he/25 416, 8.7.2017. (in Hebrew)

  2013b. www.acri.org.il/he/wp-content/uploads/2013/08/Nazrat-Ilit080113.pdf, 8.7.2017 (in Hebrew).

Addi-Raccah, Audrey. 2002. The Feminization of Teaching and Principalship in the Israeli Educational System: A Comparative Study." *Sociology of Education* 75(3): 231–248.

Afkhami, Mahnaz, and Erika Friedl (eds.). 1997. *Muslim Women and the Politics of Participation*. Syracuse: Syracuse University Press.

Agbaria, Ayman K., and Muhanad Mustafa. 2012. "Two States for Three Peoples: The 'Palestinian-Israeli' in the Future Vision Documents of the Palestinians in Israel." *Ethnic and Racial Studies* 35(4): 718–736.

Aharoni, Yair. 1991. *The Israeli Economy: Dreams and Reality*. London: Routledge.

Ahmed, Leila. 1992. *Women and Gender in Islam: Historical Roots of a Modern Debate*. New Haven: Yale University Press.

Al-Haj, Majid. 1995. *Education, Empowerment, and Control: The Case of the Arabs in Israel*. Albany: State University of New York Press.

2004. *Immigration and Ethnic Formation in a Deeply Divided Society: The Case of the 1990s Immigrants from the Former Soviet Union in Israel*. Leiden: Brill.

2005. "Whither the Green Line? Trends in the Orientation of Palestinians in Israel and the Territories." *Israel Affairs* 11(1): 183–206.

Albin, Cecilia. 1997. "Securing the Peace of Jerusalem: On the Politics of Unifying and Dividing." *Review of International Studies* 23(2): 117–142.

Algan, Yann, Christian Dustmann, Albrecht Glitz, and Alan Manning. 2010. "The Economic Situation of First and Second-Generation Immigrants in France, Germany, and the United Kingdom." *The Economic Journal* 120(Feb.): F4–F30.

Ali, Nohad. 2004. "Political Islam in an Ethnic Jewish State: Historical Revolution, Contemporary Challenges and Future Prospects." *Holy Land Studies* 3(1): 69–92.

2013. *Representation of Arab Citizens in the Institutions of Higher Education in Israel*. Tran: Miriam Schlusselberg. Haifa: Sikkuy.

Allen, Christopher, and Jørgen S. Nielsen. 2002. *Summary Report on Islamophobia in the EU after 11 September 2001*. Vienna: European Monitoring Centre on Racism and Xenophobia.

Alyan, Nisreen, Ronit Sela, and Michal Pomerantz. 2012a. "*Policies of Neglect in East Jerusalem*." Jerusalem: Association for Civil Rights in Israel.

Alyan, Nisreen, Ronit Sela, Talia Ramati, and Tamar Luster. 2012b. *Failed Grade: East Jerusalem's Failing Educational System*. Jerusalem: Ir Amim and the Association for Civil Rights in Israel.

Amara, Muhammad. 2003. "The Collective Identity of the Arabs in Israel in an Era of Peace." *Israel Affairs* 9(1): 249–262.

Amin, Shahina, and Imam Alam. 2008. "Women's Employment Decisions in Malaysia: Does Religion Matter?" *The Journal of Socio-Economics* 37(6): 2368–2379.

Anwar, Zainah (ed.). 2009. *Wanted: Equality and Justice in the Muslim Family*. Selangor: Musawah, Sisters in Islam.

Arar, Khalid, and Kussai Haj-Yehia. 2013. "Higher Education Abroad: Palestinian Students from Israel Studying in Jordanian Universities." *Journal of Applied Research in Higher Education* 5(1): 95–112.

Aronoff, Myron J. 2000. "'Americanization' of Israeli Politics: Political and Cultural Change." *Israel Studies* (1): 92–127.

Artstein, Yael. 2002. "The Flexibility of the Israeli Labor Market." In A. Ben-Bassat (ed.), *The Israeli Economy, 1985–1998: From Government Intervention to Market Economics*, 379–422. Cambridge MA: MIT Press

Asali, Muhammad. 2006. *Why Do Arabs Earn Less Than Jews in Israel?* Jerusalem: Maurice Falk Institute for Economic Research in Israel.

Ashkenasi, Abraham, 1992. *Palestinian Identities and Preferences: Israel's and Jerusalem's Arabs*. Westport, CT: Praeger Publisher.

Avraham, Eli, Gadi Wolfsfeld, and Issam Aburaiya. 2000. "Dynamics in the News Coverage of Minorities: The Case of the Arab Citizens of Israel." *Journal of Communication Inquiry* 24(2): 117–133.

Ayalon, Hanna, and Yossi Shavit. 2004. "Educational Reforms and Inequalities in Israel: The MMI Hypothesis Revisited." *Sociology of Education* 77(2): 103–120.

Ayalon, Hanna, and Avraham Yogev. 2005. "Field of Study and Students' Stratification in an Expanded System of Higher Education: The Case of Israel." *European Sociological Review* 21(3): 227–241.

Badran, Ahmad. 2012. *Elite Track Passes through the Barrier of Religion*. M.A. Thesis, University of Haifa, Haifa.

Badran, Margot. 1996. *Feminists, Islam, and Nation: Gender and the Making of Modern Egypt*. Princeton: Princeton University Press.

Bar-Tal, Daniel. 1996. "Development of Categories and Stereotypes in Early Childhood: The Case of the 'Arab' Stereotype Formation, Stereotypes and Attitudes among Jewish Children." *International Journal of Intercultural Relations* 20(3/4): 341–370.

  1998. "The Rocky Road toward Peace: Societal Beliefs Functional to Intractable Conflict in Israeli School Textbooks." *Journal of Peace Research* 35(6): 723–742.

Bar-Tal, Daniel, Eran Halperin, and Neta Oren. 2010. Socio-Psychological Barriers to Peace Making: The Case of the Israeli Jewish Society." *Social Issues and Policy Review* 4(1): 63–109.

Bar-Tal, Daniel, and Yona Teichman. 2005. *Stereotypes and Prejudice in Conflict: Representations of Arabs in Jewish Society*. New York: Cambridge University Press.

Bardasi, Elena, and Janet C. Gornick. 2000. *Women and Part-Time Employment: Workers' "Choices" and Wage Penalties in Five Industrialized Countries*. Institute for Social and Economic Research, University of Essex.

Baron, Beth. 1994. *The Women's Awakening in Egypt: Culture, Society, and the Press*. New Haven: Yale University Press.

Baron, Beth. 2005. *Egypt as a Women-Nationalism Gender and Politics*. Berkeley: University of California Press.

Bäuml, Yair. 2007. *A Blue and White Shadow: The Israeli Establishment's Policy and Actions among Its Arab Citizens, the Formative Years, 1958–1968*. Haifa: Pardes (in Hebrew).

  2010. "61 Years of Surveillancing Abandonment: Deciphering the Code of the Israeli Establishment Policy towards the Arab Citizens." In Chana Katz and Erez Tzafadia (eds.), *Abandoning State – Surveillancing State: Social Policy in Israel, 1985–2008*, 35–54. Tel Aviv: Resling (in Hebrew).

2011. "The Military Government." In Nadim Rouhana and Areej Sabbagh-Khoury (eds.), *The Palestinians in Israel: Readings in History, Politics, and Society*, 48–56. Haifa: Arab Center for Applied Social Research, Mada al-Carmel.

Bell Daniel. 1976. *The Coming of Post-Industrial Society: A Venture in Social Forecasting*. New York: Basic Books.

Ben-Bassat, Avi (ed.). 2002. *The Israeli Economy, 1985–1998: From Government Intervention to Market Economics*. Cambridge MA: MIT Press.

Ben-David, Yosef. 1999. "The Bedouin in Israel." *Israeli Ministry of Foreign Affairs*. Available at https://ssl.haifa.ac.il/download/files/542/,DanaInfo=.ac pthDfiG2t±14510822.pdf.

Ben-Eliezer, Uri. 1998. *The Making of Israeli Militarism*. Bloomington: Indiana University Press.

Ben-Porath, Guy. 2008. "Political Economy: Liberalization and Globalization." In Guy Ben-Porath, Yagil Levy, Shlomo Mizrahi, Arye Naor, and Erez Tzfadia (eds.), *Israel since 1980*, 91–116. New York: Cambridge University Press.

Ben-Porath, Yoram. 1966. *The Arab Labor Force in Israel*. Jerusalem: Maurice Falk Institute for Economic Research in Israel.

(ed.). 1986. *The Israeli Economy: Maturing through Crisis*. Cambridge: Harvard University Press.

Ben-Ze'ev, Efrat, and Issam Aburaiya. 2004. "'Middle-Ground' Politics and Re-Palestinization of Places in Israel." *International Journal of Middle East Studies* 36(4): 639–655.

Beneria, Lourdes. 1982. "Accounting for Women's work." In her (rd.), *Women's and Development: The Sexual Division of Labor in Rural Societies*, 119–147. New York: Praeger.

Bental, Benjamin, Yuval Yonay, and Vered Kraus. 2017. "Ethnic and Gender Earning Gaps in a Liberalized Economy: The Case of Israel." *Social Science Research* 63: 209–226.

Bergstrom, Theodore C., and Mark Bagnoli. 1993. "Courtship as a Waiting Game." *Journal of Political Economy* 101(1): 185–202.

Bernasco Wim, Paul M. de Graaf, and Wout C. Ultee. 1998. "Coupled Careers: Effects of Spouse's Resources on Occupational Attainment in the Netherlands." *European Sociological Review* 14(1): 15–31.

Bernhardt, Eva M. 1993. "Fertility and Employment." *European Sociological Review* 9(1): 25–42.

Bernstein, Deborah S. 1998. "Strategies of Equalization, a Neglected Aspect of the Split Labor Market Theory: Jews and Arabs in the Split Labor Market of Mandatory Palestine." *Ethnic and Racial Studies* 21(3): 449–475.

Blau, Francine D., and Lawrence M. Kahn. 1996. "Wage Structure and Gender Earnings Differentials: An International Comparison." *Economica* 63, 250: S29–S62.

Blossfeld, Hans-Peter, and Catherine Hakim. 1997. *Between Equalization and Marginalization: Women Working Part-Time in Europe*. Oxford: Oxford University Press.

Blossfeld, Hans-Peter, and Johannes Huinink. 1991. "Human Capital Investments or Norms of Role Transition? How Women's Schooling and Career Affect the Process of Family Formation." *American Journal of Sociology* 97(1): 143–168.

Bloul, Rachel. A. D. 2008. "Anti-Discrimination Laws, Islamophobia, and Ethnicization of Muslin Identities in Europe and Australia." *Journal of Muslim Minority Affairs* 28(1): 7–25.

Bobo, Lawrence, and Susan A. Suh. 1995. *Surveying Racial Discrimination: Analyses from a Multiethnic Labor Market*. New York: Russell Sage Foundation.

Bolzendahl, Catherine I., and Daniel J. Myers. 2004. "Feminist Attitudes and Support for Gender Equality: Opinion Change in Women and Men, 1974–1998." *Social Forces* 83 (2): 759–789.

Boneh, Dan. 1983. *Facing Uncertainty: The Social Consequences of Forced Sedentarization among the Jaraween Bedouin, Negev, Israel*. Ph.D. Dissertation, Brandeis University.

Boqa'i, Nihad. 2005. "Patterns of Internal Displacement, Social Adjustment and the Challenge of Return." In Nur Masalha (ed.), *Catastrophe Remembered: Palestine, Israel and the Internal Refugees*, 73–112. London: Zed.

Boserup, Ester. 1970. *Women's Role in Economic Development*. London: Earthscan.
1990. "Economic Change and the Roles of Women." In Irene Tinker (ed.), *Persistent Inequalities: Women and World Development*, 14–25. New York: Oxford University Press.

Brek, Jad. 2011. *The Construction of Suicide and Its Meaning in the Druze Community in Israel: Perceptions, Reactions, Ways of Coping*. M.A. Thesis, University of Haifa, Haifa.

Brewster, Karin L., and Ronald R. Rindfuss. 2000. "Fertility and Women's Employment in Industrial Nations." *Annual Review of Sociology* 26: 271–296.

Bronstein, Eitan. 2005. "The *Nakba* in Hebrew: Israeli-Jewish Awareness of the Palestinian Catastrophe and Internal Refugees." In Nur Masalha (ed.), *Catastrophe Remembered: Palestine, Israel and the Internal Refugees*, 214–242. London: Zed.

Brooks, Clem, and Catherine Bolzendahl. 2004. "The Transformation of US Gender Role Attitudes: Cohort Replacement, Social-Structural Change, and Ideological Learning." *Social Science Research* 33(1): 106–133.

Browne, Irene. 1999. "Latinas and African American Women in the US Labor Market." In Irene Browne (ed.), *Latinas and African American Women at Work: Race, Gender, and Economic Inequality*, 1–32. New York: Russell Sage Foundation.

B'Tselem. 2013. "Revocation of Residency in East Jerusalem." Updated August 18, 2013. On line, www.btselem.org/jerusalem/revocation_of_residency.

Cabili, Diana Mae. 2011. *Islamophobia in America*. An Honors Program Thesis, University of South Florida, St. Petersburg.

Carmi, Shulamit, and Henry Rosenfeld. 1974. "The Origins of the Process of Proletarianization and Urbanization of Arab Peasants in Palestine." *Annals of the New York Academy of Sciences* 220: 470–485.
1992. "Israel's Political Economy and the Widening Class Gap between Its Two National Groups." *Asian and African Studies* 26: 15–62.

Cattan, Henry. 1981. "Status of Jerusalem under International Law and United Nations Resolutions." *Journal of Palestine Studies* 10(3): 3–15.

CBS. 1994. *The Standard Classification of Occupations.* Technical Publication No. 64. Jerusalem: Central Bureau of Statistics.

1998. *Statistical Abstract of Israel.* Vol. 49. Jerusalem: Central Bureau of Statistics.

2000. *Statistical Abstract of Israel.* Vol. 51. Jerusalem: Central Bureau of Statistics.

2002. *Statistical Abstract of Israel.* Vol. 53. Jerusalem: Central Bureau of Statistics.

2003. *Statistical Abstract of Israel.* Vol. 54. Jerusalem: Central Bureau of Statistics.

2004. *Statistical Abstract of Israel.* Vol. 55. Jerusalem: Central Bureau of Statistics.

2005. *Statistical Abstract of Israel.* Vol. 56. Jerusalem: Central Bureau of Statistics.

2007. *Statistical Abstract of Israel.* Vol. 58. Jerusalem: Central Bureau of Statistics.

2009. *Statistical Abstract of Israel.* Vol. 60. Jerusalem: Central Bureau of Statistics.

2010. *Statistical Abstract of Israel.* Vol. 61. Jerusalem: Central Bureau of Statistics.

2011. *Statistical Abstract of Israel.* Vol. 62. Jerusalem: Central Bureau of Statistics.

2012. *Statistical Abstract of Israel.* Vol. 63. Jerusalem: Central Bureau of Statistics.

2013. *Statistical Abstract of Israel.* Vol. 64. Jerusalem: Central Bureau of Statistics.

2014. *Statistical Abstract of Israel.* Vol. 65. Jerusalem: Central Bureau of Statistics.

2016. *Statistical Abstract of Israel.* Vol. 67. Jerusalem: Central Bureau of Statistics.

N.D. "Transition to a Monthly Labour Force Survey Questions and Answers." Available at www.cbs.gov.il/publications/labour_survey04/labour_force_sur vey/answer_question_e_2012.pdf.

Charrad, Mounira M. 2001. *States and Women's Rights: The Making of Postcolonial Tunisia, Algeria, and Morocco.* Berkeley: University of California Press.

2007. "Contexts, Concepts, and Contentions: Gender Legislation as Politics in the Middle East." *HAWWA* 5(1): 55–72.

2011. "Gender in the Middle East: Islam, State, Agency." *Annual Review of Sociology* 37: 417–437.

Cheshin, Amir, Bill Hutman, and Avi Melamed. 1999. *Separate and Unequal: The Inside Story of Israeli Rule in East Jerusalem.* Cambridge: Harvard University Press.

Choshen, Maya. 2002. "Jerusalem in Our Times: Past, Present, Future." In Marshall J. Breger and Ora Ahimeir (eds.), *Jerusalem: A City and Its Future,* 17–60. Syracuse: Syracuse University Press.

Choshen Maya, and Michal Korach. 2011. *Jerusalem: Facts and Trends 2011.* Publication No. 413. Jerusalem: Jerusalem Institute for Israel Studies.

Cinar, E. Mine (ed.). 2001. *The Economics of Women and Work in the Middle East and North Africa.* Amsterdam: JAI.

Clark, Kenneth, and Stephen Drinkwater. 1998. "Ethnicity and Self-Employment in Britain. *Oxford Bulletin of Economics and Statistics* 60(3): 383–407.

2000. "Pushed Out or Pulled In? Self-Employment among Ethnic Minorities in England and Wales." *Labour Economics* 7(5): 603–628.

Cohen, Adir. 1985. *Ugly Face in the Mirror: Reflection of the Jewish-Arab Conflict in Hebrew Children's Literature.* Tel Aviv: Reshafim (in Hebrew).

Cohen, Hillel. 2003. "Land, Memory, and Identity: The Palestinian Internal Refugees in Israel." *Refuge* 21(2): 6–13.

2005. "The State of Israel *versus* the Palestinian Internal Refugees." In Nur Masalha (ed.), *Catastrophe Remembered: Palestine, Israel and the Internal Refugees*, 56–72. London: Zed.

2007. *The Rise and Fall of Arab Jerusalem, 1967–2007*. Jerusalem: The Jerusalem Institute for Israel Studies and Ivrit (in Hebrew).

2010. *Good Arabs: The Israeli Security Agencies and the Israeli Arabs, 1948–1967*. Trans. Haim Watzman. Berkeley: University of California Press.

Cohen, Uri. 2007. University vs. Society in a Period of Nation Building: The Hebrew University in Pre-State Israel." *Historical Studies in Education* 19(1): 81–110.

2014. *Academy in Tel Aviv: Te Growth of a University*. Jerusalem: Magnes (in Hebrew).

Cohen, Yinon. 2015. "Spatial Politics and Socioeconomic Gaps between Jews and Palestinians in Israel." *Israeli Sociology* 17(1): 7–31 (in Hebrew).

Cohen, Yinon, and Haya Stier. 2006. "The Rise in Involuntary Part-Time Work in Israel." *Research in Social Stratification and Mobility* 24: 41–54.

Cohen, Yinon, Yitchak Haberfeld, Guy Mundlak, and Ishak Saporta. 2003. "Unpacking Union Density: Membership and Coverage in the Transformation of the Israeli IR System." *Industrial Relations* 42(4): 692–711.

Connor, Phillip, and Matthias Koenig. 2015. "Explaining the Muslim Employment Gap in Western Europe: Individual-Level Effects and Ethno-Religious Penalties." *Social Science Research* 49: 191–201.

Cooke, Lynn Prince. 2011. *Gender-Class Equality in Political Economies*. New York: Routledge.

Courbage, Youssef. 1999. "Reshuffling the Demographic Cards in Israel/ Palestine." *Journal of Palestine Studies* 28(4):21–39.

Coursen-Neff, Zama. 2003. "Discrimination against Palestinian Arab Children in the Israeli Education System." *International Law and Politics* 36: 101–162.

Crompton, Rosemary. 2006. *Employment and the Family: The Reconfiguration of Work and Family Life in Contemporary Societies*. Cambridge: Cambridge University Press.

D'Addato, Agata V., Daniele Vignoli, and Sutay Yavuz. 2008. "Towards Smaller Family Size in Egypt, Morocco and Turkey: Overall Change over Time or Socio-Economic Compositional Effect?" *Population Review* 47(1): 21–40.

Dahan, Momi. 2002. "The Rise of Earning Inequality." In A. Ben-Bassat (ed.), *The Israeli Economy, 1985–1998: From Government Intervention to Market Economics*, 485–517. Cambridge MA: MIT Press.

Dahan-Kalev. 2001. "Tensions in Israeli Feminism: The Mizrahi Ashkenazi Rift." *Women's studies International Forum* 24(6): 669–684.

Dale, Angela, Edward Fieldhouse, Nusrat Shaheen, and Virinder Kalra. 2002. "The Labour Market Prospects for Pakistani and Bangladeshi Women." *Work, Employment & Society* 16(1): 5–25.

Danziger, Leif, and Shoshana Neuman. 1999. "On the Age at Marriage: Theory and Evidence from Jews and Moslems in Israel." *Journal of Economic Behavior & Organization* 40(2): 179–193.

Daoud, Suheir Abu Oksa. 2009. *Palestinian Women and Politics in Israel*. Gainsville: University of Florida Press.

Davis, Shannon N., and Theodore N. Greenstein. 2009. "Gender Ideology: Components, Predictors, and Consequences." *Annual Review of Sociology* 35: 87–105.

Dinero, Steven C. 1997. "Female Role Change and Male Response in the Post-Nomadic Urban Environment: The Case of the Israeli Negev Bedouin." *Journal of Comparative Family Studies* 8: 248–261.

2004. "New Identity/Identities Formulation in a Post-Nomadic Community: The Case of the Bedouin of the Negev." *National Identities* 6(3): 261–275.

2010. *Settling for Less: The Planned Resettlement of Israel Negev Bedouins*. New York: Berghan.

DiPrete, Thomas. 1989. *The Bureaucratic Labor Market: The Case of the Federal Civil Service*. New York: Plenum.

Dirasat, Van Leer Jerusalem Institute, and Sikkuy. 2014. *Arabic and Arab Culture on Israeli Campuses: An Updated Look*. Written by Thair Abu Ras and Yael Maayan. Available at: www.dirasat-aclp.org/files/present-yet-absent-inter net-eng(1).pdf.

Disney, Richard, and Amanda Gosling. 1998. "Does It Pay to Work in the Public Sector?" *Fiscal Studies* 19(4): 347–374.

Doeringer, Peter B., and Michael J. Piore. 1971. *Internal Labor Markets and Manpower Adjustment*. Lexington: Heath.

Durkheim, Émile. 1984. *The Division of Labor in Society*. Houndsmill: Macmillan.

Dwairy, Marwan. 2004. "Culturally Sensitive Education: Adapting Self-Oriented Assertiveness Training to Collective Minorities." *Journal of Social Issues* 60(2): 423–436.

Efrati, Noga. 2012. *Women in Iraq: Past Meets Present*. New York: Columbia University Press.

Erdreich, Lauren. 2006. "Strategies against Patriarchy: Sexualized Political Activism of Palestinian Israeli Women on Campus." *Israeli studies* 11(1): 35–58.

2008. "Degendering the Honor/Care Conflation: Palestinian Israeli University Women's Appropriation of Independence." *Ethos* 34(1): 132–164.

Esping-Andersen, Gosta. 1990. *The Three Worlds of Welfare Capitalism*. Cambridge: Polity.

1996. *Welfare States in Transition: National Adaptations in Global Economies*. London: Sage.

Fairlie, Robert W. 2007. "Entrepreneurship among Disadvantaged Groups: Women, Minorities and the Less Educated." In Simon Parker (ed.), *The Life Cycle of Entrepreneurial Ventures, International Handbook Series on Entrepreneurship*, Vol. 3, 437–475. New York: Springer.

Falah, Ghazi, Michael Hoy, and Rakhal Sarker. 2000. "Co-Existence in Selected Mixed Arab-Jewish Cities in Israel: By Choice or by Default." *Urban Studies* 37(4): 775–796.

Falah, Ghazi-Walid. 1983. "The Role of the British Administration in the Sedenterization of the Bedouin Tribes in Northern Palestine, 1918–1948." Working Paper. University of Durham, Centre for Middle Eastern and Islamic Studies, Durham.

1985. "How Israel Controls the Bedouins in Israel." *Journal of Palestine Studies* 14(2): 35–51.

1989a. "Israeli 'Judaization' Policy in Galilee and Its Impact on Local Arab Urbanization." *Political Geography Quarterly* 8(3): 229–253.

1989b. "Israeli State Policy toward Bedouin Sedentarization in the Negev." *Journal of Palestine Studies* 18(2): 71–91.

1990. "Arabs versus Jews in Galilee: Competition for Regional Resources." *GeoJournal* 21(4): 325–336.

1993. "Trends in the Urbanization of Arab Settlements in Galilee." *Urban Geography* 14(2): 145–164.

1995. "Pluralism and Resource Allocation Among Arab and Jewish Citizens in Israel." In Nur Masalha (ed.), *The Palestinians in Israel: Is Israel the State of All Its Citizens and "Absentees"?*, 83–108. Tran. Nur Masalha. Nazareth: *Galilee Center for Social Research*.

1996. "Living Together Apart: Residential Segregation in Mixed Arab-Jewish Cities in Israel." *Urban Studies* 33(6): 823–857.

2003. "Dynamics and Patterns of the Shrinking of Arabs' Lands in Palestine." *Political Geography* 22: 179–209.

Fargues, Philippe. 1989. "The Decline of Arab fertility." *Population* 44(1): 147–175.

2000. "Protracted National Conflict and Fertility Change: Palestinians and Israelis in the Twentieth Century." *Population and Development Review* 26(3): 441–482.

Feagin, Joe R., and Melvin P. Sikes. 1994. *Living with Racism: The Black Middle-Class Experience*. Boston: Beacon Press.

Fenster, Tovi. 1999. "Space for Gender: Cultural Roles of the Forbidden and the Permitted." *Environment and Planning D: Society and Space* 17: 227–246.

Fernández, Raquel. 2007. "Women, Work, and Culture." *Alfred Marshall Lecture, Journal of the European Economic Association* 5(2): 305–32.

Fernández, Raquel, Alessandra Fogli, and Claudia Olivetti. 2004. "Mothers and Sons: Preference Formation and Female Labor Force Dynamics." *The Quarterly Journal of Economics* 119(4): 1249–1299.

Filler, Nicole, and M. Kent Jennings. 2015. "Familial Origins of Gender Role Attitudes." *Politics & Gender* 11(1): 27–54.

Firro, Kais M. 1992. *The History of the Druzes*. Leiden: Brill.

1999. *The Druzes in the Jewish State: A Brief History*. Leiden: Brill,

2001. "Reshaping Druze Particularism in Israel." *Journal of Palestine Studies* 30: 40–53.

First, Anat. 1998. "Who Is the Enemy: The Portrayal of Arabs in Israeli Television News." *Gazette* 60(3): 239–254.

Fleischmann, Fenella. 2011. *"Second-Generation Muslims in European Societies: Comparative Perspectives on Education and Religion."* Ph.D. Dissertation, Katholieke Universiteit Leuven.

Fleischmann, Fenella, and Jutta Höhne. 2013. "Gender and Migration on the Labour Market: Additive or Interacting Disadvantages in Germany?" *Social Science Research* 42(5): 1325–1345.

Folbre, Nancy. 1991. "The Unproductive Housewife: Her Evolution in Nineteenth-Century Economic Thought." *Signs* 16(31): 463–484.

Forman, Geremy, and Alexandre (Sandy) Kedar. 2004. "From Arab Land to 'Israeli Lands.' The Legal Dispossession of the Palestinians Displaced by Israel in the Wake of 1948." *Environment and Planning D* 22: 809–830.

Friedman, Eyal, and Michael Shalev. 2010. "Loyalty Benefits." In Chana Katz and Erez Tzafadia (eds.), *Abandoning State – Surveillancing State: Social Policy in Israel, 1985–2008*, 55–75. Tel Aviv: Resling (in Hebrew).

Frisch, Hillel. 1993. "The Druze Minority in the Israeli Military: Traditionalizing an Ethnic Policing Role." *Armed Forces* 20: 51–67.

Fuwa, Makiko. 2004. "Macro-level Gender Inequality and the Division of Household Labor in 22 Countries." *American Sociological Review* 69(6): 751–67.

Gans, Haim. 2008. *A Just Zionism: On the Morality of The Jewish State*. Oxford: Oxford University Press.

Gavison, Ruth. 1999. "Jewish and Democratic? A Rejoinder to the Ethnic Democracy Debate." *Israel Studies* 4(1): 44–72. (872393)

Gelber, Yoav. 1995. "Druze and Jews in the War of 1948." *Middle Eastern Studies* 31(2): 229–252.

Ghanem, As'ad. 1998. "State and Minority in Israel: The Case of the Ethnic State and the Predicament of Its Minority." *Ethnic and Racial Studies* 21(3): 428–448.

2001. *The Palestinian Arab Minority in Israel: A Political Study*. Albany: State University of New York Press.

Ginat, Joseph. 1998. "Preservation and Change in Bedouin Societies in Israel." In Joseph Ginat and Anatoly Khazanov (eds.), *Changing Nomads in a Changing World*, 171–201. Sussex: Academic Press.

Glass, Jennifer, Marta Tienda, and Shelley A. Smith. 1988. "The Impact of Changing Employment Opportunity on Gender and Ethnic Earnings Inequality." *Social Science Research* 17(3): 252–276.

Golan, Arnon. 2003. "Jewish Settlement of Former Arab Towns and Their Incorporation into the Israeli Urban System (1948–1950)." *Israel Affairs* 9(1–2): 149–164.

Golden, Lonnie, and Eileen Appelbaum. 1992. "What Was Driving the 1982–88 Boom in Temporary Employment?" *American Journal of Economics and Sociology* 51(4): 473–493.

Goldin, Claudia. 1990. *The Gender Gap: An Economic History of American Women*. New York: Cambridge University Press.

1994. "The U-Shaped Female Labor Force Function in Economic Development and Economic History." *NBER Working Paper 4707*. Cambridge, MA: NBER.

2006. "The Quiet Revolution that Transformed Women's Employment, Education, and Family." *NBER Working Paper 11953*. Cambridge, MA: NBER.

Goldscheider, Calvin. 1996. *Israel's Changing Society: Population, Ethnicity, and Development*. Boulder: Westview.

Gornick, Janet C., and Jerry A. Jacobs. 1996. "A Cross-National Analysis of the Wages of Part-Time Workers: Evidence from the United States, the United Kingdom, Canada and Australia." *Work, Employment & Society* 10(1): 1–27.

1998. "Gender, the Welfare State, and Public Employment: A Comparative Study of Seven Industrialized Countries." *American Sociological Review* 63(5): 688–710.

Gornick, Janet C., and Marcia K. Meyers. 2003. *Families that Work: Policies for Reconciling Parenthood and Employment*. New York: Russell Sage.

Gozansky, Tamar. 2014. *Between Expropriation and Exploitation: Status and Struggles of Arab Workers in Palestine and Israel*. Haifa: Pardes.(in Hebrew)

Guiso, Luigi, Paola Sapienza, and Luigi Zingales. 2003. "People's Opium? Religion and Economic Attitudes." *Journal of Monetary Economics* 50(1): 225–282.

Gregory, Mary, and Sara Connolly. 2008. "Feature: The Price of Reconciliation: Part-Time Work, Families and Women's Satisfaction." *The Economic Journal* 118(526): F1–F7.

Grinberg, Lev Luis. 1991. *Split Corporatism in Israel*. Albany: State University of New York Press.

Haberfeld, Yitchak, and Yinon Cohen. 2007. "Gender, Ethnic, and National Earnings Gaps in Israel: *The Role of Rising Inequality*." *Social Science Research* 36: 654–672.

Habib, Jack, Judith King, Assaf Ben Shoham, Abraham Wolde-Tsadick, and Keren Lasky. 2010. "Labour Market and Socio-Economic Outcomes of the Arab-Israeli Population." OECD Social, Employment and Migration Working Papers, No. 102, OECD Publishing. http://dx.doi.org/10.1787/5k mjnrcfsskc-en

Haddad, Yvonne Yazbeck, and John L. Esposito (eds.). 1998. *Islam, Gender, and Social Change*. New York: Oxford University Press.

Haidar, Aziz. 1990. *The Arab Population in the Israeli Economy*. Tel Aviv: International Center for Peace in the Middle East.

1991. *Social Welfare Services for Israel's Arab Population*. Boulder: Westview.

1995. *On the Margins: The Arab Population in the Israeli Economy*. London: Hurst & Company.

2009. "The Arab Labor Force in Israel: Inclusive and Exclusive Processes in the Labor Market." In Rassem Khamaisi (ed.), *Arab Society in Israel: Population, Society, Economy*, Vol. 3, 252–279. Jerusalem and Tel Aviv: Van Leer Jerusalem Institute and Hakibbutz Hameuchad (in Hebrew).

Haiduc-Dale, Noah. 2015. "Rejecting Sectarianism: Palestinian Christians' Role in Muslim-Christian Relations." *Islam and Christian-Muslim Relations* 26(1): 75–88.

Hajjar, Lisa. 1996. "Making Identity Policy: Israel's Interventions among the Druze." *Middle East Report* 200: 2–6, 10.

2001. "Speaking the Conflict, or How the Druze Became Bilingual: A Study of Druze Translators in the Israeli Military Courts in the West Bank and Gaza." *Ethnic and Racial Studies* 23(2): 299–328.

2004. "Religion, State Power, and Domestic Violence in Muslim Societies: A Framework for Comparative Analysis." *Law & Social Inquiry* 29(1): 1–38.

Hakim, Catherine. 1996. *Key Issues in Women's Work: Female Heterogeneity and the Polarisation of Women's Employment*. Vol. 4. A&C Black.

Hakim, Catherine. 1997. "A Sociological Perspective on Part-Time Work." In Hans-Peter Blossfeld and Catherine Hakim (eds.), *Between Equalization and Marginalization: Women Working Part-Time in Europe*, 22–70. Oxford: Oxford University Press.

Haklai, Oded. 2011. *Palestinian Ethnonationalism in Israel*. Philadelphia: University of Philadelphia Press.

Halabi, Rabah. 1997. *The Druze Educational System, 1975–1995: Preference or Control Policy?* M.A. Thesis, The Hebrew University, Jerusalem (in Hebrew).

2004. *Israeli and Palestinian Identities in Dialogue: The School for Peace Approach*. Trans. Deb Reich. New Brunswick: Rutgers University Press.

Halabi, Usama. 1995. "The Impact of the Jewishness of the State of Israel on the Status and Rights of the Arab Citizens in Israel." In Nur Masalha (ed.), *The Palestinians in Israel: Is Israel the State of All Its Citizens and "Absentees"?*, 7–33. Tran. Nur Masalha. Nazareth: Galilee Center for Social Research.

2001. "The Legal Status of Palestinians in Jerusalem." *Palestine Israel Journal of Politics, Economics and Culture* 4(1); https://ssl.haifa.ac.il/,DanaInfo=.awxy CtnpGw0q±details.php?id=505.

Han, Shin-Kap, and Phyllis Moen. 1999. "Work and Family over Time: A Life Course Approach." *The Annals of the American Academy of Political and Social Science* 562(1): 98–110.

Hananel, Ravit, and Rachelle Alterman. 2015. *National Land Ownership and Policy in Israel: The Values and Considerations Guiding Israel's Land Policy*. Tel Aviv: Hakibbutz Hameuchad (in Hebrew).

Hanieh, Adam. 2003. "From State-Led Growth to Globalization: The Evolution of Israeli Capitalism." *Journal of Palestine Studies* 32(4): 5–21.

Hargreaves, Linda. 2009. "The Status and Prestige of Teachers and Teaching." In Lawrence J. Saha and Anthony Gary Dworkin (eds.), *International Handbook of Research on Teachers and Teaching*, 217–229. New York: Springer.

Hasan, Manar. 2005 "The Destruction of the City and the War against the Memory: The Conquerors and the Conquered." *Theory and Society* 27: 197–207 (in Hebrew).

Hassan, Yousef. 1992. *Changes in Druze Settlements in Consequence of Their Integration into the Israeli Security System*. M.A. Thesis, Department of Geography, University of Haifa.

2001. *The Social Geography of the Druze in Israel: Systems of Socio-Spatial Interaction*. Ph.D. Dissertation, Tel Aviv University.

Hasson, Nir. 2010. "3,374 East Jerusalem Residents Were granted Citizenship in the Last Decade." *Haaretz*, 20.10.2010. www.haaretz.co.il/magazine/1.184 5812 (in Hebrew).

Hasson, Nir. 2012a. "The Educational Transit Station of East Jerusalem Residents on Their Way to Receive Work in Israel." *Haaretz*, 28.8.2012. www.haaretz.co .il/news/education/1.1810790 (in Hebrew).

Hasson, Nir. 2012b. "Blue ID: On High Demand in East Jerusalem." *Haaretz*, 29.12.2012. www.haaretz.co.il/magazine/1.1895168 (in Hebrew).

Hatem, Mervat F. 1992. "Economic and Political Liberation in Egypt and the Demise of State Feminism." *International Journal of Middle East Studies* 24(2): 231–251.

1993. "Toward a Critique of Modernization: Narrative in Middle East Women Studies." *Arab Studies Quarterly* 15(2): 117–122.

Hendin, Ayala. 2011. *Arab Students' Integration in the Israeli Higher-Education System*. Jerusalem: The Federmann School of Public Policy, Hebrew University. http://public-policy.huji.ac.il/.upload/Orange%20Serie/Ailla_Han din_Orange.pdf (in Hebrew).

Hermansen, Are Skeie. 2013. "Occupational Attainment among Children of Immigrants in Norway: Bottlenecks into Employment—Equal Access to Advantaged Positions?" *European Sociological Review* 29(3): 517–534.

Hertz-Lazarowitz, Rachel. 2003. "Arab and Jewish Youth in Israel: Voicing National Injustice on Campus." *Journal of Social Issues* 59(1): 51–66.

Hertz-Lazarowitz, Rachel, and Tamar Zelniker. 2004. Can Peace Education Be Enhanced via Participatory Research? Three Case Studies at Haifa University 2001–2003. *Peace Research* 36(1): 119–134.

Herzl, Theodor. 1960[1902]. *Old New Land*. Trans. Lotta Levensohn. New Preface: Emanuel Neumann. New York: Bloch and Herzl.

Herzog, Hanna. 2004a. "Absent Voices: Citizenship and Identity Narratives of Palestinian Women in Israel." In Adriana Kemp (ed.), *Israelies in Conflict: Hegemonies, Identities, and Challenges*, 236–262." Brighton: Sessex Academic Press.

2004b. "'Both an Arab and a Woman': Gendered, Racialized Experiences of Female Palestinian Citizens of Israel." *Social Identities* 10(1): 53–82.

2005. "Shifting Boundaries: Palestinian Women Citizens of Israel in Peace Organizations." In André Levy and Alex Weingrod (eds.), *Homelands and Diasporas: Holy Lands and Other Places*, 200–219. Stanford: Stanford University Press.

Herzog, Hanna, Smadar Sharon, and Inna Leykin. 2008. "Racism and the Politics of Signification: Israeli Public Discourse on Racism towards Palestinian Citizens." *Ethnic and Racial Studies* 31(6): 1091–1109.

Herzog, Hanna, and Taghreed Yahia-Younis. 2007. "Men's Bargaining with Patriarchy: The Case of Primaries within Hamulas in Palestinian-Arab Communities in Israel," *Gender & Society* 21(4): 579–602.

Hijab, Nadia. 1988. *Womanpower: The Arab Debate on Women at Work*. Cambridge: Cambridge University Press.

2001. "Women and Work in the Arab World." In Suad Joseph and Susan Slyomovics (eds.), *Women and Power in the Middle East*, 41–51. Philadelphia: University of Pennsylvania Press.

Hlihel, Ahmed. 2008. "Singlehood among Arab Women: Causes Widening the Phenomenon in Israel Center and North." In Adel Manna (ed.), *Arab Society in Israel: Population, Society, Economy*, Vol. 2, 283–312. Jerusalem and Tel Aviv: The Van Leer Jerusalem Institute and Hakibbutz Hameuchad (in Hebrew).

Hochschild, Arlie. 1989. *The Second Shift: Working Parents and the Revolution at Home*. With A. Machung. New York: Avon.

Holland, Jennifer A., and Helga A. G. de Valk. 2014. "Differences in Labour Force Participation by Motherhood Statusamong Turkish Second Generation and Majority Women across Europe." Working Paper 2014/1. Nederlands Interdisciplinary Demographic Institute (NiDi).

Hosni, Djehane, and Adriana Chanmala. 2001. "Female Endangerment: The Case of the Middle East and North Africa." In E. Mine Cinar (ed.), *The Economics of Women and Work in the Middle East and North Africa*, 33–49. Amsterdam: JAI.

Hovsepian, Mary. 2004. *Sewing Other People's Clothes: Gender, Nation, and Subcontracting across the Border between the Palestinian Territories and Israel.* Ph.D. Dissertation, University of Wisconsin, Madison (Sociology).

Huang, Chong, Hongbin Li, Pak Wai Liu, and Junsen Zhang. 2009. "Why Does Spousal Education Matter for Earnings? Assortative Mating and Cross-Productivity." *Journal of Labor Economics* 27(4): 633–652.

Huber, Joan. 1991. "Theory of Family, Economy, and Gender." In Rae Lesser Blumberg (ed.), *Gender, Family and Economy: The Triple Overlap*, 35–51. Newbury Park: Sage.

ILO. 2014. Key Indicators of the Labor Market (KILM). Online database for Researchers. 8th ed. Prepared by the ILO. www.ilo.org/empelm/what/WC MS_114240/lang–en/index.htm.

Imseis Ardi. 2000. "Facts on the Ground: An Examination of Israeli Municipal Policy in East Jerusalem," *American University International Law Review*, Vol. 15, 1040–1069.

Index Mundi. 2015. www.indexmundi.com.

Jabareen, Youssef. 1998. "Law and Education: Critical Perspectives on Arab Palestinian Education in Israel." *American Behavioral Scientist* 49(8): 1052–1074.

Jabareen, Yousef T., and Mohanad Mustafa (eds.). 2013. *Local Government in Palestinian Society in Israel: Political, Management, and Legal Aspects.* Haifa: Pardes.

Jacobs, Jerry A. 1989. "Long-Term Trends in Occupational Segregation by Sex." *American Journal of Sociology* 95(1): 160–173.

Jacobsen, Joyce P. 2007. *Economics of Gender.* 3rd ed. Malden, MA: Blackwell.

Jad, Islah. 2013. "The Debate on Islamism and Secularism: The Case of Palestinian Women's Movements." In Rochelle Davis and Mimi Kirk (eds.) *Palestine and the Palestinians in the 21st Century*, 142–157. Bloomington: Indiana University Press.

Jakubowska, Longin. 1992. "Resisting 'Ethnicity': The Israeli State and Bedouin Identity." In Carolyn Nordstrom and JoAnn Martin (eds.), *The Paths to Domination, Resistance, and Terror*, 85–105. Berkeley: University of California Press.

Jamal, Amal. 2002. "Beyond "Ethnic Democracy": State Structure, Multicultural Conflict and Differentiated Citizenship in Israel." *New Political Science* 24(3): 333–351.

2004. "The Ambiguities of Minority Patriotism: Love for Homeland versus State among Palestinian Citizens of Israel." *Nationalism and Ethnic Politics* 10(3): 433–471.

Joseph, Suad (ed.). 2000. *Gender and Citizenship in the Middle East.* Syracuse: Syracuse University Press.

Joseph, Suad, and Susan Slyomovics (eds.). 2001. *Women and Power in the Middle East.* Philadelphia: University of Pennsylvania Press.

Ju'beh, Nazmi. 2007. "East Jerusalem: 40 Years of Occupation." *Palestine Israel Journal of Politics, Economics and Culture* 14(1): 16–23.

Justman, Moshe. 2002. "Structural Change and the Emergence of Israel's High-Tech Sector." In A. Ben-Bassat (ed.), *The Israeli Economy, 1985–1998: From Government Intervention to Market Economics*, 445–484. Cambridge MA: MIT Press

Kadman, Noga. 2015. *Erased from Space and Consciousness: Israel and the Depopulated Palestinian Villages of 1948*. Trans. Dimi Reider. Bloomington: Indiana University Press.

Kalekin-Fishman, Devorah. 2004. *Ideology, Policy and Practice: Education for Immigrants and Minorities in Israel Today*. New York: Kluwer.

Kalleberg, Arne L. 2000. "Nonstandard Employment Relations: Part-Time, Temporary and Contract Work." *Annual Review of Sociology* 26(1): 341–365.

Kalleberg, Arne L., and Barbara F. Reskin. 1995. "Gender Differences in Promotion in the United States and Norway." *Research in Social Stratification and Mobility* 14: 237–264.

Kaminker, Sarah. 1997. "For Arabs Only: Building Restrictions in East Jerusalem." *Journal of Palestine Studies* 26(4): 5–16.

Kanaaneh, Rhoda Ann. 2002. *Birthing the Nation: Strategies of Palestinian Women in Israel*. Berkeley: University of California Press.

2009. *Surrounded: Palestinian Soldiers in the Israeli Military*. Stanford: Stanford University Press.

2010. "A Good Arab in a Bad House: Unrecognized Villagers in the Israeli Army." In Rhoda Ann Kanaaneh and Isis Nusair (eds.), *Palestinians in Israel Revisited*, 39–52. Albany: SUNY Press.

Kanaaneh, Rhoda Ann, and Isis Nusair (eds.). 2010. *Displaced at Home: Ethnicity and Gender among Palestinians in Israel*. Albany: State University of New York Press.

Kandiyoti, Deniz. 1991a. "Introduction." In Deniz Kandiyoti (ed.), *Women, Islam and the State,"* 1–21. Houndmills: Macmillan.

1991b. *Women, Islam and the State*. London: Macmillan.

1992. *"Women, Islam and the State: A Comparative Approach."* In Juan R. I. Cole (ed.), *Comparing Muslim Societies: Knowledge and the State in a World Civilization*, 237–260. Ann Arbor: University of Michigan Press.

Kane, Emily W. 2000. "Racial and Ethnic Variations in Gender-Related Attitudes." *Annual Review of Sociology* 26(1): 419–439.

Karayanni, Michael Mousa. 2007. "The 'Other' Religion and State Conflict in Israel: On the Nature of Religious Accommodations for the Palestinian-Arab Minority." In Winfried Brugger and Michael Karayanni (eds.), *Religion in the Public Sphere: A Comparative Analysis of German, Israeli, American and International Law*, 333–377. Berlin: Springer.

Karshenas, Massoud. 2001. "Economic Liberalization, Competitiveness, and Women's Employment in the Middle East and North Africa." In Djavad Salehi-Ishfahani (ed.), *Labor and Human Capital in the Middle East*, 147–192. Reading: Ithaca.

Karshenas, Massoud, and Valentine M. Moghadam. 2001. "Female Labor Force Participation and Economic Adjustment in the MENA Region." *The Economics of Women and Work in the Middle East and North Africa* 4: 51–74.

Katz, Kimberly. 2008. "Administering Jordanian Jerusalem: Constructing National Identity." In Tamar Mayer and Suleiman A. Mourad (eds.), *Jerusalem: Idea and Reality*, 245–265. London: Routledge.

Kedar, Alexandre (Sandy). 2001. "The Legal Transformation of Ethnic Geography: Israeli Law and the Palestinian Landholder 1948–1967." *NYU Journal of International Law and Politics* 33: 923–1000.

Keddie, Nikki R. 1991."Introduction: Deciphering Middle Eastern Women's History." In Nikki R. Keddie and Beth Baron (eds.), *Women in Middle Eastern History: Shifting Boundaries in Sex and Gender*, 1–22. New Haven: Yale University Press. Haifa HQ1726.5.W66

Keshet, Yael, and Ariela Popper-Giveon. 2017. "Neutrality in Medicine and Health Professionals from Ethnic Minority Groups: The Case of Arab Health Professionals in Israel." *Social Science and Medicine* 174: 35–42.

Keshet, Yael, Ariela Popper-Giveon, and Ido Liberman. 2015. "Intersectionality and Underrepresentation among Health Care Workforce: The Case of Arab Physicians in Israel." *Israel Journal of Health Policy Research* 4(1): 18.

Khalidi, Raja. 1988. *The Arab Economy in Israel: The Dynamics of a Region's Development*. London: Croom Helm.

Khalidi, Rashid. 2006. *The Iron Cage: The Story of the Palestinian Struggle for Statehood*. Boston: Beacon Press.

Khamaisi, Rasem. 2011. "National Priority Areas." In Nadim Rouhana and Areej Sabbagh-Khoury (eds.), *The Palestinians in Israel: Readings in History, Politics, and Society*, 111–118. Haifa: Arab Center for Applied Social Research, Mada al-Carmel.

Khan, Azra. 2001. "Education in Jerusalem: A Study in Disparity." *Palestine Israel Journal of Politics, Economics and Culture* 8(1); https://ssl.haifa.ac.il/,DanaInfo= .awxyCtnpGw0q±details.php?id=173.

Khattab, Nabil. 2002. "Ethnicity and Female Labour Market Participation: A New Look at Palestinian Enclave in Israel." *Work, Employment and Society* 16(1): 91–110.

2003. "Segregation, Ethnic Labour Market and the Occupational Expectations of Palestinian Students in Israel." *British Journal of Sociology* 54(2): 259–285.

2005. "Ethnicity, Class and the Earning Inequality in Israel 1983–1995." *Sociological Research Online* 10(3).

Khawaja, Marwan. 2003. "The Fertility of Palestinian Women in Gaza, the West Bank, Jordan and Lebanon." *Population* 58(3): 273–302.

Khazanov, Anatoly. 1998. "Pastoralists in the Contemporary World: The Problem of Survival." In Joseph Ginat and Anatoly Khazanov (eds.), *Changing Nomads in a Changing World*, 58–67. Sussex: Academic Press.

Khazoom, Aziza. 2003. "The Great Chain of Orientalism: Jewish Identity, Stigma Management, and Ethnic Exclusion in Israel." *American Sociological Review* 68(4): 481–510.

Khoudja, Yassine, and Fenella Fleischmann. 2015. "Ethnic Differences in Female Labour Force Participation in the Netherlands: Adding Gender Role Attitudes and Religiosity to the Explanation." *European Sociological Review* 31(1): 91–102.

Khoudja, Yassine, and Fenella Fleischmann. 2017. "Labor Force Participation of Immigrant Women in the Netherlands: Do Traditional Partners Hold Them Back?" *International Migration Review* 51(2): 506–541.

Khoury, Nabil F., and Valentine M. Moghadam (eds.). 1995. *Gender and Development in the Arab World – Women's Economic Participation: Patterns and Policies*. London: Zed.

Kimmerling, Baruch. 1983. *Zionism and the Economy*. Cambridge, MA: Schenkman.

  2001. *The Invention and Decline of Israeliness: State, Society, and the Military*. Berkeley: University of California Press.

Kimmerling, Baruch, and Joel Migdal. 1993. *Palestinians: The Making of a People*. New York: The Free Press.

  2003. *The Palestinian People: A History*. Cambridge: Harvard University Press.

Klein, Menachem. 2001. *Jerusalem: The Contested City*. London: Hurst & Company.

  2004. "Jerusalem without East Jerusalemites: *The Palestinian as the 'Other' in Jerusalem.*" *The Journal of Israeli History* 23: 174–199.

  2005. "Old and New Walls in Jerusalem." *Political Geography* 24: 53–76.

Knesset. 2009. *Data on Students from the Arab Sector in Institutions of Higher Education*. Jerusalem: The Research and Information Center, The Knesset (in Hebrew).

Knouse, Stephen B., Paul Rosenfeld, and Amy Culbertson (eds.). 1992. *Hispanics in the Workplace*. Vol. 142. Newbury Park: Sage Publications.

Köbrich Leon, Anja. 2013. "Does Cultural Heritage Affect Employment Decisions: Empirical Evidence for Second Generation Immigrants in Germany." Working Paper Series in Economics, No. 270, University of Lüneburg.

Kolberg, Jon Eivind. 1991. "The Gender Dimension of the Welfare State." *International Journal of Sociology* 21(2): 119–148.

Koopmans, Ruud. 2016. "Does Assimilation Work? Sociocultural Determinants of Labour Market Participation of European Muslims." *Journal of Ethnic and Migration Studies* 42(2): 197–216.

Korn, Alina. 2000. "Crime and Legal Control: The Israeli Arab Population during the Military Government Period (1948–66)." *British Journal of Criminology* 40: 574–93.

Kraus, Vered. 1992. "The Role of Industrial Sectors on Gender Inequality in Earnings." *Research in Social Stratification and Mobility* 11: 153–175.

  2002. *Secondary Breadwinners: Israeli Women in the Labor Force, 1955–1995*. Westport: Praeger.

Kraus, Vered, and Yuval Yonay. 2000. "The Power and Limits of Ethnocentrism: Palestinians and Eastern Jews in Israel, 1974–1991." *British Journal of Sociology* 51(3): 525–551.

Kressel, Gideon M. 2003. *Let Shepherding Endure: Applied Anthropology and the Preservation of a Cultural Tradition in Israel and the Middle East*. Albany: SUNY Press.

Kretzmer, David. 1990. *The Legal Status of the Arabs in Israel*. New York: Westview Press.

Kristal, Tali. 2013. "Slicing the Pie: State Policy, Class Organization, Class Integration, and Labor's Share of Israeli National Income." *Social Problems* 60(1): 100–127.

Lamont, Michèle, and Mario Luis Small. 2008. "How Culture Matters: Enriching Our Understanding of Poverty." In Ann Chin Lin and David R. Harris (eds.), *The Colors of Poverty: Why Racial and Ethnic Disparities Persist*, 76–102.

Lapidoth, Ruth. 2002. "Jerusalem: Some Legal Aspects." In Marshall J. Breger and Ora Ahimeir (eds.), *Jerusalem: A City and Its Future*, 61–90. Syracuse: Syracuse University Press

Law-Yone, Hubert. 2003. "From Sedentarization to Urbanization: State Policy towards Bedouin Society in Israel." In Duane Champagne and Ismael Abu-Saad (eds.), *The Future of Indigenous People: Strategies for Survival and Development*, 175–183. Los Angeles: UCLA American Indian Studies Center.

Leibovitz, Joseph. 2007. "Faultline Citizenship: Ethnonational Politics, Minority Mobilisation, and Governance in the Israeli 'Mixed Cities' of Haifa and Tel Aviv-Jaffa." *Ethnopolitics* 6(2): 253–263.

Lesch, Ann Mosely. 1979. *Arab Politics in Palestine, 1917–1939: The Frustration of a Nationalist Movement*. Ithaca: Cornell University Press.

2006. *Origins and Development of the Arab-Israeli Conflict*. 2nd ed. Westport: Greenwood.

Lester, Bijou Yang. 1996. "Part-Time Employment of Married Women in the USA." *American Journal of Economics and Sociology* 55(1): 61–72.

Levy, Gal. 2005. "From Subjects to Citizens: On Educational Reforms and the Demarcation of the "Israeli-Arabs." *Citizenship Studies* 9(3): 271–291.

Levy, Natalie, and Yossi Shavit. 2015. "A Chronicle of Disappointment: Integration between Arabs and Jews in a Jewish-Israeli Elementary School." *Israeli Sociology* 16(2): 7–30.

Lewando-Hundt, Gillian. 1984. The Exercise of Power by Bedouin Women in the Negev." In Emanuel Marx and Avshalom Shmueli (eds.), *The Changing Bedouin*, 83–123. New Brunswick: Transaction.

Lewin, Alisa C. 2012. "Marriage Patterns among Palestinians in Israel." *European Journal of Population* 28(3): 359–380.

Lewin, Alisa C., and Haya Stier. 2002. "Who Benefits the Most? The Unequal Allocation of Transfers in the Israeli Welfare State." *Social Science Quarterly* 83(2):488–503.

Lewin-Epstein, Noah, and Moshe Semyonov. 1992. "Local Labor Markets, Ethnic Segregation, and Income Inequality." *Social Forces* 70: 1101–1109.

1994. "Sheltered Labor Markets, Public Sector Employment, and Socioeconomic Returns to Education of Arabs in Israel." *American Journal of Sociology* 100(3): 622–651.

Lewin-Epstein, Noah, and Haya Stier. 1987. "Labor Market Structure, Gender, and Socio-Economic Inequality in Israel." *Israel Social Science Research* 5(1–2): 107–120.

Lewis, Jane. 1992. "Gender and the Development of Welfare Regimes." *Journal of European Social Policy* 2(3): 159–173.

2001. "The Decline of the Male Breadwinner Model: Implications for Work and Care." *Social Politics* 8(20): 152–169.

Lewis, Jane, Trudie Knijn, Claude Matin, and Ilona Ostner. 2008. "Patterns of Development in Work/Family Reconciliation Policies for Parents in France, Germany, the Netherlands, and the UK in the 2000s." *Social Politics: International Studies in Gender, State & Society* 15(3): 261–286.

Lissak, Moshe. 1999. *The Mass Immigration in the Fifties: The Failure of the Melting Pot Policy*. Jerusalem: The Bialik Institute.

Lithwick, Harvey. 2002. Making the Bedouin Towns Work. Jerusalem: The Center for Social Policy Studies in Israel.

    2003. "Urbanization Policy for Indigenous Peoples: A Case Study of Israel's Negev Bedouins." In Duane Champagne and Ismael Abu-Saad (eds.), *The Future of Indigenous People: Strategies for Survival and Development*, 184–202. Los Angeles: UCLA American Indian Studies Center.

Lustick, Ian. 1980. *Arabs in the Jewish State: Israel's Control of a National Minority*. Austin: University of Texas Press.

    1993. *Unsettled States, Disputed Lands: Britain and Ireland, France and Algeria, Israel and the West Bank-Gaza*. Ithaca: Cornell University Press.

    1996. "The Fetish of Jerusalem: A Hegemonic Analysis." In Michael N. Barnett (ed.), *Israel in Comparative Perspective: Challenging the Conventional Wisdom*, 143–172. Albany: SUNY Press.

    2008. "Yerushalayim, al-Quds, and the Wizard of Oz: The Problem of Jerusalem after Camp David II and the Aqsa *Intifada*." In Tamar Mayer and Suleiman A. Mourad (eds.), *Jerusalem: Idea and Reality*, 283–302. London: Routledge.

Maayan, Yael. 2013. *From a Racialized Space to Social Sustainability: Faculty Members' Perceptions of Their Influence on Campus Climate*. M.A. Thesis, University of Haifa.

Maman, Daniel, and Zeev Rozenhek. 2009. "Contested Institutionalization of Policy Paradigm Shifts: The Adoption of Inflation Targeting in Israel." *Socio-Economic Review* 7: 217–243.

    2012. "The Institutional Dynamics of a Developmental State: Change and Continuity in State—Economy Relations in Israel." *Studies in Comparative International Development* 47: 342–363.

Mandel, Hadas, and Moshe Semyonov. 2006. "A Welfare State Paradox: State Interventions and Women's Employment Opportunities in 22 Countries." *American Journal of Sociology* 111(6): 1910–1949.

Manna, Adel. 1997. *Double Marginality – Palestinian Israelis in Jerusalem*. Jerusalem: The Jerusalem Institute for Israel Studies (in Hebrew).

    2008. "Change and Continuity in the Lives of Arab Citizens in Israel – A Snapshot." In Adel Manna (ed.), *Arab Society in Israel: Population, Society, Economy*, Vol. 2, 13–37. Jerusalem and Tel Aviv: Van Leer Jerusalem Institute and Hakibbutz Hameuchad (in Hebrew).

Maoz, Asher. 1994. "Application of Israeli Law to the Golan Heights Is Annexation." *Brooklyn Journal of International Law* 20(2): 355–396.

Maoz, Ifat. 2000a. "An Experiment in Peace: Reconciliation-Aimed Workshops of Jewish-Israeli and Palestinian Youth." *Journal of Peace Research* 37(6): 721–736.

2000b. "Multiple Conflicts and Competing Agendas: A Framework for Conceptualizing Structured Encounters Between Groups in Conflict—The Case of a Coexistence Project of Jews and Palestinians in Israel." *Peace and Conflict: Journal of Peace Psychology* 6(2): 135–156.

Maoz, Ifat, Dan Bar-On, Zvi Bekerman, and Summer Jaber-Massarwa. 2004. "Learning about 'Good Enough' through 'Bad Enough': A Story of a Planned Dialogue between Israeli Jews and Palestinians." *Human Relations* 57(9): 1075–1101.

Mara'i, Tayseer, and Usama R Halabi. 1992. "Life under Occupation in the Golan Heights." *Journal of Palestine Studies* 221(1): 78–93.

MARD. 2016. The Authority for Bedouin Settlement and Development in the Negev, Ministry of Agriculture and Rural Development, www.moag.gov.il/ag ri/yhidotmisrad/reshut_technun/technun_kafri/rashut_buduim/Population/def ault.htm.

Margalioth, Sharon Rabin. 2004. "Labor Market Discrimination against Arab Israeli Citizens: Can Something Be Done?" *New York University Journal of International Law and Politics* 36: 845–884.

Margalit, Meir. 2001. "A Chronicle of Municipal Discrimination in Jerusalem." *Palestine Israel Journal of Politics, Economics and Culture* 8 (1); www.pij.org/details.php?id=172.

Marini, Margaret Mooney, and Pi-Ling Fan. 1997. "The Gender Gap in Earnings at Career Entry." *American Sociological Review* 62(4): 588–604.

Marteu, Elisabeth. 2005. "Some Reflections on How Bedouin Women of the Negev Relate to Politics: Between Political Marginalization and Social Mobilization." *Bulletin du Centre de recherche français à Jérusalem* 16: 271–286.

Marx, Emanuel. 1967. *Bedouin of the Negev*. Manchester: Manchester University Press.

1978. "The Ecology and Politics of Nomadic Pastoralists in the Middle East." In Wolfgang Weissleder (ed.), *The Nomadic Alternative: Modes and Models of Interaction in the African-Asian Deserts and Steppes*, 41–74. The Hague: Mouton.

Masalha, Nur al-Din. 1992. *Expulsion of the Palestinians: The Concept of "Transfer" in Zionist Political Thought, 1882–1948*. Washington, D.C.: Institute for Palestine Studies.

(ed.). 2005. *Catastrophe Remembered: Palestine, Israel and the Internal Refugees: Essays in Memory of Edward W. Said*. London: Zed.

2012. *The Palestine Nakba: Decolonising History, Narrating the Subaltern, Reclaiming Memory*. London: Zed.

Mastnak, Tomaž. 2010. "Western Hostility toward Muslims: A History of the Present." In Andrew Shryock (ed.), Islamophobia/Islamophilia: *Beyond the Politics of Enemy and Friend*, 29–52. Bloomington: Indiana University Press.

Matras, Judah. 1973. "On Changing Matchmaking, Marriage, and Fertility in Israel: Some Findings, Problems, and Hypotheses." *American Journal of Sociology* 79(2): 364–388.

Mattar, Ibrahim. 1983. "From Palestinian to Israeli: Jerusalem 1948–1982." *Journal of Palestine Studies* 12(4): 57–63.

Mazawi, André Elias. 1994. "Palestinian Arabs in Israel: Educational Expansion, Social Mobility and Political Control." *Compare* 24(3): 277–284.

1996. "Patterns of Competition over School-Management Positions and the Mediation of Social Inequalities: A Case Study of High Court of Justice Petitions against the Appointment of Principals in Public Arab Schools in Israel." *Israel Social Science Research* 11(1): 87–114.

1999. "Concentrated Disadvantage and Access to Educational Credentials in Arab and Jewish Localities in Israel." *British Educational Research Journal* 25(3): 355–370.

McCarthy, Justin. 1990. *The Population of Palestine: Population History and Statistics of the Late Ottoman Period and the Mandate*. New York: Columbia University Press.

McGahern, Una. 2011. *Palestinian Christians in Israel: State Attitudes towards Non-Muslims in a Jewish State*. Milton Park, Abingdon, Oxon: Routledge.

Medzini, Arnon. 1998. "Bedouin Settlement Policy in Israel, 1964–1996." In Joseph Ginat and Anatoly Khazanov (eds.), *Changing Nomads in a Changing World*, 58–67. Sussex: Academic Press.

Meir, Avinoam. 1997. *As Nomadism Ends: The Israeli Bedouins of the Negev*. Boulder: Westview.

Meir, Avinoam, and Ayelet Baskind. 2006. "Ethnic Business Entrepreneurship among Urbanizing Bedouin in the Negev, Israel." *Nomadic Peoples* 10: 71–100.

Melly, Blaise. 2005. "Public-Private Sector Wage Differentials in Germany: Evidence from Quantile Regression." *Empirical Economics* 30(2): 505–520.

Memmi, Albert. 1965. *The Colonizer and the Colonized*. New York: Orion.

Mernissi, Fatima. 1985. *Beyond the Veil: Male-Female Dynamics in Modern Muslim Society*. London: Al Saqi.

Miaari, Sami, and Nabil Khattab. 2013. "The Persistent Wage Gaps between Palestinians and Jews in Israel, 1997–2009." In Nabil Khattab and Sami Miaari (eds.), *Palestinians in the Israeli Labor Market: A Multi-Disciplinary Approach*, 61–84. New York: Palgrave Macmillan.

Miaari, Sami, Asaf Zussman, and Noam Zussman. 2011. "Ethnic Conflict and Job Separations." *Journal of Population Economics* 25(2): 419–437.

Misra, Joya, Stephanie Moller, and Michelle J. Budig. 2007. "Work-Family Policies and Poverty for Partnered and Single Women in Europe and North America." *Gender & Society* 21(6): 804–827.

Mitchell, Thomas G. 2000. *Native vs. Settler: Ethnic Conflict in Israel/Palestine, Northern Ireland, and South Africa*. Westport: Greenwood Press.

Moen, Phyllis, Mary Ann Erickson, and Donna Dempster-McClain. 1997. "Their Mother's Daughters? The Intergenerational Transmission of Gender Attitudes in a World of Changing Roles." *Journal of Marriage and the Family* 59(2): 281–293.

Moghadam, Valentine M. (ed.). 1993. *Identity Politics and Women: Cultural Reassertions and Feminisms in International Perspective*. Boulder: Westview.

1998. *Women, Work, and Economic Reform in the Middle East and North Africa*. Boulder: Lynne Rienner. Haifa HD6981.9.M67 1997

2000. "Economic Restructuring and the Gender Contract: A Case Study of Jordan." In Marianne H. Marchand and Anne Sisson Runyan (eds.), *Gender and Global Restructuring: Sighting, Sites and Resistances*, 99–115. London: Routledge.

2003. *Modernizing Women: Gender and Social Change in the Middle East*. Boulder: Rienner.

2004. "Enhancing Women's Economic Participation in the MENA Region." In Hebe Handoussa and Zafiris Tzannatos (eds.), *Employment Creation and Social Protection in the Middle East and North Africa*, 237–280. Cairo: The American University in Cairo Press.

Mor-Sommerfeld, Aura, Faisal Azaiza, and Rachel Hertz-Lazarowitz. 2007. "Into the Future: Toward Bilingual Education in Israel." *Education, Citizenship and Social Justice* 2(1): 5–22.

Morris, Benny. 1987. *The Birth of the Palestinian Refugee Problem*. Cambridge: Cambridge University Press.

Motzafi-Haller, Pnina. 2001. "Scholarship, Identity, and Power: Mizrahi Women in Israel." *Signs* 26(3): 697–734.

Motzafi-Haller, Pnina. 2012. *In the Cement Boxes: Mizrahi Women in the Israeli Periphery*. Jerusalem: Magnes (in Hebrew).

Mourad, Suleiman Ali. 2008. "The Symbolism of Islam in Early Islam." In Tamar Mayer and Suleiman A. Mourad (eds.), *Jerusalem: Idea and Reality*, 86–102. London: Routledge.

Mueller, Richard E. 2000. "Public-and Private-Sector Wage Differentials in Canada Revisited." *Industrial Relations: A Journal of Economy and Society* 39 (3): 375–400.

Musallam, Sami F. 1996. *The Struggle for Jerusalem: A Programme of Action for Peace*. Jerusalem: Passia.

Nahmias, Petra, and Guy Stecklov. 2007. "The Dynamics of Fertility amongst Palestinians in Israel from 1980 to 2000." *European Journal of Population* 23(1): 71–99.

Nassar, Issam. 2008. "Jerusalem in the Late Ottoman Period: Historical Writing and the Native Voice." In Tamar Mayer and Suleiman A. Mourad (eds.), *Jerusalem: Idea and Reality*, 205–223. London: Routledge.

Negrey, Cynthia. 1993. *Gender, Time, and Reduced Work*. Albany: State University of New York Press.

Nets-Zehngut, Rafi. 2008. "The Israeli National Information Center and the Collective Memory of the Israeli-Arab Conflict." *Middle East Journal* 62(4): 653–670.

Noland, Marcus. 2005. "Religion and Economic Performance." *World Development* 33(8): 1215–1232.

Nousiainen, Kevt, Anne Maria Holli, Johanna Kantola, Milja Saari, and Linda Hart. 2013. "Theorizing Gender Equality: Perspective on Power and Legitimacy." *Social Politics* 20(1): 41–64.

Nurieli, Benny. 2005. "Strangers in a National Space: Arab-Jews in the Palestinian Ghetto in Lod." *Theory and Criticism* 26: 13–42 (in Hebrew).

Nusair, Isis. 2010. "Gendering the Narratives of Three Generations of Palestinian Women in Israel." In Rhoda Ann Kanaaneh and Isis Nusair (eds.), *Displaced at Home: Ethnicity and Gender among Palestinians in Israel*, 75–92. Albany: SUNYP.

Obermeyer, Carla Makhlouf. 1992. "Islam, Women, and Politics: The Demography of Arab Countries." *Population and Development Review* 18 (1): 33–60.

OCHA. 2011. *Barrier Update*. Office for the Coordination of Humanitarian Affairs, Occupied Palestinian Territory, United Nations.

Ofer, Gur. 1967. *The Service Industries in a Developing Economy: Israel as a Case Study*. New York: Praeger and the Bank of Israel.

Okun, Barbara S. 2013. "Fertility and Marriage Behavior in Israel: Diversity, Change, and Stability." *Demographic Research* 28: 457–504.

Okun, Barbara S., and Friedlander, Dov. 2005. "Educational Stratification among Arabs and Jews in Israel: Historical Disadvantage, Discrimination, and Opportunity." *Population Studies* 59(2): 163–180.

Oppenheimer, V. K. 1988. "A Theory of Marriage Timing." *American Journal of Sociology* 94(3): 563–591.

Or, Theodor. 2006. "The Report by the State Commission of Inquiry into the Events of October 2000." *Israel Studies* 11(2): 25–53.

Or Commission. 2003. *Report of the State Commission to Investigate the Clashes between the Security Forces and Israeli Citizens in October 2000*. Jerusalem: The Judiciary. http://elyon1.court.gov.il/heb/veadot/or/insi de_index.htm (in Hebrew).

Owen, Roger. 1982. *Studies in the Economic and Social History of Palestine in the Nineteenth and Twentieth Century*. London and Oxford: Macmillan/St. Anthony's College.

Ozacky-Lazar, Sarah. 2000. "From Hebrew *Histadrut* [Federation] to Israeli *Histadrut* [Federation]: The Integration of Arabs in the Organization." *Iyunim Bitkumat Israel* 10: 381–419 (in Hebrew).

Pampel, Fred C., and Kazuko Tanaka. 1986. "Economic Development and Female Labor Force Participation: A Reconsideration." *Social Forces* 64(3): 599–619.

Pappé, Ilan. 1988. *Britain and the Arab-Israeli Conflict, 1948–1951*. Basingstock: Macmillan.

1992. *The Making of the Arab-Israeli Conflict, 1947–1951*. London: Tauris.

2004. *A History of Modern Palestine: One Land, Two Peoples*. NY: Cambridge University Press.

2006. *The Ethnic Cleansing of Palestine*. Oxford: Oneworld.

2011. *The Forgotten Palestinians: A History of the Palestinians in Israel*. Newhaven: Yale University Press.

Parsons, Leila. 2000. *The Druze between Palestine and Israel, 1947–49*. Houndmills: Macmillan.

Paternoster, Raymond, Robert Brame, Paul Mazerolle, and Alex Piquero. 1998. "Using the Correct Statistical Test for the Equality of Regression Coefficients." *Criminology* 36(4): 859–866.

Patinkin, Don. 1967. *The Israel Economy: The First Decade*. Jerusalem: The Maurice Falk Institute for Economic Research in Israel.

Pearson, Ruth. 1992. "Gender Issues in Industrialization." In Tom Hewitt, Hazel Johnson and David Wield (eds.), *Industrialization and Development*, 222–47. Oxford: Oxford University Press.

Peled, Alisa Rubin. 2001. *Debating Islam in the Jewish State: The Development of Policy toward Islamic Institutions in Israel*. Albany: State University of New York Press.

Peled-Elhanan, Nurit. 2010. "Legitimation of Massacres in Israeli School History Books." *Discourse and Society* 21(4): 377–404.

 2012. *Palestine in Israeli School Books: Ideology and Propaganda in Education*. London: I. B. Tauris.

Peleg, Ilan, and Dov Waxman. 2011. *Israel's Palestinians: The Conflict Within*. Cambridge: Cambridge University Press.

Peters, Francis Edward. 2008. "Jerusalem: One City, One Faith, One God." In Tamar Mayer and Suleiman A. Mourad (eds.), *Jerusalem: Idea and Reality*, 14–26. London: Routledge.

PEW. 2016. *Israel's Religiously Divided Society*. Downloaded Dec. 15, 2016 from www.pewforum.org/2016/03/08/israels-religiously-divided-society/.

Piterberg, Gabriel. 2013. "The Zionist Colonization of Palestine in the Context of Comparative Settler Colonialism." In Rochelle Davis and Mimi Kirk (eds.), *Palestine and the Palestinians in the 21st Century*. Bloomington, IN: Indiana University Press.

Podeh, Elie. 2002. *The Arab-Israeli Conflict in Israeli in Israeli History Textbooks, 1948–2000*. Westport: Bergin & Garvey.

Popper-Giveon, Ariela, and Yael Keshet. 2016. "'It's Every Family's Dream': Choice of a Medical Career Among the Arab Minority in Israel." *Journal of Immigrant and Minority Health* 18(5): 1148–1158.

Popper-Giveon, Ariela, Yael Keshet, and Ido Liberman. 2015. "Increasing Gender and Ethnic Diversity in the Health Care Workforce: The Case of Arab Male Nurses in Israel." *Nursing Outlook* 63(6): 680–690.

Portes, Alejandro and Leif Jensen. 1989. "The Enclave and the Entrants: Patterns of Ethnic Enterprise before and after Mariel." *American Sociological Review* 54: 929–949.

Portugese, Jacqueline. 1998. *Fertility Policy in Israel: The Politics of Religion, Gender, and Nation*. Westport: Praeger.

Posusney, Marsha Pripstein, and Eleanor Abdella Doumato. 2003. "Introduction: The Mixed Blessing of Globalization." In Eleanor Abdella Doumato and Marsha Pripstein Posusney (eds.), *Women and Globalization in the Arab Middle East: Gender, Economy, and Society*, 1–22. Boulder: Lynne Rienner.

Quigley, John. 1996. "Sovereignty in Jerusalem." *Catholic University Law Review* 45(3): 765–780.

Rabinowitz, Dan, and Khawla Abu-Baker. 2008. *Coffins on Our Shoulders: The Experience of the Palestinian Citizens of Israel*. Berkeley: University of California Press.

Rashad, Hoda. 2000. "Demographic Transition in Arab Countries: A New Perspective." *Journal of Population Research* 17(1): 83–101.

Rashad, Hoda, and Magued Osman. 2003 [2001]. "Nuptiality in Arab Countries: Changes and Implications." In Nicholas S. Hopkins (ed.), 20–50. Cairo:

The American University in Cairo Press. Republication of *Cairo Papers in Social Science* 24(1–2), Spring-Summer, 2001.

Rashad, Hoda, Magued Osaman, and Farzaneh Roudi-Fahimi. 2005. *Marriage in the Arab World*. Washington, D.C.: Population Reference Bureau.

Read, Jen'nan Ghazal. 2004. "Family, Religion, and Work among Arab American Women." *Journal of Marriage and Family* 66:1042–1050.

Read, Jen'nan Ghazal, and Sharon Oselin. 2008. "Gender and the Education-Employment Paradox in Ethnic and Religious Contexts: The Case of Arab Americans." *American Sociological Review* 73(2): 296–313.

Remennick, Larissa. 2007. *Russian Jews on Three Continents: Identity, Integration, and Conflict*. New Brunswick: Aldine Transaction.

Rindfuss, Ronald R., and Karin L. Brewster. 1996. "Childrearing and Fertility." *Population and Development Review* 22, Supplement: 258–289.

Reiter, Yitzhak. 2003. "Higher Education in Jerusalem." In Abraham (Rami) Friedman and Rami Nasrallah (eds.), *Divided Cities in Transition: Publication I*, 189–195. Jerusalem: The International Peace and Cooperation Center and the Jerusalem Institute for Israel Studies.

Rekhess, Elie. 1998. *The Arabs in Israeli Politics: Dilemmas of Identity*. Tel Aviv: Moshe Dayan Center for Middle East and Africa Studies, Tel Aviv University (in Hebrew).

2007a. "The Arabs of Israel after Oslo: Localization of the National Struggle." *Israeli Studies* 7(3): 1–44.

(ed.). 2007b. *Together but Apart: Mixed Cities in Israel*. Tel Aviv: Moshe Dayan Center for Middle East and Africa Studies, Tel Aviv University (in Hebrew).

2008. "The Palestinian Political Leadership in East Jerusalem after 1967." In Tamar Mayer and Suleiman A. Mourad (eds.), *Jerusalem: Idea and Reality*, 266–282. London: Routledge.

Rempel, Terry. 1997. "The Significance of Israel's Partial Annexation of East Jerusalem." *Middle East Journal* 51(4): 520–534.

Reskin, Barbara F., and Patricia A. Roos. 1990. *Job Queues, Gender Queues: Explaining Women's Inroad into Male Occupations*. Philadelphia: Temple University Press.

Robson. Laura. 2011. *Colonialism and Christianity in Mandate Palestine*. Austin: University of Texas Press.

Romann, Michael. 1978. "Jerusalem since 1967: A Profile of a Reunified City." *Geopolitics* 2(6): 499–506.

Romann, Michael, and Alex Weingrod. 1991. *Living Together Separately: Arabs and Jews in Contemporary Jerusalem*. Princeton: Princeton University Press.

Roos, Patricia A. 1985. *Gender and Work: A Comparative Analysis of Industrial Societies*. Albany: State University of New York Press.

Rosenfeld, Henry. 1968. "Change, Barriers to Change, and Contradictions in the Arab Village Family." *American Anthropologist* 70(4): 732–752.

1978. "The Class Situation of the Arab National Minority in Israel." *Comparative Studies in Society and History* 20: 374–407.

Rosenfeld, Rachel A., and Gunn Elisabeth Birkelund. 1995. "Women's Part-Time Work: A Cross-National Comparison." *European Sociological Review* 11(2): 111–134.

Rosenfeld, Rachel A., and Arne L. Kalleberg. 1991. "Gender Inequality in the Labor Market: A Cross-National Perspective." *Acta Sociologica* 34(3): 207–225.

Rosenhek, Zeev. 1999. "The Exclusionary Logic of the Welfare State: Palestinian Citizens in the Israeli Welfare State." *International Sociology* 14(1): 117–137.

Rosenhek, Zeev, and Michael Shalev. 2000. "The Contradictions of Palestinian Citizenship in Israel, Inclusion and Exclusion in the Israeli Welfare State." In Nils A. Butenschon, Uri Davis and Manuel S. Hassassian (eds.), *Citizenship and the State in the Middle East: Approaches and Application*, 288–315. New York: Syracuse University Press.

Rosmer, Tilde. 2012. "Resisting 'Israelization': The Islamic Movement in Israel and the Realization of Islamization, Palestinization, and Arabization. *Journal if Islamic Studies* 23(3): 325–358.

Ross, Michael. 2008. "Oil, Islam, and Women." *American Political Science Review* 102(1): 107–123.

Rouhana, Nadim N. 1989. "The Political Transformation of the Palestinians in Israel: From Acquiescence to Challenge." *Journal of Palestine Studies* 18(3): 38–59.

1997. *Palestinian Citizens in an Ethnic Jewish State: Identities in Conflict*. New Haven: Yale University Press.

1998. "Israel and Its Palestinian Citizens: Predicaments in the Relationship between Ethnic States and Ethnonational Minorities." *Third World Quarterly* 19(2): 277–296.

2006. "'Jewish and Democratic'? The Price of a National Self-Deception." *Journal of Palestine Studies* 35(2): 64–74.

Rouhana, Nadim N., and Areej Sabbagh-Khoury. 2015. "Settler-Colonial Citizenship: Conceptualizing the Relationship between Israel and Its Palestinian Citizens." *Settler Colonial Studies* 5(3): 205–225.

Sa'ar, Amalia. 1998. "Carefully on the Margins: Christian Palestinians in Haifa between Nation and State." *American Ethnologist* 25(2): 215–239.

2004. "Many Ways of Becoming a Woman: The Case of Unmarried Israeli-Palestinian 'Girls'." *Ethnology* 43(1): 1–18.

2006. "Feminine Strength: Reflections on Power and Gender in Israeli-Palestinian Culture." *Anthropological Quarterly* 79(3): 397–430.

2007. "Maneuvering between State, Nation, and Tradition: Palestinian Women in Israel Make Creative Applications of Polygyny." *Journal of Anthropological Research* 63(4): 515–536.

2016. *Economic Citizenship: Neoliberal Paradoxes of Employment*. New York: Berghahn.

2017. "The Gender Contract under Neoliberalism: Palestinian Israeli Women's Labor Force Participation." *Feminist Economics*.

Sa'di, Ahmad H. 2001. "Control and Resistance at Local Level Institutions: A Study of Kafr Yassif's Local Council under the Military Government." *Arab Studies Quarterly* 23(3): 31–47.

2003a. "The Incorporation of the Palestinian Minority by the Israeli State, 1948–1970: On the Nature, Transformation and Constraints of Collaboration." *Social Text* 21(2): 75–94.

2003b. "The Koenig Report and Israeli Policy towards the Palestinian Minority, 1965–1976: Old Wine in New Bottles." *Arab Studies Quarterly* 25(3): 51–61.

2004a. "Construction and Reconstruction of Racialised Boundaries: Discourse, Institutions and Methods." *Social Identities* 10(2): 135–149.

2004b. "Identity in a Context of Conflict: The Question of Palestinians in Israel." In A. Kemp, Uri Ram, David Newman, and Oren Yifahel (eds.), *Israelis in Conflict: Hegemonies, Identities and Challenges*. Brighton: Sussex Academic Press.

Sabbagh-Khoury, Areej. 2011. "The Internally Displaced Palestinians in Israel." In Nadim Rouhana and Areej Sabbagh-Khoury (eds.), *The Palestinians in Israel: Readings in History, Politics, and Society*, 27–46. Haifa: Arab Center for Applied Social Research, Mada al-Carmel.

Sabella, Bernard. 1996. "Palestinian Christians: Challenges and Hopes." www.al-bushra.org/holyland/sabella.htm.

2007. "The Socio-Economic Impact of the Wall on East Jerusalem." *Palestine-Israel Journal of Politics, Economics, and Culture* 14(1): 29–36.

Sadiqi, Fatima, and Moha Ennaji (eds.). 2011. *Women in the Middle East and North Africa: Agents of Change*. London: Routledge.

Said, Edward W. 1978. *Orientalism*. New York: Pantheon.

1995. "Projecting Jerusalem." *Journal of Palestine Studies* 25(1): 5–14.

Samergandi, Rogayah S. A. 1992. *A Study of Factors that Contribute to the Discrepancy between the High Number of Women Receiving College Education and the Low Number of Women Participating in the Labor Force in the Kingdom of Saudi Arabia: A Qualitative Exploratory Study*. Ph.D. Dissertation, University of Michigan.

Savitch, Hank V., and Yaakov Garb. 2006. "Terror, Barriers, and the Changing Topography of Jerusalem." *Journal of Planning Education and Research* 26: 152–173.

Schellekens, Jona, and Zvi Eisenbach. 2007. "The Predecline Rise in Israeli Muslim Fertility." In Jona Schellekens, and Jon Anson (eds.), *Israel's Destiny: Fertility and Mortality in a Divided Society*, 541–555. New Brunswick: Transaction.

Schnell, Izhak. 1994. "Urban Restructuring in Israeli Arab Settlements." *Middle Eastern Studies* 30(2): 330–350.

Schnell, Izhak, and Michael Sofer. 2002. "Unbalanced Embeddedness of Ethnic Entrepreneurship: The Israeli Arab Case." *International Journal of Entrepreneurial Behaviour & Research* 8(1/2): 54–68.

Schnell, Izhak, and Michael Sofer. 2003. "Embedding Entrepreneurship in Social Structure: Israeli-Arab Entrepreneurship." *International Journal of Urban and Regional Research* 27(2): 300–318.

Schnell, Izhak, Michael Sofer, and Israel Drori. 1995. *Arab Industrialization in Israel: Ethnic Entrepreneurship in the Periphery.* Westport, CT: Praeger.

Schölch, Alexander. 1982. "European Penetration and the Economic Development of Palestine, 1856–82." In Roger Owen (ed.), *Studies in the Economic and Social History of Palestine in the Nineteenth and Twentieth Century,* 10–87. London and Oxford: Macmillan/St. Anthony's College.

(ed.). 1983. *Palestinians over the Green Line: Studies on the Relations between Palestinians on Both Sides of the 1949 Armistice Line since 1967.* London: Ithaca.

Schwarz, Walter. 1959. *The Arabs in Israel.* London: Faber and Faber.

Scott, Jacqueline, Duane F. Alwin, and Michael Braun. 1996. "Generational Changes in Gender-Role Attitudes: Britain in a Cross-National Perspective." *Sociology* 30(3): 471–492.

Semyonov, Moshe. 1980. "The Social Context of Women's Labor Force Participation: A Comparative Analysis." *American Journal of Sociology* 86(3): 534–550.

Semyonov, Moshe, and Noah Lewin-Epstein. 1994. "Ethnic Labor Markets, Gender, and Socioeconomic Inequality: A Study of Arabs in the Israeli Labor Force." *The Sociological Quarterly* 35: 51–68.

Sewell, Jr., William H. 1992. "A Theory of Structure: Duality, Agency, and transformation." *American Journal of Sociology* 98(1): 1–29.

Shafir, Gershon. 1989. *Land, Labor and the Origins of the Israeli-Palestinian Conflict, 1882–1914.* Cambridge: Cambridge University Press.

Shalev, Michael. 1992. *Labour and the Political Economy in Israel.* Oxford: Oxford University Press.

2000. "Liberalization and the Transformation of the Political Economy." In Gershon Shafir and Yoav Peled (eds.), *The New Israel: Peacemaking and Liberalization,* 129–159. Boulder: Westview.

Shalev, Michael, and Amit Lazarus. 2013. "The Welfare State as an Employer: An Unacknowledged Avenue of Opportunity for Palestinian Women in Israel." In Nabil Khattab and Sami Miaari (eds.), *Palestinians in the Israeli Labor Market: A Multi-Disciplinary Approach,* 153–182. New York: Palgrave-Macmillan.

2016. "Horizontal Inequality in Israel's Welfare State: Do Arab Citizens Receive Fewer Transfer Payments." In Nabil Khattab, Sami Miaari, and Haya Stier (eds.), *Socioeconomic Inequality in Israel: A Theoretical and Empirical Analysis,* 225–252. Houndmills: Palgrave Macmillan.

Shami, Seteney, Lucine Taminian, Soheir A. Morsy, Zeinab B. El Bakri, and El-Wathig M. Kameir (eds.). 1990. *Women in Arab Society: Work Patterns and Gender Relations in Egypt, Jordan and Sudan.* Providence, RI and Paris: Berg/UNESCO.

Shamir, Ronen. 1996. "Suspended in Space: Bedouins under the Law of Israel." *Law and Society Review* 30: 231–257.

Shamir, Shimon. 2005. *The Arabs in Israel: Two Years to the Publication of the Or Commission Report.* Tel Aviv: Moshe Dayan Center for Middle East and Africa Studies, Tel Aviv University (in Hebrew).

Sharabi, Hisham. 1988. *Neopatriarchy: A Theory of Distorted Change in Arab Society*. New-York: Oxford University Press.

Sharkansky, Ira. 1987. *The Political Economy of Israel*. New Brunswick: Transaction.

Shavit, Yossi. 1989. "Tracking and the Educational Spiral: Arab and Jewish Patterns of Educational Expansion." *Comparative Education Review* 33: 216–231.

1990. "Segregation, Tracking, and the Educational Attainments of Minorities: Arabs and Oriental Jews in Israel." *American Sociological Review* 55(1): 115–126.

1992. "Arabs in the Israeli Economy: A Study of the Enclave Hypothesis." *Israel Social Science Research* 7: 45–66.

Shdema, Ilan. 2012. "The Role of Socio-Economic Factors in Changing Relations between Muslim and Christian Arabs in Israel between 1967 and 2010." *Islam and Christian–Muslim Relations* 23(4): 515–530.

Sheleff, Leon. 1994. "Application of Israeli Law to the Golan Heights Is Not Annexation." *Brooklyn Journal of International Law* 20(2): 333–354.

Shenhav, Yehouda. 2006. *The Arab Jews: A Postcolonial Reading of Nationalism, Religion, and Ethnicity*. Stanford: Stanford University Press.

Shenhav, Yehouda, and Yael Berda. 2009. "The Colonial Foundations of the State of Exception: Juxtaposing the Israeli Occupation of the Palestinian Territories with Colonial Bureaucratic History." In Adi Ophir, Michal Givoni, and Sari Hanafi (eds.), *The Power of Inclusive Exclusion: Anatomy of Israeli Rule in the Occupied Palestinian Territories*, 337–377. New York: Zone Books.

Sheridan, Lorraine P. 2006. "Islamophobia Pre– and Post–September 11th, 2001." *Journal of Interpersonal Violence* 21(3): 317–336.

Shlaim, Avi. 1988. *Collusion across the Jordan: King Abdullah, the Zionist Movement, and the Partition of Palestine*. Oxford: Clarendon.

Shmueli, Avshalom, Itzhak Shnell, and Arnon Soffer. 1983. *The Little Triangle: Transformation of a Region*. Haifa: The Jewish-Arab Center and the Institute of Middle Eastern Studies, University of Haifa.

Shohat, Ella. 1988. "Sephardim in Israel: Zionism from the Standpoint of Its Jewish Victims." *Social Text* 19–20: 1–35.

Shor, Eran, and Yuval Yonay. 2011."'Play and Shut Up': The Silencing of Palestinian Athletes in Israeli Media." *Ethnic and Racial Studies* 34(2): 229–247.

Shoshana, Avihu. 2016. "The Language of Everyday Racism and Microaggression in the Workplace: Palestinian Professionals in Israel." *Ethnic and Racial Studies* 39(6): 1052–1069.

Shryock, Andrew (ed.). 2010. *Islamophobia/Islamophilia: Beyond the Politics of Enemy and Friend*. Bloomington: Indiana University Press.

Simpson, Wayne. 1980. "A Simultaneous Model of Workplace and Residential Location Incorporating Job Search." *Journal of Urban Economics* 8(3): 330–349.

1987. "Workplace Location, Residential Location, and Urban Commuting." *Urban Studies* 24(2): 119–128.

Siniora, Hanna. 2001. "The Declining Economy of East Jerusalem." Interview with Hanna Siniora. *Palestine Israel Journal of Politics, Economics and Culture* 8(1); https://ssl.haifa.ac.il/,DanaInfo=.awxyCtnpGw0q±details.php?id=179.

Smits Jeroen. 2007. "Family Background and Context Effects on Educational Participation in Five Arab Countries." NiCE Working Paper 07–106. Nijmegen: Nijmegen Center for Economics, Radboud University Nijmegen.

Smits, Jeroen, Wout Ultee, and Jan Lammers. 1996. "Effects of Occupational Status Differences between Spouses on the Wife's Labor Force Participation and Occupational Achievement: Findings from 12 European Countries." *Journal of Marriage and the Family* (581): 101–115.

Smooha, Sammy. 1978. *Israel: Pluralism and Conflict*. Berkeley: University of California Press.

1982. "Existing and Alternative Policy towards the Arabs in Israel." *Ethnic and Racial Studies* 5: 71–98.

1997. "Ethnic Democracy: Israel as an Archetype." *Israel Studies* 2(2): 198–241.

1999. "The Advances and Limits of the Israelization of Israel's Palestinian Citizens." In Kamal Abdel-Malek and David C. Jacobson (eds.), *Israeli Palestinian Identities in History and Literature* 9–33. New York: St. Martin's.

2002. "The Model of Ethnic Democracy: Israel as a Jewish and Democratic State." *Nations and Nationalism* 8(4): 475–503.

2004. *Index of Arab-Jewish Relations 2004*. Haifa: University of Haifa, Jewish-Arab Center.

2010. *Index of Arab-Jewish Relations in Israel 2003–2009*. Haifa: University of Haifa, Jewish-Arab Center.

Soen, Dan, and Aharon Shmuel. 1987. "The Israeli Bedouin: Political Organisation at the National Level." *Middle Eastern Studies* 23(3): 329–347.

Sonbol, Amira El-Azhary. 2010. "A Response to Muslim Countries' Reservations against Full Implementation of CEDAW." *HAWWA* 8: 348–367.

Sorek, Tamir. 2003. "Arab Football in Israel as an 'Integrative Enclave'." *Ethnic and Racial Studies* 26(3): 422–450.

2005. "Between Football and Martyrdom: the Bi-Focal Localism of an Arab-Palestinian Town in Israel." *The British Journal of Sociology* 56(4): 635–661.

2008. "Cautious Commemoration: Localism, Communalism, and Nationalism in Palestinian Memorial Monuments in Israel." *Comparative Studies in Society and History* 50(2): 337–368.

Spierings, Niels. 2014. "How Islam Influences Women's Paid Non-Farm Employment: Evidence from 26 Indonesian and 37 Nigerian Provinces." *Review of Religious Research* 56(3): 399–431.

Spierings, Niels, Jeroen Smits, and Mieke Verloo. 2009. "On the Compatibility of Islam and Gender Equality: Effects of Modernization, State Islamization, and Democracy on Women's Labor Market Participation in 45 Muslim Countries." *Social Indicators Research* 90: 503–522.

Spierings, Niels, Jeroen Smits, and Mieke Verloo. 2010. "Micro and Macrolevel Determinants of Women's Employment in Six Arab Countries." *Journal of Marriage and Family* 72(5): 1391–1407.

Starrels, Marjorie E. 1992. "Attitude Similarity between Mothers and Children Regarding Maternal Employment." *Journal of Marriage and the Family* 54(1): 91–103.

Steiner, Talya. 2013. *Combating Discrimination against Arabs in the Israeli Workforce*. Policy Paper 97. Jerusalem: The Israel Democracy Institute.

Stier, Haya, and Noah Lewin-Epstein. 2000. "Women's Part-Time Employment and Gender Inequality in the Family." *Journal of Family Issues* 21(3): 390–410.

Stier, Haya, and Meir Yaish. 2014. "Occupational Segregation and Gender Inequality in Job Quality: A Multi-Level Approach." *Work, Employment & Society* 28(2): 225–246.

Strawczynski, Michel, and Joseph Zeira. 2002. "Reducing the Relative Size of Government in Israel after 1985." In A. Ben-Bassat (ed.), *The Israeli Economy, 1985–1998: From Government Intervention to Market Economics*, 61–83. Cambridge MA: MIT Press.

Suleiman, Ramzi. 2002. "Minority Self-Categorization: The Case of Palestinians in Israel." *Journal of Peace Psychology* 8(1): 31–46.

Swidler, Nina. 1980. "Sedentarization and Modes of Economic Integration in the Middle East." In Philip Carl Salzman (ed.), *When Nomads Settle: Processes of Sedentarization as Adaptation and Response*, 21–34. New York: Praeger.

Swirski, Shlomo. 1999. *Politics and Education in Israel: Comparisons with the United States*. New-York: Falmer.

2008. "Transparent Citizens: Israeli Government Policy toward the Negev Bedouins." *Hagar: Studies in Culture, Polity and Identity* 8(2): 25–45.

Swirski, Shlomo, and Yael Hasson. 2005. *Transparent Citizens: Government Policy toward the Negev Bedouins*. Tel Aviv: Adva Center (in Hebrew).

Tamari, Salim (ed.). 1999. *Jerusalem 1948: The Arab Neighbourhoods and Their Fate in the War*. Jerusalem: Institute of Jerusalem Studies and Badil Resource Center.

2003. "Contested City in a Sacred Geography." In Abraham (Rami) Friedman and Rami Nasrallah (eds.), *Divided Cities in Transition: Publication I*, 119–138. Jerusalem: The International Peace and Cooperation Center and the Jerusalem Institute for Israel Studies.

Tarrow, Norma. 2008. "Human Rights and Education: The Case of the Negev Bedouins." *Hagar: Studies in Culture, Polity and Identity* 8(2): 137–158.

Thornton, Arland, Duane F. Alwin, and Donald Camburn. 1983. "Causes and Consequences of Sex-Role Attitudes and Attitude Change." *American Sociological Review* 48(April): 211–227.

Tibawi, Abdul Latif. 1969. *A Modern History of Syria: Including Lebanon and Palestine*. London: Macmillan.

Tilly, Chris. 1996. *Half a Job: Bad and Good Part-Time Jobs in a Changing Labor Market*. Philadelphia: Temple University Press.

Tilly, Louise A., and Joan A. Scott. 1978. *Women, Work and Family*. Holt, Rinehart & Winston.

Tinker, Irene (ed.). 1990. *Persistent Inequalities: Women and World Development*. New York: Oxford University Press.

Troen, S. Ilan. 1992. "Higher Education in Israel: An Historical Perspective." *Higher Education* 23: 45–63.

Tsimhoni, Daphne. 1993. *Christian Communities in Jerusalem and the West Bank since 1948: An Historical, Social, and Political Study.* Westport: Praeger.

2001. "Israel and the Territories – Disappearance: Disappearing Christians of the Middle East." *The Middle East Quarterly* 8(1): 31–42.

Tucker, Judith E. (ed.). 1993. *Arab Women: Old Boundaries, New Frontiers.* Bloomington: Indiana University Press.

United Nations. 2013. *The Palestinian Economy in East Jerusalem: Enduring Annexation, Isolation and Disintegration.* United Nations conference on trade and development. UNCTAD/GDS/APP/2012/1.

2017. United Nations, Department of Economic and Social Affairs, Population Division, www.un.org/en/development/desa/population/publications/data set/fertility/wfd2015.shtml.

Voicu, Mălina, Bogdan Voicu, and Katarina Strapcova. 2009. "Housework and Gender Inequality in European Countries." *European Sociological Review* 25(3): 365–377.

Walby, Sylvia. 1986. *Patriarchy at Work: Patriarchal and Capitalist Relations in Employment.* Cambridge: Polity.

2010. *The Future of Feminism.* Cambridge: Polity.

Waldinger, Roger, Howard E. Aldrich, and Robin Ward. 1990. *Ethnic Entrepreneurs: Immigrant Business in Industrial Societies.* Newbury Park: Sage.

Weber, Max. 1958. *The Protestant Ethic and the Spirit of Capitalism.* New York: Scribner.

Weiner-Levy, Naomi. 2006. "The Flagbearers: Israeli Druze Women Challenge Traditional Gender Roles." *Anthropology and Education Quarterly* 37(3): 217–235.

2008. "On Cross-Cultural Bridges and Gaps: Identity Transitions among Trailblazing Druze Women." *Gender and Education* 20(2): 137–152.

2009. "' . . . But It Has Its Price': Cycles of Alienation and Exclusion among Pioneering Druze Women." *International Journal of Educational Development* 29(1): 46–55.

2011. "Patriarchs or Feminists? Relations between Fathers and Trailblazing Daughters in Druze Society." *Journal of Family Communication* 11(2): 126–147.

Weingrod, Alex, and Adel Manna. 1998. "Living along the Seam: Israeli Palestinians in Jerusalem." *International Journal of Middle East Studies* 30(3): 369–386.

Weller, Paul, Alice Feldman, Kingsley Purdam, and Ahmed Andrews. 2001. *Religious Discrimination in England and Wales.* London: Home Office Research, Study 220. London: Development and Statistics Directorate, Home Office.

Wesley, David A. 2006. *State Practices & Zionist Images: Shaping Economic Development in Arab Towns in Israel.* New York: Berghahn.

White, Michelle J. 1977. "A Model of Residential Location Choice and Commuting by Men and Women Workers." *Journal of Regional Science* 17(1): 41–52.

Whitehouse, Gillian. 1992. "Legislation and Labour Market Gender Inequality: An Analysis of OECD Countries." *Work, Employment & Society* 6(1): 65–86.

Wiemer, Reinhard. 1983. "Zionism and the Arabs after the Establishment of the State of Israel: A Study of Zionist Conceptions for Arabs in the Jewish State." In Alexander Schölch (ed.), *Palestinians over the Green Line: Studies on the Relations between Palestinians on Both Sides of the 1949 Armistice Line since 1967*, 26–63. London: Ithaca.

Wilensky, Harold L. 1968. "Women's Work: Economic Growth, Ideology, Structure." *Industrial Relations: A Journal of Economy and Society* 7(3): 235–248.

Winckler, Onn. 2003. "Fertility Transition in the Middle East: The Case of the Israeli Arabs." *Israel Affairs* 9(1): 37–67.

Wolkinson, Benjamin W. 1999. *Arab Employment in Israel: The Quest for Equal Employment Opportunity*. Westport, CT: Greenwood Press.

World Bank. 2016. EDSTATS. Data calculation engine, available on: http://datatopics.worldbank.org/Education/wDataQuery/QProjections.aspx.

Yaish, Meir, and Vered Kraus. 2003. "The Consequences of Economic Restructuring for the Gender Earnings Gap in Israel, 1972–1995." *Work, Employment & Society* 17(1): 5–28.

Yakobson, Alexander, and Amnon Rubinstein. 2009. *Israel and the Family of Nations: The Jewish Nation State and Human Rights*. Milton: Routledge.

Yiftachel, Oren. 1992. *Planning a Mixed Region in Israel: The Political Geography of Arab-Jewish Relations in the Galilee*. Aldershot: Avebury.

   1997. "Israel: Metropolitan Integration or 'Fractured Regions'? An Alternative Perspective." *Cities* 14(6): 371–380.

   1999. "Between Nation and State: 'Fractured' Regionalism among Palestinian-Arabs in Israel." *Political Geography* 18: 285–307.

   2000. "Social Control, Urban Planning and Ethno-Class Relations: Mizrahi Jews in Israel's 'Development Towns'." *International Journal of Urban and Regional Research* 24(2): 418–438.

   2003. "Bedouin Arabs and the Israeli Settler State: Land Policies and Indigenous Resistance." In Duane Champagne and Ismael Abu-Saad (eds.), *The Future of Indigenous People: Strategies for Survival and Development*, 21–47. Los Angeles: UCLA American Indian Studies Center.

   2006. *Ethnocracy: Land, Politics and Identities in Israel/Palestine*. Philadelphia: University of Pennsylvania Press.

Yiftachel, Oren, and Avinoam Meir (eds.). 1998. *Ethnic Frontiers and Peripheries: Landscapes of Development and Inequality in Israel*. Boulder: Westview.

Yiftachel, Oren, and Michaly D. Segal. 1998. "Jews and Druze in Israel: State Control and Ethnic Resistance." *Ethnic and Racial Studies* 21(3): 476–506.

Yiftachel, Oren, and Haim Yacobi. 2003. "Urban Ethnocracy: Ethnicization and the Production of Space in an Israeli 'Mixed City'." *Environment and Planning D: Society and Space* 21: 673–693.

Yonay, Yuval P., and Vered Kraus. 2001. "Strategies of Economic Endurance: Israeli Palestinians in the Ethnic Economy and the Public Sector." *Research in Social Stratification and Mobility* 18: 207–247.

2011. "Ethnicity, Gender, and Exclusion: Which Occupations Are Open for Israeli Palestinian Women." Paper presented in the International Sociological Association RC28 in Iowa City, August 5–9, 2011.

2013. "Ethnicity, Gender, and Exclusion: Which Occupations Are Open to Israeli Palestinian Women." In Nabil Khattab and Sami Miaari (eds.), *Palestinians in the Israeli Labour Market: A Multidisciplinary Approach*, 87–110. New York: Palgrave Macmillan.

2017. "The Role of the State and the Pliability of Tradition: Israeli Palestinian and Middle-Eastern Jewish Women in the Labor Force." *Research in Social Stratification and Mobility* 50: 29–39.

Yonay, Yuval P., and Eran Shor. 2014. "Ethnic Coexistence in Deeply Divided Societies: The Case of Arab Athletes in the Hebrew Media." *The Sociological Quarterly* 55: 396–420.

Yonay, Yuval, Meir Yaish, and Vered Kraus. 2015. "Religious Heterogeneity and Cultural Diffusion: The Impact of Christian Neighbors on Muslim and Druze Women's Participation in the Labor Force in Israel." *Sociology* 49(4): 660–678.

Youssef, Nadia. 1971. "Social Structure and the Female Labor Force: The Case of Women Workers in Muslim Middle Eastern Countries." *Demography* 8: 427–439.

Zeedan, Rami. 2015. *Battalion of Arab: The History of the Minorities Unit in the IDF from 1948 to 1956*. Ben Shemen: Modan.

Zeedani, Said. 1995. "Democratic Citizenship." In Nur Masalha (ed.), *The Palestinians in Israel: Is Israel the State of All Its Citizens and "Absentees"?*, 66–82. Trans. Nur Masalha. Nazareth: Galilee Center for Social Research.

Zlotogora, J., H. Habiballa, A. Odatalla, and S. Barges. 2002. "Changing Family Structure in a Modernizing Society: A Study of Marriage Patterns in a Single Muslim Village in Israel." *American Journal of Human Biology* 14(5): 680–682.

Zuo, Jiping, and Shengming Tang. 2000. "Breadwinner Status and Gender Ideologies of Men and Women Regarding Family Roles." *Sociological Perspectives* 43(1): 29–43.

Zureik, Elia. 1979. *The Palestinians in Israel: A Study in Internal Colonialism*. London: Routledge & Kegan Paul.

Zussman, Asaf. 2013. "Ethnic Discrimination: Lessons from the Israeli Online Market for Used Cars." *Economic Journal* 123(November): F433–F468.

Index

age at marriage, 50, *51f*, 156, *157f*
Arab cultural heritage, 226–227
Arab Palestinians, 10, 26, 27, 32–33, 34
Ashkenazi Jews, 17, 20, 225–226

Bedouins
    economic activity, 126
    education, 123–124, *128f*,
        128–129, 171
    employment opportunities, 124–125
    history of Naqab, 120–121
    living in Israel, 119
    polygyny, 137
    state-planned towns, 121–123
    unrecognized villages, 121, 136–140,
        137f, 138f
Bedouin women, 26, 121, 125–127,
    136–140, *137f, 138f*
    divorce rates, 137
    education, 131–134, *138f*, 138–139
    employment characteristics, 134–136
    labor force participation, 129–134, *131f*,
        132f
    marriage, 130, 137
    work experience, 136–140, *137f, 138f*
birth cohorts
    cohort replacement, 205
    part-time employment, 86–88, *87f, 88t*
    patterns in LFP, 64–66, *65t*, 78
"blaming the victim" tendency, 7
British Mandate, 14, 120, 145, 202

child rearing, 3, 76, 89–90, 186
Christians
    Anglicans, 201
    Druze relations, 178
    as enhancers to women's employment, 74
    fertility rate declines, 53–54, *54f*
    in Jerusalem, 155
    level of educational attainment, 44, 47,
        48–50
    marriage age statistics, 50–52, *51f*

Maronites, 201
Muslim relations, 25
never-married women, *52t*, 52–53
pro-Jewish bias of state policies, 181
Christian women
    background on, 201–203
    earnings, 215–216
    education, 206, 207–208, 216
    employment, 208, 210–217, *214f*
    labor force participation, *204f, 206f, 207f*,
        207–210, 217
    marriage and, 203, 208
    politics of employment, 240–241
    tertiary education, 207–209
Cohen, Adir, 21
cohort replacement, 205
communal agricultural settlements, 31
commuting, 91–94, *93f*, 105, 188, 233–234
Compulsory Education Law (1949), 39, 41,
    45–46, 123–124
concentration index, 96–97
counterfactual earnings, 104, 168–169
cultural factors
    Arab cultural heritage, 226–227
    Christian women's labor force
        participation, 201
    labor force participation role, 4–7
    Muslim women's labor force
        participation, 4–7
    religious culture, 2

development towns, 27, 30, 43
discrimination against Arabs and Muslims
    in Europe, 8
divide-and-rule policy, 25, 202
divorce rates, 137
Druze
    background, 19, 25, 178–182
    Christian relations, 178
    military draft, 179–180
    particularism, 179, 236–237
Druze women

children, impact of, 186
earnings, 193–194
education, 179, 192, 194, 232–233
employment, 186–194, *187f*, *190f*, 195
fertility rates, 53–54, *54f*, 182
labor force participation, 182–186, *183f*, *185f*, 190
level of educational attainment, 44–45, 47, 48–50, 182
marriage and, 50–52, *51f*, 181, 182
never-married women, *52t*, 52–53
occupational enrollment, 188–192
part-time employment, 186–188, *187f*
social control of, 195–196
tertiary education, 48, 184, 186

earnings, 167–168
Christian women, 104, 168–169
Druze women, 103–104, 193–194
gender gaps, 101–103, 166–167, 169, 196, 216
in Jerusalem, 154
Muslim women, 35, 101–104, *102t*, 106, 166–169
East Jerusalem, 146, 147
economic branch enrollment, 95–97, 165
economic impact of Muslim women in workforce, 6
education. *See also* Tertiary education
academic, 98–99, 105–106, 166
attainment trends, 44–50, *45f*, *46f*, *47f*, *49f*, 129, 182
of Bedouins, 40, 123–124, *128f*, 128–129, 131–134, *138f*, 138–139, 171
of Christians, 206, 207–208, 216
compulsory education, 123–124
divided in Jerusalem, 148–151
of Druze, 179, 192, 194, 232–233
expansion, 41–42
gender differences, 159–160
husbands' level of education, 73–74, 76
labor force participation, 34–35, 68–71, *69f*, 131–134
of Muslims in Jerusalem, 157–160, *159f*, 161, *162f*, 170
private schools, 41
secondary education, 41, 78, 128, 132–133, 158
structure of, 39–41
tertiary education, discrimination, 42–44
education, tertiary
Bedouin women, 128–129, 131
Christian women, 207–209

discrimination against, 42–44
Druze women, 48, 184, 186
Jewish women, 66
labor force participation and, 70, 79
Muslim women, 131–132
politics of employment, 232
educational system
Israeli matriculation diploma, 150
Ministry of Education, 39, 149
employment. *See also* Labor force participation; Occupational enrollment trends; Part-time employment; Politics of employment
Bedouin women, 124–125, 134–136
child rearing and, 3, 76
Christian women, 208, 210–217, *214f*
commuting trends, 91–94, *93f*, 105, 188, 233–234
Druze women, 186–194, *187f*, *190f*, 195
gender differences, 136, 161, 164, 168
Muslim women, rates of, 5, 64–66
Muslim women of Jerusalem, 154–156, 161, *162f*, 164–169, 170
patterns in, 9
trends in, 62–64, *63f*, 91–94, *93f*
worker well-being and success, 94
work experience of Bedouin women, 136–140, *137f*, *138f*
Eretz Israel (The Land of Israel), 13
ethnic composition, 19–20, 99–100
European Jews, 17, 20

family composition and labor force participation, 71–73, *72f*
family structure and Palestinian women, 50, *51f*, *52t*, *54f*, *55f*
fellaheen Bedouins, 122–123
fertility rates
Bedouin women, 127, 138
Christians, 53–54, *54f*
declines, 53–54, *54f*
Druze women, 53–54, *54f*, 182
Jewish women, *54f*, 55
Muslim women, 53–54, *54f*, 156–157, *158f*
Palestinian women, 50, *51f*, *52t*, *54f*, *55f*
foreign workers, 37
full-time employment, 84

Gapso, Shimon, 29
garment industry workers, 95, 191
Gaza Strip, 13, 15, 50, 120, 149, 152
gender differences
academic education and occupation, 99, 106, 166

gender differences (cont.)
  age at marriage, 52, 156
  counterfactual earnings, 104
  earnings gaps, 101–103, 166–167, 169,
    196, 216
  economic control, 125–126
  in education, 159–160
  employment, 136, 161, 164, 168
  industrial branch employment, 96
  labor force participation, 130, *183f*, 184
  occupational enrollment trends, *97f*,
    99–100, 189, 191–192
  part-time employment, 86, 186
  social stratification, 95
  unemployment, 139
  working from home, 92
gender equality, 16, 49, 73–74
gender ideologies, 5
Green Line, 61
  in jerusalem, 149, 162
Growth and Effectiveness Measures of
    Schools (GEMS tests), 42

Halachic Law, 19
health services jobs, 165
Hebrew language, 42, 232
Hebrew University of Jerusalem, 150
High Follow-Up Committee, 41–42
high-tech industry, 36
The Histadrut, 30, 31
hyper-inflation, 30

industrialization, 30, 38
industrial restructuring, 36
industrial sector employment, 96,
    134, 189
institutionalization of colonial
    regime, 14
intergroup relations, 20–23, 25–26
internal refugees, 15
Intifada, First, 152, 240
Intifada, Second, 153–154
involuntary part-time work, *90f*, 90–91, 236
Islam, women under, 2
Islamist movements, 8
Israeli economy, 30–37
Israeli-Palestinian conflict, 170
Israeli Palestinian women. *See also* Bedouin
    women; Christian women; Druze
    women; Muslim women
  education, 40
  labor force participation, 204
  residential segregation, 26
  social services employment, 35
  university graduates, 33

Israeli relations with Palestinian minority
  ethnic composition, 19–20
  historical background, 13–15
  intergroup relations, 20–23, 25–26
  Israeli economy, 30–37
  Jewish and Democratic state, 15–19
  neoliberalism, 36–37
  Palestinian attitudes, 23–24
  Palestinian standing, 31–33
  pro-Jewish bias of state policies, 181
  public sector, 34–36
  residential segregation, 26–30
  self-employment, 34
'Israelization' of Palestinians, 23
Israel/Jewish democratic state, 15–19

Jerusalem. *See also* Muslim women of
    Jerusalem
  Christians in, 155
  East Jerusalem, 146, 147
  educational divide in, 148–151
  educational programs in, 149
  employment problems, 154
  Green Line, 148, 161
  annexation of West Bank territories,
    146–147, 151
  Jerusalemite women, 157, 159, 167,
    238–239
  Mount Scopus enclave, 145
  municipal jurisdiction of, 19
  Old Quarter, 145
  Palestinian citizenship rights in, 147–148
  Palestinian-Jewish conflict, 152,
    153–154, 240
  separation barriers in, 153–154, 240
  West Jerusalem, 145
Jerusalem Education Administration, 150
Jerusalemite women, 157, 159, 167,
    238–239
Jerusalem/Palestinian residents, 20
Jewish-controlled political parties, 16
Jewish women
  academic education and occupation,
    98–99, 106
  commuting trends, 91–94, *93f*
  counterfactual earnings, 104
  earnings gaps, 101–103, *102t*, 106
  fertility rates of, *54f*, 55
  labor force participation, 63, 66–67,
    204f, 205
  level of educational attainment, 47, 70, 79
  occupational enrollment trends, 97–98,
    212–213
  part-time employment, 86, *88t*, 89, 105,
    213–215

public sector employment, 96, 103
tertiary education, 66
work outside of home, 1
Jordan, 6, 15, 36, 44, 120, 169
    annexation of West Bank, 15, 145, 146
    ceasefire agreement with, 61
    Hashemite regime, 151
    Israeli Palestinians' academic
        studies, 149
    Jordanian educational programs in
        Jerusalem, 149

labor force participation (LFP). *See also*
    Employment
    age factors, 130, *131f*
    Bedouin women, 129–134, *131f, 132f*
    birth cohort patterns, 64–66, *65t*, 78
    Christian women, *204f, 206f,*
        207f–210, 217
    common explanations, 1–4
    discrimination and, 7–8
    Druze women, 182–186, *183f, 185f*, 190
    education, 34–35, 68–71, *69f,*
        131–134
    employment trends, 62–64, *63f*
    family composition, 71–73, *72f*
    fertility rates of Palestinian women, 50,
        51f, 52t, 54f, 55f
    gender differences, 130, *183f*, 184
    health services, 34–35
    husbands' level of education, 73–74, 76
    increases in, 85
    Jewish women, 63, 66–67
    marriage and, 66–68, *67f*, 130
    Muslim women of Jerusalem, *160f,*
        162f, 163
    Muslim women part-time employment,
        84–91, *87f, 88t, 90f*, 105, 213–215
    overview, 8–12
    patterns by birth cohorts, 64–66, *65t*
    place of residence, 74–76, *75f*
    politics of employment, 232–242
    rates of participation, 234
    role of culture, 4–7
    single women, 66–68, *67f*, 77
labor force surveys (LFSs), 10
Law of Compulsory Education. *See*
    Compulsory Education Law
The Law of Return, 17
locality of residence, 209
logistic regression technique, 89

Mandatory regime. *See* British Mandate
manufacturing sector employment, 95, 165,
    189–191

marriage
    age at marriage, 50, *51f*, 156, *157f*, 182
    Bedouin women, 130, 137
    Christian women, 203, 208
    Druze women, 181
    effect on part-time employment, 89
    labor force participation and, 66–68,
        67f, 130
    Muslim women of Jerusalem, 156,
        157f, 163
    never-married women, *52t*, 52–53
MENA countries, 54, *55f*, 118, 227, 228
military draft, 179–180
military rule of Palestinians, 15–16
Mizrahi Jews, 20–21, 203, 225–226
Mount Scopus enclave, Jerusalem, 145
Muslim Palestinians, 27, 34
Muslim women
    earnings trends, 101–104, *102t*
    employment and commuting trends,
        91–94, *93f*, 105
    employment problems in Jerusalem, 154
    employment rates, 5, 64–66
    fertility rate declines, 53–54, *54f*
    marriage age statistics, 50–52, *51f*
    never-married women, *52t*, 52–53
    occupational enrollment, 94–100,
        97f, 189
    tertiary education, 131–132
Muslim women of Jerusalem
    before annexation, 151
    characteristics of, 156–160, *157f, 158f,*
        159f
    earnings, 166–169
    education, 157–160, *159f*, 161, *162f*, 170
    employment characteristics, 164–169
    employment conditions, 154–156, 161,
        162f, 170
    fertility rates, 156, *157f, 158f*
    labor force participation, *160f, 162f*, 163
    marriage, 156, *157f, 158f*, 163
Muslim women part-time employment
    labor market standing, 84–91, *87f, 88t,*
        90f, 105, 213–215
    multivariate analysis of, 89–90
    trends in, 86–89, *87f, 88t*, 213–215
    voluntary/involuntary work, *90f*, 90–91

Nakba, 14, 15, 61, 202, 203
Naqab (Negev), 62, 119, 124, 140
Nazareth-Illit, 29
neoliberalism, 36–37
never-married women, *52t*, 52–53
nomadic peoples, 118
nurses, 36, 98–99, 135, 192, 212, 235

occupational enrollment
   academic education, 98–99, 105–106
   agricultural occupations, 97, 125,
      190–191
   clerical occupations, 98, 135, 191
   Druze women, 188–192
   ethnic composition, 99–100
   gender differences, *97f*, 99–100, 189,
      191–192
   Jewish women, 97–98, 212–213
   managerial occupations, 98
   manual occupations, 97
   Muslim women, 165–166, 189
   non-manual occupations, 98
   politics of employment, 234–235
   professional jobs, 191
   service occupations, 98, 191
   technical occupations, 97, 191
oil industry in MENA countries, 7
Old Quarter, Jerusalem, 145
Or Commission, 18–19
Oslo Accords, 149, 152
Ottoman period, 120

Palestinian Authority, 152–153
Palestinians, 10, 26, 27, 32–33, 34. *See also*
      Discrimination against Palestinians;
      Israeli Palestinian women; Israeli rela-
      tions with Palestinian minority
   citizenship rights in Jerusalem, 147–148
   discrimination/racism against, 18–19,
      20–23, 32–34, 232, 235, 241–242
   divided education in Jerusalem, 148–151
   employment discrimination against,
      32–33, 38
   'Israelization' of Palestinians, 23
   marginalized minority, 9
   military rule of, 15–16
   in the Occupied Territories, 180
   'Palestinization' of, 23, 24
   Jews' fears of Palestinians'
      repatriation, 27
   residential segregation, 26–30
   socio-economic status of, 154
   standing of, 31–33
   work outside of home, 1
'Palestinization' of Palestinians in Israel,
   23, 24
part-time employment. *See also* Muslim
      women part-time employment
   Druze women, 186–188, *187f*
   gender differences, 86, 186
   involuntary part-time work, *90f*,
      90–91, 236

Jewish women, 86, *88t*, 89, 105,
   213–215
   marriage effect on, 89
   Muslim women, labor market standing,
      84–91, *87f*, *88t*, *90f*, 105,
      213–215
   politics of employment, 235–236
   voluntary part-time work, *90f*, 90–91,
      188, 236
patriarchal societies, 48
patrilocality, 28–29
politics of employment
   Bedouin women, 237–240
   Christian women, 240–241
   discrimination in work remuneration,
      241–242
   Druze particularism, 236–237
   exclusion/blocked women, 238–239
   Jewish women, 240–241
   labor force experience, 232–242
   occupational enrollment, 234–235
   part-time employment, 235–236
   public sector employment, 235
   puzzle of, 225–228, *229t–231t*
   secondary education, 232–233
   tertiary education, 232
polygynous relationship, 5, 137
private sector. *See* Sector of employment
profit-maximization logic, 94
public sector employment. *See* Sector of
   employment

residence concerns with labor force
      participation, 74–76, *75f*
residential segregation, 26–30
Rosenfeld, Henry, 31

sales jobs, 191
school segregation, 29
secondary breadwinners, 7
sector of employment (private/public), 85,
   94, 96, 103, 166, 190, 235, 210
sedentarization, 125
self-employment, 34
sensitivity training, 42
separation barriers in Jerusalem,
   153–154, 240
"Seyag" area, 121
Shari'a (Islamic law), 2
single women labor force participation,
   66–68, *67f*, 77
Smooha, Sammy, 16, 22
social stratification, 95
socio-economic differences, 202, 203

socio-economic status of Palestinian
    residents, 154
Soviet Union immigrants, 19
state-planned towns in the Naqab,
    120–123, 134, 136, 140

teachers, 35, 41, 91, 98–100, 103
    Bedouin, 124, 126
    Christian, 211–213
    Druze, 188, 191, 192
    in Jerusalem, 149, 165
teaching jobs, 135, 191
Triangle area, 27, 62, 75

UN Convention on the Elimination of All
    Forms of Discrimination against
    Women (CEDAW), 2
UN decision about Jerusalem, 146
unemployment, 139
UN General Assembly, 146
unionization, 95
universities and colleges. *See* Educational
    system
UN partition decision, 145
unrecognized villages of Bedouins, 121
urbanization, 122

village land appropriation, 28
Vision Documents, 24
voluntary part-time work, *90f*, 90–91,
    188, 236

welfare services jobs, 85, 165
West Bank, 149, 152,
    153–154
Westernized education, 202
West Jerusalem, 145
white-collar jobs, 103, 136, 211
women's place in the economy
    educational attainment trends, 44–50,
        45f, 46f, 47f, 49f
    educational system development, 39–44
    family structure/fertility, 50, *51f, 52t,*
        54f, 55f
worker well-being and success, 94
work experience of Bedouin women,
    136–140, *137f, 138f*
World War I, 202
1948 war, 14, 15, 27, 61, 120
1973 war, 30
1967 war, 15, 19, 146, 151

Zionist movement, 14, 21

Lightning Source UK Ltd.
Milton Keynes UK
UKHW020213060720
366013UK00008B/68